All about Spirituality

ALL ABOUT SPIRITUALITY

Practical Way for Self Realisation

Ashok Tyagi

SP SHIPRA
SHIPRA

Price: Rs. 1600; US$ 80

ISBN: 978-93-86262-25-7

First Published in India in 2017

All About Spirituality: Practical Way for Self Realisation

Published by:
SHIPRA PUBLICATIONS
LG 18-19, Pankaj Central Market,
I.P. Ext., Patparganj, Delhi-110092, India
Tel.: +91 11 2223 5152/6152
E-mail: info@shiprapublication.com
www.shiprapublication.com

Preface

This book is intended to ignite the dormant fire of pursuing Spirituality among inclined fence sitters. Many of us can relate to matured adults unmindfully engaged in an unending race for chasing material pursuits and recognitions. To get more and more of what is already achieved appears to be a fair and responsible effort towards living a happy and successful life for most of us. Few people are keen about a life focused on bliss and fulfillment akin to an awakened being. Walking down that lane is constrained by lack of right knowledge and guidance. In the absence of fine tuned receptors required to interpret the signals in any profound manner, our inner voice remains unheard. In addition there is another big trouble. Most of us do not wish to walk out of our cocoon of material possessions acquired and worldly bonds nurtured all through our life. Apparently, pursuing ultimate liberation by giving up all that is accumulated is not the option any more. But, in spite of all known challenges, pursuing our fundamental humanity quintessentially is our obligation as much as right.

Today, more than ever, we need to be told successful stories and ways to deal with attractions of material world without giving up our claim for liberation. We need proper direction to cross over the bridge of living normal life and aspiration for connection with deep within, the universe and Supreme. Also required is exposure to tools and techniques to be used for undertaking that path. All through the journey, we also require proper knowledge for correctly interpreting our own signs over this entire progression. This book addresses all these issues and much more besides my personal experience of similar journey that started over ten years and continues. Yes without my own fascination with this subject and confrontation with the enumerable challenges on each step, I would never have ventured to write this book.

This book is not for quickly running from cover to cover and tossing into a shelf of personal library. No, to take advantage, one must be an active practitioner besides being a reader. Reading alone can excite a person to take up the higher cause of human life and nothing more. The hesitant starters, who are unable to interpret their signals with clarity and conviction, will get to measure their spiritual development similar to identifying their position on a ladder connecting the floor with the roof. Just for clarity, most topics in this book are aimed at householders in the age bracket of late forties to mid-sixties. Exceptions apart, people below forties haven't experienced full range of life pressures; while people in their seventies and beyond may have reached a different stage of spiritual accomplishments where many of the principles discussed may not appeal to them with similar intensity of logic as applicable to people in their fifties with a few years plus or minus.

Speaking in terms of Vedic system of Ashram Vyavastha, this book is aimed for the benefit of people who have enjoyed the offerings of Grihastha ashram, and are eligible to move on to Vanprashtha ashram. Age brackets lose relevance once the target audience is linked to Ashram Vyavastha. Specific stage is rather based on mental makeup and level of attachments with the worldly affairs of the practitioners rather than their physical age. For example, a person well past sixty but still attracted to money making will still get defined as a pure Grihastha, whereas a thirty year-old dedicated to pursuing spirituality and engaged in selfless social service, with detachment from family, shall safely get classified as a Vanprasthi. So, this book is for everyone falling in between 'matured Grihastha' and 'neo-Vanprasthi'.

The target reader may be a professional, business executive, teacher, bureaucrat, or any other accomplished person from other occupations. Most importantly, this initiative works more with achievers; people falling under higher percentile curve of real life achievements, those who have tasted success in their chosen occupations, and have been touched by their deeper desire of searching for higher objectives of human life. Those who are still struggling to make their professional mark, and have yet to get internal reminders for higher human goals aren't expected to find enough energy and drive to engage in prescribed learning and practicing spirituality.

This book is designed to achieve four distinct objectives. The first is to serve as a course material for developing detailed understanding on all the concepts involved. Secondly, it should work as a compass pointing constantly towards the real purpose of human life. Here it also works as a road map to help one identify location on the spiritual journey. Thirdly, is works as a troubleshooting guide as and when practitioners feel grounded for one reason or the other. Finally, this book seeks to enable the reader cum practitioner cultivate their self-awareness and motivate them to seek their own self-realization in real practical surroundings.

I humbly accept errors and omissions and take full responsibility for the same.

Please share your views, suggestions, experiences and inputs at indotyagi@gmail.com

Surabaya, **Ashok Tyagi**
April 2017

Contents

Part II

Developing Understanding of Spirituality

PART III

SPIRITUAL EVOLUTION AND PRACTICE

PART IV

UNDERSTANDING SELF BEFORE SELF REALISATION

Introduction

At a point in life, some people can be seen developing the feeling of "*been there, done that*". Based on modern societal standards, they have done well professionally, enjoyed materialistic pleasures, and experienced benefits of position and recognition. By this stage in life, a person is generally through being a doting parent to children, a dedicated partner to spouse, and such other familial responsibilities. Enough financial resources are accumulated to avoid worries about paying the bills for rest of the life, wanderlust is quenched to some extent; so is the case with pursuing passions and hobbies. Probably, from now on, such persons are likely to get more of what they have already got. But deep within, each one of them knows it well that all is not right — that something is missing. Some vague feeling lingers inside, a deep void of some sort. Their mind keeps pondering same thoughts in endless cycles. What is next? What else is there to pursue? Questions like these refuse to vacate their mental space just like adamant tenants. This very yearning, cultivated properly and sincerely, can turn into a launch pad for a huge transformation of human life.

Let us now look to another side of the real-life scenario. Doing better on personal and professional fronts, setting superior goals, maintaining proper work-life balance, and bringing balance among money, purpose, passion, success, and relationships are all the resolutions made and broken over growing years. Earning a living, following traditions, staying in touch with others, attending to habits are all mundane aspects of our lives that eat up a substantial chunk of total time. Life gets reduced to a bundle of mechanical routines. A good portion of remaining waking hours is spent in rekindling memories of good and bad experiences, chasing pleasures, worrying about fears, and nursing hurts and anxieties, or convincing others to follow a beaten path. In the process, the need for transformation remains a mirage in desert where it is always in sight, but keeps moving with every step on the way.

By the way, a successful career with higher position or materialistic abundance, unfortunately, doesn't have any direct connection with living a happy and meaningful life. What constitutes a fulfilling life is indeed very old question, and has kept brilliant philosophers engaged over millennia. To explore and realize the hidden facets behind this critical question, one must become an aspirant; aspire to overcome ignorance; to see through the glitz of everyday life; to cross over man-made boundaries; to explore the depths of human spirit, and above all, to realize the fundamental human nature consisting of pure love, peace, and joy. "Spiritual Seeking" is that very noble purpose for living a happy and blissful human life, here and now.

But this seeking calls for plenty of dedication, commitment, and transformative changes in the way life is lived. The tough challenges of '*seeking*' lie on one side of this prism while the other side involves strong motivations for looking beyond sense gratification, getting rid of known attachments, and exploring the dormant universe lying right within the inner core of humans. Seeds of such critical seeking, however, germinate only in soil well primed with acceptance for everything new without biases or judgement. *Seeking* also necessitates a mind free from conflicts, confrontations, divisions or fragmentations. *Seeking* brings people face to face with their inherent tendencies underlying the expressions of love, hate, pain, pleasure, jealousy, envy, anger, animosity, misery, and joy. Baby steps taken over years provide access to the very source code, and make one aware of the real Self.

Challenges coming in the way of right *seeking* need a tremendous amount of courage and conviction to overcome. What is required is learning, practising, and realization for many new subjects and concepts including but not limited to working of emotions, states of mind, response system, ego, consciousness, wisdom, accessing truth through self-experiences, determination of personal values and principles, and expanding one's own real capabilities. More importantly, simply knowing leads to nowhere. It calls for inexhaustible hunger to practice it with uncompromising attitude, to work as hard as it takes to succeed. Practice must be followed with more practice. True, the real world of today is a very difficult place as there are fights, riots, social unrests, and innumerable divisions in society and at multiple levels. Living in such a vitiated environment has its own baggage for everyone, but great individuals look past their surroundings and concentrate on superior objectives of human life. Unwanted developments in their surroundings only strengthen their resolve to go beyond the visible and deeper than the surface. Yes, it has never been easy for anyone and will never be.

The *seeking* soon gets focused on finding the real *truth* as against its popular versions and vitiations. Modern day living adversely impacts the capability to recognize truth, the real, and the ultimate truth. One gets entangled in multiple versions of truth circulating in all directions. This dichotomy results in increasing queues before so-called teachers and preachers who are getting abundant followers lining up for their blessings, and that too on chargeable basis. Enumerable options are available to teach newer and easier ways of finding enlightenment. Supply of such instant variety of truth sharers is on the rise daily in India, almost everywhere, and in all cultures and religions. Interestingly, while people are unable to see the truth, the teachers and preachers are expanding their empires in an unprecedented manner. They are laughing all the way to the bank. Their most important marketing mantra is their promise to let people access ultimate liberation comfortably and quickly.

Real *seeking,* once grown to right levels, helps realizing that the real truth is hidden inside each human and one need not search it outside. With long practise of righteous *seeking*, the seeker achieves significant advancement in the spheres of morality, ethics, empathy, and compassion. In turn, such advancements result in proper germination of the seeds of *spirituality* — the subject matter of this book.

Spirituality is generally sold commercially with endless versions abounding. But *spirituality* itself is like a liquid resource which can take as many forms and shapes as the number of people dealing with it. Irrespective of what shape it takes, there can be no methods that ensure advancement in spiritual seeking by following instant variety of preachers, cult leaders, and pseudo gurus. Opinions given by others are dissenting. Suggestions and solutions offered by them are compellingly attractive, but practically unworkable. Ways shown by most of them are incessantly rooted in blind orthodoxy and reliance on outdated belief systems that don't address current day realities. Popular scriptures (barring a few) of all cultures are fossilized. Practice of yoga and meditation are marketed and packaged like fast foods. How can one blame the serious, sincere common man in the street in failing to seek genuine guidance? He is completely exasperated with his life, terribly disillusioned, and pathetically forced to be resigned to his fate. His dilemma is indeed well founded.

Pursuing *spirituality* is best begun with the realization that each person holds the entire universe within her/his own inner core, and that core can only be accessed by own individual efforts without any dependence on others. One needs to take complete responsibility for transformation sans crutches or hand-holding by others. Self-reliance, self-dependence, and self-perseverance are the keys required to unlock this magnificent hidden treasure that genuinely belongs to humanity. Yes, travel down this road is like a roller coaster ride; eventually the results are worth every effort. One is required to understand, learn, and practise a clearly laid out step-by-step approach for the long journey ahead. Experiences of people who have already travelled down that path with success can at best help us in avoiding some pitfalls or detours and, in turn, enhance chances of being successful at the end. One must focus on self to the exclusion of all others. It is subhuman if one's present self is not better than his/her former self. Quest for *spirituality* helps us realign our sense of self. It helps us in realizing that we are greater and more powerful than we have known ourselves to be. *Spirituality* allows us to realize that human life is much more than goods, grades, glories, galleries, gadgets, and gratifications. *Spirituality* alone allows us to fine tune our own inner wavelength and listen to its voice with requisite clarity and intensity.

But *spirituality* needs to be practised hard spanning over years and decades. Practising it calls for some very tough choices on the way. Human beings are a product of choices, and not so much of nature or nurture. Pursuing *spirituality* is no exception to this simple rule. To begin with, searching *spirituality* demands a great deal of our time and energy. The choice to commence this search is better made when one is physically capable and mentally strong. Postponing this choice for later years is like batting in a T20 game with the mindset of test cricket; soon your remaining overs are going to be over. Don't wait for formal retirement because working and earning alone can't define human life. Finding meaning in life and going after that meaning is what life is all about. Directed by deep conscience and driven by disciplined passion, pursuing *spirituality* is destined to bring clarity to the actual purpose of living.

The process of exploring one's spirituality begins with advancing self-awareness. It requires ability to observe oneself (something that has been integral part of entire life thus far) as an absolutely unknown entity. It is amazing to note the gigantic difference in 'self' and 'Self'. It also requires full stretching of neuro-plasticity of one's mind and training it to work with logic, and reason with compassion by shunning ego-laced thought process and responses. This process is not very different from training a strong, but recalcitrant horse. Advanced self-awareness elevates a person to "*Aham Brahmasmi*" (I am Brahman) by bridging the entire gap standing between a single soul and *Parambrahm*. This journey of advancement, however, calls for several iterations of self-recognition leading to self-awareness to self-regulation, and finally to self-realization. Reiterations require sinking of memories, drowning of attachments, and deactivation of tendencies generating unwanted thoughts. Needless to mention that the process of self-awareness leading to self-realization is bound to offer many challenges. But those challenges shall also expose one to some exciting revelations and wow moments.

During spiritual evolution, one is called upon to understand and overcome ego, a temporary combination of physical body, mind, life and intelligence. Individual ego is said to be masked by ignorance and treats itself as unique. This sense of uniqueness, *ahamkara,* prevents the harmony with the universe resulting in mental agonies. Interestingly, individual's intelligence itself will later be used as a tool for submerging that very uniqueness by proper tuning and regulation. The same intelligence that forms ego must be developed for proper wisdom and intuition. But this ego-laced intelligence avoids engaging in logical reasoning. It is only with hard practice that the same intelligence gets converted to spiritual wisdom and accepts applying logic based reasoning on all live issues. Ultimately, practising *spirituality* leads consciousness to rise to higher levels where one feels interconnected with the deepest part of self, each other, ecology, and finally with the universal consciousness.

Bridging this false ego brings us to our integral self, allowing us to live in this world with a different outlook of connection and oneness. Once the real Self is realized, the human body does not remain a burden anymore. The whole world appears friendly and supportive. Living permanently in such a situation is called living in bliss. This state, once achieved, leaves no room for contemplating about Creator, Administrator or Supreme as all those boundaries get erased forever. Such a person lives in the flesh without going after flesh. Such a person continues interacting and participating in this very world without doing any evil. Without developing additional limbs or anything, this person continues to be normal being with all his actions aimed at universal good. Such a person lives and dies just like any other normal person, but all doubts are shed from his mind. He need not differentiate among Moksha, Nirvana or normal life as any different as these are just words for him without much relevance. Reaching this stage precisely ought to be the ultimate purpose of every living human being.

None of this, however, is going to happen on its own. There is also no point in waiting for a miracle or divine blessings. This should be approached in a step by step manner and achieved through one's own efforts, dedication, patience, and perseverance. The path is full of disillusionments. No wonder many people abandon their seeking mid-way. One must guard against any image or fascination associated with seeking *spirituality* as there is nothing romantic about it. In reality it involves hard work. The seeker must maintain a distance from many joys and pleasures of physical life. There is a Tibetan saying that "*engaging in virtuous practice is like pushing a donkey uphill, while engaging in destructive activities is as easy as rolling boulders downhill...*". Surely, it calls for sufficient preparations to overcome challenges of an arduous journey never undertaken before.

If, and only if, one is ready to walk down this rigorous route, here is an effort to show a way based out of practical experience of a fellow traveler who, at best, may be travelling a few notches ahead of beginners. Sharing of freshly acquired experiences with other *karma yogis* is the precise purpose of writing this book. Inviting others to learn and practice techniques capable of providing transformative results is the sole motivation for this effort. To help the reader comprehend theoretical understanding followed by ways to practice that knowledge, this virtual journey is divided in logical sequences. The idea is to encourage *karma yogis* towards searching, exploring, and realizing spiritual capability without giving up connections with the immediate family in particular, and the world in general.

All through the early stages of writing of this book, discussions were held with several people from the target audience to know about their perceptions about spirituality. The most obvious finding was constant confusion of spirituality being perceived as an extension of their religious thoughts in some way or the other. Generally, people find it difficult to look at spirituality as a standalone knowledge stream. In appreciation of this, a detailed commentary is included in the book exclusively to map out religions and spirituality as being mutually exclusive to each other. The second critical finding was the desire to pursue spiritual progress without giving up comforts as well as work and family focused life. Clearly, modern day seekers are in no mood to hang up their gloves despite realizing pitfalls associated with modern day life. They are too scared to give up the social life that they have been part of. One can feel certain amount of excitement and interest in taking spirituality as an add-on subject but certainly not as a replacement of existing life. Some such questions have been listed with proper answers as an annexure to the book.

The book starts with the simplest and most common desire shared by entire humanity of living a happy and blissful life. Soon it explores the realities about the complexities involved behind the simple desire of being happy. Then it deals with contemporary and ancient systems suggested for pursuing that desire. In between, it also deals with the role of emotions as a cause and effect forming motives, initiatives and responses. These initial pages should be found useful for living normal life more effectively and developing clarity about right priorities to be followed. Initial chapters are dedicated to relatively younger generation and to make them aware that search of spirituality is simply a logical extension of living a fulfilling human life.

Having paved the way for a fulfilled life, the book invites the reader to check his/her location on the spiritual awakening curve to map the status by interpreting signs with understanding and clarity.

At this stage, it also provides a complete overarching view of the entire spiritual horizon to help one prepare for a possible journey. To dispel reservations about other popular concepts, *spirituality* has been explained by placing it on a similar platform. This journey is going to unfold many unseen treasures about which one may have had a vague inkling rather than deep understanding. Effort has been made to help the practitioner explore around these treasures without losing sight of the onward journey. Being a journey without predefined destination, the beauty lies in enjoying the scenery on the way. Exploring own truth, being in the know about awareness, and being conscious of consciousness are just some critical milestones imbedded en route.

In between the ongoing journey, the book deals with various practices generally used for enriching the spiritual growth. This is where yoga and meditation are explained regarding their contribution towards *seeking*. Practising meditation in its true sense is the most effective technique for developing spirituality all through its evolved state. Hence, any discussion on spirituality will remain incomplete without a fair discussion about meditation. However, in recent times, like yoga, meditation has also been over-simplified with varying versions and variety of servings. Effort has been made to make the reader aware of the pristine form of meditation, an art that should be learned and perfected through individual dedication. While most readers may have had some exposure to meditation already, the chapter on meditation might have some fresh and effective learning on offer.

Practical spirituality being what it is, one might come across, at times, strong words being used for teachings, teachers, or religions. These references are to be taken as general comments with the understanding that exceptions are very well recognized. But just for the sake of exceptions, the bulk of the available supply of teaching and preaching can't be considered gospel truth far beyond comments. The idea is to bring home clarity by calling spade a spade without mincing words. The committed reader will soon realize that the book demands more of unlearning rather than new learning. This unlearning is by far the biggest challenge and roadblock for most people. The most important contribution of this book may be the practical interpretation for self-realization. As against the traditional concepts, the practical self-realizations shall certainly help in living life in the present — here and now. It calls for exploring truth based on self-awareness and self-contemplation rather than secondhand knowledge from external sources. A life lived in such an environment is expected to be full of love, peace, and joy. This indeed is living in heaven, a heaven that exists right here on this very earth in the middle of all the chaos and confusion.

This beautiful journey is bound to pass through some stunning scenic surroundings on the sides. Consequently, each traveler will constantly be enriched through the journey irrespective of reaching the destination. This journey encompasses a beautiful landscape having multiple track routes. Each traveler is at liberty to explore his/her own route depending on his or her individual likings and energy available to be invested for the cause. So, let there be no worry about the destination. It is enough if one can enjoy each passing landmark at leisure and individual's own pace.

Finally, there is a word of caution. Some sections may not seem interesting to read or practice due to the conceptual complexities around the doctrines involved. But to achieve cleanliness of a place, spider webs need to be removed even when it is difficult to access high places. Everything covered under the subject matter of interest, irrespective of complexities in its comprehension, needs to be perceived and comprehended to overcome the fear of unknown. Difficult concepts and doctrines, therefore, need not hinder our path of wisdom.

Part I

Happiness: The Most Plausible Human Desire

Background

If one is to recall moments of solitude, multiple and varied thoughts will be recounted to occupy the imaginative space. Such thoughts comprise about hits and misses of material life, fears of failure at work, criticism or harsh words by people around etc. Such thoughts may partly gravitate around spouse or children, who are indeed an integral part of one's existence. One might recollect worries related to work where others failed to appreciate inputs and genuine suggestions. It may also be obvious to think about past interactions with special people one admired, loved or was influenced by; the twinge of not being able to spend quality times with loved ones; chances to spend time at places craved to visit; financial opportunities missed that had potential of multiplying net worth. This list of '*that was not to be!*' situations indeed keep playing live in our thoughts as a record player without an off button ... The list is long, almost endless ... This is the harsh reality of modern day life and needs to be faced squarely.

Our mental systems are unable to delete the recordings of wrong shots called even in distant past at critical junctures in life where alternate decisions had the potential to change our destiny. For example, the job offer from a small company that wasn't accepted while later that company became a big success, the team that wasn't joined but later it won championship, or the person one didn't marry who later became so much more successful and famous. One also gets filled with remorse for committing mistakes or wrong judgements made or misplaced reliance on people who proved untrustworthy. We are also unable to erase the memories of those countable few chances of feeling thrilled when we believed that the world could be conquered. Those moments of victory or achievements or recognition certainly were our moments of climbing over Mount Everest. As human beings, we are naturally inclined to desire a longer list of hits than misses. But this is real life of real people and mere fantasies or desires have no relevance at the end of the day. Sometimes, the logical mind reminds that spending so much of time and energy on these hits and misses is not productive, but this divine understanding fails to bring end to constant cycle of thoughts.

If one identifies himself/herself with such a typecast, there is a genuine question to be asked. Is it all right to lead a life filled with so much of repetition, contradictions, and reiteration? Does it not lead to undesired negativity and pessimism? The next logical step is to question one's willingness to surrender against this critical battle as a frustrated and tired soldier. Similarly, we have another list of equally pressing suspicions. One wishes to spend scarce moments of solitude in enriching the life to come rather than past. One wishes to aim for fulfilling engagements to live a life filled with peace and happiness, and to take control of life to change its direction by reinventing right motives and passions, and invest energies in lasting happiness and fulfillment.

Yes, a happy and fulfilling life is definitely possible, right here, amidst this very chaotic world. It is possible to replace the sub-human status many live with a life full of peace and tranquility suitable for a noble person. It is indeed possible to retrain normal human mind so that it is stable, works on selected thoughts at a time, and operates under a tight command as against a normal mind that continues its pendulum like movements switching from one thought to another in an endless manner. Improved command over the mind is destined to replace anger laced lethargic reactions, stressing mood swings, and constant chattering with a peaceful, quiet, and happy state. Incidentally, that is the original state of mind bestowed by Supreme to every living being at the time of birth. In short, it is indeed possible to regain original state of being by going back to where it all started in the first place.

But all this is not possible without making sincere efforts. One must learn and identify right actions/initiatives and make determined efforts to avail that divine right of living. One must be flexible to make changes required, be ready to embrace what works and give up what doesn't. One needs to learn many new things and, more importantly, unlearn lot of things already learned the wrong way. One is required to sink bundles of attachments, relations, belief systems, trophies, memories, experiences, titles, habits, judgements, and other such superfluous deadweights. Interestingly, most things required are self-centric without requiring mercy of others. Now, that by itself is no mean feat. After all, our chances of gaining success are always more when there is no dependence on others. But, one must remember that there are no quick fix solutions out here. It will require an approach with an absolute open mind and an unwavering determination to practice all the techniques and use all the recommended tools. There is no miracle substance that can be consumed in prescribed doses to create the magic. Neither is there some blessing to be received from any guru. Please don't even believe if any shortcuts are promised, as none exist whatsoever.

Also, remedies suggested for this transformation are not exotic cocktails or out of the world methods. All we have are a few proven remedies with modern adaptations which have already brought success for many aspirants over generations. The real-life situations of today are entirely different from what these used to be just couple of hundred years ago. The industrial revolution that started in 1760 changed the way people lived, learned, ate food, worked, and enjoyed their life almost completely. So, due to these drastic changes applicable to modern living, the historical solutions are no longer advisable to be used without required innovative adaptations. The idea is to draw on the source and universal spirit of ancient solutions and innovate newer remedies to ensure effectiveness in modern times.

But pursuing these remedies require constant practice and concerted efforts spanning over years and decades rather than months or days. Also required is unwavering commitment and fully focused dedication. On course of this journey, the seeker should be prepared for disappointments and be ready to go through numerous frustrating episodes. A seeker is required to deal with stubbornness of old habits, discouragements by people in close vicinity, and nagging feeling of results not being commensurate with efforts. Interruptions and obstructions will make their unwanted appearance on the scene regularly. This quest for searching and pursuing right purpose in life is not for the weak hearted or for those who are prone to give up easily. It was never easy for anyone at any time in history. Only a handful people trod this path in ancient times and fewer do it today. Let us start with the simplest, and most universal, desire of a normal human to live a happy and blissful life.

Happiness: The Default Setting for Every Human

Due to its relative importance in human lives, philosophers and scientific researchers have always remained occupied with focus on different aspects of happiness. Beside intellectuals of all shades and hues, most cultural and religious experts keep commenting ways and means of enhancing happiness all the times. His Holiness, the Dalai Lama addressed a large audience in Arizona, USA some years ago. Following excerpts from that lecture bring about the critical importance for pursuing happiness in our lives, and he said:

> "I believe that the very purpose of our life is to seek happiness. That is clear. Whether one believes in religion or not, whether one believes in this religion or that religion, we are all seeking something better in life. So, I think, the very motion of our life is towards happiness ..."

Living a happy life is the commonest aim shared by entire humanity. Nature itself has programmed human beings to desire happiness as a default setting. But growing years vitiate it by taking away that very happiness. It isn't as though nothing gets done as every person, at individual level, keeps trying various things centered on happiness for most efforts. People go from one relationship to another or from one job/position to another basically to seek the desired happiness. They work really hard to develop babies, buildings, biases, bonds, and bank accounts in one or the other sequence just to enhance their happiness in one or the other ways. They walk the extra mile to eat well, exercise well, grow flowers, and undertake vacations on beaches or hills. Some also try yoga, pranayam, meditation, and other such recommended remedies. There is nothing wrong in working hard to seek happiness. The problem lies in the belief that such initiatives are capable of enhancing happiness. Some even succeed in thinking that they actually got happiness. But majority are forced to settle for occasional periods of happy moments and that too at superficial levels. What is advised is to see through the misconceptions and unrealistic expectations that these externally focused issues are capable of providing the longer lasting happiness at a wholesome level.

But without exception, almost everyone rates pursuing happiness in life as an important objective with variation in terms of additional frills by the side. So, people know about happiness, they wish to have it and they also try hard to pursue it. But do they get it right? Do they get it in sufficient proportions? This is where an interesting twist occurs.

Considering happiness as a universal desire, individual happiness levels should logically be in close proximity to each other. But that is not so in reality as we see wide gaps in happiness levels of different individuals. Interestingly, these variations exist among all categories of age, caste, creed, culture, nationality, race, education, income, religion, gender or some such typical categorizations that divide human societies into brackets. Forget difference among different individuals, happiness of every single individual varies drastically from one time to another on the same day. Wide variations are seen even when external circumstances remain unchanged. The reality of large variations calls for greater understanding for entire gamut of human happiness. Surely, there ought to be critical issues involved in preventing generalization about happiness.

To begin with, happiness means different things to different people. It may probably be due to different psychological levels and orientations. Investigating likely reasons of vast differences leads to more questions than answers. In short, happiness is a subjective phenomenon. This relativity prompts us to check as to where we stand and why. Studying the dynamics of happiness as a subject will allow us to gain knowledge which will be used to bring desired transformation at our deeper level. Later, this genuine curiosity will also drive us to seek how we can bring changes to improve our scoring to desired levels. Many people in the past have done it, and now it may be our turn to explore the same and transform our own lives.

Suddenly, simple and innocent happiness is turning out to be a complex and intriguing subject!

Happiness can't be Bought or Acquired

In these times of instant gratification, the first idea that crops up in our mind is 'can I buy it?' Yeah, one can buy material things and many other traded items as much as one can afford. There are plenty of sensory pleasures on offer and people are seen chasing them all the time. But such acquired objects or pleasures are known to quickly change into a source of anguish, which is soon followed by remorse. Acquired happiness is always short-lived, and is necessarily accompanied by its shadow sibling called sadness. So, opting for it is a losing proposition. Material possessions are linked to happiness only initially. Ultimately these end up becoming irritants in life. Real happiness can't be bought or owned by anyone for long lasting spells. Money can only buy toys which are either broken soon or outgrown rather quickly, in almost all cases. Neither can it be earned as a matter of right, nor acquired through inheritance. No one can consume it in excess. It is not like money that we can store it for use at a later day. One can feel it only when it is there. Interestingly, contrary to the principle of things depleting after sharing, happiness increases when shared with and passed on generously among others. Also, its source is unlimited where one can harness as much as one can. As such, there are no constraints whatsoever on the supply side of the equation.

Happiness as a Roadblock to Creativity

As an extension of the old, but popular fable of sour grapes, some people try justifying lack of happiness by calling it as an essential shadow of unhappiness. Such people loudly advocate their acceptance for lack of happiness as an essential life element. For them being unhappy is being practical to face miseries of life as incidental. They argue that happy people stop growing and lose ability to stand against dangers as they become carefree. In their opinion, lack of happiness is essential to inspire people to try their best. In a way, they argue that pursuing happiness is an undesirable aim. This sounds completely untrue as happiness sharpens the focus of our entire response system, and brings an unusual sense of purity allowing us to observe and appreciate things with positive attitude and clear perspective. Happiness provides greater push to our natural motivational instincts to strive to do better and better, to survive and pass our genes to the next generation. It allows us to concentrate on harmonious and qualitative aspects of our actions. All achievers from every field can be traced to be happy individuals besides being proficient in their respective arenas. Surely, unhappiness is not so essential for human survival so as to be given prime place in our life.

Infants and children can be seen enjoying their happiness during their early days. But it keeps reducing as they start learning more and more about this real world. Growing process exposes children to contrasting experiences and learning about approval and rejections, winning and losing, success and failures, pleasures and pains. These exposures bring them face to face with unavoidable divisions present in human life and certainly erode their ability to enjoy free environment as they did earlier. On the other hand, we do come across many adults who continue enjoying access to their original form and remain happy even in their adult life just like a child. So, pressures of modern day may be a major cause of interruptive happiness spells for grownups, but not so for everyone.

Do we have ways and means of allowing adults to retrieve that original fun-filled happiness space? Surely, there are ways, but before one explores those ways, there is a need to penetrate more into it and develop better understanding of all the nuts and bolts involved.

Understanding Real Happiness

Despite it being so common, its impact and intensity, and hence its definition, varies from person to person. To a poor man on the street, happiness in life may mean a big pot of money to spend. But it means something entirely different to a person blessed with deep pockets. Its meaning is altogether different to a yogi than it is to a householder. Different sets of definitions emerge when happiness gets linked with religious beliefs, cultural backdrops, educational status, age brackets, and genders besides philosophical, emotional or psychological orientations of people. But the simplest and easiest view to understand is that of happiness coming from spiritual orientation, where it is taken as a feeling or state of mind referring to experiencing real life from moment to moment with love, grace, and gratitude.

One needs to understand that happiness is less dependent on what we got, and more with what we are in terms of our approach and attitudes towards real life. Happiness always resides in person's deeper core and can be accessed with proper preparations. Those who are busy searching it outside are never going to find it, just like the famous saying about the musk deer searching everywhere to trace the source of the scent which actually comes from its own belly. Placing undesirable hope on enhancing happiness quotient by focusing on material affluence, people, titles, relationships, gadgets, or events is doomed to certain failure.

Happiness, incidentally, is not something reserved for humans alone as animals also share this quest. Animals' quest for happiness, however, is restricted to sense of survival and gratifying physical demands like hunger, sleep, safety, procreation, rearing children, etc. In contrast, human beings are blessed with the thinking faculties that enable them to experience happiness at an even deeper level. This unique faculty brings added responsibility on human beings. Letting go of this capability actually brings humanity on a par with its lesser blessed species. It is another way of saying that indulging in physical level happiness alone is akin to living life like animals.

Levels of Happiness

Sense gratification indeed results in immediate happiness. Besides direct sense organs, sense gratifications also include many subjective matters. But the strongest of all these is certainly the lure for sexual encounters, and it is not difficult to understand why. Our evolutionary process has hinged on priority for survival and healthy rate of procreation. To help evolution continue, nature has deliberately bundled the procreation process with intense pleasures to excite consenting adults to come together, get attracted to each other, have sex with ultimate enjoyment, and finally reproduce. But for the pairing of enjoyment with sex, many species might have disappeared by now. Secondly, by their natural instinct, human beings wish to avoid complexities to the extent possible, and sex is more direct than all other gratifications. Sense gratification is most immediate and direct — it is obvious, visible, and provides experience in an instant. Therefore, it is called first level of happiness. First level of happiness is intense, but short-lived and a person gets tired of such gratifications sooner or later. Expiration of these pleasures is inevitably destined to leave behind a strong feeling of emptiness. This is the precise reason that many people can see through their full cycle, and decide to abstain from the same. It is exactly like the famous idiom that tells that what you gain on the roundabout will be lost on the swings.

Second level of happiness is associated with gratification for ego. Our ego is our best companion for life, as it never leaves us alone even for a moment. Feeling of being the smartest, funniest, most admired, resourceful, and well connected are all known to drive most of us towards the sense of worthiness. The sense of superiority reigns supreme under this level. If I consider myself better than others, I feel happy and vice versa. Issues surrounding 'I, me and mine' certainly occupy the major part of our mental space. So, happiness on this 'I' level is certainly more important than the physical level of gratification. But ego is also very deceptive and deceitful. It can befool its own owner by using the weapons at its command consisting of guilt, insecurity, anger, and judgement. Ego keeps the intelligence and wisdom of its owner preoccupied in managing the repercussions arising out of the weapons used. At this level, ego actually becomes a great destroyer of happiness. So, there may be a false kick to begin with, but ultimately one gets the bagful of unhappy situations.

Next in line is level three of happiness and it involves feelings and emotions such as love, care, commitment, concern towards, and acceptance of others. Here the person is bestowed with a sense of compassion allowing for focus on others. Above all these, there is level four where the person grows above all things transient and starts consciously exploring its relationship with the Supreme, called with whatever name and forms. Needless to say, any person with intelligence should focus only and only on third and fourth level of happiness by deliberately staying away from the first two levels. Pursuing third and fourth levels of happiness is the real subject matter of this book, and will take up bulk of space in the following pages, chapters, and sections.

Transient vs Enduring Happiness

Permanent happiness can be expected out of only permanent things. But we know well that all the worldly things are temporary in nature. So, happiness associated with such things in undeniably temporary in nature. We see a beautiful red rose in a garden, and instantly feel happy about it. But the flower is bound to fade and lose all its petals within hours. What will happen to our happiness coming out of that flower when that very flower is no more? We ought to apply the logic and reasoning that we are blessed with as humans. Logic supports the argument or proposition that the transient is never preferable at the cost of permanent. Yes, enduring happiness is quite elusive, but hope keep inspiring us to pursue it despite overwhelming odds. That hope is kept alive by our genetic inheritance of 'being human'.

If it was not so, we would not find people going for healthy food or engaging in socially acceptable behaviour or resisting temptations for casual sex. If transient was to be the main motto, our children would never study hard to secure higher grades. Just imagine parents allowing their children to pursue games and sports at the cost of study. No, parents are always after the children to focus on studies, so that in the long run they acquire high qualifications, good positions coupled with better earnings or pay and perks. Most of us appreciate the long-term perspective over short-term thrills. It is difficult to imagine the plight of the society if people were to be chasing short-term gratifications alone.

Happiness and Misconceptions

Happiness as a subject matter is shrouded by several misconceptions. For example, many of us look at it as an individualistic trait and fail to see its connection with the role played by other people around us. Others play a critical role in our achievement and enjoyment of happiness, whether we admit it or not. Giving overriding emphasis to ourselves is incomplete and short-lived. Similarly, we must realize that inner peace, the peace of heart, is so much more essential to feel happy.

Happiness is also not about getting big things right. People do say that they will be happy when such and such target is achieved. But when you meet them post such targets, they generally remain as empty as before. Crossing of milestones does not result in long lasting happiness. Didn't we have two more milestones decided soon after crossing the first one? Didn't we aspire to get another or bigger object to expect the same joy and happiness? There is never an end to such objects and there is no real joy linked with events or objects. Actually, happiness is all about getting small things right. If you are optimistic in attitude, kind in approach, cooperative towards others, and have your empathy and compassion in place, you are more likely to focus on your efforts, and still feel happy irrespective of final outcomes.

Yet another misconception is that happy people don't feel sad or they are blessed not to feel grief or failures. It is completely wrong. Happy people are as vulnerable to these human conditions as others. The difference is that they don't lose hope and don't fall prey to despair. They remain confident that even under the most testing situations things will get better. Happiness is not about blessings from high powers. It is all about choices being made at every step and every moment. It is indeed linked to the attitude of each individual. Like all other natural bounties from Mother Nature, access to the source of happiness is free for every living being without any discrimination whatsoever.

Another very important aspect of happiness is the understanding that it is indeed under our own control. Factors governing our happiness quotient, with few exceptions, certainly fall within our own control. Despite humanity in general undergoing constant testing, quite a few of us enjoy success in our pursuit of living a happy and fulfilled life during challenging times as well. This goes to prove that factors of human happiness and its fulfillment are beyond human hardships, conflicts, and all other types of visible or physical difficulties.

It is clear that below the reality of this carefree feeling of being

Total Happiness Pyramid

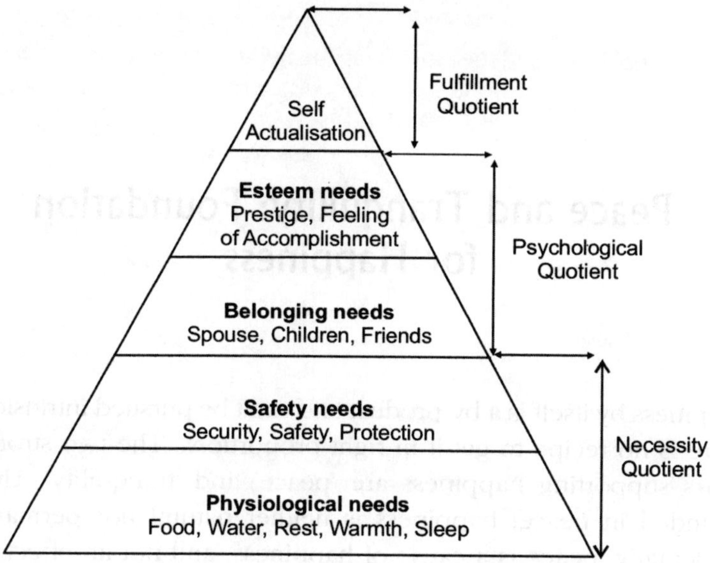

happy, there are layers and layers of issues that need to be scanned with proper microscopic lenses. After all, our objective is not only to know about it from the outer surface, but to identify real drivers and learn how to activate them properly to ensure more and more enduring spells of happiness as against smaller episodes. Potential factors can be listed as financial prosperity, social support system, people and relationships, visible signs and underlying currents, internal and external factors, mental or emotional attitudes, original or acquired traits, etc. These factors contribute in varying proportions to our happiness just as numerous spices are used to ensure enhanced but balanced aroma, appearance as well as taste in traditional Indian cooking. All these factors both supplement and complement each other in a unique manner. Surely, their interplay is going to help us gain a better hold on our well-being.

Peace and Tranquility: Foundation for Happiness

Happiness by itself is a by-product and can't be pursued intrinsically. There is no recipe to get it in right proportions. The two strongest pillars supporting happiness are 'peace' and 'tranquility'. Unless grounded in peace, happiness is neither natural nor permanent. Incidentally, peace is a cause of happiness, and not an effect. The moment one understands this link clearly, new doors open to cement happiness. As long as we remain restless, no other feeling can lead us to happiness. You might bring the whole world to the feet of an internally disturbed person, but he just can't get anything out of it. So, what is this inner peace that can put a spanner in all our efforts of seeking happiness? Speaking theoretically, it simply means 'being in a mental and physical state of ease'. In even simpler words, it is just opposite of being in the stressful state, the same stress that we are so well aware of. Peace, the real subject that we are attempting to unravel is also not about decibels levels alone. The peace we talk here is not about visiting a beautiful tourist destination or relocating to the mountains or a valley. It is neither sitting in isolation without any work to do nor living a retired life in a small town away from the challenges of modern day life. No, all such adventures may be classified as entertainment or escapism rather than peace. What we are talking is internal peace.

We know well that germination of the best seed and its evolution into a strong tree depends on the availability of quality soil, besides moisture and proper nutrients. Inner peace is that very soil (environment) which enables the growth of the plants of happiness in our life. We see plenty of challenges, people, emotions, and situations in our daily life that constantly create stress from morning till night. Life will always have issues and that is true for everyone and at every point of time. But still one should search for inner peace. Consuming antidepressant or sleeping pills is not the solution. That can only bring relief to the body but can't help a bit in attaining the desired state of mind. The basic solution for regaining lost inner peace lies in an underrated simple word called 'acceptance' — acceptance of self, of one's prevailing conditions (howsoever precarious these might be), acceptance of everything around us, including people and situations as these are. This ability of being at ease with one's surrounding is the starting point of the journey having a destination named happiness. You accept a thing and it brings harmony; but when we develop any dislike for it or be judgemental about the same and we get stress straight away.

Another source of stress is attachment with the past or desire to have specific outcomes in future. So long as we keep holding on to the past or remain in pursuit of changing the future, we are actually busy destroying our ability to live in the present. Concentrating on the present is the only remedy to repair our internal fractures, flows, and weaknesses. Focus on the present alone will convert such negative aspects into beautiful blessings. Over the centuries millions and billions have fought the battle of human life, so it is pointless to believe that our own situations are compelling enough to lose our inner peace. Whosoever believes in that is actually fooling himself. After all, what new can happen to us that has not happened to others in the past? The real problem is that, in our ignorance, we take our life and our very existence too seriously. None of us is comparable to a tiny tip of the smallest particle of this universe? So why should our problems and pressures be so huge?

Contrary to general perception, the real peace need not be associated with a *rishi* or a *yogi* alone. No, they don't have exclusive copyright over it. As a virtue, it is open to every human being. All of us, the common people, living our normal life, right here and now, with all its complications and pressures have equal right to access the very source of internal peace. All it takes is to know how to look for it.

Understanding Internal Peace

Internal peace means living life with a balanced state where energies operating in our heart and mind are in equilibrium; where our thoughts and actions are in perfect synch with each other, where there are no ripples of tension or divisions. This internal peace requires a perfect harmony between our emotions and mental capabilities. It presupposes that our logical reasoning is at play while controlling entire thought process. Peace is where moods and reactions are without any restlessness, disturbance, or anxiety.

This state is developed by evolving clean, clear, and complete perceptions about issues surrounding our life and accepting these as they are. Peace brings strong transformational powers. It allows harmonious and perfectly balanced mental conditions to operate irrespective of external factors. Peace provides us the ability to remain calm and undisturbed even in unpleasant or challenging circumstances. Peace is all about attitude focused on our inner self rather being dependent on people, places, objects, or environment. This is not about what the world offers to us but about our own response to the situations offered by the world. A person having internal peace can certainly overcome real life difficulties by facing them with perfect knowledge and evolving the right response to deal with it. Such a person is not guided by quantum of results, but by quality of responses.

This is a state that is not accidentally blessed or gifted to us. It is to be practised and acquired. One must realize that 'internal peace' is very much a skill. But it is not just another set of skills. It requires sustained learning and unlearning of wrong things. It also requires greater self-control and hard practise before it gets accessed. Dependent neither on external conditions or situations, it matures in our mental space when there is no negativity, fears or worries. Further, we ought to remember that peace, together with joy, ecstasy and bliss, are intrinsic to our being human. It is very much a part of our DNA. Also, that we are solely responsible for both its presence and absence in our life. It is a mistake to assume that things or people or situations are responsible for our peace or joy. No, they aren't and they can't be. Joy and peace are already lying there in the depth of our own being. All we need to do is to ignite it or let it get activated by removing overburden covering it. Coming together or falling apart due to external situations or persons or objects impacts our intrinsic peace only temporarily, and only when we allow these to do so.

Peace enables us to take stock of situations dispassionately. Peace lets us remain strong and capable of helping others as much as the need exists. Peace tells us to take care of the only thing that we have control over — our real self. There is no point in worrying about the A to Z of this world when you have no control over it. It is only our peace that helps us channelize our energy into our responses rather than reactions. It is peace that inspires us to do as best as we can in all spheres of life and do that without linking the results to our success. Peace makes us stronger in our efforts and strong efforts always lead to higher achievements. Fears, anxieties and worries are negative emotions and drain our personal energy, resulting in the weakening of our efforts, and thereby lowering our level of achievements. A peaceful mind also enables us to thrust away lust that comes from a mind filled with temptations. Only a tired mind allows temptations to have the upper hand. A peaceful mind generates strength and freedom alike and allows mind to prevail over attractions of transient sense gratifications.

Impact of Peace on Thoughts

Peace and tranquility make it conducive for our mind to generate responsive thoughts as against reactive thoughts. Peace works as a stimulus feeding to positive thoughts delinked with the external situations. Peace keeps the negative factors like jealousy and hurt under check. A tranquil mind activates the filter that identifies situations where the person facing them has no or little influence. It makes the mind differentiate in externally dependent problems, failures and challenges and those falling within one's own ambit. Let us remember that feeling of hurt or failure on one side, and positive resolve to face it on the other side, are alternate choices made by different people for a single challenge. Thus, it is response rather than the situation that makes the difference.

This transformation that can reverse the entire order of 'action-hope-happiness' to 'happiness-action-surety' is the search that we ought to find with knowledge, with wisdom and most importantly with practice. It is this source of perennial happiness that ultimately guides us to gain control over our thoughts. In turn, our thoughts will influence our actions. Actions, when carried out with full strength but no attachment bring success. The linear equation is really so simple.

Plight of Modern Day Karma Yogis

Our age is full of striking contradictions. On the one side, we have new and better technologies attracting billions of consumers while on the other we have billion others not having even enough food, drinking water and access to basic hygiene and sanitation, leave alone healthcare and education. On one side, we have ever enlarging product range of assured luxuries including houses, automobiles, electronic gadgets, and equipment promising enhanced happiness. On the other hand, we have modern day curses like obesity, diabetes and depression impacting more and more people while showing up at younger ages. We have increasing knowledge and decreasing tolerance. We are turning towards self-reliance with increased mutual distrust. Economic independence is rising, but so is dependence on gadgets and possessions. Bank balances are rising but accumulation of relationships is falling. Houses are becoming bigger while families are getting smaller. Questions relating to how much is enough and what is good time to apply brakes are getting blurred. The whirlpool of these contradictions keeps us in constant spin depriving us of peace and tranquility.

Most people in the age bracket of forties and fifties are generally engaged in generating and accumulating the wealth in one form or the other. Their next priority is the desire to improve the quality of life for self as well as those who are dependent on them. These priorities suck all their energies and initiatives in a manner that, forget about family and friends, they are hardly left with any quality time exclusively for themselves. They are so busy that they have no time to even consider whether what they are pursuing is exactly what they sincerely desired to achieve in the first place. You try to put across the basic and fundamental learning of great sages that 'material needs alone are not enough to fulfill ultimate human needs' and they will look baffled as if someone has just interrupted them in their worship unnecessarily. This tendency is on the rise much more in recent decades. Almost everyone can be seen racing faster than even before with no finish line in sight.

But all is not lost. One can still rely on old lighthouses for proper navigation. The real art lies in realization of the need to change the course and wisdom to spot the lighthouse from your position in the open ocean.

"Happiness is your nature. It is not wrong to desire it. What is wrong is seeking it outside when it is inside."

— Ramana Maharishi

As a recap of main learning until now we can quickly list the following key takeaways for augmenting our focus on our very desire of enhanced happiness of longer duration and more frequent spells.

a) Our happiness is a matter of our earning rather than a gift or blessing of others; genes, God, parents, society, and environment included.
b) Evolving mental controls to keep temptations for material possessions in check is a prerequisite for seeking happiness.
c) Pushing tendency of pursuing sensory gratification out to avoid remorse that necessarily follows like a shadow, needs to be practised always.
d) We alone have absolute control over our happiness. It is linked with our internal attitude rather than what this world offers.
e) Acceptance for surroundings is the prerequisite for searching peace.
f) Focus must be on the present, where the past and the future are considered undesirable distractions.

Each one of us desirous of enhancing happiness quotient is required to work on all these areas. But before we do that, let us differentiate which individual factor needs to be worked on, and whether there is any priority list that can be followed for better scoring. As we have limited energy and time, a clearly prioritized order will help us get to our destination faster.

Ashta Aishwarya

After differentiating happiness from thrills, enjoyments, and gratifications, we now move on to deal with factors enhancing our happiness. It is indeed a far deeper question than what appears on the surface and needs a cautious approach. Surprisingly, most people fail to recognize the factors involved comprehensively in happiness, especially their sequencing and relative importance. Besides appreciating the right factors, we shall also have to settle nagging issues as to what provides us more happiness or less, what we should hold on to, and what to discard. After all, we have a big basket of issues to deal with.

"*Aishwarya*" is a word from *Sanskrit* that refers to happiness enhancing bounties in general. While there is no exact parallel word in English to convey its real power, it can be loosely translated to mean power, wealth, prosperity, and riches all put together. There are several *Aishwaryas* and each one of these plays out differently for different people or at different times for the same person. But collectively these *Aishwaryas* accumulate a major portion of all possible happiness enhancers for majority of mankind. While we do deal with these *Aishwaryas* in our daily life, but at times we fail to appreciate these factors in proper perspective out of sheer ignorance or lack of realization.

Most people place financial abundance on top of such list. But in reality, monetary prosperity is just one of the several *Aishwaryas* and certainly not the most critical. As such, to feel happy and blessed, we must develop correct understanding and recognize other equally compelling contributors. This approach will help us establish proper balance among all these competing factors. Ability to do so is the art and science of achieving long lasting happiness and fulfillment in an adult's life.

> "People take different roads seeking fulfillment and happiness. Just because they are not on your road, does not mean they are lost." – Dalai Lama

Actually, searching fulfillment is not a modern-day problem. It has been around for a long time. Our ancestors have faced this very dilemma and have evolved the concept of "*Ashta Aishwarya*", eight specific and well-defined areas in ancient Indian scriptures. It will indeed be interesting to see if these factors have lost their shine over the centuries or they still hold their relevance. The sequencing of these factors, however, may appear to be a matter of individual choice. There is no "one size fits all" combination of *Aishwaryas*. The order used below is said to have evolved over thousands of years of experiences, and analysis of human tendencies by Indian ancient sages. But everything changes over long periods. Our society today is radically different from what it was a long time back. That change may need to be reflected in the order to keep pace with modern day realities. Change of order apart, it will be difficult for anyone to reject any of the individual *Aishwaryas* explained below as irrelevant, that much can be said with certainty. So, one is advised to suspend any urgent desire to question the efficacy of the order while reading through the following lines.

It will be seen that pursuing any one *Aishwarya* is not the end by itself. Rather it is just a single important step towards a fulfilling life. Another important point to remember is *Aishwaryas* have been recommended for Grihastha Ashram alone. Other stages of life have altogether different objectives to pursue and seeking happiness is not to be sought there as a direct purpose. The basic objective of studying all the *Aishwaryas* is to seek guidance to gain equilibrium in apportioning our available time, energies, and efforts.

Let us look at the recommended order of *Aishwaryas* for a householder one by one.

First Aishwarya

Personal Achievements

Every human life, in a way, is just a sum of multiple experiences acquired over long period. Some of these are exciting while many others are not. Some of our experiences impact our life for a short period, while only a countable few leave long lasting imprint. Our achievements signify the relevance of our entire existence. As a human spirit, each one of us needs our own accomplishments to survive and thrive. We need to achieve successes and collect as many triumphs as we can. A collective list of our triumphs, together with their volume, and significance define our life. Recollection of our successes brings happiness as many times as we think about them.

Apart from big successes, we also enjoy some smaller, but touching moments in life. Aspiring for something with great intensity, writing your heart out to someone special, catching a good discussion with someone you admire, cooking a special dish and enjoying it with loved ones, reading an enlightening piece of literature, watching a touching movie, visiting a dream destination, are but some examples of events that get hard coded on our mental hard disc with long lasting impressions. These personal experiences may not be that great in terms of contributing to conventional standards of success, but a person having a large collection of these treasures knows their real worth. These are moments that provide great satisfaction and bring meaning to our life.

Achievement-oriented events shape our success at the professional level as well. Coming up with a unique solution to a sizeable problem faced by the organization, completing an important project on time and within budget, trying new things ahead of others and seeing them succeed, acquiring some genuinely enjoyable piece of knowledge or skill, getting recognized by the fraternity for professional contribution in one's own chosen field, reaching the heights of one's own occupation commensurate with capacity and capability are examples from professional field that make it fulfilling. Using an illustration from cricket, all the scoring need not be by hitting sixes and fours. Every great batsman accumulates his runs even in ones and twos while waiting for juicy balls to come his way. In cricket, the emphasis is on enhancing total score — be it with boundaries or singles. The scoreboard always depicts the total runs scored. The same principle holds true for collecting achievements in our life to fuel our happiness. Similarly, in real life big achievements and trophies will always be few and far between, so we should also accumulate smaller achievements regularly.

Such accomplishments provide a feel of being a winner, and a raw sense of achievement. These can never be acquired in exchange of money, or even if one tries to buy them, (for example obtaining social recognitions/awards in exchange of something) that genuine feeling associated with personal success, can never be acquired. Your achievements create a special aura that remains with you even when you are with a crowd. The dreams of an achiever are always more positive than that of an under-achiever simply because achievements remain with you even when you are in deep sleep.

However, for achievements to lead to happiness there is a condition attached. You can't hope for happiness until and unless your achievements are connected to your core values and vision for life. Also, simply getting something by chance is no achievement. The achievements must be those which were earned hard, where you could put in your very best. One should differentiate between success and achievements as the latter is possible even in failures. Similarly, achieving something when one is addicted to achievement will fail to bring in joy and happiness. After all, happiness is less of an event, and more about the process of celebrating efforts.

In addition, these experiences and achievements need to be peeped, protected, polished, and preserved regularly. At the end of our working lives, accumulation of the right kind of experiences is the difference between happy people and those who are not. Certainly, those who have a larger balance in deposits of experiences will be happier than the rest. Let each one of us create as many great moments in life while remaining at the pinnacle of our professional life to preserve strong memories of these achievements, so that their fragrance lingers with us for the rest of our lives.

Second Aishwarya

Obtaining Right Wisdom and Knowledge

Knowledge is information acquired through study or from other sources, but it is objective as well as subjective in character. Objective knowledge is based on measurable facts, while subjective knowledge arises from the realm of personal perspectives, opinions, and assumptions that differ from person to person. In other words, objective knowledge can be learned from books or from teachers, but subjective knowledge has to be assimilated from real life. Grounded on indisputable facts, objective knowledge alone can qualify as right knowledge. In any case, every person should remain in learning mode all through his/her adult life because no matter how much one has learnt; there will always be more questions than one can ever answer. The bulk of the knowledge we acquire over the years is actually incomplete and subjective in nature. Such knowledge is barely skin deep. The moment you scratch under the surface, much remains unknown. In the initial stages of your contemplative process itself, you start seeing through the layers of subjective beliefs and assumptions that hamper your perceptions from acquiring real knowledge.

Continuous learning, however, needs to be focused on avoiding subjective knowledge which involves opinions and personal interpretations that clog the mind with worldly affairs, and pushes peace and equanimity out of bounds. Learning is not to be restricted only to the earlier stage of our life. One comes across many young adults who start believing that there is nothing more for them to learn anymore. That is an ignorant approach. One is always advised to keep learning until the last. If you don't know how to use the newly acquired knowledge, it doesn't matter as it will seldom go unused. We might be surprised by how a newly found skill or knowledge can impact our life and the life of others around us in some significant way. Some people go to the other extreme and equate stoppage of learning to mental death.

When we turn fifty, many of us begin facing a fresh set of unknown questions from within. Am I here to do the same nine to five job month after month? Do we have a greater purpose in this life? What lies beyond all the physical things that we see around us? What supreme power is controlling and guiding the prevailing order in the universe? Between means and ends, which is more critical and what should we focus on? Questions like these do not bother us so much in the earlier stages of life. To deal with these new questions, one is asked to look for altogether different sources of knowledge far beyond the conventional sources of texts, books, dictionaries, or search engines. Traditional tools prescribed for obtaining right knowledge are scriptures, prayers, yoga, contemplation, and meditation. But the most important tool required to secure new objective knowledge is fixing the gaze inside one's own heart and mind. Initial success in acquiring the ability to focus inward itself exposes us to the realization as to how little we know.

This new-found knowledge acquired through contemplation by focusing on the inner self is called wisdom. Wisdom is to be gained through experience, and it exists largely at the intuitive level. It is only wisdom that generates moral and ethical strength. This wisdom also facilitates adherence to a stricter code of behaviour. Pursuing wisdom will lead one to an incredible sense of calmness, peacefulness, and happiness that was never experienced earlier. Acquiring right knowledge (*vidya*) and getting rid of ignorance (*avidya*) has been described as responsible behaviour for every enlightened individual. The concept of *avidya* includes delusion and false knowledge, and is said to be responsible for several root causes of miseries, the *kleshas*.

Avidya is also directly identified with the ego's glorification. Ego appears a natural tendency of the human mind, and one should accept it as an essential part of human existence. But ego is known to superimpose itself over the voice of the soul successfully. In that state, it justifies subjective knowledge as being more important than objective knowledge. This very tussle can be seen among many people who say that they are perfectly happy even in situations where they don't even understand the real meaning of happiness. The line used quite frequently 'Ignorance is bliss' is more often used for people harbouring '*avidya*'. Without exception, search for real happiness will necessitate eliminating this ignorance, and obtaining desired wisdom by pursuing all prescribed methods.

True wisdom may also be understood as knowledge and intelligence coupled with moral integrity. Morality may not have been so important to people living life under the shadow of subjective knowledge. But the role of morality must be realized with advancing age. It is wisdom that makes us understand that ultimately means are as important as the ends. Acquiring wisdom through determined effort and strict discipline also results in bringing the mind and senses under control. A person, who acquires proper objective knowledge by following moral and ethical means, is the real wise person, and is always happier than any unenlightened character, unless of course, you are talking of the camel that puts his neck in the bush and believes that it can't be seen by the external world. People not having right knowledge keep swinging from one extreme to another, and from one moment to other. But right knowledge facilitates contentment replacing the lust for acquisitions, possessions, and temptations. It unleashes moral strength to become a strong shield in temptation-filled situations. Eventually, such people alone can enjoy long lasting peace and tranquility followed by happiness and bliss.

Third Aishwarya

Wellbeing of Spouse, Children, and Immediate Family

Accepting another person or persons in our life, at any stage, is essentially a life changing experience. This statement applies best to one's spouse and children. Some people take the support of their spouse as given. Such a situation may prevent them from appreciating the link between wellbeing of their spouse and their own fulfillment. Thinkers, however, have always found a deep connection between the two. In eastern societies, the individuality of most husbands and wives is so truly intertwined that one can't help considering one's spouse as one's own extension. They end up sharing their successes and failures as a combined entity. The husband's promotion provides the kind of thrill to the wife as if she herself has been recognized for her individual performance. Similarly, recognition of the wife within important circles or her personal achievements brings pride to the husband in equal proportions.

Some of us, however, make the mistake of supposing that no special efforts are required to make this wonderful relationship flourish. That is a totally wrong assumption. Both husband and wife must contribute to their relationship all their life. To make each other stronger and act like a shield protecting the other against their weaknesses is a struggle to be endured all through. A simple reality check of proper investment in marriage is to assess how much one helped the other become a better person. Just list out ten points where you worked hard to help your spouse become better or an improved person, and you will know how much credit you deserve for the success of this special relationship. Not helping the spouse to grow is like pulling yourself back. At the end of the day, it is a two-legged race and the happiness of a couple depends on joint efforts.

Similarly, well-being of children and their individual achievements are another important source of fulfillment for parents, especially in the Asian context. You can't imagine a parent being happy when their children are not performing to their potential. Parents can't feel safe if their children are in some sort of danger. As a parent, we see a lot at stake when it comes to the progress of our children, be it at their school results, professional education, achievements in extra curriculum activities, and advancements in career. Success tasted by a child is always as thrilling to their parents as if it was their own. We are genetically engineered by nature to feel that way.

The factor adding value to our happiness about our children, however, is commensurate with how much we contribute towards children getting all they could. Children are generally raised when parents are in their midlife. That stage in life has many pressing time demands of its own. Despite that, responsible parents can find time to invest on their children. Time invested is the real measure of your discharging parental obligations. Simply creating better physical environment is not enough for ideal grooming of children. Seeking financial and material support from parents is more a child's right than a parent's obligation. The argument that "I was busy in advancing my career to provide better resources to children" doesn't cut ice here. In reality, advancing one's career is for one's own self and not so much for the children or spouse for that matter, and we better understand that.

How much time could you invest on them during their growing years is what is going to add to your happiness and satisfaction. Did you stand by them during their important milestones? Did you ensure that their value system was never contaminated by the socially acceptable lies, double speak, or foppish behaviour? Was your physical support available to them for mooring their boats during storms? Were you there to offer your shoulder to them during their testing situations? Were you all ears when they wanted to share some of their burdens? Could you motivate them by being a coach on occasions when they wished to learn new things? Were you able to be around them whenever they desired? Answers to all these questions depend on how much time you had for them when they needed it. You can draw your own answer sheet and count your score to see if you secured a distinction. It is really that simple. But it is never too late. One can try amending the situation at any stage of life. Be well informed that your children are part of your happiness, and more than your money, they appreciate your spending more of your time with them. And, unfortunately, if you think that they are eying your wealth more than your time, the signal is worse than you might have imagined initially. Such a situation conclusively proves that the damage is done, and crisis point has been reached requiring admission to intensive care.

The role of a happy family in one's own fulfillment is placed very high and it certainly appears critical the moment we decide to look around us. Look at the most successful people that you may know, and invariably you can spot their common link. Most of them have a well-knit family support system working as a sturdy foundation for their success. Members of such families are found enjoying each other's company irrespective of their material fortunes. Clearly, their source of happiness is linked to their accounts of mutual interdependence and support systems, and quite delinked with the size of their bank balance.

Family is the foundation that holds the structure which houses health, wealth, wisdom, and experiences. Hence, our family deserves our constant emotional and physical support to continue having meaning in living a fulfilling human life. Nothing should ever be allowed to come in the way of helping members of the family if we are aiming to reach a higher level of personal happiness. It is foolhardy to pursue potential wealth building opportunities by sacrificing health and family. What matters more for the family is your time than your money. As it is, your time is by far the most precious gift to your dear ones. Your time is the real part of your life because it is exhaustible, and it never comes back. Essence of real love for family is how much of our life we give to them. Giving time to money making and justifying that money will be used for our beloved is never the same thing.

Fourth Aishwarya

Sound Physical and Mental Health

Let us compare a happy life to a journey involving a drive through a road having beautiful scenery on either side. For such a journey, physical health is like the vehicle being used by the passenger. Important body organs are comparable to parts of the vehicle ranging from tires to engine to seat to steering wheel to windscreen etcetera. As a passenger, none of us will be comfortable taking a long journey in a vehicle which is not well kept. If the above cited parts of the vehicle are known to be less than perfect, we will be very fearful even before the journey begins. Such a poor vehicle will turn out a big handicap for the best of driver in terms of distance covered and time taken for crossing milestones. Continuing the same example, wealth can be imagined just like gas and lubricant required for smooth running of the vehicle. Yes, the vehicle can't move without the gas, but abundance of gas for a dilapidated vehicle is unlikely to let you reach to your destination either.

Nothing really matters without good health. Feeling any form of happiness is possible for only those blessed with sound physical health. Taking good care of it, therefore, ought to be high in priority for every adult. Many of us take our body for granted, and keep thinking that it will always remain subservient to us as a humble attendant irrespective of atrocities we commit. That is not true at all. This body is a unique creation of God and is designed with lot many safety margins, but it constantly keeps score of all the ills and atrocities that we expose it to. Similarly, it keeps score of all the good things that we do for it in terms of food, lifestyle, and exercises. And again, good physical health also requires a good portion of our time.

Eating well and at regular intervals, enjoying right sleep cycles, regular exercises, periodical check-ups to identify unwanted variations, abstaining from use of alcohol, tobacco, and such other substances, proper protection against environment one lives in, are some of the factors or personal choices that we continually make each day. These measures ultimately combine and reflect on our physical health. Not that we have not known it until now, but regular reminders are a must even for those who are otherwise quite conscious about it. Some of the curses of modern day life arise out of mismatch in our lifestyle and food intake. Food is not as generic in nature as it sounds, since it must match our physical surroundings and the way we spend our time every day. So, food better be different even for different members in the same family. It should be different for people in different stages of their life, and it should be different for similar people but who work in different professions.

On an average, most of us have better awareness about health issues these days. But all is not well. The idea of undergoing regular check-ups and using medications to keep warning signals within required range is but only a poor substitute to appropriate lifestyle to ensure pure health without dependence on medical prescriptions. We also come across many people who conveniently find refuge for faults in health issues in their gene pool. There are only a few ailments that are hereditary, while most others relate to life style choices. Well, if my father was not trained to take work related stress too well, and I also continued with the same attitude, there is a genuine question about this problem being hereditary or my own creation? On the contrary, if an elder had a particular problem, it should be a strong reason for the next generation to make sure that special care is taken from beginning to ensure that preventive actions are taken to avoid repetition. Blaming it on others or external factors is behaviour called escapism.

Money can't buy good health. So, spoiling health to earn more is a bad bargain. There is a common saying about ignorance of this situation where a person '*spends his health to earn money in his earlier life and is forced to spend his money to regain health in later part of life.*' In this way, in the end he is left with neither money nor health, and exhausts his most limited resource — time. Unfortunately, many of our friends and acquaintances can be seen walking on this very road unmindful of known consequences.

Besides physical health, mental health brings forth another aspect critical to happiness. Depression and anxiety resulting in psychological problems and complaints are common symptoms of imperfect mental health. As a modern-day curse, we have more people impacted by varying levels of mental health related issues in cities everywhere. Till sometime back, mental health used to carry a stigma attached with it but not now. Mental health has a key role to play in evolving individual responses required to face challenges in life. Almost everyone goes through plenty of stressful situations in life. Avoiding it completely is not a practical proposition. Getting into financial difficulties, death of a loved one, chronic medical condition, and traumatic experiences are all part of normal human life. However, we see different people facing these situations differently. While some take these very seriously and end up spoiling their life up to a point of no return, few others take them rather positively and face them with courage. They can be seen resuming their normal life in due course. Different responses to similar situations point towards mental health of the persons concerned.

How to take care of your mental health better? Well, first thing is the acceptance of the problem, and have the courage to go and consult a trained therapist. In case no symptoms of excessive anxiety exist, one can work on raising self-dignity and respect to higher levels. This might require self-acceptance, keeping mild targets, and promoting positivity in thinking. Positivity requires being in the company of good people, and avoiding those who don't add value to your life. Another important aspect is to avoid stressful situations and walking away from doubts and delusions. A clean and clear mind is a healthy mind. Happiness is never far from such a person. The techniques explained later under the chapters on Self-awareness and Meditation are known to work wonders for improving mental health as well.

Fifth Aishwarya

Money and Material Wealth

After taking care of your achievements, wisdom, family, and health, Material wealth figures as an important blessing to enjoy this world. No one can say that money or wealth is a bad word, or that it has no relevance. Money is a great facilitator and helps in enhancing quality and standards of living. Money certainly reduces mortality and allows one to have access to worldly comforts. Financial sufficiency is a must even to pursue philosophical objectives. Wealth takes care of all types of energies essentially required to pursue every other thing in life. No one can enjoy a comfortable life, let alone help others in any form without money. Money is a unique form of energy that can be used, exchanged, stored, shared, donated, preserved, and passed on to the next generation. It is also unique in the sense that, beyond a point, it works itself, and keeps growing of its own if directed and monitored properly, unlike any other form of energy. This is evident from the fact that the growth of financial fortunes is generally higher for high net worth individuals and organizations.

Wealth is a powerful resource. It builds empires on one hand, and destroys nations on the other. It helps getting dreams come true, but also brings unwanted nightmares. It makes most people happy and few others miserable. At the lower levels, its availability improves satisfaction. But beyond the initial levels, it loses its link with increasing satisfaction almost completely. One of its biggest flaws is being addictive in nature to the extent of being insatiable. Entire human history is full with examples of the inability of people in drawing the line as how much is enough. That is why prophet after prophet has advocated against pursuing mindless accumulation of material resources. Such accumulation certainly risks undermining the importance of other pressing objectives of human life.

We all know that God has given us limited time within which we pursue our objectives. But acquisition of wealth eats up substantial time of its accumulators. No amount of material wealth helps us buy even a single moment of extra time. Time indeed is the ultimate limited resource of every person. It deserves to be spent very wisely. Surely, we ought to act judiciously. We must restrain against mindless accumulation of wealth. We must ensure that only a part of our time goes into making money. Going after it at the cost of other important activities will prove worthless for overall score of our real happiness.

Sixth Aishwarya

Company of Real Friends

Constant access to real friends you care about and share interests with is surely life fulfilling. It is so easy for anyone to lower their guard among friends, because you know that they like you for what you are and there are no conditions attached. Friends are great teachers of the values such as sharing, caring, affection, trust, and sacrifice. Friends always provide free and frank opinions and suggestions. Their words leave unconditional impact on because you can believe them completely. More often, friends know each other better than even respective parents, and it helps them to pass suggestions about you without turns and twists. Having a reliable friend is a certain source of driving away all your unwanted pressures and depression. In their presence, we end up forgetting all our sorrows and tensions. Nothing comes better than friends when it comes to sharing even the darkest secrets, as you know that they will never shortchange you for any petty gain. Your friends reduce your sorrows and enhance your happiness by sharing unquestioningly. Every normal human being improves self-esteem in the company of friends. Surely, having good friends enriches you in more ways than one.

But friends that are being talked about here are real friends. The difference between mutual affection bound relationship and benefit seeking tail-waggers needs to be discerned with appropriate clarity. We are talking of someone who is there to support you no matter what. A real friend trusts you completely and does not judge you. Without putting you down, she/he calls a spade a spade without fear or favour. The label of friendship is very serious matter and should not be approached casually. The real friend is the person who has his/her own achievements in place, and has unwavering opinions and views. He/she ought to have proven to be loyal to you over longer periods of good and bad times. Without the test of time, no one can be called a real friend. A true friend can bring a smile to your face even in gloomy circumstances. The company of friends has a unique aura where calm and peace can exist even amidst chaos. Their company makes you gather courage to face every worry of the world. No amount of money, power or position can make you enjoy that serene feeling which comes only among friends. Having a couple of such friends is a real blessing for living this life with happiness.

Friendships driven and coloured by wealth, power or position survive only until the others are dependent on you. Once you lose that or they find some other person whose status is higher than yours, all your so-called 'friends for benefits' just run away. Only real bonding based friendships last longer irrespective of rise or decline of status on either side. So, presence of feeling of affection and absence of selfishness are necessary pre-conditions before naming any relation as genuine friendship, the friendship relevant to be measured as an *Aishwarya*. It is critical to understand that friendship is a double-edged sword as an inappropriate friend can lead you in the wrong direction and can drain your resources rather than being pillar of support.

Seventh Aishwarya

Security, Safety, and Freedom

It is a bit difficult to realize, but a secured environment where one feels safe and protected from all fears and failures, goes a long way in nurturing the feeling of happiness deep within. For a person tormented with multiple fears for physical safety of lives and possessions, thinking about happiness is a challenge. Survival is the only thing that occupies the total mind space of a person in fear. Fears related to security and safety may relate both to the physical environment as well as emotional conditions. Anxiety can be the only tenant living in such a space. It is natural to expect to be loved, desired, and feel good about ourselves. The greatest and the bravest of us requires someone seconding and convincing us about our goodness. But all these feelings, so critical to our happiness, presuppose a safe, sound, and secured environment in which we operate. Unsafe and insecure environment results in a feeling of vulnerability or inferiority. As such, there is no possibility of perfect and complete happiness out there. All one expects is ever threatening negative vibrations, which only lead to desperation and resultant chaos.

Turning our vision to emotional safety, we often come across people suffering from regular and spiked mood swings. This is another kind of unsafe environment killing or camouflaging complete happiness. In modern times, these symptoms are given scary names like depression, bipolar disorder, attention deficit hyperactivity disorder, or dementia. Generally speaking, all these disorders have their common root in fears for security and safety. Forget about neighbours, people at the workplace, people in public sphere, or any and every person in power, under such situations the person concerned is not able to trust even family members.

Next in line is the issue of freedom. Freedom and happiness also are inter-connected. Freedom here means the possibility of making a choice without being inhibited by others in any way. It is not that humans can make any kind of choice without any restriction whatsoever. Even when one makes a choice, humans can't fly or suspend sleep for a very long time or live forever. But within the gambit of possible options, the very possibility of making a choice from available options itself is a big opportunity. Freedom of choice can be classified further in terms of economic, political, religious, or social etc. A normal human enjoys being part of a free environment where he doesn't have to look towards any other person for making a choice. So, happiness asks the seeker to make choices about conditions of his living, choices about his emotional balance, and finally choices about professional work so that life is lived in a secure, safe, and free environment. This particular *Aishwarya* is more dependent on surroundings and situations and offers only a limited role to the individual concerned to make big changes. To this extent, our total happiness is largely dependent on our circumstances.

Eighth Aishwarya

Pursuing Passions

Passion is a word associated with multiple meanings. As an *Aishwarya*, passion is not to be read as desire, lust, fantasy, or longing. Passion is not being used here to refer to impulse, or rage, or any self-indulgent activity loosely called hobby. What is being discussed is fervour or enthusiasm capable of channelizing physical and mental energies to achieve excellence in some area of interest and relevance. Passion here will mean the process of building strong capabilities acquired over longer periods of time. Passion is acquired by gaining mastery by working on natural skills of the individual, the mastery which translates into enhanced performance levels. Above all, passion here is called so only when a certain degree of expertise is achieved in the chosen field. It is only then that it becomes an outlet for self-determining needs. Pursuing passion starts with identification of the activity that thrills the person, and exploring whether for that minimum skill exists in the person for such an activity. Then there are long and tiring spells of dedicated *'sadhana'* needed to achieve mastery over the activity. It doesn't matter what the activity is. It might be as simple as cooking, music, camping, tracking, bird watching, or whatever. It must be able to inspire the person to aim for perfection and lead the pursuer to bliss.

This passion is pursued not for competing with someone, or winning and losing associated with sports, but for relaxation and devotion. Excelling in sports or such other competitive activities also involve hard preparations on one's own talents and natural abilities, but the underlying focus there is winning. Losing in sports involves a lot of heartburn and agony that takes sports of all types out of our definition of passion for the present discussion. Passion requires constant learning and growing without set targets. Pursuing passion keeps validating the values and beliefs of the pursuer. Pursuing passion over a long period leads to a sense of freedom where there are no bounds or limitations.

Joy derived from pursuing passion is always longer lasting, unlike hobbies or competitive sports which are at best to be taken as instant mood upgrades. Besides impact over happiness, passions are known to boost positivity by reducing negative feelings. That is the precise reason that most accomplished passion pursuers have a calm and serene aura, and are generally seen to be above typical segregations. It is for this reason that we must encourage youngsters to find their passion and pursue it with vigour to be real achievers. On one hand, it would help them face the negativity hurled by external environment, and on the other hand, it would provide enjoyment.

Important Takeaways

1. Developing understanding of these Aishwaryas underscore that happiness and fulfillment are more about earning rather than just getting it as a boon or blessing. In this world, no one gets anything substantial without working hard and seeking happiness is no exception. You desire it, you understand its right source, you give your best, and finally you get it. This is the only recipe. If anything falls in our lap without working for, it can't thrill us.
2. Placing dependence on one or two Aishwaryas alone can't enhance our score to desired levels. For example, assume these eight factors to be independent questions in a Board's Examination where all of them carry roughly similar marks. Now, no one can expect to score a perfect 100 without successfully attempting answers to all the questions. The

scoring for our happiness is no different. We ought to work on all or most of these simultaneously if we wish to gain higher scores. It is that simple.

3. The single most important takeaway is to realize the limitation of financial wealth as an overarching Aishwarya. Money doesn't have the power to cure all our ailments. Those of us who are blessed with sufficient resources will immediately vouch for the fact that they fail to gain complete happiness even after having plenty of wealth and monetary abundance. We should, therefore, revisit our time allocation and adjust our life in a manner where we find sufficient time for pursuing other Aishwaryas.
4. No Aishwarya is to be compromised and none is to be taken for granted. Leaving one for another will create discord and bring imbalance. Our time, energy, and initiatives are required for improving our health, for attending to the well-being of our children and spouse, for chasing our long-forgotten passion, besides making money or improving our achievements or enhancing our wisdom. Sincere efforts made over longer periods will certainly bring parity among all factors and will place us higher on the percentile curve of happiness and fulfillment. Efforts, more efforts, and better-informed efforts are required to bridge the void of peaks and valleys which exist among different factors.

Decoding Critical Quotients and their Link to Happiness

Having dealt with the 'What' part of the happiness, we shall now look at its 'How' and 'Why' aspects. Analyzing these aspects will necessitate understanding of psychological issues in terms of what is workable and what is not. While going over the list of priorities that one should observe in life to seek happiness, the questions that are likely to create ripples across our thought process are that we are limited by our capabilities, and there is only so much that one can do. We must investigate, if it is so. Many scientific studies have been carried out in the field of psychology in the last 3-4 decades, which have not only decoded many unknown factors, but also listed improvements that can be learned with proper knowledge and practice. These new insights enable the person to upscale his/her psychological orientation and learn how to alter their responses to real life circumstances like never before. Let us look deep into the matrix of such new insights focused around these four different dimensions called Physical, Intellectual, Emotional, and Spiritual Quotients or PQ, IQ, EQ, and SQ respectively.

Human beings are blessed with multiple types of intelligences. Each intelligence type has its own strength and weaknesses for an individual at any given point in time. But presence or absence of one type of intelligence or its degree does not necessarily get correlated to other intelligences. It is to the credit of Howard Gardner, who in 1983 came out with his "Theory of Multiple Intelligences" where physical, intellectual, emotional, and spiritual intelligences came out as the main types of intelligences. These are interrelated and build on each other as overall intelligence levels of any individual person undergo changes enriched by academic achievements, self-learning, and professional pursuits or simply by normal life experiences. All these dimensions have their own importance, and impact on our lives in uniquely different ways. Knowing about their respective qualities will help us understand ourselves and others surrounding us with better clarity. That learning will also help us gain real control on how to improve our happiness quotient.

Physical Intelligence (PQ)

Our body is undoubtedly the sole equipment that is used to experience and interact with this existential world of forms and figures. Our body is the medium that helps us resonate with vibrations of energy required to carry out every small and big action. This alone is the antenna used for receiving all types of signals from external world. Our body also works as a diagnostic kit used for experiencing all symptoms, feelings, emotions, pains, and pleasures alike. Physical intelligence operates in various situations involving use of physical powers, effective hand-eye coordination, and skills used for managing body fluidity. For example, activities involving sportsmen, warriors, performers, and dancers require perfection of PQ to excel over normal standards. PQ is also important for overhaul wellbeing, personal health, and contributes towards longevity.

Improvements in PQ require good knowledge about fitness, nutrition, and bodily wellness. Diet is the fuel that operates the entire body. It must have a proper mix of carbohydrates, proteins, and minerals. The numbers indicating calories and fat content are all too important to ignore. Management of portions and timing for our meals must be valued like worship. Eating on time, and eating frequently in small proportions are two golden ground rules that are frequently ignored in modern life. Regular intake of all types of vegetables and fruits in sufficient proportions are highly recommended. These items contain some unique combination of nutrients, and preferring only selective items is like depriving yourself from life supporting ingredients.

Consuming locally grown items need special mention due to its critical contribution for sustaining harmony with the climatic conditions/variations of our live environment. Over centuries, Mother Nature has mastered how to grow most suitable foodstuff for survival of living beings in respective geographies. It has also combined remedies for meeting variations due to change of seasons. Alas, this unique gift of Mother Nature no more gets its due respect and recognition. With the shopping center culture, consumers have no means to know what stuff is grown locally and what comes from entirely different climatic conditions. One simple step to overcome is to ensure that fruits and vegetables are procured only from local bazaars rather than malls.

Increased awareness of observing, identifying, and responding to signals from body, in terms of hunger, depression, fatigue, pains or frustrations is yet another critical ability impacting PQ. We do great injustice to our physical body by ignoring subtle indications being conveyed by it from time to time. Human body is said to be one of the most rugged machines fitted with required standby systems. It is also said to be fitted with auto correct mechanism in sufficient capacity. Nothing breaks down suddenly or abruptly. All we need to do is pay attention to signals coming from this mean machine. Regular checkups and commitment to bring improvements in required areas at the right time is the responsibility of the proud owner of this machine. Diagnosed at the right time, many course corrections required can, in most cases, be applied even without opting for medical interventions. Ignoring the message from our own body is open invitation to complications of varying intensities. Needless to mention that almost every curative process involving human body comes with avoidable side effects, and hence should be desisted as much as possible. Having seen place of health at higher priority in the '*Ashta Aishwarya*' list, it is expected that we behave with responsibility and stay away from committing tyranny over our body. This body is the only equipment at our disposal for all possible experiments to improve our afterlife, let alone the present life.

Intellectual Quotient (IQ)

Next, we shall look at the dimension of our intelligence. IQ measures human abilities such as grasping power and 'retain and recall' power for factual knowledge. IQ leads us to think, to establish cause and effect analysis, logic applying abilities, use of problem solving techniques, and our management with numbers and words. In short, it is the maturity curve achieved over the growing process. There were times when IQ was considered as God's gift. Later it got established that it could be enhanced, to some extent, by practices such as stilling the mind each day and single point focusing. IQ is especially important for children, young adults, and adults, while its usefulness continue to remain relevant over all ages.

Opinions are sharply divided among researchers about IQ impacting quotient of happiness and their views range from one extreme to another. But generally speaking, we can find the correlation only at casual level. Some people also warn about high IQ people suffering from superiority complex coming in the way of dealings with other people considered by them as less smart. Others also suggest that more the knowledge you have, broader are your experience and greater will be your concerns such that you will drag down your Happiness Quotient with higher IQ. But faculties managed by IQ are too critical to be ignored and aiming for higher IQ is crucial even if there is no direct impact on level of happiness.

Mr. Shirzad Chamine, a seasoned strategy trainer and a lecturer at Stanford and visiting Professor at University of San Francisco, has introduced another concept called Positive Intelligence (PI) that further supplements the IQ concept. PI, in his approach outlines the struggle between our friendly mental forces and enemy mental forces, similar to a 'Good Cop and Bad Cop' scenario. Part of our intelligence deals with wisdom, insights, mental powers that goes to make us Good Cop. On the other hand, we have inherent Bad Cop syndrome where part of our intelligence work in automatic and habitual mind patterns having its own voice, beliefs, and assumptions. In that avatar, it doesn't mind working even against own interest; and is capable of working in self-sabotage mode.

The Bad Cop side remains occupied in negative thoughts like criticizing others, controlling situations, creating stronger arguments in support of bad behavior, justifying habits, stands taken in different situations, and identifying threats to sharpen survival instincts. As such, it remains engaged in promoting negative attitudes. On the other hand, the Good Cop side engages in thoughts revolving around empathy, innovation, and creativity. Both are essential but in proper balance. Good Cop serves us well by taking care of our interest as a good friend and does not mind pooh-poohing whenever required.

Thus, it promotes a positive attitude, and we all know it too well that working with positive mindset enhances an individual's performance at all levels of productivity, creativity, and engagement bringing in higher success. Success precedes happiness. The PI advocators call for working on habits that bring our Bad Cop under control and promote our Good Cop, so that our mind remains occupied more often with positivity and vigor. The following lines of Mr. Shirzad Chamine best summarize the whole concept:

> "With Positive Intelligence you can significantly improve the percentage of time that your mind is acting as your friend, rather than as your enemy. This will permanently shift the balance of power inside your mind so you can achieve more of your vastly untapped potential — and help others do the same."

The ways suggested for controlling our mind and how to make it work as our friend are important focus areas of this book, and shall be explained in great details in subsequent chapters. Actually, this single step is the most significant initiative for bringing critical changes in one's life.

Emotional Intelligence (EQ)

Emotional Intelligence is the ability to identify and manage emotions of self as well as others and includes three distinct components. Firstly, it covers the ability to identify the emotion correctly. Secondly, EQ involves harnessing emotions by applying the same for problem solving and finding right solutions. Lastly and most importantly, it includes ability to regulate one's own emotions as well as cheering up others around. Emotions are at the center of almost all aptitudes and attitudes in human life. Almost every human interaction involves interplay of emotions. Emotions like fear, worry, guilt, shame, embarrassment, disgust, helplessness are all part of our normal daily life and must be dealt with by each one of us. Right use of EQ helps to develop empathy with others, overcome challenges, and most importantly defuse conflicts. This results in avoidance or at least minimizing of stress. Thus, it facilitates a stress and friction free engagement and makes interaction with others smooth. In addition, matters such as self-management, self-confidence, self-initiatives, self-improvements are all part of management of our emotions and are directly linked to our EQ.

When emotions are at work, instincts take over our ability to react and respond. Instinctive responses are based on limited range as speed rather than rationality is the underlying objective. Therefore, an emotional person generally uses only limited knowledge to make a quick choice from the options of flight, fight, or freeze. Once a person is able to keep emotions in check, his/her choice of options is extended to include all rational and logical options as well. Even our memory is deeply influenced by emotions. Same past event will generally be recollected in a different manner depending on our prevailing emotional state at the time of recollection of the event out of our stored memory.

In addition to self, EQ governs our ability to work towards relationship building, inspiring others to excel, manage change, resolve mutual conflicts, contribute in teams, and learn from each other. Emotions have a direct and substantial role in our happiness and work in a cause and effect relationship. The entire structure of our existence involving family, friends, and workplace generate a number of emotions all the time that keep creating ripples bringing us face to face with more emotions. As a result, management of emotions works as a key to the door of happiness.

Spiritual Intelligence (SQ)

The concept of Spiritual Intelligence got a proper focus when Ms. Danah Zohar, the British American author, introduced this concept in 1997. She extended the segregations of different kind of Intelligences elaborated earlier by Howard Gardner. SQ relates to the intelligence that addresses and solves problems relating to deeper meaning and values of humanity. This intelligence allows us to house principles and belief systems, and helps us find our ultimate purpose in life. It will be out of place to call human beings the most unique creatures on this earth, unless spiritual intelligence is considered. Ultimately, SQ is used in expanding the horizon of human awareness to maximum possible dimensions.

Ms. Zohar defined specific principles underlying SQ including self-awareness about beliefs and values dear to one, living in present with spontaneity without bindings from past, taking actions based on well thought out principles and vision, developing sense of belonging among relationships and connections, having reliance on deep empathy and compassion, celebrating diversities rather than raising walls around differences, recognizing one's own small existence in this big world with all humility and developing curiosity by asking the question "Why" as a general tendency to deal with all fundamental issues. The challenges involved in understanding these factors together with developing techniques to bring about changes in awareness form a significant part of our efforts aimed at unravelling all the mysteries involved.

Brahmakumari Shivani, a well-known face of Brahma Kumari movement, provides an even more concise explanation of SQ. She says, "*Spiritual Intelligence is the expression of innate spiritual qualities through thoughts, actions, and attitudes.*" She beautifully differentiates between spirituality and Spiritual Intelligence by defining spirituality as 'to know' who you are, and Spiritual Intelligence as 'to realize' how to live life with that awareness. Supporting pillars of Spiritual Intelligence include self-awareness, wisdom, empathy, and compassion. All these pillars need to be constructed with sufficient strength before attempting to superimpose spirituality, and that is no mean feat. At this stage, it should suffice to understand that SQ is a personal endowment which helps in maintaining inner and outer peace and tranquility irrespective of surroundings being stressful or ridden with conflicts and divisions. It takes significant practice over long periods before one can aim to develop this intelligence to its matured levels.

Spiritual Intelligence also works at the helm of specific individual characteristics such as flexibility, tolerance, and inclusive approach. SQ makes the person capable of maintaining a calm attitude even in testing situations, and provides courage to go against even defined and well-established conventions. Understanding of our own world view and value systems is, therefore, integral to working of our SQ. Control over personal ego, setting up vision of life, desire to get guidance of Supreme Self, having and sustaining faith mechanism are a few other critical areas of human life where SQ plays the all-important role. Due to its overarching influence, Spiritual Intelligence is rightly said to connect a person to the transpersonal.

Conclusion

In a way, each of the intelligences mentioned above reflects an individual's ability to manage and monitor personal capability, be it physical, emotional, intellectual, or spiritual. Varying levels of these intelligences are possessed by each one of us and that proportion is what makes us unique in our own way. A holistic approach to successful and happy life requires combinations of all these intelligences in sufficient and balanced proportion. These intelligences influence each other to feed and support at all critical junctures. Like Aishwaryas, no single intelligence is expected to help succeed beyond a point in life.

The most important point to take home is that all these intelligences are not to be taken as unalterable. Because these can very well be scientifically decoded, these are no more a black box filled with unknown facts. These can be worked around with proper knowledge and regular practice. Each one of us, therefore, must feel responsible for understanding and improving on these intelligences to seek complete and permanent happiness in our life. Leaving these to the vagaries of destiny is not right because it is possible to improve so much with one's own initiatives and commitment. The understanding of this reality is the difference between an awakened individual and one who is not. Interestingly, working on improvements on these intelligences are beneficial to us irrespective of what engages us in terms of our occupation. You might be a professional manager, or a leader, or a sports personality — these are relevant to you for making you a complete person. So, we have more than one reason to try our best to bring perfect equilibrium among all.

Emotions — Unique Interrelation of Body and Mind

Long-term happiness, the subject matter of our study, is not dependent on any single factor. Each of the Aishwaryas that we discussed contributes in particular aspects and work as domain specific contributor. Similarly, working on each of the Intelligences discussed help is expanding the scope of our understanding and responses. But global life satisfaction requires continued flow of frequent positive emotions to keep irrigating our life. Our emotions and their interplay over longer periods shape our feelings, attitudes, passions, and drives. More and more discussions about human happiness will bring us face to face with all aspects of emotions. Therefore, digging deep to gain an understanding of all emotions will be of great help towards living a fulfilled life.

Emotions hold key to our feelings or way of thinking or ways in which we take actions on a moment-to-moment basis. Knowing, understanding, classifying, identifying, segregating, and their relative impact on genders, are all important aspects of emotions that need to be dealt with. Detailed study about emotions shall lead us to learn how to navigate them and bring them under desired self-regulation to obtain final outcomes on desired lines. Because of overarching effects of emotions on our psychic life, study of emotions as a separate subject will enlighten us on many aspects of the 'how' and 'why' parts of our happiness. Incidentally, emotions are no more an area of imagination or crystal ball gazing as was the case until few decades ago. Human emotions are now a very well researched subject with tons of scientific works. Advanced researchers have carried out detailed studies by penetrating the psyche of human beings. These works have allowed scientists to gain many clear insights.

The very word emotion is rooted in 'motion' and emotions are indeed energies in motion. Its root is also linked to 'motivation', which makes it self-explanatory as something that motivates us and guides us to move on. Emotions bring biological changes in our system at subconscious level. Such changes lead to increase and decrease in levels of working of our brain. Emotions operate on a very wide spectrum and swing from the most negative to the most positive extremes. Negative emotions like worries and sadness pull down our energy and enthusiasm, while the reverse goes for positive emotions. People have been saying that human have two separate minds where one is identified with thinking, while the other with feelings; but newer studies suggest that after all, these two compartments are not as isolated from each other and enjoy a somewhat master-slave relationship.

Thanks to scientific developments such as brain-imaging technologies, the studies on human emotions have unraveled many earlier mysteries. These studies have provided increasing access to the complex systems operating on our thinking, feeling, imagining, and dreaming. The new neurological advancements allow peep into the entire spectrum of emotions like never before. In short, our emotions help us decide on direct action in situations where knowledge based mental processes are unable to initiate action at the required speed. Why are we interested in this? Well simply because their interplay runs through the entire process of our happiness; from the very impulse of initial thoughts or desires, to likes and dislikes to actions and reactions, to feelings to more thoughts and actions linked in an unbroken chain.

Emotions have a key role in prompting us with the ability to face dangers and embrace situations, which could not have been left to human intellect alone. To that extent, emotions have helped human survive all through its evolution process by letting him act faster in situations involving dangers, fear, and group dynamics. Each human emotion is hard wired to ignite a specific push to one or other quick physical motion. Since, all these impulses got imbedded in human DNA over millions of years of human evolution to its current form, maneuvering around emotions is not going to be child's play. Based on the long history of survival, our systems (physical, psychological, and mental) got habituated to generating automatic reactions like hands reaching for available weapon or object in self-defense while sensing unknown danger, or impulse to run away when attacked by any wild animal, or searching for immediate escape to avoid facing an apparently stronger enemy. Today we may find such situations undesirable, but one can well imagine the importance of these responses in situations when, not so long back in the history, humans were living amidst wild animals in the open.

Emotions Explained

Being an integral part of our own life, qualitatively, anyone can talk volumes about emotions. But many of us might like to know how emotions actually operate on a physical level. Emotions are impulses to immediately act with full power against a newly emerged or fast emerging situation. The impulse instantly directs all energies at the command of the body to a specific organ or set of organs. For example, we see a snake, and we are gripped by fear and danger. Our nervous system increases oxygen to our muscles and raises our heart rate instantly, so that we can deal with the situation with our full strength.

In case of anger, the blood flow gets enhanced to hands; while fear involves the flow directed to legs and muscles so that we can get away from the situation faster. Sadness, on the contrary, results in a sharp drop in our energy and enthusiasm. Tender emotions of love and sex enhance level of relaxation by working just the opposite to rush of blood to hands or legs. No wonder, we are in a most vulnerable situation if we have to defend ourselves physically when we are feeling relaxed under the influence of tender emotions. Similarly, surprise results in wide opening of the eyes to instantly allow sharper vision of the scene in front.

Before going further, it will be interesting to have a look at all types of emotions and their categorizations in general. In his book titled 'Emotional Intelligence — Why it can matter more than IQ', the bestselling author, Daniel Goleman, who is considered an authority for his writings on emotions, has defined emotions as "*feeling and its distinct thoughts, psychological and biological states, and range of propensities to act. There are hundreds of emotions, along with their blends, variations, mutations, and nuances. Indeed, there are many more subtleties of emotions than we have words for.*"

He has also attempted to classify the main emotions and their family to provide us best possible overview and it goes as under:

- *Anger:* fury, outrage, resentment, wrath, exasperation, animosity, annoyance, irritability, hostility, and at the extreme of this group are hatred and violence.
- *Sadness:* grief, sorrow, gloom, self-pity, loneliness, dejection, and at the extreme end of this group sits depression.
- *Fear:* anxiety, apprehension, nervousness, concern, edginess, misgiving, terror, and the extreme of this group are phobia and panic.
- *Enjoyment:* happiness, joy, relief, contentment, bliss, delight amusement, sensual pleasure, thrill, euphoria, ecstasy.
- *Love:* acceptance, friendliness, trust, kindness, affinity, devotion, infatuation and adoration.
- *Surprise:* shock, astonishment, amazement, wonder.
- *Disgust:* contempt, disdain, aversion, distaste, revulsions.
- *Shame:* guilt, embarrassment, remorse, humiliation, regret, mortification.

This above classification can by no means be said to be exhaustively complete, as many more emotions can be identified because of innumerable blends of one or more of the basic emotions. Such blends give rise to some deadly emotional impacts. For example, jealousy a commonly found modern day deadly emotion is a combination of fear, anger, and sadness all put together. Similarly, we have some other critical emotions of hope, faith, courage, and forgiveness which have shades of many base emotions.

Soon, we shall be looking at these groups in some detail to enhance our understanding about how these operate and affect our lives. With well-developed understanding, there are better chances for us to sharpen our self-awareness with reference to how and why it is necessary to correlate our emotions with our basic desire of seeking happiness. In due course, we also intend to look at possible ways and means to work on channelizing and regulating our emotions in constructive ways to gain a better hold on our own life systems.

Lastly, we ought to remember that basic emotions developed all through the evolutionary process of humanity. In initial stages, the pace of evolution of emotions was very slow as were most other factors. But the industrial revolution brought major changes in the living conditions of humanity. These changes were not only drastic; their speed also has been supersonic. While this resulted in substantial comforts and protections available to us like never before; it also brought fundamental changes in our food, work, and living. Just imagine that factory farmed animal products which account for the bulk of meat and dairy supplies seen in shopping malls across the world were inconceivable just a hundred years ago. Growth hormones, antibiotics, genetically modified feed given to animals, and spraying of pesticides, chemicals, and drugs on plants have converted our dairy, vegetables, fruits, and even grains into entirely different products compared to what our ancestors consumed. Besides food, attractions of better work take away majority of people from their place of birth and known surroundings. Such changes can't but leave their imprints on our emotions that shadow our life conditions albeit with a time lag.

No wonder that newer set of emotions suitable for survival in new conditions could not evolve at the same speed. That is why we come across increased instances of the modern miseries such as hypertension, diabetes, cancer, heart problems, arthritis, obesity, and respiratory diseases. These ailments never took such chronic proportions in long history of humanity. But of late these have suddenly assumed gigantic proportions due to difference in speed of life changes and emotional evolution. Study of emotions and developing capability to deal with them effectively, should help us confront these new nuances more effectively.

Emotions versus Feelings and Passions

All emotions can be safely bifurcated as positive or negative. Obviously, seeking happiness as focus of our life requires suppressing negative emotions, and promoting positive ones. There are some proven techniques that are effective in getting the recommended suppression and promotion of emotions in desired direction, and we will soon be discussing such tools and techniques in essential details. But before we do that, let us also draw a distinction between emotions and feelings as well as emotions and passions. This segregation will clear out the smoke surrounding pure emotions. Correct understanding of each of these will prove important when we wish to work on underlying subjects extensively and with profoundness.

While feelings and emotions are used intermittently as synonymous but technically speaking feelings are direct experience of our sense organs. Feelings involve physical pains and pleasures, while emotions originate from mental processes and have more to do with thoughts and actions. Examples of feelings include taste by use of tongue, sight by use of eyes, smell through use of nose, experiencing temperature being hot or cold by use of hands, and experiencing pressures by use of entire body in general. Similarly, pain felt with a cut on the body is a feeling as it is physical and real, as against pain felt by failure in reciprocity of love or pain due to loss of a loved one, which are purely emotional in nature. As such feelings are much more direct and limited in nature, and don't offer too much room for playing around with. They have a direct and proportional relation. As such, their impact on most human beings are within a narrow band. But emotions being part of mental processes, drastically vary from one person to another. Emotions leave much room for exerting controls and regulations. So, in brief we can very well conclude that feelings are largely uncontrollable, but emotions are invariably within our control provided we know how to exert such controls.

Similarly, we should also bring clarity between passions and emotions. Unlike specific use of the word passion while dealing with it as an Aishwarya, it is used here in rather its general nature. Passions are intense, compelling, and strong desires for something or someone. Passions are much more than just enthusiasm or excitement. These are ambitions materialized into actions by putting as much heart, mind, body, and time in chasing something as possible. Passion is a strong impulse that causes the person to act ignoring dangers and risks even in a tight situation. Strong romantic or sexual desire for someone is also covered under this definition for the same reason.

Passion, as the underlying impulse or desire, is not guided by a sense of judgement of right versus wrong. The pursuer of passion is ostensibly incapable of controlling the urge to act by judicious and reasoned out judgement of 'should' or 'should not'. No wonder, negatively inclined passions are feared so much for their likely consequences over the wellbeing of the person possessed by them. On the other side, positively inclined passions can contribute towards success to the person's life. Passions therefore are weapons that work wonder but only for those who know how to command them and guide their energy towards right targets as passions are full of potential threat of getting misfired incurring self-damage in equal proportions.

The interplay of emotions and passions can be understood by comparing them with different kinds of driving skills under two different settings. Emotions are like driving a car on a city street with lots of red lights and crossings, where there are many other road users and vehicles commuting to and fro in different directions. The driver is advised to navigate his vehicle considering all these aspects from moment to moment, and continues his journey towards destination. Passions, on the other hand, are compared to driving a racing car at full speed on a racing track where the driver is focused on obtaining maximum possible speed and leaving behind other participants. He focuses on speed by ignoring entire surroundings off the track and pushing his adrenaline at full pace. One can imagine potential impact on the driver in case of collisions in these two separate settings. So, passions bring fervour and thrills, but incapacitates you from enjoying the scenery at the sides (concerns about surroundings) or care for people travelling with you (relationships).

But it is not to be concluded that passion has only negative connotations. Passions fueled by positive emotions work for human life like spices work towards enhancing taste in the food. Surely, the human life becomes much more colourful with flowers of passion spreading their beauty and smell. The real issue about passions, therefore, is to ensure that these are grounded only towards positive emotions. Equally important is the condition that the person should drive passions, rather than passions driving the person.

While bringing clarity among general terms, we should also shed some light on temperaments, moods, and attitudes in order to appreciate their direct linkage with the subject of emotions. Temperament refers to someone's nature, which affects their normal behaviour on a permanent basis. It is a combination of mental, physical, and emotional traits of persons, their natural disposition. To some extent temperament refers to individual differences in the quality and intensity of emotional reactions, activity levels, and intensity of attention. Temperament has more to do with the genes of a person rather than an individual's own choice. But, good news is that temperament can be tempered by developing awareness and following regular practices of specified techniques.

Moods, on the other hand, are just temporary states of human mind and people get over them pretty fast depending on intensity and influence of surrounding circumstances. Attitude refers to a settled and rigid way of thinking or feeling of a person about some situation or thing or person. Attitude is clearly visible in a person's own behaviour. Attitude gets directly reflected in an individual's personal choice of actions and responses to challenges, punishments, incentives, as well as rewards. To that extent, it is absolutely voluntary. However, it does not have a range of degrees like temperament, and is known to oscillate between fixed corners marked as positive and negative.

Having understood the individual components of this complex web, we should be able to appreciate the challenges in perceiving and working on bringing any fundamental changes in any of these, so that our basic aim of seeking happiness remains on track.

The Emotional and Rational Mind

Further study of emotions necessitates understanding of segregation of human mind into two separate identities of being rational and emotional. One must be clear about their mutual interactive working. Appreciation of rational and emotional minds will help us on the 'how' part of regulation or controls over emotions. Normally, both these minds are expected to work in tandem and harmony but that is not entirely feasible always. The emotional mind should better operate as the younger brother, where it should feed inputs for the consideration of its big brother, the rational mind. As a person responsible for taking action, the rational mind is expected to consider those inputs, have its own feedback, fall back on its own experiences, process it, and finally decide on the action required. But it is easier said than done. There are times when these brothers are not on speaking terms with each other. This is generally a situation where passions run high. Passions are like spoilt friends of the younger brother. They have, by definition, fast friendship with the emotional mind but are completely disliked by the rational mind. In the company of passions, the younger brother bypasses his elder brother's authority and decides to take direct action. Such actions create situations where the big brother is forced to seek excuse and repentance as to why it did not control action at the right time. This is why life is termed as a comedy for those who think (happy ending) and tragedy for those who feel (unhappy ending).

The understanding of dual faculties of rational and emotional minds is deeply linked to the evolution of human brain as an organ that took thousands of years to evolve to its present condition. In the most primitive state of human existence, human beings also had faculties like other species. The faculties pertained to regulating breathing, metabolism, and other such basic movements like synchronization of hand and leg movements during walking. Survival was the sole purpose and thinking or learning was on a slow burner. These conclusions are not mere imagination or fantasies, but based on the researches which concluded that the limbic system of our mind, the one that handles emotions, is the oldest part of human mind, while the cortex system which manages thinking is a new development and is one of the youngest parts of the human mind.

Development of cortex came as a big differentiator among different species. It became a powerful tool facilitating learning and memorizing among human beings. Higher memorizing capability made a big difference to human survival. Humans learned to adapt to changing conditions like what food to eat and what to refrain from, to take a path or avoid (to keep away dangers). It also helped to differentiate between other species in terms of which one was to be protected, and which one to be attacked or killed. Further organic development of neo-cortex enabled those activities which are today associated exclusively with human beings such as long term planning, thinking, devising, and learning. Evolution of cortex is also considered the beginning of a new set of emotions exclusively among human beings. It may be noted that primal emotions like fear are associated with pre-mammal ancestors equally, and are common among wild animals and even reptiles. Newer experiences led to newer learning. Newer learning enabled newer emotions in a step-by-step process. This process continues even today. The interlinked process of thinking, acting, realizing the impact, and comparing it with the expectation, and thinking again continued over generations and centuries, and kept etching on human DNA in a never-ending process.

This understanding is to be kept in the background to remember that anything formed with such a long history will certainly require extraordinary efforts to accept alterations. Nothing should be expected to happen quickly. Undoubtedly, major life-changing efforts necessitate regulating our emotions as well as thinking process. Individuals who can accept this reality, and keep working with deep commitment succeed in their efforts to achieve their potential. Others perish on the sides by living a subhuman life entrenched in stereotyped living. The choice about which path to follow is purely individual. This may sound a harsh statement to some, but it is the bitter truth. To maintain and sustain human superiority over all other living beings, it is imperative that each one of us contributes to our evolutionary process by sincerely making efforts to improve our genes; to become better humans than our own heritage.

In any case, at no point of time one may dismiss emotions as something unwanted or a hurdle in our life. Emotions are fundamental traits associated with being human, and serves several physical and psychological purposes. Emotions add colour to our lives and bring in depth and differentiation. Emotions motivate us to behave in specific ways and introduce uniqueness to each one of us. If all human beings are not alike like all elephants are to each other, it is primarily because our range of emotions is far more comprehensive and expanded than other species. Individual creativity and expressions that are unique to each one of the human beings is largely because of our individual set of emotions. Surely, there is no wishing away emotions.

Working of Emotions

To begin with, there are not very large variations among different individuals. But experiences of each individual during their growing up years, and their specific surroundings impact the level of their sensitivity towards each basic emotion which will necessarily be different from others. Later, these very sensitivities metamorphose into distinctive emotional reactions. Because variations in a child's emotional response are introduced in childhood, all cultures of the world emphasize letting children grow in a comfortable, peaceful, and happy environment. As a direct example of these factors, we can easily trace emotionally disturbed children coming from broken families or violent societies.

Biochemical reactions created by emotions generate responses resulting in changing the physical state of our body. Distinct facial and bodily expressions are also associated with specific emotions. That is why individual emotions generate similar expressions irrespective of which part of the world an individual comes from. Language, culture, skin colour variations are no barrier to emotional expressions of human beings. This is where Darwin's theory of evolution contributed much value. Another point to remember is that emotional expressions are quite reflective in nature. It has been registered during studies that most people unconsciously imitate, at least in parts, the emotions on display in immediate surroundings. This fact reestablishes that human beings are social animals, and their behaviours are programmed to operate on group basis as much as on individual basis.

Further, more than words or sounds, emotions are on display through non-verbal indications like gestures, tones, facial expressions etc., which get picked up by each other without requiring major efforts. This is where a highly charged positive mood works in lifting spirits of the entire group. A normal classroom can be a good example to appreciate this aspect, where the energy and enthusiasm of a single teacher spreads to entire class in both ways.

Interaction of Emotions among Genders

Yet another aspect of emotions is their large variation between genders; both in terms of intensity in experiencing as well as in expressing them. Of course, one can argue about variations in emotional stimulus, the context, and the response format, but few things can be generalized easily. It is concluded that for most emotions, women experience a larger span of the emotional interplay at either extreme. It seems to be a deliberate design of Mother Nature to let females feel greater intensity for most emotions. The explanation for these variations link this gender difference to roles expected by nature in procreation and rearing children during infancy. But for higher sensitivity and emotional intensity imparted to females, survival of many infants would have been at stake.

These variations are imprinted on the human genes. Males need to develop the humility to understand and accept this fact, as nothing much can be done about this reality. Neither should they consider emotions insignificant as they need to confront emotions many times during any given day. Exceptions apart, ladies are quick to spot emotions together with the complexities involved. They pick emotions quickly and experience them at deeper levels. Even their personal recollection of emotional episodes is different from their male counterparts. In order to exercise emotions at the ground level, women are ready to bear pains more willingly. Women have a larger limbic system which keeps them more in touch with their emotions, and makes them more expressive about them. Men generally can be seen thinking more logically. Women have a wholesome view of thinking and understanding. They don't mind their emotions influencing their decision-making.

The differences of emotional interplay among genders exist even before pressures of real life conditions start impacting their behaviours while growing into adulthood. These differences are emanating due to different set of emotional equations governing both genders right from the time they are born. It is our choice that we ignore them, or face them as natural phenomena and apply them while seeking solutions involving members from different genders. Sure, there will be some who would like to interpret this situation from the gender inequality perspective, but that will be just like closing eyes from the reality thinking that it will disappear if we turn our face away.

Girls are genetically equipped to take up their role of emotional manager. This starts early in all their interactions with others and continues subsequently all through their adulthood as well. Normally, the husband is unable to spot this subtle difference during the initial years of their marriage because of his poor emotional judgement. He is naturally programmed to remain dominated by his rational mind while the wife takes over the role of emotional-in-charge. The differences due to different emotional orientations remain buried during the early stage called 'honeymoon period' largely because of over compensating influence of physical attraction laced by sexual gratification.

While a lot can be said about gender based emotional disparity, a word of caution is generally reserved for the male. The open suggestion to their entire clan is to understand and appreciate basic difference in emotional hard wiring in female species blessed by Mother Nature itself. This hard coding prompts them to accord more importance to communication and discussions. The real meaning of discussion here is to patiently listen and show agreement in as polite manner as possible by forgetting all the differences that the man may hold in the point under discussion. Surely, it may sound as words from Linda Goodman or John Gray (author of *Men Are from Mars, Women Are from Venus*). They and many other authors about relationships gained huge popularity and following by writing about this natural variation in the basic orientation of these two genders.

The practical message for husbands regarding the topic of seeking happiness is 'please keep talking, keep appreciating, and keep reassuring your better half without keeping count or showing any sign of impatience'. To further insure your happiness, please extend this support more at times when the wife is unhappy. When the wife is in good mood, she has higher capacity to understand and appreciate good things in her life. But during her unhappy phase, her vision for love and affection becomes cloudy. This is when she becomes shortsighted about every good thing, and all she can see is doom and gloom all around. Hence, female unhappiness needs to be handled with silken gloves. Men are different; they can take a whole load of troubles without much problem as long as their ego is not trampled. If you can spot the strength and conviction of these words of wisdom coming out of personal experience, so be it!

There is yet another important difference which is particularly relevant in the modern world where both spouses are qualified, and earning their own money. This point revolves around financial status and independence. Men normally have a simple view about money, and believe that it provides a solution to all problems that one can have. Interestingly, their position about money remains the same whether they are poor or rich. But women's awareness for her emotional satisfaction is said to be linked with financial riches. With the rise of financial fortunes, her expectation of emotional support also rises in equal proportion. Increasing instances of marital discord among couples where both are financially independent are the result of this less appreciated emotional difference between the genders.

The interplay of feelings between the genders is a universal phenomenon among all cultures and all geographies, and has been around since time immemorial. This is also not restricted to the household alone, and applies equally to workplace interactions. The idea behind touching this matter in such details is to recognize and reinforce this reality as it has humongous impact on very presence and sustenance of happiness between married couples, and thereby extending to the entire family.

Emotions and Medical Solutions

Emotions have also been found to play an important role in efficacies of specific medical treatments. One comes across people making tall claims about emotional and mental controls are enough for treating specific diseases, as if to conclude that control over emotions and attitudes is capable for curing all illnesses. Surely, that seems too much to be acceptable. Some others may point out that the very origin of illnesses is due to imbalance in emotions. It is safe, however, to ignore both these extreme positions for the middle path that says that emotions do help in faster and stronger recovery in select cases.

Several scientific studies carried out in last few decades conclusively prove that there is an interlinked impact of mental and emotional states on the central nervous system, immune system, and other aspects of physical functioning of human body. Let us first look at the immune system as it was until recently considered independent, and unlinked even with the all-important nervous system. As we may know, immune cells travel across our body through the blood stream contacting each and every body cell. Immune cells are expected to attack unrecognized cells, thereby protecting our body from unwanted viruses, bacteria, and more importantly, cancerous cells. However sometimes immune cells fail to correctly identity even helpful cells. Based on such incorrect identity test, even harmless cells get attacked. This is how we get different types of allergic reactions.

All along it has been believed that the immune system operates all by itself on a stand-alone basis. Even the human mind was believed not to have any control over the working of the immune system. But recent studies conclude that negative emotions like stress and anxiety release adrenaline, and initiate other chemical reactions which adversely impact even the immune system through the nervous system. Long periods of persistent negativity under negative emotions such as pessimism, hostility, suspiciousness, and sadness have been established to work as agents for multi-timing the effects on diseases like asthma, arthritis, headaches, peptic ulcers as well as heart diseases. That is why this group of negative emotions is now referred as toxic emotions. Incidentally, toxic emotions impact growth of these diseases as much as, say, smoking or high cholesterol, in causing heart diseases. This claim is based on findings of Mr. Daniel Goleman mentioned in his book 'Emotional Intelligence — Why it can matter more than IQ'.

Comments on Major Emotions

Having gained a broad understanding of emotions, and having seen their significant impact on all systems linked with our physical and mental well-being, it would be interesting to consider in depth a few important emotions. This understanding of individual emotions, and their broader group will significantly help us practising with ways and means available for regulating our emotions. We will try to pick up those few emotions which impact us more often, and have a direct impact on the subject of our interest.

Anger

The inner world of people is always shaped by their thoughts, emotions, behaviours and attitudes. Anger is simply accepted as the most common negative emotion having its origin in a mismatch between external world and one's inner world. Generally, it starts with some small irritated issue arising due to strong disliking for alternate views and actions. Those strong dislikes germinate due to too much importance given to own false sense of ego. As we know, focus on ego induces our own strong likes to the exclusion of likes of others. The root cause of anger, therefore, goes to over emphasis on 'my way of thinking' being superior to 'other's way of thinking'. It does not matter who is right or who is wrong. The very over-emphasis of only one way being the right way leads to rigidity. In such situations, other alternates are just kicked out of acceptance. Many sufferers of anger blame it on prevailing injustice and disappointments but such people are actually pleading their own case and announcing their own judgement.

Anger has worst kind of impact on health of human heart. Violent and hostile behaviour, so common expression of frequent anger, is more dangerous for heart than higher blood pressure. In addition, anger fuels to other ailments like sleeplessness, degenerative disorders with most obvious symptom being increased blood pressure. Categorized as one of the strongest negative emotions it is a big drain on our mental energy pool. Anger is a blatant display of sidelining our cherished uniqueness of having discriminative awareness, the supreme gift to humanity. No other creature in this universe enjoys this boon of discriminative awareness; indeed it makes us what we are. Anger snaps away this very power from us in no seconds and deprives human to exercise the judgement by discriminating between good or evil, right or wrong, positive or negative, short term or long term.

It doesn't matter the least that situation being reacted is justified or otherwise. Even with thousand strong and genuine reasons to lose temper, anger will always have higher negative consequences for self than others. Further, it does not matter if you let it burst out in the open or bottle it up. Once anger comes up in your system, you get exposed to its negative consequences without fail. As such the theory about venting it out being safer than bottling it inside is nothing but a totally misconstrued myth. The only advice here is to eliminate it all together from your system. Please remember that sulking, exasperation and revenge are just variants of this base toxic emotion and are all equally malignant.

Anger snaps our connection with others and pulls us down below the animal level; animals don't even know what anger is. Anger adds to irrationality in our entire system and affects our very existence in more ways than visible to naked eye. Anger is based on cognitive habits, which are undoubtedly very hard to break. But it is not impossible to overcome it. Most modern anger management programs available talk about numerous simple looking steps being enough to control this beast. Their suggestions include taking a break from the situation, breathing deeply, moving to a happy space, switching mind to some different subject or going to positive self-talk. But these are all Band-Aid category solutions and presuppose that the person infested holds control for deciding what to do and what not to do, which is hardly the case.

What should be done to control it? Well it requires working around the very root of it i.e. by controlling one's likes and dislikes and by increasing the circle of your acceptance for others. It has to be understood that you can't prevent many undesirable situations to arise. One must graduate to accept that others have a right to exist and their likings and actions are equally well thought out. One is required to accommodate view point of others; one must become truly democratic in approach and believe that others are equally engaged in searching for their happiness. Above all, one is required to work on patience. Motivating self can overpower anger by seeking proper Self-awareness and by working on empathy and compassion for others. All these steps will be discussed in the coming chapters. Let us, at this stage, remain focused in understanding of major emotions being faced by us in our day to day life.

Fear and Anxiety

Fear collectively refers to group of emotions such as apprehension, worry and nervousness. It occurs due to perceived risk associated with some potential happening in future; 'what will happen if...' syndrome. The risks may be for life, health, status, power, wealth, security or some such other subject of attachment. The root cause behind fear is perceived danger. Many people are known to have varying level of fear from multiple factors such as snakes, spider, flying, heights, criminals and violence. Unfortunately, fear is highly contagious and people catch it, more often than not, from others or simply by reading about it or seeing it happening with others. Fear is our alarm system to prevent any potential harm. So long as the danger is real, it prompts us to be cautious, to pay attention and take next step carefully. But when it is not rooted in reality, it becomes an unnecessary drag on energy and results even in nervous disorders.

Anxiety, on the other hand, is directly related to unwanted feelings typically about some imminent event or something with an uncertain outcome. Normally, anxiety is experienced before confronting something challenging. While in past, these challenges were to do with basic survival, of late these got limited to tests, examinations, job interviews or such other occasions where there are equal chances of alternate outcomes. While a normal level of anxiety is motivating in so far as it helps us prepare better to face the perceived challenge but factors like expecting too much out of our lives and fear of failures are situations responsible for fuelling this simple disorder to unacceptable levels. One of the most common expressions of anxiety among adults emanate from higher attachment with outcomes of events to happen only in desired direction or seeing self made predictions about even casual events falling apart.

Going through anxiety can continue without being noticed. It is because its symptoms are very common and are accepted as normal in modern day living. Initially, anxiety affects physical working such as sleep disturbances, digestive system disorders, loss of appetite and irregular bowel movements. But continuity and intensity of anxiety bouts start undermining the intellect in due course of time. At that level, anxiety starts impacting general performance of the person in negative manner. For example, even a good student with excessive anxiety invariably makes mistakes while attempting questions that otherwise were well prepared for.

Further higher levels of intensity of anxiety leads to panics and ultimately go to become phobia. In reality, the subject causing anxiety is more perceived than actual where the reality of situation has nothing to do for aggravating the situation. Anxiety engulfs the victim by artificial projection of perceived dangers associated with 'what if' scenarios. In real life we do come across people who were unfortunate to experience some negative encounter some times in the past. Even with passage of time some of them fail to overcome the negative shadow of the encounter. But expecting that negative happenings will keep repeating all the times is beyond the real world. Unfortunately, some people become victim of anxiety even when they have not been exposed to any bad experience themselves and they have been having best of things going for them on most personal fronts.

Such people need to be reminded that this world, in spite of all its deficiencies, is still a very good place to live happily. By any count, there are more good things happening than bad even today. Some people end up making lower efforts but suffer due to expectations of higher results. They tend to do so under influence of being unrealistic. Few others develop the compulsions of jumping to negative conclusions far too quickly. Yet another reason for many to get into unnecessary bouts of anxiety relates to expecting reoccurrence of worst-case scenario far too often. While there are situations that call for worst-case preparedness but in most other cases, hope is better emotion to inculcate and pursue.

Why we need to be cautious about all this? Well, most inclement doubts and fears have paralyzing affects on quality of life and thereby on our objective of leading a happy life. These suck a great deal of emotional energy out of life and soon start interfering with our normal working. Unfortunately, in its modern day form, anxiety is impacting many people coming from different age groups in varying shades of Obsessive Compulsive Disorder (OCD). Out here, anxiety generates repetitive, distressing and disruptive thoughts and ends up robbing the emotional sphere from its positive feelings and emotions. Unfortunately, real life demands of modern day living generate too much pressure on our mental and physical systems.

Disgust

Disgust can be understood as a strong feeling of a thing having very unpleasant appearance, taste, smell, sound or feel; basically all feelings linked with human primary sense organs. Charles Darwin identified disgust as a sensation that refers to something revolting. One way of expressing disgust is to look at it as glamour in negative. It pushes people away from it as much as glamour attracts them. The common thread, however in disgust and glamour is curiosity. If hatred is said to be a moral emotion, disgust gets related to aesthetic category of emotions.

Originally evolved as a self protection mechanism, disgust developed as a quickest possible response to offensive foods that may cause harm to human organism, e.g. response we get as we put rotten dish in our mouth or by consuming stale drink. As a primary emotion, it is present even among infants who are programmed to tighten their face or vomit out the food to give a clear indication to the parents that food is not to their liking. Disgust is perhaps the most visible emotion and facial expressions of a person could easily be detected. Disgust can be quickly spotted due to unique annoyance that one feels for a thing to be inappropriate, for example, disturbing feeling arising from very visibility of human body discharges like faeces, vomit, mucus, and sexual fluids.

Sometimes something which is so much accepted among ourselves, can be disgust for a foreigner. For example, the Indian food, spicy and greasy at it may be, is so much loved by foodies in most places but some people look at its strong smell and fat content in disgust. *Gulab Jamun* is one of my all times favourite sweet dish that finds its own space even after most sumptuous food. But I was astonished to see the reaction of one of my foreign guest after eating his first *Gulab Jamun* because he finds it so sweet and oily. Come on, *Gulab Jamun* and disgust? Yes, it is that much relative.

In modern times disgust is more prevalent in our day-to-day life in form of 'mine versus others'. Most instances of disgust impacting our life are based on lack of appreciation or lack of exposure to other cultures or our false sense of superiority. Slurping is considered bad manners in many cultures and most of us are uncomfortable with the slurping sound especially when we all are eating food together. But there are cultures where a guest's liking of the food is judged by the sounds made by him in his slurping. There, the intensity of slurping is an indication of trust placed by your guest in you and show of his confidence that the food is safe and tasty. You try eating food in English style there and the message to the host will go that your caution is coming out of your lack of trust in them.

'Mine versus others' is also strong basis for acceptance or otherwise for this group of emotions. What explains the fact that the same person, who will do anything to engage a beautiful girl for a passionate mouth-to-mouth deep kiss, can show total disgust in using her toothbrush? If protecting your dental cavity from hers is to be cited as possible motive for the need of caution in using toothbrush, what was to happen when you were dying to prolong the deep kiss? This is purely because the kiss was common while the toothbrush is entirely hers; the sense of asymmetry. Because our own shit, just because it is ours, doesn't smell as bad as it does to others. Did you just felt disgusting? Hold on, if discussions about violence need not be violent and discussions for anger need not be angry, why is that discussions about disgust are proving so disgusting? Surely, it won't if you consider this your own discussion, and that is the precise point being made.

In its morality linked domain disgust speaks of the sense of identity. It is a strong declaration that I accept what is mine but I assert what falls outside my area or whatever is alien. Disgust, therefore, is a declaration that here is something that I don't associate myself with. To that extent, it is an expression of my values, fears and anxieties lest some contact with such object leave me contaminated. People familiar with the Indian social problem of untouchability may appreciate this connect right away. Disgust is also classified as an aversive emotion belonging together with fear and hatred. Disgust is negatively correlated to aggression. Aggression motivates a person to approach and attack while disgust motivates the person to withdraw and seek protection. Throughout recent history, disgust has, unfortunately, played a big differentiating divide by creating voids among whole lot of ethnicities and sectarian divides. What else could have explained the Nazis demeaning Jews to the extent that they did?

On emotional level, disgust works as a barrier for empathy. It leads to intolerance for everything alien. Normal approach for anything new should be to accept or desire to know the same in full detail. It should lead to ideas such as: a) here is something new, b) let me know it in detail, c) let me learn about it, d) let me understand it with full knowledge, and e) may be that I am able to relate it with something we already are familiar with. This curious approach is not too much asking from human beings for things belonging to their very fellow beings. But disgust laden conventions have suppressed all curiosity by aggressively stopping any contact and thereby eliminating all the chances of knowing, understanding and establishing commonalities.

This lesson will help us a lot in our subsequent endeavours that, under any situation, if bridges need to be built ever for bringing people together, individually and collectively, the disgust will have to be dispensed with by sending it into deep sleep.

Shame and Guilt

Shame is an emotion having undesired but significant impacts on lives for many of us. It is a very complex emotional response that all human beings acquire during early childhood itself. Shame is quite a normal feeling about our behaviour. Shame result in feeling let down and also fear of ridiculing from others. It is a basic part of being human and remains rather harmless and leaves no big scars so long as it is well acknowledged and gets dealt with instantly. But accumulating too much shame for too longer periods is known to affect psychologically and, in extreme cases, becomes terminal. Embarrassment and shyness are to be taken as its first cousins.

Guilt, on the other hand, is self-disapproval by failing on norms set by the person concerned. It is generated internally and some people may come under its influence even without committing a wrong. Mere generation of thoughts about some inappropriate possibility of bad conduct is good enough a trigger for guilt. To some extent, healthy guilt keeps us on right course as it works as a good gate keeper to ward unwanted thoughts entering in our mental space. Good thing is that it works well even when we are all alone without possibility of being watched. Guilt can operate on several levels like:

- Where we did something morally wrong.
- Where we allowed something to happen that we should have prevented.
- Where something happened which was totally out of controls but we still remain under guilt as why we could not have done something.

The line between shame and guilt is rather thin. One can feel shame and guilt for the same behaviour but with a different underlying emotion. For the same wrongdoing, shame will illicit the response of "I am bad" while response from guilt will be "I did something bad". There is yet another key differentiator among this group of emotions. Shame is failing on social standards and appears only when such failure gets exposed. Guilt, being a matter about internal values, gets self diagnosed. Embarrassment, on the other hand, is one step further because it involves public humiliation.

No other emotion affects self-identity as much as shame. It induces doubts about self. Such doubts lower confidence. This results in lower desire for taking initiatives in future restricting progress and relationship building. Shame and guilt stand as a roadblock in open arm interaction with others and also spoil basic spirit of intimacy. The more influencing situation of loneliness and feeling of alienation and inferiority, all have their roots in shame and guilt. Depressions, addictions, sexual and eating disorders are all germinating out of shame and guilt. In modern times, these emotions are slowly influencing increasing numbers. There are strong reasons for many of us to stand firm and ward off these subtle but powerful breakers out of our way of seeking happy life.

This set of emotions is generally called as 'Moral Emotions' or 'Social Emotions' precisely because these have direct relation with self-consciousness, a trait that is identified most distinctly only among human beings. Let us also look at another important debate centered on this set of emotions and it is about the tussle between actual deeds and thoughts about wrong deeds. Many of person's thoughts are indeed uncomfortable and each one of us might have come across these now and then. There is no wishing away these thoughts just like that. Sure, we come across many teachings, especially of religious colours, asking for controlling such thoughts. But it is best to consider such teaching simply as good words and not feasible for implementation. Ultimately, we need to develop the habit of simply ignoring such thoughts. Surely, we know how human mind operates; mind is a free bird and is designed to fly without any respect and regard for no-fly zones. Free flights of our mind are actually important for our ongoing mental processes.

So long as our bad thoughts make us go through our discomfort, it is good enough to believe that right guards are in place and working well. Discomfort is definite proof that our judgement between right and wrong is up and running. But enjoying bad thoughts or indulging with them in any way is morally and ethically bad. If so is the case, there is need for you to understand and realize that this is a dangerous signal awaiting catastrophe. Similarly, feeling too much shame for everything ongoing in the vicinity is not going to help anyone in anyways. As normal human beings, we should be aware about our very small and insignificant role in this world where we are just a tiny miniscule unimportant character. Our entry on this stage called universe is designed for a fraction of time and space. Under this situation, taking responsibility of making this entire play succeed is a foolish approach.

Let us conclude our understanding of this emotion with a note for the parents of young children. Please be very careful while criticizing or punishing your children with the objective of straightening them out. Frequently criticized, severely punished, constantly neglected or abused children end up registering these activities as a message that they are inadequate, unworthy and inferior. These feelings lead them to low self-esteem and force them to be highly sensitive and fearful. They become afraid and convinced that they don't know the right rules and also fear their actions will be considered inappropriate. Their feeling of being terminally bad is not productive and sows early seeds of destructive behaviours. Bullying about making efforts to cover up their shortcomings and failures from being exposed is only a tip of the iceberg of things to come in future. I hope that parents having young children or grand parents having active role in supervising their grand children must develop this understanding very strongly and help their loved ones remain firmly grounded in confidence, courage and honour. This is the least we can ensure for them to create a healthy environment for them to bloom to their potential.

Love, Acceptance and Trust

Let us start with love, the quintessential emotion of great impacts and repercussions. We can visualize it easily to be many things rolled into one. Poets, philosophers, neurologists, biologists, scientists, meta-physicians have remained busy, since time immemorial, with their respective lenses focused on love. But first and foremost, love is an emotion, a supreme emotion with great power and energy, and the warmest of all emotions. In addition to being a pure emotion, love is also a cognitive experience. It is an open attitude, the one that has no prefixed perceptions and ideas, the one which comes out from the spring of human heart without any traces of prejudices, hate or dislikes; the one centered on other beings in the surroundings.

Love in any of its forms is beyond the logical working of mind as it necessarily involve human heart; it can never be limited to only thoughts or thinking process. It is a very expansive concept with multiple facets and meanings and many co-related qualities. Important thing is to realize that love has many shades. When pursued for furthering self objectives, it is called passion; pursued for physical gratification and it becomes lust; pursued with affection for other human, it becomes relationship; pursued for selfish attachment, it becomes romance; pursued with non-judgmental attitude, it becomes acceptance; pursued for divinity, it becomes devotion; pursued for shared beliefs, it becomes religion and pursued just for pleasure, it becomes sex. It is because of its varying shades that it is so complicated to appreciate and realize love in simple terms.

Real love, however, is not about self at all. The love that we intend discussing here must necessarily involve other people; there is no emotional love unless other beings are involved into it. Focus on self brings it down to limited motives and takes its real power away. Love, with reference to own self will be treated as a negative emotion as it is bound to ignore interest of others. The only exception to this rule is love for one's own soul, where love becomes complete even without any other person involved; love for own soul actually becomes Spirituality, the very subject matter of this book.

Real love is when happiness, security and well being of other(s) are as real to us as our own; it may be more but not less. In its true form, love has unique affect where distinctions between the person and others start disappearing, where there is a feel and acceptance of similarity without any differentiations or divisions. In its real definition, love is best expressed as under:

- Love expressed as sharing and enriching life of a dear one is *Friendship*.
- Love expressed for affirming achievement of others is *Celebration*.

- Love expressed for lifting burden of others is *Help.*
- Love expressed as repenting other's action is *Forgiveness.*
- Love expressed for views and life of others is *Respect.*
- Love expressed by focusing on narrative of others is *Attention.*
- Love expressed by standing with someone even in bad times is *Loyalty.*
- Love created for making something for others is *Creativity.*

We should also look at love as a special attitude. Here again it is necessarily filled with inclusiveness, acceptance and trust involving others. Attitude of love determines all our standpoints or perspectives for interacting with everything around. This attitude brightens up our life and help us expand our self-awareness to its complete potential and its linkage with the universe. That way love makes us feel even larger than real. So, love in its true sense carries lot of responsibility and is much loaded word and, hence, shouldn't be used with a casual approach.

Acceptance of its own is an imposing emotion. It means embracing something or someone in its entirety, giving it our full support and approval. It is about sharing, about taking part together with a deeper feeling of involvement. Hence, it is much bigger than just being indifferent to something or someone. Acceptance involves being in confirmation with our original goodness. To that extent, it is first step of the ladder whose later steps include love. No one can attempt to reach to a higher step without first climbing over acceptance. Acceptance suggests that our mind has agreed to be non-judgemental and agree to take the outcome of the event at par with best possible outcome. Later we will see full spectrum of acceptance as the corner stone for achieving true self-awareness. Overriding presence of this emotion is capable of ensuring that many toxic emotions are deprived of their venomous effects.

Lastly, let us look briefly at the emotion of trust. Trust involves believing in the reliability, ability, truth or strength of somebody else. Thus, trust is a double-edged sword and needs to be used sparingly. On its positive side, it is important for forming relationship with others while on the negative side, its success or failure depends on others. It is seen so often that betrayal is not standing far from trust. So fate of our trust hinges on the quality of trustworthiness of the person we wish to trust. But trust also works as a side step for growing towards total love with the caveat that trust requires a fine blend of optimism and realism. Due to its proximity with betrayal, it is advisable to seek solutions to situations such that there is no need to bring trust in action. So, trust is a unique emotion which better remains with us without it being used.

Surprise, Shock and Astonishment

This group of emotions covers incidences of happening of something unexpected. Depending on the pendulum swing from extreme positive to extreme negative, the emotions covered here are called stunned, astonished, amazed and dazzled. Surprise is sitting happily in the center occupying the most neutral position. Surprise is basically a cognitive emotion, which need to be combined with some or the other emotions like joy, fear or grief to help determine its true underlying feeling. Since it must strike with one or more of other emotion, surprise by itself is regarded as the only neutral emotion.

The unique features of this group are their shorter duration of influence and unique facial expressions when impacted. Surprise has very limited span of maximum few seconds after which some other dominant emotion is bound to take over the situation. The moment surprise is struck, our eyes get opened wide to facilitate a wider scan of the situation in quickest possible time. The initial cognition combined with better scan, helps us to come up with an immediate decision about what to do next. Every instance of surprise has a shock value and blinds our response system for a split second. Response to surprise is directly linked with individual's ability for handling multi-tasking where someone with good ability comes up with multi-prong actions to thwart the potential dangers.

Shock, on the other hand, can be understood as a sudden or violent disturbance of mind, body or senses. The suddenness of this emotion can induce wide range of physical and emotional reactions. At times, these reactions are beyond your own imaginations. Shock is quickly taken over by either of the other toxic emotion of anger, anxiety, guilt, shame or fear. Victim of shock is well advised to make efforts to bring back normalcy ASAP. Rest and relaxation are best advised.

If shock represents extreme side of the pendulum in negative sphere, astonishment can be taken as the other extreme in positive sphere. Astonishment refers to the feeling of awe or admiration of higher scale. Just imagine a city dweller getting opportunity to spend a comfortable night in a desert far away from the city. The feeling that he/she may get after looking at millions of stars in the sky will be called astonishment. Accumulating as many astonished moments as possible is like adding on the kitty of your happy experiences which shall get engraved on your memory.

Enjoyment – Joy, Contentment and Sensual Pleasure

Lastly, we will briefly take up these emotions with similar grouping but with quite different orientations. Let us begin with enjoyment, which is a state of well being defined by positive feelings ranging from contentment at the bottom and intense ecstasy at the top. As per Mr. Martin Seligman, a psychologist of repute from Princeton University, the entire spectrum of enjoyment can be classified under following five categories:

a) *Pleasure*: Consisting of meeting of physical needs above the basic minimum level like tasty food, warm climate and a hot bath in winter.
b) *Engagement*: Involvement of deeper level towards pursuing some absorbing, satisfying and challenging activity of choice.
c) *Relationship*: Presence of strong social ties with other beings having inter-dependence and level of trust.
d) *Meaning*: A perceived quest of belonging to something bigger.
e) *Accomplishment*: Feeling of having realized some tangible goals set earlier by working hard over longer period of times, something normally considered difficult where several others fail.

Joy is sweetness of life similar to sugar being the essence of a flavoured drink. In a way, it is a reward for a job well done; icing on the cake. For a man working as an employee for salary, joy is similar to the bonus conferred on him for his contribution for performance of the company. It is something that is worked upon and not a gift, bribe or buy-out. Joy can be gentle or intense, simple or complex, momentary or enduring at the same time. Another interesting point of enjoyment is that it needs company for proper accentuation and is best experienced within community. In reality, joy is a great inspiration for doing things to one's best potential and ability.

Contentment is being satisfied with one's life situation at a given point of time. Taking it as stagnation or giving up in testing situations of real life will be an absolute mistake. It requires wholehearted acceptance of whatever condition prevails in one's life. It is again a positive emotion and is deeply linked to entire concept of happiness. The most important part of contentment is that it is deep rooted in proper understanding of insatiability of human desires.

Contentment is being at peace with the results of choices made and results obtained. Finally, contentment is absence of attachments with sense objects and transient attractions. This emotion, when properly worked, becomes a noble virtue and overshadows entire spectrum of one's thoughts and attitudes. It is highly praised by Ancient Indian traditions and is taken as a must for worthwhile attempt for seeking permanent happiness.

Sensual Pleasure

We grew old listening that sex is an essential biological requirement like hunger, thirst and sleep. But is it really so? Can someone die for not having sex? Therefore, it is absolutely wrong to take it as a biological need. Let us first see what makes it an emotion. Basic components of something being classified as an emotion are that it should be cognitive, evaluative, motivating and generate one or the other feeling. And all these are very much associated with the desire for sensual pleasure. Imagination and thoughts play most crucial role for different stages of seeking, experiencing and enjoying sex.

Other components like un-stability of mind, heightened intensity and relative brevity of the actual encounter make sexual experience at par with many other emotions. The degree of variation for its desire between different beings is another differentiating factor to group it as an emotion. So, we better get prepared to look at it in the same manner that we wish to look at, say, anger or fear or disgust.

Another myth surrounding sensual pleasure relates to its perceived extension of universal emotion of love. But it has nothing to do with love, which is but a very profound attitude. Unlike sex, love is neither available on demand, nor it can be bought over or dispensed with easily. Love is about giving and caring rather than gratifying and indulging. At best sex desire may be considered as essential component of a romantic relationship which by itself is just a miniscule fraction of a much greater emotion called love. However, all said and done, presence of sexual desire with other aspects of romantic love, make for a complex but highly satisfying and fulfilling experience and there can be no denying to this fact. This is why desire for sex occupies the top of the pile when it comes to irresistible temptations of human life.

Romantic Relationship

Infatuations and overpowering lust is known to be underlying basis of romantic relationships in modern times. Higher Emotional quotient also is traced among people falling for makeshift and short-lived physical attractions. This dependence on temporary factors invariably proves unreliable in many cases for a long lasting relationship. Irrespective of intensity level of these transient forces, the initial passion eventually cools down. Hence, such relationships carry the risk of turning into disillusioned state rather quickly. In many such cases, it is seen culminating to parting ways or shows of never ending domestic discord. Decades ago all these were thought to be only Western world's problem but that does not seems to be the case anymore.

Emotional balance plays a very crucial role in romantic couples to ensure fulfilling relationship because that balance start playing on other ingredients desired for success together. Romantic relationships require presence of mutual respect, interdependence and mutual support to succeed. Especially in Asian context, social conduct of the romantic partners in relationship plays a dominant role for success of relationships other than physical attraction and gratification.

General

Having looked at key emotions in sufficient details, one is expected to become conscious about particular emotion in action at a particular time. Right understanding should also lead to being aware if a particular emotion is positive, pleasant, comforting or coming from other side comprising of negative, unpleasant and discomfort. The emotional scale among different individuals is often seen swinging from the extreme pleasure to extreme discomfort. Developing in-depth understanding of emotions allows the person to prepare for facing them as they are. Emotions have to be worked around and can't be thrown away as some unwanted baggage.

Focus on emotions also gets reflected under dimension of internal or external. People having higher internal focus are called introverts while those having emotional focus on external objects or other persons are branded as extroverts. The very classification between introverts or extroverts is based on dominance of single or multiple emotions. The dominant emotions of introverts are generally identified out of shame, contentment, guilt, admiration and embarrassment while emotions found dominant among extroverts are out of anger, fear, liking and disgust. Presence of a dominant emotion doesn't mean that they don't get impacted by other emotions. All it suggests is that sensitivities for or influence of other emotions is not so strong on their personality.

Another interesting classification of emotions hinges on the level of intensity involved. Intensity level depends on how deeply one person feels about a particular emotion. Individuals are blessed with varying level of intensity. For example, same situation may cause one person small irritation but some other person may develop deep disgust out of that very situation; one may develop only a dislike while some other person can take that to the level of hate. Talking about gender impact, studies have also found that, in general, females display wider intensity scale of most emotions in comparison to males.

Surely, emotions are, at the same time, most pleasant and most painful forces in human life. Emotions drive us to most of the good and not so good initiatives that we undertake. Emotions are also at work when we ignore or suppress intellectual and logical arguments and take a call by going against reasoning. All chances taken, all dices rolled, all beginnings made are having emotions playing at the very root.

Regulation/Control of Emotions

Having acquired sufficient knowledge about the key emotions, the next obvious question staring at us is how to overcome their influence. For sure, the time invested in developing understanding for different emotions will get justified only when we are able to do something about it. Else it will be just an academic discussion. Our emotions are like driving a car on the expressway where speed provides a lot of excitement. Over speeding also involves thrill of taking over other vehicles. And there are lots of objects on and around the road which also attract our attention constantly. It is natural for a driver to feel temptations for switching lanes from left to right and from fast to slow and vice versa in order to ease out of the traffic. But, a good driver is one who remains focused on basics and is able to set aside temptations of over speeding as well as frequent lane changing. Such a driver reaches at his destination with better certainty, without tiring himself and without exposing his vehicle to unnecessary road risks. Ultimately 'lane driving always proves to be sane driving'.

Bookstores are filled up with volumes suggesting theories after theories explaining ways and means for exercising control over emotions for ensuring a better social and personal life. But controlling emotions is better said than done. Points recommended by these books at random include suggestions such as:

- Don't react to situation right away to avoid regret later on.
- Replace your thoughts with alternate thoughts to redirect your attention.
- Look out for another healthy outlet to engage your focus.
- Expand your thinking and look out for the bigger picture.
- Identify your emotional triggers (including spouse, children, friend, parent, sibling or who so ever) and forgive them.
- Get over negative ideas and make a better choice.
- Refrain from judging the situation and yourself.
- Repeat self-calming verbal statements to restore your normalcy.

Special precaution is required for handling negative emotions (anger, hate, rage, bitterness and envy, etc.) as these have potential of getting out of hand rather quickly. Denying, intensifying, weakening, curtailing, masking, replacing and completely hiding are the options that sounds good but prove totally impractical. How can a person under siege by strong emotions can have logical thinking to try out and exercise any of the impractical suggestions made by such self-help books? As a rule, emotions can't be ignored, controlled or avoided.

All one can do about emotions is regulation. And the best approach for regulating emotions with some chances of success is when situations are understood with balanced mix of practicality and logic. People who have been making attempts with some seriousness towards suppression of emotions will stand testimony to the fact that all their efforts could yield was decreased expression of emotions and nothing beyond. All said and done, regulating emotions seems to be the only practical approach with least adverse impacts. The moment one understands the strong genetic base of emotions, avoiding and fighting them will be quickly concluded as a losing battle.

Regulating emotions, however, is not something that can be acquired by reading few books or undertaking some lessons or practising some set of exercises. Ability to get over the emotions involves a great preparation in terms of ethical and moral readiness. This capability will require a new approach to know our own inner self; enlightenment about self-awareness and most importantly finding the real purpose of your life. You need to go through a daily emotional fitness routine. You also have to evolve your own philosophy of acceptance; holding on what is under your control and letting go everything outside your control. Now, all these steps sound simple and harmless but those who have tried practising these will appreciate the depths and challenges involved in finding a way through. For example, any attempt to enhance self-awareness is expected bit-by-bit, step-by-step, by learning, by practising, by perfecting, by gaining few new habits and by forgoing a lot.

> "Ultimately, managing emotions is simply a question of making choices.
> The only problem is that there are too many choices to be made for too long a period."

Practising regulation of emotions, in a way, is just like acquiring a new life changing skill by discarding the one that has been used by us for many years. Anyone can imagine the dedication and perseverance required in acquiring an altogether new skill set. Regulating emotions also demands similar efforts. Yes, it calls for big changes. Those big changes are really difficult to pursue as we human do have a long and failed history of struggle in making big changes. There is no harm in admitting this reality. But some do succeed in doing so. Many of such people must be known to us within our own families or immediate society. Those who succeed, how different are they from us? Don't we aspire to be like them, is it so impossibly difficult for us to make serious attempt in emulating their success? Not many can answer this in negative.

Keeping the details for later, one should be happy to know at this stage that the practice of right meditation is known to do wonders for achieving success in managing emotions. As one of its several significant advantages meditation empowers us to separate our self from the situation. This separation provides a strong ground for the practitioner to understand self with enlarged clarity like never before. It is a different matter; however, that right meditation itself has its own challenges that need to be dealt with before expecting results.

In conclusion, the process of bringing desired regulation over emotions is feasible and doable in spite of it being a slow and painful process. Surely, it demands a great deal of commitment and dedication. But before exploring actual techniques let us also glance over several other recommendations that are available for accessing a happy and fulfilled life. These recommendations can be safely grouped as ancient and contemporary.

Contemporary Tools for a Fulfilled Life

Happiness is the most sought after emotion by most human beings simply because it is a state of well being involving positive feelings that range from contentment at the bottom to intense joy at the very top. All these states are naturally inclined to the original internal constitution of human being where one never gets tired. Being a subject matter of intense impact on humanity, people before us as well have identified areas where a person can work proactively. Hence, there is no need to leave our happiness to unseen forces. If you think you should be happier and you are sincere to work in that direction, there are tried and tested initiatives which are said to work as much as prescription drugs cure for many other serious ailments.

Let us first quickly look at broad factors that actually influence our happiness quotient in the first place. It is here that work done by Ms. Sonja Lyubomirsky, a long time professor in the department of Psychology at the University of California and author of *The How of Happiness* (2007) comes very handy. Her findings deal with underlying sources of happiness impacting planes in exact proportions. The scientific studies that are basis of her conclusions were carried by her and her team covering over two and half decades. Her work by far is most respected when it comes to assigning the weights of factors impacting happiness level. The length and width of the studies makes it a genuinely serious study to believe findings without much murmur.

Keeping intriguing details aside, she concluded that as much as fifty per cent factors governing human happiness are in the genes where not much can be done about. But the next forty per cent factors impacting individual's happiness fall within the category where self-controls are responsible for happiness levels. In short, forty per cent factors are established to be directly related to the interests and activities that we can choose to engage and relate to what we think and what we do. She concluded that it is only the last ten per cent of individual's happiness that is affected by real life circumstances and situations that have external factors lying beyond control of the particular individual. Contrary to this, general idea of most people was to believe that lack of happiness is attributed largely to external factors. Crux of this study is to let us know that as much as forty per cent of factors fall well within the direct ambit where we ourselves have direct say and our own regulation can bring desired changes irrespective of given genetic tendencies and external influences. Well not hundred per cent but there is a sufficient leverage in our hands to carry out course corrections of our own destiny.

It is in this background that we shall now list out contemporary solutions available at the command of a normal person of today; a person who is not very religious, not averse to his share of enjoyment, flexible in approach and attitude and, at best, believe in a mix of Eastern and Western traditions. The target person is well educated, well placed, well informed, has open mind and sees himself more as a global citizen and does not wish to remain tied down under traditional bands of geography, religion, caste, creed, colour, language, nation, sectarian or rural/urban backgrounds. The solutions discussed here are based on scientifically based researches carried out in recent times. The time span of studies relied is last twenty-five years i.e. the period falling in between 1990 to 2015. Most scientific researches, studies and analysis have been carried out under very controlled environments. Hence, these studies need to be considered fairly reliable and relevant for our modern day. Suggestions from these studies could be self tested by any serious seeker to realize its effectiveness.

The well-being studies relied for this section suggest three major influence areas. First, we have factors providing due focus on general life satisfaction. Second, we have factors effecting specific individuals own well-being. These may be different for each person and one has to do a lot of self-talk and self-check to identify the real motivators.

Third and last, we have suggestions intended towards pruning down factors having negative influences kicking in pains, anger and such other feelings, which drain out personal happiness.

Let us try to list out the steps for enhancing our score or frequency of happy moments or the regularity of such spells:

Training the Mind before Regulating its Working

Recommendations for training of human mind for superior benefits are nothing new. Cultures after cultures can be seen throughout the history suggesting its populace to go for proper training of mind. So, it is not a new phenomenon. It is considered necessary to acquire higher control over actions, reactions, and thoughts. A trained mind is supposed to channelize mental energy and thought process towards desired direction in a controlled manner. Training of mind is taken as a strong tool even for self development of skills by modern day management gurus as mind training contributes to developed imaginations.

Now, several recent scientific researchers confirm that human brain has neuro-plasticity and can be trained to be more empathetic, appreciative and compassionate. We all are fully aware now that specific kind of feeling is related to our habit of thinking. For example, if one thinks that he or she is not as good as some other person being compared; such person actually starts feeling sad. It also works in reverse direction. If you think that your senior within family, immediate society or at work is a nice person and likes you, your happiness remains intact even when he comes out tough on you. Our thoughts allow us to believe or overlook several things about people we like. Conversely, there are situations where casual remarks made by very own siblings result in lot of heartburns injecting pains for longer period.

Of course, training the mind is neither easy nor impossible. One is called upon to pay close attention to his intimate emotional responses to understand the under currents, understand the real meaning of currents and deal with the real issues. Few sittings in a quite space away from every day pressures are required to make sincere beginning. Few sittings later, one can expect to become familiar with his/her own natural impulses to the given situations.

This will soon result in learning about personal drivers that work behind our reactions. We are deliberately refraining from calling these sittings as meditation or by any other name as these are intended for beginners without any formal training or supervision and without really understanding the process required to realize meditation. Calling such sessions straight away as meditation will qualify as a casual reference to meditation. Meditation is indeed a life changing practice and deserves serious understanding before being called so.

To begin with, you just need to find time and a peaceful corner and sit with closed eyes and watch your mind hopping from one subject to another without applying any control or regulation. Just become a silent observer, a neutral and unbiased observer. Only precaution is to avoid the tendencies of bringing live your past or your so-called ideal outcome of particular situations. Tendencies relating to both past and future hinder our neutral position of being a pure observer. One practical tip that might work for some is to develop ability to observe our own thoughts as if we are actually watching thoughts of some other person.

With sufficient sittings over weeks and months, you should be able to clearly identify the emotions associated with your thoughts at a given point of time. Let those relate to either negative or positive sides as that doesn't matter at all. At this stage you are testing waters and should not be worried for swimming into it. Just to extend the same example, please look at the cleanliness, temperature, smell, turbulence, currents, etc., as if some other person may have to swim out there. Regulation will be the next stage. Every time you come across thoughts generating negative feeling, you should question such feeling and convince yourself logically and explore options having positivity even in that tough situation. What we are intending doing here is to calm the emotional brain and hand over the subject matter to our logical brain, the one that is known to have optimistic approach without losing hope even at worst of times.

It might sound a bit tough for the beginners but those of us, who have practised true self-awareness exercises for some time, will vouch that practical success is perfectly feasible. One-by-one and step-by-step, each of the negative feeling could get replaced by positive feeling reassuring self that entire environment is positive enough and conducive to our happiness, which is indeed a statement of reality. This is precisely how the feeling of "All is well" approach brings slow but sure positive results (reference is being made to the concept used in the famous Hindi movie named 'Three Idiots'. Thanks to this movie that the concept of "All is well" got popularized in a very effective manner).

Every person in a positive environment is prompted to work out his own mantra for calming down the thoughts. What is required is to apply the same formula every time there is an agitating or disturbing situation. Over time, such response becomes our second nature and original thoughts and feelings itself will move from negativity to positivity germinating the seeds of happiness. How much time it takes is, however, dependent on level of negativity, our level of commitment, quality of our observation practices and physical and moral fabric of the practitioner. As a general rule, while dealing with changes involved with your own inner matters, please try not operating with fix time lines as that might only spoil your efforts. You are advised to focus on efforts rather than results and hold your patience with the repeated reminder that if it works for others and you are making as sincere efforts, why this will not work for you?

A good point to start on our journey of exercising control over thoughts is the sound knowledge that human brain is hard coded for accepting change. Let accepting change may not be a barrier. Our brain has been accepting changes all the time. Original programming of our brain being for positive emotions of peace, joy and happiness is surely one of the most reassuring understandings that we should cement. This is in fact one of its most unique quality. It is individual's life pressures, modern-day stresses, negative swings of emotions that act upon the brain to generate negative thoughts and feelings. Cognitive therapy is very well validated treatment for counteracting effects of stresses and is advised for whomsoever so desire. As per Wikipedia's page on 'Cognitive therapy':

> 'This therapy is based on the cognitive model, which states that thoughts, feelings and behavior are all connected, and that individuals can move towards overcoming difficulties and meeting their goals by identifying and changing unhelpful

or inaccurate thinking, problematic behavior and distressing emotional responses."

Restrain Selfish Motives

Undoubtedly, today is the time for individualism in general. Earlier individualism was associated exclusively with the Western World but now the same has well spread in other parts of the world especially in urban areas. Each person is seen working to support one's own life and aiming for one's own happiness. No doubt people are working harder and can be seen making their best efforts to fulfill their dreams. Today, nobody feels happy to live life of a parasite thriving at the expense of others. Male or female, young or old, everybody wish to be their own masters, at least financially. Like it or not, but this shift of focus away from society/joint family setups to individuals/nuclear family setups is fueling to an increasing selfishness.

People are increasingly getting trapped in 'I, me and mine' syndrome. The modern idea of making it big and quick, feeds on the premise that one ought to be inherently selfish without bothering too much for being aggressive or hostile. This focus limits their view on short term and drives people to seek instant gains. They are willing to opt even for quick-fix approach. People seek personal benefits even with willing violations of morals and ethics. In short, ends have become more important than means.

But a true seeker has to get away from these ill methods. Forget who is watching and forget what others are doing as that is not important for you. You better learn as quickly as possible that a ground prepared with selfishness can and shall germinate only on negative tendencies. The seeds of positive tendencies are unable to develop roots where selfishness rules. Many prevalent social ills of lying, cheating, assaulting, revenge seeking, looting, short changing are all but examples of weeds growing on selfishly fertile ground. These negative tendencies are bound to leave unnecessary imprint on your heart, mind and soul. History is witness that no one could gain happiness or bliss by walking on the road of selfish laced approach. You are welcome, however, to try being the first exception?

Unfortunately, even when you are working selfishly, there is none to put you on trial or book you under some offence or catch you red-handed. But these negative imprints are bound to eventually haunt your conscience and bite you day in and day out, including during sleep. Remember that your conscience is keeping absolute count of all your actions and thoughts. Listen to it with attention and respect before it gets suppressed and gets covered with overburden of your evil deeds. The haunting of your conscience is bound to impact your happiness and only negatively. Let us always remember that selfishness and happiness can't co-exist together, period! By acting selfishly, you are invading on the laws of happiness.

We have to remind ourselves that helping others and caring others are natural impulses of human beings. Every time one goes against it, there will be unseen stress and every time you help a needy and stand for others, your soul gets relaxed and your heart feels melting. In any case, you will be called intelligent when your ultimate purpose gets achieved. If leading a happy and fulfilled life is your purpose, going for selfish motives and actions is certainly being less than intelligent. One really wishes that we are smart and real selfish to serve our genuine nature of extending love, peace and support to all. Let us immediately start accepting and caring others. That will make us happy at heart and help us realize the real spirit of being selfish. Let helping others and making our heart happy becomes indirect route to reach our destination. After all, seeking happiness was the purpose behind our being selfish in the first place?

Even if it sounds like a discourse by a religious preacher in a congregation, the fact remains that pursuing selfishness or being violent or being hostile to others is not our natural state and each one of us must move away from such situations as soon as possible. Recommended way is to pursue, attain and enjoy your happiness while being in harmony with others. So long as your actions and thoughts are in conflict with well being of others, your own true happiness will keep eluding you.

Access Your Compassion and Gentleness

Undoubtedly, normal life of today generates tons of tensions and anxieties. Tensions are drowning normal folks of today neck deep. Modern life inflates only two things — stress and ego. One comes across overflowing egos at almost every social setting. Egos have indeed become very fragile. Touching of vehicles in crowded roads in any city in India is a common sight for egos getting hurt leading to aggressive behaviours between two unknown people. Tempers run high even between total strangers. Patience seems to be out of stock at all times. People are running in cross directions without any finish line in view. It is understandable that it is hardly a perfect environment for seeking fulfillment and blissful happiness.

As we have seen earlier anger, envy and greed were already there with us. These negative tendencies worked like holes in our reservoir of happiness. All our efforts to fill up our reservoir fail to yield desired results. Now focus on self and materialistic objects create environment where conflict arise easily. With addition of conflict, the holes emptying our reservoir of happiness get further widened. Thus our reservoir gets empty at faster speed. The requirement was additional supply of happiness to get brimful but what we end up getting are leakages draining it thick and fast. Interestingly, quite a few of us are not even aware of these taps and their capacity to drain out whatever little accumulation we had in our happiness tank. This is the precise situation facing many of our friends today.

Anger, agitation and frustration are the only fruits that can be plucked when we lock compassion and empathy in the closet. Affection travels in 'to and fro' manner; true affection shown by person in front gives us the more calmness than our own emotion of affection present in our own heart. Someone may argue that anger and conflict also arise from our own heart. Yes, these negative emotions also have same source and this reality can't be wished away but that is where our nature of being human comes into play. If we fail to apply prudence of our judgement over situations in our own lives, what is the point in being human?

It seems that many of us have forgotten that all human beings are blessed with compassion and gentleness as an underlying true nature of humanity. And even if we knew it, we certainly didn't believe it as real. We are known as social animals and we realize it every day that only so much can be enjoyed without others. We may like it or not but the fact is that human can't do much without each other. The burning question is why all our affection and compassion get limited to handful of people within our immediate family. What stops us from connecting with entire humanity at large? Sure, the world is so big but why we forget to look at people coming in our contact as parallel souls. Should we not look at the milkman, the lift operator, the vegetable vendor, and the courier boy and many more such people first as our fellow travellers on their journey called human life. True that there may be many others who may not look at us as fellows but what about those where we are in position to extend the olive branch?

Anger, violence and aggression are part of our nature only on superficial level. At deeper level we are blessed with love, compassion and gentleness. We may use examples to justify negative flow of anger or frustration on real life situations but these emotions are not part of normal human nature. Basic nature is where you wish to remain for a long time and temporary nature is what you regret being and where you wish to make a quick exit. We can each take a moment to introspect and see if we wish to have a serene calm environment or the opposite of it. Flared emotions are a big barrier in seeking mutual solutions. As human beings, we can always bring together better results when we let compassion and gentleness prevail. Indians of present generation have to learn that how much happiness they let go simply by losing compassion. Let me elaborate why Indians in particular have to re-learn their lessons in compassion and gentleness by way of a real life example.

Altercations between occupants of two random vehicles involved during road accidents are a common sight in most Indian cities. People involved can be seen screaming at high decibel and blaming each other. Surely there are impacts of delay for work, problems involving insurance claims, visits to workshop and many days without access to vehicle. But irrespective of strong reasons to flare tempers on either side, what is the role of abuses and verbal fighting? During my stay in Indonesia, I was once driven by one of my young manager on a highway. Something happened in front of our vehicle. This person in front car applied sudden breaks but got hit by our vehicle. The impact was sizable on both the vehicles. In situation like this, my Indian experience alarmed me of some big altercation. But to my dismay, both car owners got down quickly, inspected each other's car, said sorry to each other, asked if repairs were well covered in the insurance, and shook hands. Still sitting in the car, I was rather surprised seeing these two smilingly exchanging name cards for future contact. Needless to mention, they both co-operated each other in claim settlements for each other and became good acquaintances for life.

Gentleness and compassion, if cultivated well, have great power either in uplifting our happiness or to be a barrier for controlling leakages from our reservoir of happiness by other negative emotions, justified or otherwise. Please forget that being compassionate is a favour on others. Sorry, the biggest beneficiary of your compassion is you yourself. If you fail to look at this emotion like this, the losses are all yours.

Contemporary Happiness Management Sequence

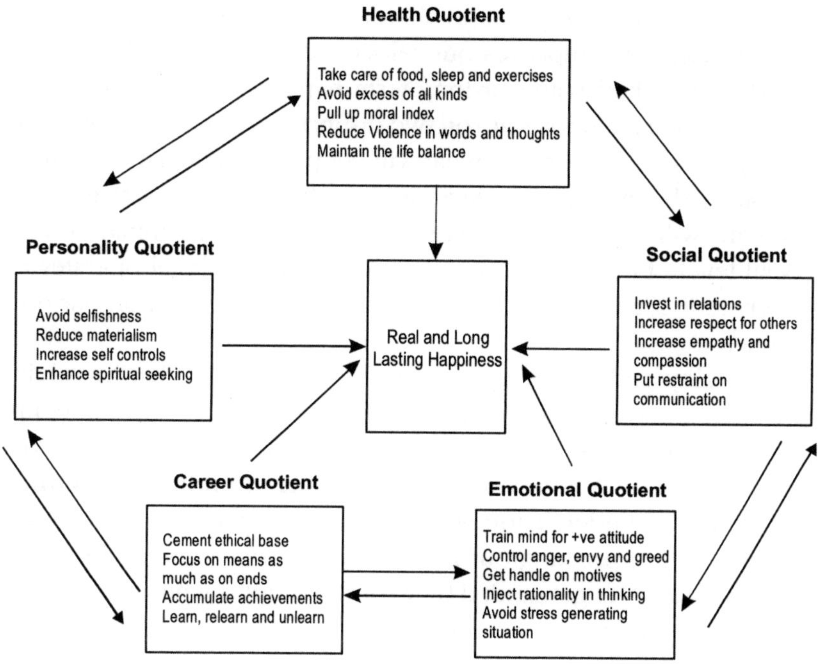

Holding on Morality and Ethics with Rock solid Firmness

Morality here is the distinction between being 'right or wrong' and 'good or bad' human behaviour. It is well established that positive management of moral and social Emotions, consisting mainly shame, guilt, embarrassment and pride, influences our virtuous activities. Strong moral and social virtues encourage each one of us to resist greedy temptations of taking shortcuts with violation of moral behaviour. Just to understand the two more clearly, morality revolves around how we ought to treat others while ethics revolves around how we ought to live ourselves. One can come up with the simple question as to why should we follow morality? Well, it is advised for the sake of our long term self-interests and short term psychological satisfaction. Both these aspects are, unfortunately, integral for your search of fulfilled life.

Riding on morality and ethics, good behaviour maintained over longer period of times results in happy situation where our brain develops new neurons. These neurons help in conditioning our brain for developing positivity in our thoughts and actions. There is nothing surprising out here as this is how human brain has evolved to its present form over its evolutionary process. So morality and ethical behaviour improves our self-consciousness which in turn is too deeply linked with our long term happiness. Feelings for self-conscious behaviour operate on two distinct levels. First level involves perceptions held by others; what will people think? What my parents will say? What will be the reaction of my friends and relatives? How my wife will take it? These are all thoughts that germinate out of social level of our consciousness. Second distinct level operates on purely individual basis where our thoughts reflect back on our own character.

Morality and ethics operate in invisible ways. This invisibility prompts many of us to think that morals and ethics are just insignificant. In reality, these have much penetrating impact on our entire psyche. Whenever we violate the morality and ethics, knowingly or under ignorance, nagging thoughts and feelings are bound to keep pricking our inner core creating stress and tension. One should never get guided by wrong examples where some other people are seen happy even with known records of immorality and unethical behaviours. We should be least concerned with others. Our happiness is nothing to do with what others do or don't, it is all about us and no one else. If you do wrong, you will always have realization of that, and your conscience will bite you and you will be deprived of your happiness.

Happiness can never be taken as an end by itself. Happiness without moral and ethical surrounding is just transient and will be followed by pangs of pains, sufferings, regrets and self-tortures. An immoral and unethical action does provide a momentary excitation and stimulation but the guilt and disgust that follows is capable of draining our real happiness for longer times. In fact, maintaining morality strictly is an integral part of the definition of happiness that we all are after. The entire structure of happiness rests on the foundation of morality and ethics. Even small damage to this foundation is good enough to shake the entire superstructure of happiness. Focus on morality is one of the most important objectives of all popular religions and they all play big role in spreading moral values among all their followers.

Unwavering commitment towards moral and ethics requires strong self-discipline and self-control. Are we saying it as anything new? No, it is nothing new as Gautam Buddha spoke about it some 2500 years back in much detail. Problem with humanity is that it keeps forgetting whatever is comparatively difficult to practise.

Investing Energy in Relationships, Duties and Purpose

In Sanskrit all these points can be summarized in a single word "*Swa-Dharma*", the right focus on individual's essential obligations. Every adult carries unique responsibilities towards family, parents as well as immediate society. This thought is well ingrained on our psychic self that our personal share of happiness is to be expected only after attending our obligations towards our dependents and close relatives dutifully. Our own personal happiness is just a by-product that comes into existence automatically while attending to family and social obligations. Present generations may be living in nuclear family structures but welfare of parents and siblings is never very far from thoughts of responsible adults even today. One is in better position to appreciate this fact after getting exposure to the family systems prevalent in different cultures in other parts of the world.

Investing in relationships is considered better investment than investing in equity markets and stocks provided, of course, the returns are measured in terms of overall happiness. But the word relationship is being used here has nothing to do with the present day common parlance associated with it. Relationship referred here is pure concept of connectedness for care and concern within a close circle of family and well wishers. These relationships also operate just like stocks. Most of us have had our exposure in stock markets and know very well that some stocks give us short-term returns, some other will mature over longer period, some investments are good just for discussions among friends, some are volatile while some are fundamentally rock solid. Some will give better income while some other may give only capital appreciation. We also know that few of the investments might depreciate over years while few others may even get de-listed. But if we are well invested, our spread is well distributed among various segments and our time horizon is long term, we should be making money over the entire portfolio. Now, each one of the previous two hundred odd words can be repeated verbatim for relationships. The gains and returns from relationship are in terms of personal well being and feeling of worthiness. Hence, those who are well invested in relations of multiple types and for longer periods, their supplies of personal happiness are rather assured over longer horizon.

Simplifying Life by Shunning Complications

Let us face the fact that human life is not too elusive or a big mystery in any way. Most of the problems we face in daily life are manmade. Having understood so much, it should be easy for us to keep it as simple as possible. Surely, life is known to throw many overwhelming issues, issues that are strong enough to submerge our entire existence for a while. But people who are able to keep it simple are able to swim back to normalcy faster. One of the preliminary steps towards simplifying our life is a two-letter word "NO". One should have the conviction to use this strong word for guarding against everything that has potential to overwhelm our life. 'No' for setting unachievable targets, 'no' to people seeking help that is beyond us, 'no' to things that are not part of our plan, 'no' to even good things if there are chances of drowning down, 'no' for those plans that soak peace out of our life, 'no' to things that immerse us so deep that we have no time to stop for smelling roses of our garden (to be read as success and growth of our kith and kin). Each one of us can recount instances where we landed in difficulty under pressure from others of one or the other kind. But those who can say 'no' with clarity and conviction are saved from enumerable pressures and many more problems that otherwise would have emerged later.

Next point relates to chasing materialism in general. Pursuing materialism is myth as all it leads to momentary pleasures similar to one that kids get whenever they get their new toys. Worrying for this car and that house and those vacations and pursuing brands are all unwanted complications that sink us deep into unending spins. Forget siblings, cousins, neighbours and colleagues and let them chase what is good for them. What is the point in leading a second hand life of doing what others have done beforehand? Mother Nature never wanted human beings to be exactly similar to each other so why do we even wish to be like others? Human beings are unique but only if we appreciate and use our ability for reasoning and logical thinking with best of our abilities and efforts. Alas, this very blessing, not possessed by other known species, remains under used with most of us at most of the time.

Avoiding excesses of all kinds is yet another strong step for simplifying life. Leading a simple, disciplined and regulated life makes us stronger to absorb occasional pressures that life offers to us here and there. Discipline in speech, in eating, in work, in exercises, in entertainment, in thinking and practically in every other thing we ever do allows us to develop ability to examine and engage uncertainties of life as it unfolds. Those of us, who are unable to avoid excesses, are exposed to sink when the flow is faster. Some may say that simple thing like thinking about something important should not be bad even if it is in excess. They are welcome to explore the meaning of worrying. Even thinking too much for things that are beyond our control, is a big barrier for happiness. Avoidance of excesses from our life will fill it with harmony and balance. Remember that harmonious sounds from multiple instruments remaining in balance is called symphony. Now we all know that symphony of soothing music leads us to peace and relaxation. Simplicity is the biggest requirement for a symphony, period.

Someone will find it difficult to conclude that steps mentioned above are difficult to follow or aren't expected to lead a happy life. Neither of these is dependent on others, people and circumstances included. All you need is to have a strong will and firm resolve that this is my life and I am entitled to live it with better control on its outcome rather than living endlessly and aimlessly like most others.

Ancient Indian Tools for a Fulfilled Life

After contemporary recommendations for happiness management, it will be interesting to go over recommendations made by sages and scriptures of Ancient India over two thousand years back. Indian sages achieved tremendous progress towards theoretical explanations of the world and thought processes of human mind together with religious contemplation. They mastered intellectual progress ahead of most others at any other place in human history. They scaled superlative heights in learning details about human psyche through systematic practices and systems. With all the progress claimed by sciences in last few centuries, mastery over human psyche achieved by Indian Sages millenniums before is indeed baffling to many people of modern times.

Indian sub continent has been blessed with constant stream of series of learned sages having divine abilities. Many of those accomplished souls could contemplate towards most subtle aspects of human hearts, minds and brains. They could very well decipher human impulse in its widest possible spectrum. Some of these findings are getting scientifically validated now with so much progress on science and technology levels. Those sages could think beyond glamour of fleshly life and anticipate need for striving appropriate human endeavours. Such endeavours catered to people in different age brackets, social backgrounds and cultural groups. They also factored in natural variations among beings like intellectual abilities and emotional orientations. Their systems got evolved over centuries and got perfected to the extent that generations of Indians kept following them with benefits of inexhaustible significance. These systems accommodated desired space for all types of human desires including exploring education, religions, social, administrative, carnal, financial and spiritual.

Besides, they also evolved social systems and structures following which, the people in general could find near perfect balance among multiple purposes of a complete, happy and fulfilled life. The beauty is that the essence of those systems remains equally relevant even today. It is mesmerizing that each passing century and decades, with all the significant transformations and technological progress by humanity, the truth contained in these Ancient learning remains as relevant as a bunch of freshly plucked roses from the garden. New breakthrough on different fronts of learning seems to play only the catching up game. Kudos to those great sages and systems perfected by them so much time ago!

The learned sages established optimum balance among different human needs and aspirations by intricately knitting out well-rounded matrix of systems. Their recommendations ensured requisite exposure of all types of attractions and attachments of the material world to every person before escalating their efforts for aiming the highest goal of human existence. They provided for milestones on the way and recommended change of gears commensurate with natural maturity expected of persons along their growing age. The intricacies conceptualized and the solutions suggested by them are indeed great examples of their wonderful imaginative caliber.

Ancient Indian System being more than Hindu, Buddhist or Jain Systems

Not identifying these systems with Hinduism or other homegrown religious traditions is a deliberate attempt and not a casual overlook. Most of the systems being referred here got evolved centuries before the origin of very word 'Hindu' surfaced on the horizon. This was the period much before Gautama Buddha and Mahavira started popularizing their individual doctrines with higher focus on some unique aspects and branched out pursuing their separate ways. Indians, in any case, ought to remember that most of their key concepts and doctrines from the land evolved out of constant communication among all homegrown movements. That spirit has never dried on Indian land. One can easily see several similar strands within all religious streams originating on Indian soil including Jainism, Buddhism, Hinduism and going well up to Sikhism. Due to this inseparable influences coming out of constant borrowing and lending, clubbing them all together under Ancient Indian system is the only justified reference to them. So what is discussed below is a somewhat combined product and no attempt is deemed necessary or feasible to look at it with the prism of any one of the religious thought from India. The caution is being flagged for people who at best are blessed with only half-baked knowledge of Indian subcontinent.

Ancient Indian systems look at the entire aspect of human happiness in its entire spectrum. To begin with, Indian systems classify the happiness at different levels like nowhere else. It has a vertical system that provides clearly demarcated stages based on intensity of happiness and it has horizontal classification. The vertical levels of happiness are classified as *'Sukham', 'Harsham', 'Ullahasam', 'Anandam', 'Paramananadam'* and finally *'Brahmanandam'*. Although, English language can 't provide exact translation for these planes but loosely speaking we can understand these steps as comfort/pleasure, joy, glee/gaiety, delight, bliss and supreme bliss. On the other hand, three horizontal silos are called *Bhautika, Mansika* and *Adhyatmika* i.e. Physical, Mental and Spiritual respectively.

At the lowest step we have Physical happiness (*Bhautika Sukham*), which is related more with physical needs, comforts, sexual and sensual enjoyment and such other bodily pleasures experienced by sense organs. This is direct, intense, immediate but very short-lived. As such, these are branded as least sought after. All you get here are physical gratification and enjoyment of luxuries. These are subjective in nature and don't impact all beings with similar intensity. These are above the level of necessities and hence are not capable to add much to the quality of life. All these enjoyments are classified under '*Sukham*'. It is fine if you get it and nothing great is lost if one fails to experience these. To the people who have not experienced these before, their absence does not impact their level of satisfaction. So, at best these are pure add-ons and nothing to do with basics.

Next in importance is Mental happiness (*Mansika Harsham*) and it involves positive feelings, thoughts and emotions. In its interplay, mental happiness is linked to sense of overall fulfillment and, more importantly, freedom from worries, afflictions and anxieties. The nearest English words that largely convey its exact meaning are delight, cheer, joy and rejoice. The Sanskrit word used for this category is '*Anand*', a mental state of feelings where everything looks relaxed, contended and pleased. Being linked to mental situation, it has nothing to do with comforts or state of physical body. Physical and mental happiness are totally independent of each other but generally have mutual impact with unidirectional correlation.

The source of mental happiness is located within and without. The all-important Creative principle imbedded in human psyche is the underlying force in action out here. Contentment, confidence, engagement and self-esteem are all the mental states that get exhibited under positive influence of this level of happiness. Simple steps advised for uplifting mental happiness are connecting with others (family, friends and neighbours included), being active all the time, continued curiosity for new learning, keeping the mind engaged in creative mode and undertaking contemplative exercises.

The third and final category is called '*Adhyatmika*' or Spiritual. The vertical levels clubbed under this category are '*Paramananda*' (ecstasy, jubilance or bliss) and '*Brahmananda*', ultimate pure wisdom of merging existence with Divine or achieving true understanding of Self and its union with the Supreme Self. This is supposed to be highest stage of human happiness and comes from freedom from all bondage and attractions. Ancient Indian systems concluded that human being felt unhappy because they are bound/ attached to impermanent things and can't easily escape from such attachments and aversions. Converging and separation of loved ones, inescapable old age, sickness and final decaying of human body, are all inevitably temporary things and source of unhappiness. Going forward, the entire build up of Buddhism got based on this very '*Dukhha*', the sadness associated with these unavoidable realities of human life. Ancient Indian systems discourage the very human desire to seek happiness in temporary things as a mirage in ultimate journey. These systems strongly recommend all human beings to put their energy in coming out of the recurrent cycle of life and death and seek the final liberation as a permanent state of happiness, the state of "*Moksha*", the never ending liberation.

In addition to this, Ancient Sages also evolved unique social structures and its stages with strong recommendations to people to grow through recommended stages and pursuing aims and objectives laid out for each stage of human life. This matrix of multiple stages and multiple objectives has guided millions and billions Indians for time immemorial. Let us quickly touch base with these structures.

Ancient Social Structures Designed for Fulfillment

Ancient systems recognized multiple objectives and stages in human life. They also recognized and accepted uniqueness of every individual in their own orientations and preferences. These unique strengths were to be the basis for their choice of occupation. Each person was prompted to choose the occupation he has best chance to excel. It was the corner stone around which initial segregations of class started taking shape. Emotional and spiritual bent of every person was also to be counted for recommending appropriate teachings. Accordingly, they established a unique class system by dividing people under four distinct groups with each class shouldering well defined social responsibilities among them. This complex matrix comprises of: 1) Ashram Vyavastha, the Four Stages of Life; 2) Varna Vyavastha; the Fours Classes of Society; and 3) Purushartha, the Four Aims of Human Life. Each one of these systems work like a valuable pearl on the necklace crafted by great sages to ensure well fulfilled human life.

Let us briefly look these groups in brief:

Life Divided in Four Stages – *Ashram Vyavastha*

Modern day life has indeed become very hectic like never before. For most of us, life is throwing new challenges each passing day. Millions are struggling for basic necessities and comforts. For few, lifestyles are getting luxurious with problems of plenty. Knowledge is expanding while wisdom is shrinking. Internet has brought the entire universe to our finger tips rather than palms, laps and tables. Distances have lost their meanings now as the whole world is considered a small village. Bank balances are rising but human values are on steep decline. Each person is running fast with no finish lines in the offing. Those who don't have are working hard to get it and those who have, want more of the same.

Presumably, it will be difficult for modern age people to appreciate a system where entire human age gets segregated in four distinct stages of roughly twenty-five years each; where different priorities are to be focused in different stages, where gears have to be changed upon completion of the stage, where one has to leave behind past life and move on to next, where attachments to physical world are to be shed voluntarily rather than being forced by someone, where one is conditioned to match his priority in line with his psychological and mental evolution, where there is both time and energy available to pursue all goals prescribed for human life with their sequence and prioritization remaining intact.

Such stages were well conceived to take care of all human aspirations; short-term, mid-term and long-term included. This system is basically designed to maintain right focus all through human life. The stages crafted under this system are completely in sync with physical abilities, learning capabilities, social demands, natural aging process of the body and maturity of mind and intellect. Basic aim behind this four-stage climb is to envisage proper gear changes with changing milestones on this beautiful journey called human life.

Sages have realized that human desires and instincts have strong pulls and pressures and drain out lot of life energy. Also that, unless it is properly guided, there remains a risk of people continuing chasing worldly desires having no time to pursue other equally pressing obligations. It appears that these words are as meaningful and relevant today as ever. The *Ashrams* work as a system of moral checks and balances. One realizes that these are universal principles and will remain relevant as long as humanity survives. Of course, with passing centuries, there may be need to redefine the dos and don'ts so that the magic of the ageless principles continue to hold their shine. Let us try to understand the Four Stages along with present day context:

Brahmacharya Ashram

This exciting first stage starts with beginning of formal education and is devoted for learning all types of subjects with underlying conditions of celibacy, chastity and obedience. This stage was to continue until the formal education continues. The subject of education was to be decided based on one's caste and opinion of the teachers. The word caste here is to be read as 'based on genetically accumulated expertise acquired over generations'. So, all through the learning stage, one was supposed to ensure that:

- Turbulent sensual desires are kept under control to avoid injuries to moral and physical health.
- Learn to remain master of senses and sense organs to avoid enslaving by their natural instincts so there are no roadblocks in the process of learning.
- Live life under strict discipline to build strong foundation for rest of the life.
- Acquire full knowledge in chosen subject matter and spiritual practices. Also, fully embrace the concept of Dharma as prescribed by scriptures.

Understanding Brahmacharya as observing celibacy alone will be a narrow view. Emphasis is on control over desires and senses. The focus here was on subject knowledge as much as on harmony with morality and spirituality. Strong and purified mind developed at this stage was to help all subsequent stages to overpower anxieties, worries, and conflicts. While an untrained mind in this stage was to remain weak and helpless to resist worldly tendencies and was seen as strong cause for loss of peace and tranquility in later life. This ability paves way for strong happiness in subsequent stages in life.

Basic principles are absolutely relevant in present context as well. One can trace any brilliant student in immediate society and can vouch that excellence in education requires following these principles even today; those students who allow dilution in these principles, also see dilution in their academic results and overall performance in subsequent life, no exaggeration.

Grihastha Ashram

This stage in life is for marrying, having children and achieving maximum heights in one's chosen occupation. Another important expectation of the stage is to accumulate sufficient financial resources for supporting everyone around as well as support for self for later part of life. This is the foundation as to why Indians are known for higher savings than rest of the world. Awakened body and mind are used to accumulate resources but without forgoing Karma credits. Natural tendencies of pursuing money, fame and power are taken care in this stage while holding on Dharma. This is also the stage for enjoying comforts, luxuries and going after sensual satisfactions within permitted peripheries. Religious rituals for this stage worked as regular reminders to let the person constantly remember that there are other important things to be done besides enjoying luxuries of life.

Gribastba stage has been given great importance as this stage actually supports (both physically and financially) people in all other stages. *Gribastba* also carries the burden of extending possible support to ascetics, teachers, philosophers and such other people engaged in different kind of social activities. The Bhagwad Gita strongly suggests householders to perform at this stage of life with a sense of sacrifice and as an offering to Gods. Thus, focus is advised to shift from self to society. This shift was to play a major role in finding fulfillment away from personal comforts and going for meeting prescribed obligations.

Because worldly experiences can make it easy to forget the difference between right and wrong, Ancient Indian scriptures prescribe overarching presence of Dharma for everything pursued in this stage. Interestingly, the directions recommended here are practical and ideal at the same time. This stage is prescribed to end when one completes his fiftieth year. Idea was to keep the second half of life for pursuing higher aims of life. This is where most people, in modern time, get into trouble. Attractions of this stage have binding spell on most people. It is so common to see many people around us who continue in this stage without plans for early termination. The lures of money, fame and power are insatiable and keep growing with passing time. One can never get enough of these. But, how can one forget that so long one continues pursuing this stage, the next stage in life remains suspended.

The continuation in *Gribastba* beyond the age of fifty years is attributed to bulk of miseries in life of most people at present. Continuing in this stage brings in conflict of interest with next generation. This can be vouched both at places of work and at homes. No wonder, the conflict so arising deprives the mental peace guaranteed by next stage of life. Firm conviction is required to end this stage on time. On a personal note, the author is a good example of a person having strong belief in the prescribed timelines. I came out of my professional career as a CEO in a midsize corporation just after completing fifty years to pursue next stage on a purely voluntary basis. No, it is not impractical even for modern times. Presumably, the lures for continuing were as strong in ancient times as at present. All I can say is that those continuing in Grihastha past their fifties are missing the freedom to live life in a rewarding and fulfilling manner. I hope that people continuing in their *Grihastha* well past the recommended physical age are aware about the fun being missed by not graduating to next stage which is full of frolic and freedom besides plenty of fun of superior nature. Sure you miss a few kicks here and there but the gains outweigh the misses by miles. Having seen both sides, I dare say that continuing in *Grihastha* beyond a point is a poor bargain for sure.

Vanprashtha Ashram

Besides physical age, scriptures prescribed that when a man of knowledge been through with his worldly obligation towards direct family, has become debt free, is well provided for basic material needs for remaining life, his skin has started getting wrinkles and hair have started turning gray, the person was to be considered eligible to withdraw from the active world and move on to next stage of life, *Vanprashtha*, the stage for spiritual preparations. From now on, all he is supposed to concentrate is systematic initiatives intended solely to make his soul happy. From this stage onward, one is supposed to work only for superior aim of human life and beyond. This is also the time to contribute wisdom and energy to help society benefit from his experience. But this giving back has to be without seeking anything in return. Such a selfless contribution is expected to keep the aspirant engaged with noble cause and lead him to experience joy and satisfaction.

Grihastha Ashram, by its very nature, involves engagements in activities carried out for pursuits of money, power and fame resulting in accumulation of Karma debits. Those debits need to be settled as a precondition for seeking everlasting peace and joy. This stage is intended for settling all pending points carried over from previous stage. Originally prescribed only for men from higher classes, the system allows a wife to accompany her husband but only if she wishes to do so voluntarily. Actually, there are examples where ladies opted for this stage and contributed in equal proportions. So, depending on the individual orientation, this stage was open for both men and women.

Literally speaking, *Vanprashtha* means 'moving on the edge of the society towards forest' but the real meaning is dissolution of attachments with worldly bondage and starting life of contemplation after giving up worldly life of luxuries. One is also expected to bring changes in food habits and from now onward one must 'eat to live' and not 'live to eat'. The knowledge and practice of detachment refines the essence of enjoyment and enhances spiritual orientation.

The best understanding for the recommended dos and don'ts of this stage is summarized by Manu Samhita Chapter 6, Shloka No. 8, which is produced below with present day meaning;

> "....He should engage in regular study, control his senses, keep friendly behavior with everyone and maintain a tranquil mind at all times. He must always give charity as best as he can, should not expect or accept any gifts from others and he should always have mercy for all living beings".

This is the time for silently giving back to society using the wisdom and experience gathered during working life. At the start of this stage, one is financially self reliant, physically strong and mentally alert. So this is a perfect platform to learn how to give up worldly pleasures and spend time in contemplation. One is advised to remain available to guide and educate someone willing, desirous and deserving to learn. Remaining time and energies are to be directed to seek spiritual knowledge and progress. Having completed more than half of life (assuming maximum age of 100 years), this stage is a big halt. It is good time to take a pause and evaluate about sufficiency of material resources for the balance life. One has to face the internal signals of tiredness from normal routine. One has to feel for a deep urge to spend time towards mentally satisfying and spiritually uplifting activities by giving up activities aimed at generating money or sustaining power.

No one should look at *Vanprashtha* as an escape or excuse for going for a simpler life away from pressures of householder's life.

No, it is not so. It is also not about obligatory retirement and idling around. It is embracing a big move and venturing into unchartered territory which calls for devotion of your physical and mental energy focused on higher cause. Moving to Vanprashtha, in real terms, requires far deeper involvement; much more than ever experienced by a *Grihastha* towards his work. It calls for use of your mind in much concentrated manner than you would have possibly done during *Grihastha*. *Grihastha* by design involves responsibilities spread over several objects and subjects. Many things seek your attention and energy without need for planning at your part. Contrary to that, *Vanprashtha* is very concentrated and completely focused exclusively on spiritual refinements and nothing else. Your own initiatives and drives replace the pulls and pressures of previous stage. Now, one can just imagine how big that simple change is.

Strict advice for a person stepping into Vanprashtha is to stay away from any and every form of attachments; money, position, recognition, revenge, habits, styles, addictions, intoxications, friends, relatives, children and grandchildren all included. All types of attachments are known to colour human thoughts and inhibit vision's clarity. You also have to be ready to lose dominance in every sphere of life. One has to be ready to give up all good and not so good things of human life. It is indeed a tough call but experience of learned sages is there to prompt, motivate and guide to enjoy the freedom of giving up. This is the time to encourage children to live life of their own. Pursuing life without selfish desire germinates a unique feeling of satisfaction and contentment that widens the entire outlook to broader dimensions.

All available energy and initiatives are to be directed only and only for enhancing spiritual orientation as a full time activity. You must be determined and ready to give up attachment to all above in a voluntary manner. It is time to lead life in your own simple way without too many frills. Numerous activities advised to be pursued include religious travelling, socially benefiting events, reading of scriptures, spending time in solitude, meditation, writing, researching, painting, bhakti, etc. Your sole purpose in pursuing any and every activity from now on is simply to seek pure joy and fulfillment. Self-satisfaction is the sole purpose of every activity as there is nothing left to prove to anyone any more.

In terms of current scenario of modern days, it is not obligatory to move to the edge of the society or shift in forests to pursue this stage. Living in forest physically but keeping the fire of desires occupying every thought can't be the right eligibility for Vanprashtha. On the contrary, remaining in the heart of the city but shunning out attachments and spending time for meditation, yoga and study of scriptures to pursue one's own spiritual progress is sure eligibility. As it is with increasing population and all the deforestation around, there are no forests available to move into in most cases. If the rest of the family is ready to accept the new life style of the aspirant and the aspirant himself has been successful in giving up attachments, one may even continue living within or nearby the family, as the case may be. But it has been seen that living amidst your family is bound to draw you towards its compulsive attractions and distractions. A much higher degree of wisdom and realization is necessitated to live inside family with burnt out attachments and it is generally not practical and never was.

The happiness and bliss of this matured person comes from living life of a recluse who talks less but listens more; who does less but experiences more; who receives nothing but enjoys in giving. During this stage, with minimum possessions and away from luxuries, one experiences happiness only in exploring his consciousness, deeper and deeper. It is a different matter, however, that exploring own consciousness is known to offer toughest resistance. No wonder, sages provided as long as twenty five years for this phase. People who have experience of practising this small initiative will vouch for the difficulties of Himalayan proportions engulfed in expanding one's own consciousness.

Interestingly, people living in this stage during the Vedic times made great contributions towards advancement on multiple fronts. Composition of Upanishads, the running of forest academies (the than equivalent of the Harvard, the Stanford, the MIT and the Cambridge of today), evolving Ayurveda, composition of best of literature, defining concepts in theology and Indian philosophies are all credited to people from Vanprashtha stage. Maharishi Panini, Vyasa, Charaka, Sushruta, Bhardwaja, Kashayap, Patanjali, Kanaka, Kapila are names of some of these acclaimed sages of olden times who contributed to various fields while living in their *Vanprashtha*. Surely, people remaining engaged in accumulating material wealth or enjoying luxuries of life can't be expected to contribute on social fronts.

Some of the unwanted fears and frustrations gripping our present day society can be attributed to overlooking of this great tradition. Today, most of the people are seen continuing with Grihastha ashram until their limbs stop working. This results in a big vacuum of true knowledge and wisdom being sought. That is directly reflective in the void of seeking spiritual progress. This also results in conflict with younger generations, which is the root cause of many unwanted diseases, anguish, afflictions and distresses prevalent in modern societies. I wish more and more people take this route and realize all the fun they are missing in continuing as *Grihastha.*

Sannyasa Ashram

Successful completion of Vanprashtha stage of life helps the person towards dissolving all the ignorance of separate existence. This in turn unites him with universal humanity. Expected around the age of seventy five, the graduation to Sannyasa allows him to develop total indifference to the necessities of life. The person develops capability to withstand harsher austerities including towards hunger, climate, physical conditions and dependence on beings. All through this Ashram, the person remains engaged in deep meditation. The only aim for such a person is to understand subtle nature of supreme self and issues pertaining to transmigration in terms of life after death.

Now, he should be completely in control of his own destiny. Having dissolved all of his attachments and bonds with things, places or family, he rejoices every opportunity of consoling others, motivating others and guiding others for pursuing the Dharma filled life. It is not that such persons become useless and are only awaiting death. Actually, a Sannyasi on the path of Dharma has already lost any fear of death, as he is able to see reality beyond human life. Yes, physical body is deteriorating but the soul is at its best. His discipline, wisdom, spiritual attainments are all helping him to connect with the supreme reality like never before.

Discontinuation of Ashram system, over the centuries, resulted in widespread fears and frustration among various sections of the society where people feel threatened for their position, where no one has time left to pursue spirituality, accumulation of Karmic debits are going unnoticed and are sowing seeds for lack of happiness. Social stigma, poor health, financial dependence, family compulsions, fear of criminals were some other practical reasons that resulted in more and more people losing interest in this system besides lure of living the life of a house holder.

Adaptation suitable for present day—Continuing to live the life of a Grihastha is, in any case, easiest of all options. It is simply the path of least resistance. No wonder that most people are happy continuing in there without contemplating any break. No serious human effort is required to remain attached with attractions, aspiring or enjoying luxuries, pursue selfish tendencies of sensual and sensuous gratifications; anybody and everybody can do that. It is only few brave hearts who are able to see through the lure of worldly attractions and gather courage to dedicate themselves for the search of unknown bliss. Pursuing higher objectives of contemplation and spiritual evolution was never prescribed, in any case, for all and sundry. Even in Ancient times, not every householder was heading towards forest in his fifties. It was always the responsibility of those blessed few who could think beyond the obvious. Blessings, guidance and a bit of prompting from divine power is always desired for such plunge. Present day situation is no exception of that rule. The only change is that number of people trending down this route today is abysmally low in proportionate terms to total populace.

Let us quickly look at how we can interpret the Ashram system applicable in current times. Not much needs to be said about getting proper education, raising family and achieving professional heights. One should start accumulating financial resources to support later life. This can be done by investing in annuities, pension funds, investment portfolios or investing in real estate options as the case may be. Idea is to ensure a regular stream of money to support basic necessities of normal life even after opting the life of a *Vanprasthi*. In the meantime, the person should make his best efforts to help society and world in general so that better environment is left behind for following generations. Soon after completing fiftieth year, one should slow down and evaluate and identify mentally satisfying and spiritually uplifting activities.

One should channelize all available energies only for such

activities. Making peace with the fact that there was only so much to achieve and so much to accumulate, is the biggest possible hurdle one is required to cross this void. One must understand that switching over to soul pleasing activities is not escape but critical diversion of energies for higher cause. Undertaking mentally and spiritually satisfying activities results in wonderful positive impact on entire spectrum of quality of life by improving physical/mental health, change in attitude towards life, quality of interaction with family and relationships of all types and bringing in higher meaning to human life. This is happiness all about. Finally, after hitting seventy-fifth year of life, one must completely withdraw from all types of activities, as it is time for complete relaxation. From now onwards, all you should focus is to find God within.

Each stage of life is like a new railway junction in a long journey. The passenger travelling has to prepare his baggage well in advance to get down as soon as the station arrives. As he knows the distance covered and expected time for his station, all the preparation is possible well in advance and certainly before the train hits the station. Starting new stage in life is like boarding a new train for next destination. So, soon after getting down from the previous train (previous stage of life), you try finding out the platform number and timing for the next train. Depending on your knowledge, you reorganize your possessions to make your future travel comfortable. Soon after boarding the new train you make your way in, look out for your sitting space, try to take stock of new surroundings, try to open communication with immediate co-passengers and generally make yourself comfortable before starting to enjoy the new journey all over again. Before you realize, you become one of them.

Roughly same routine is repeated after you arrive at the destination for yet another stage. On the way, you go through many stations where some earlier passengers keep getting down and new passengers keep getting in all the time. Once again, well before arrival of your next junction, you are expected to prepare for getting down with all your belongings checked out and all garbage and stuff, not required subsequently, well disposed off. This preparation helps each passenger to ensure that they get down at the right place without leaving behind any important stuff and also to immediately head for the new platform for taking train appropriate for yet another new destination. Most important junction in our life is when we need to end our journey of *Gribastba Asbram* and start *Vanprasbtba*. This is like changing from trunk route broad gauge to isolated and less travelled route on a narrow gauge.

Society Divided in Four Classes – *Varna Vyavastba*

Everybody even remotely connected with Indian society is likely to know about the Indian Class system, where entire population is divided among four watertight segregations called Brahmins (responsible for all education and religious activities), Kshatriyas (responsible for military, ruling and administration), Vaishyas (responsible for land holding, industry, trade and commerce) and Sudras (responsible for cultivation and menials manual jobs, remaining category). To begin with, Class was decided for every person based on professional and occupational disposition and their natural orientation suitable for specific occupation. Everyone was free to choose the profession one was good at. It was much later that caste became hereditary. A plethora of enumerable sub-castes emerged within these four classes to deal with new variants of initial basic occupations to keep pace with increasing number evolving over in due course.

Besides India, one can also trace class segregations among ancient cultures like Egyptians, Arabs, Tartars and few others. But the pyramid shaped hierarchical system of India is distinctly unique. This system has contributed greatly to specializations in all fields as people acquired proficiencies in their respective professions. So long this system was operative with purity, India made tremendous progress in all spheres including all types of arts, crafts, industries, education and sciences. Later, due to multiple reasons, this system got corrupted as social and economic expansions resulted in manifold increases in number of occupations/professions and walls got raised along regional, linguistic and sectarian divides.

Initial segregation was based on the cardinal principle that people should specialize in their respective professions and no one should be useless to the commonwealth of the state. Thanks largely to this system; India avoided lapsing into a state of barbarism as experienced around that time in history among those cultures where anyone could do anything without any social restrictions. Since wars were common in those days, aggressions in other societies, lead to crippling of entire population. In India, on the contrary, only one Class was engaged in wars, leaving other three classes to remain engaged in their professions. As a result, wars were less disastrous in India as compared to most of the other states, where wars completely destroyed cultures and ethnicities.

While there may not be a direct relation of Class/caste system for human happiness but the class system, indirectly contributed towards social, financial, religious, educational and spiritual prosperity achieved by Ancient India. This prosperity, in turn, contributed to the well being of society.

Life Dedicated for Four Aims – *Purushartha*

This is yet another important part of complex structure created by Ancient Indian sages to ensure peace and happiness for society at large. Here, we shall look at four different aims recommended for achieving a fulfilling human life. These aims, superimposed over four stages of life discussed earlier, provide the mantra for securing full realization of strong and positive attitudes, wisdom, happiness and tranquility.

Purushartha literally means "*Purpose and Significance of Human Life*". Ancient Indian culture provided great value for its practitioners by prescribing them four distinct purposes of life with well-defined stages in life when these purposes ought to be fulfilled. Purushartha serve as right pointers in the life of a human being. Depending upon his attitude, sincerity and dedication applied to pursue these; these aims set him free from the allurement of human life. And we know well that human efforts focused in right direction under a well defined objective always end up in superior results. This golden rules applies to all endeavours that we can think of.

Logical appreciation of these aims has very convincing rationale in guiding us living a meaningful life even today. Surely, this is going to make us aware about our sense of purpose. These aims inspire us to work hard keeping sense of duty and fulfillment intact. Each one of us must have realized that different stages in life have their own needs and priorities. Attention and approval from peers and parents may be very important to a teenager. But a young adult is seized with advancements in career, financial prosperity, and accumulation of material objects of luxury and physical gratifications. Similarly, an older person wishes for a higher level of life satisfaction, obedience shown by next generation and better health more than anything else. This changing nature of human priorities is well incorporated in these goals. In a way, these goals work as perfect guide for showing us the right direction at every stage of our life journey.

Sequencing of these aims is of prime importance and can't be deviated. One was to move from one to another without jumping over to the next goal. Skipping any goal was recommended against completely. It was strongly argued that actual experience of earlier aims is essentially desired to help realize ultimate aim of liberation leading to permanent happiness. And it is not difficult to see why it was recommended like that. Contemplation and seeking liberation are comparatively harder pursuits. The actual experience of householder's life, coupled with maturity intellect linked with advancing age is essential to prepare an individual for doing that.

Now let us focus on each of these pious aims:

Very First Aim of Life – Dharma

As a word, Dharma is used in almost all eastern religions. But it means different things to different people. As such, it is almost impossible to translate it in English. English words like duty, faith, religion, righteousness, sacred law, justice, ethical obligations and morality do refer to particular shades of Dharma but fail to capture the true gist as meant in Vedic traditions. Dharma is to be taken as a divine constitution that defines individual roles and responsibilities in the social and moral contexts. More accepted definition of Dharma could be taken as below:

> "Obligatory duty as prescribed by Vedas expected to be performed by an individual in accordance of the rules prescribed with relation to his age, caste, capability, capacity and profession without any desire, preference or attachment with the result of such duty"

The fact is that Dharma is a concept rather than a single word and must be understood accordingly. In broader term, it is the secret glue or binding force that upholds and regulates the entire creation just as the law of gravity upholds the entire universe. Dharma is an organizing principle for human beings. It defines harmony and balance maintained by human behaviour. It includes behaviour while living in solitude or out there in public. In addition to beings, it does cover human behaviour towards entire cosmos and its parts. To put simply, it is all about moral duties and virtuous behaviour of a human with one and all beings and non-beings such that the equilibrium holding this Universe together remain sustained forever. Therefore, any action by any person in any way harming the prevailing balance will fall on the wrong side of Dharma.

Well how do we learn and practise Dharma? Most obvious way is knowledge acquired and wisdom gained by study of scriptures. But most importantly, it is practised by listening to our inner core and relying on its advice by seeking proper guidance under any testing situation. Facing a *Dharma Sankat,* a moral ambiguity with reference to a situation in life or dilemmas are normal for human life and most of us get exposed to them at different times. The *Yaksha Prashna* episode from Mahabharata where Yudhisthira finds all his brothers dead and provide *Dharma Sangat* answers to critical questions of '*Yaksha*' is by far the best example how to face moral ambiguity even under most testing circumstances.

Indian scriptures describe Dharma as the natural universal law whose observance enables human beings to live life with contentment and happiness. Living with Dharma is expected to save them from all kinds of degradation and sufferings. It is supposed to be sacred, inviolable and pervasive. Every individual undertakes it in harmony with divine injunctions and sense of morality and justice. "Dharma" is much wider than Religion and each one of us have to re-understand this principle with greater clarity. So, Dharma is first aim for a fulfilled human life. It is an overriding principle for every other activity at every step and must be pursued in every stage of life. There is nothing in human life that must fall on the other side of Dharma.

Second Aim of Life – Artha

With literal meaning referring to wealth and prosperity, it is recognized as quite essential for the overall happiness and well being of any individual living worldly life. Wealth is special kind of energy and absolutely essential to enjoy a decent life. Another way to define it as an aim in life is to say that Artha is working for and achieving success in terms of wealth and power. Financial resources alone can't explain full significance of Artha, as it is much wider than money. Various forms of Artha can be briefly listed as under. The sequence is not accidental but a well-defined prioritization:

- *Inner Wealth* – Positive mindset, self respect, internal peace; something that should be but is rarely valued as highest possible wealth; Contentment is part of this wealth which is more than or equal to cumulative wealth of the world.
- *Physical Wealth* – Ability and capacity to undertake all physical activities with vigour. So long as this wealth is there, options for collecting subsequent types of wealth always remain.
- *Relationship Wealth* – Well knit family, capable and respecting children, circle of reliable and loyal friends and personal community. Sometimes it is wrongly taken as an obligation.
- *Professional Wealth* – Actualizing highest potential by reaching at pinnacle of pursued profession by attaining everything possible to attain commensurate with ones intellectual potential. It includes trophies and accolades accumulated over the years as due recognition.
- *Economic Wealth* – Money or everything convertible to money, freedom to acquire things required for pursuing what one really likes and generally to be used for making life easier for self as well others around.

Contrary to commonly held belief, Ancient Indian culture called for accumulating financial resources for human life. It is only the greed for wealth that was always, and at every stage of life, considered as bad. Selfless desire for creating and preserving wealth within the ambit of Dharma was highly recommended. It may be noted that only righteously acquired wealth can be considered as the correct meaning of *Artha.* Any part of wealth acquired by foul means or dubious methods is considered *Anartha*, just the opposite of *Artha.* So, wealth is not acceptable unless its means of acquisition are as per accepted norms of right Dharma.

Wealth is taken as divine energy. Abundance of this divine energy is held desirable. Some ignorant commentators are seen failing to appreciate the fact that Indian ethos do not glorify poverty at all. Yes, it does advocate austerity, simplicity and detachment towards everything considered materialistic in nature. Mantras after mantras contained in Vedas can be seen making oblations to various Gods for bestowing wealth. It can also be seen that right up to the time that Indian territories got captured by foreign aggressors during later part of first millennium AD, India was enjoying glorious prosperity and its riches made the whole world envious. However, Ancient Indian traditions emphasized that being poor or rich should be taken just as an experience without getting attached to it. So, one should become indifferent to comforts/discomforts or having/not having of life caused by it. What is advocated is moderation and balance in pursuits of both material and spiritual goals of one's life.

The important learning contained here is that it is ok to earn, enjoy and accumulate all types of resource. However, fixation on economic wealth alone is strongly advised against. Another important condition is that wealth accumulation is done within the time frame of Grihastha Ashram and by remaining within the periphery of Dharma. Subject to these two conditions, each person is obliged to focus on full spectrum of wealth, materialistic pursuits included, and still keeping his claim intact for achieving happiness and fulfillment of life. No one should have problem with such an approach. These two conditions are equally relevant even today because psyche of human hasn't changed so much over last few thousand years. Wealth acquired or hoarded in violation of these simple conditions is the source of negative tendencies attached with being materialistic. Hence, such a person is doomed to an unfulfilled life devoid of real happiness.

Third Aim of Life – Kama

'*Kama*' actually means the enjoyment of legitimate desires with the help of wealth acquired with honesty. Kama again is very wide term and includes producing and enjoyment of art, music, dance, drama, literature and poetry besides carnal and sensual gratifications. Thus, Ancient systems do accept enjoyment of any and every form of pleasure. However, in terms of taking it as an objective of life, the wealth being used must have been acquired and the activity itself must fall within the gambit of Dharma. This is the only caveat applied. In other words, so long as one person has properly achieved previous two aims of life, he has no restrictions to enjoy and gratify his senses by functioning within norms compatible with Dharma.

Buddhism considers '*Kama*' as root cause of human suffering. Hence, detachment from sense objects, specially, sex is advocated as a way out from these sufferings.

Caution needs to be applied to *Kama* as it can facilitate liberation and happiness or be a great hindrance and create sufferings. It depends on how we approach it. In any case, one has to overcome *Kama* ultimately to achieve salvation; either by abstaining from it or indulging in it. Abstaining from *Kama* is the way of '*Vedanta*' and indulging in it is the way of '*Tantra*'. The first is the way of suppression while the second is the way of expression. But *Tantra* has almost entirely vanished from all major parts of Indian thoughts; hence we must stop any efforts being made by anyone equating it as a means of liberation at all. Vedantic ways, on the other hand, have continuously flourished all across the globe with more and more thinkers joining to propagate it even in new boundaries. It is like settled that liberation is possible only through the path of suppression.

Coming to sex, the most challenging activity for most human, *Kama* as aim of human life has no objection to sex so long as it is used for procreation, perpetuation of family and social order and within the boundaries of traditions, social norms and scriptures. The uncontrollable passion and pleasure attached with sexual activity between adult male and female is nature's way of forcing them to produce children for future generations. Hence, sexual activity is part of social obligation and must be carried out. The condition here is that it should not be indulged just for seeking pleasure. But sexual desire is ultimate in all basic human desires and eventually one has to overcome it for seeking liberation as the final aim of life. There is no denying to this fact.

The *Puranic* stories carry many instances where Gods and Goddesses are portrayed as oversexed objects and showing how irresistible attractions overpowered Gods alike for beautiful *Apsaras.* But readers may already know it well that *Puranas* are just 'Pulp fiction' away from all types of realities. *Puranas* are like cheap literature and need to be ignored as flight of imaginations without much attention paid. *Puranas*, in any case, have nothing to do with Ancient Indian literature, which precedes *Puranas* by at least one thousand years. But the real Vedantic traditions, as explained above, have had very clear and logical views on this aspect.

Final Aim of Human Life – Moksha (Liberation)

Pursuits of Dharma regulate the life to keep an individual on the right path; pursuits of Artha and Kama add to his worldly experience and impart valuable lessons of life. The pursuit of Moksha, the final and most important aim in human life is pursued for complete liberation from the unending cycle of birth and death. Following Dharma starts in early student life and continues all through. Pursuing twin aims of Artha and Kama are reserved in the householder stage. Seeking Moksha is considered as most important among all aims of life and is recommended to start only after seeking experiences of all other three aims. This is, together with *Dharma,* the only aim to be followed all through *Vanprashtha* and *Sannyasa Ashram.* We can imagine the importance accorded to this all-important Purushartha for which the sages have apportioned entire second half of life.

Liberation is also explained as ultimate stage of Self-realization and this point is going to be explained in sufficient details later as it is synonym with the everlasting bliss, the supreme stage of long lasting happiness that a normal householder can only dream about. All important matrix of pursuing particular aims of life in different stages of life ensure that individual is able to meet his obligations of human life without becoming obsessed with any single aim at the cost of other. This is projected as better option of securing sustained satisfaction in life with full everlasting happiness and fulfillment.

> Indian Ancient systems refrained from giving attention to temporary comforts or momentary gratifications and called upon the seekers to discharge their due obligations and invest half of their life in preparing and seeking final liberation. As a masterstroke, these teachings lay down a clear roadmap for entire human life and assure attaining happiness by catering to both material and spiritual aspirations in right steps, priority and proportions.

These teachings are in line with Indian Philosophies where the reason of the very feeling of happiness is directly linked to person's likes and dislikes for objects approached with sense organs. These objects have been identified as a trap because physical world is said to be nothing but a combination of illusions. Attachments with these illusions give rise to '*Kama*' leading to strong bondage. This bondage is shown as the aggravating cause of all sufferings.

Finally, sufferings make happiness increasingly distant. To the credit of Indian sages that no short-term option is recommended as it can only provide short-term results. They have strongly suggested the ultimate way that links the human with the perennial source of bliss. Many people have taken that route in the past with success and others are welcome with a well laid out and clearly spelt out route. It is indeed true that the route is difficult but gigantic attraction waiting at the destination makes the journey worth pursuing with all the vigour.

Pursuing happiness in the objects and attachments is likened to a mirage where every time you move, the probable source also moves as much. Indian system wards against chasing fantasy and hallucination and direct instead to pursue Spirituality, which alone assures absolute freedom from all types of '*moh*', '*maya*' and '*bhrum*'. These scriptures remind us that no one has ever been able to obtain happiness by indulging in fulfilling desires and that the only right option is to restrain our body and mind and free our dependence on them.

It is interesting to note that the enjoyment of Artha and Karma must take place before pursuing the final quest for spiritual salvation. A person must enjoy in some measure what worldly life has to offer, pay off debts to society and contribute one's bit in maintaining a healthy communal life before turning away from the transient world and attaching himself to the changeless Reality that lies veiled beyond material existence, which alone can give everlasting joy. The underlying approach sounds very forceful and practical at the same point of time. A person who has not experienced the real life situations cannot appreciate the strength of bondage and magnetic force of attractions that are being advised to be ward against. Once a person has experienced those situations, he/she is better equipped to fight the temptations and move on to other higher objectives; self-experience is the real and right experience.

Need to develop a detached attitude is the most important point to understand because right attitude makes it easy to switch from one aim or stage to another without unbalancing the life and surroundings. Look at the beauty that pursuing wealth obsessively by sacrificing pleasure is held a clear mistake. Similarly, pursuing moral duty to the exclusion of wealth and pleasure is also held incomplete. A person can achieve complete life only by being disciplined in changing stages of life along with objectives recommended for that stage in life, exceptions apart.

So long as, Indian Society gave proper emphasis on these aims and followed the four-stage, four classes and four purposes of life, it grew to its maturity and became rich, splendid and magnificent. It reached to its pinnacle in culture and civilization; it developed great literature, contributed immensely for emergence of all types of sciences, arts, crafts and industry. It also laid inspired basis of wonderful spiritual philosophies. But in due course, degradation of all cherished values set in. Old time integral harmony among various aims gave way to higher focus on Kama and Artha at the cost of Dharma. But even then, some strong basis of the old knowledge did remain and kept alive the hopes of the people even in the darkest days of Indian culture. That is why it alone, out of all ancient civilizations, still exists today having lived over five thousand years of an unbroken continuous collective life at the very land where it evolved. This feat is absolutely unique and no other culture of entire world matches Indian traditions on this important score.

The quest for *Moksha* and its value as the highest goal of human life, however, needs to be redefined and applied once again in present context to keep its relevance intact. In a way, this is going to be the core point of our endeavour in the chapters to follow.

Human Happiness and Role Play by Religions

Religion is a very subjective matter and involves emotions of people going from one extreme to another. Religions also involve too much width and depth and come in so many types of packing that a whole lot of space becomes necessary just to understand what religions are all about. But for our limited purpose, let us narrow our vision to their general perceptions where we have beliefs, worship methods and scriptures. Considering the purpose on hand, our discussion about religions is deliberately kept limited to contributions towards human happiness and fulfillments and nothing beyond. Proper understanding for this abridged objective is essential for appreciating the concepts and principles touched in this chapter as well as remaining part of this book.

Religions generally operate where believers are expected to believe the given; follow the division between right or wrong as given; where people are not encouraged thinking logically or taking responsibilities for their own choices but follow the line already set. Generally speaking, most religious people do not appreciate invoking logic and reasoning when it comes to their religious sentiments and we should have no qualm for their feeling. Let them stay blessed with their personal and private views about religions. As an important disclaimer, no attempt is made for evaluation or any comparison and certainly none of the remark is intended against any religion in particular; so please hold on to your respective beliefs as strongly as you wish without feeling offended in any way.

Readers may or may not have noticed that there has been no reference made to the role-play of religions, religious traditions and religious teachings in entire discussions thus far. No, it was just not accidental but just the way things are. It is simply because we have been focusing on human happiness and there is hardly any established contribution by religions towards level of happiness enjoyed by their followers. It might be shocking for few of us but studies after studies suggest that if some religious person is found happier in comparison to non-religious person, it is not because of religion; religion is neither a cause nor an effect. Variations in happiness index of different people are precisely because of individual attitude, upbringing, socio-economic conditions and general surroundings. Religions per say are devised for organizing and supervising life of human beings within communities with focus on morality and divinity rather than happiness. There is no religion that focuses on happiness as a standalone subject matter. That is why religions in general aren't seen adding much to their follower's happiness.

However, while on search for any possible link between religions and human happiness, one can see some indirect correlations here and there. Basically, active people in all religions are pro-social lots who have higher level of purpose and better sense of right over wrong. Those are individually better disciplined than their other counterparts. These are same qualities that are common among people who are blessed with more personal satisfaction, physical well-being and, therefore, higher level of happiness. And the fact that one finds such people among all religions, it certainly comes out individual quality than a thing even remotely connected with religious stream being followed. In other words, if we come across happy people engaged in religious circles, it is not that religion per say contributed to their happiness. Such people are seen happy even among cultures that are not religious at all.

Looking around religious societies, we can, at best, see some increased social support base of an active follower. Many religions do have social activities that extend help to those in need. These are similar to big corporations undertaking social projects under Corporate Social Responsibilities and nothing beyond. Higher level of optimism is another obvious advantage attributed to people engaged in religious activities. Such people are seen scaling up their optimism by actively participating in their religious activities including rituals, celebrations, attending to services etc. But there are several other ways where those less religious can also enhance their optimism. After all, being optimistic has never been credited to being religious.

One does come across lot many studies showing religious people having better sense of purpose, having better support systems, having larger number of friends and acquaintances. There are people concluding these factors leading to increased self-esteem etc. But that will not be a correct conclusion. All religions are practised in group based collective environment that develop into mutually dependent communities. This is a fact and needs no denial. The question is in what respect these advantages are different than those people operating in other communities? For example, groups of racing bikers, golfers, morning walkers, support groups for de-addiction or people working in political groups, have all been known to interact with each other with similar sentiments as those going to temples, visiting Mosques or Church assemblies? No one can deny that working in larger groups, any kind of groups for that matter; result in enhanced sense of identity and support base. Reality remains that this sense and support is not due to religion but due to working in the groups as social beings.

There is a large group of volunteers operating in a small town in Madhya Pradesh, India that is involved in preparing and distributing fresh breakfast for all patients and their attendants in all hospitals in their area. Besides general donors, people having birthdays of their children, anniversaries or such other auspicious occasions become cash donors to support the campaign. This free distribution is going on for over sixteen years. The group members assemble every day and prepare fresh food of good variety and visit every hospital bed for distribution. Looking at this example with logical reasoning, each one of us will agree that their group identity and sense of belonging to their initiative is in no way less than those participating in the temples or mosques of that very area. In fact it is more because breakfast need to be served everyday irrespective of rains or thunderstorms. Interestingly, the members of the group come from diverse religious backgrounds. Followers of those religions, elsewhere, can be seen fighting with each other like wars. Surely, human beings are social beings and social support network adds to human fulfillment but such a network can be in any form and shape. Common religious trappings are but just one kind of social networking.

But there is a particular area where religions are seen contributing towards individual's well-being and it relates to emphasis on moral teachings and ethical conduct. Every religion, without exception, calls upon its practitioners to follow moral values and abstain from specific social evils. The contribution of religion in the success of moral behaviours of their followers, however, needs to be clearly understood as a fringe advantage, as a side benefit rather than being a core advantage. The question is how much of morality gets added because of religions. Is it not that if somebody is good in pursuing his religion it is largely because he is basically a good person rather than because his religion makes him good? If religions were indeed good at improving morality and ethical behaviours of people, there must have been differences in crime rates of societies having religions and those not having or between those having religion A and those having religion B or C. This is precisely the reason that we have criminals, looters, rowdies, rebels, insurgents, extremists, cheaters and law offenders coming from all types of religious or non-religious followings without any marked difference.

Yet another area quoted with tremendous advantage coming from religious affiliations relates to capacity for bearing pains and frustrations during periods of natural calamities, loss of lives and such other troubled times. It is said that those having belief in super natural powers of their Gods are able to take the calamities strongly than the non-believers. It might be true because having access to strong moorings is always handy during times of trouble. People feel lighter by accepting it as 'His' desire or by accepting it as 'His' test for checking how much pain can be endured or by simply taking it as 'His' punishment.

One may concede that religions have a role to play during traumatic experiences. But does religion alone works in testing times? Or in real life, do testing times are such a common occurrence that we need to develop special tools to cope up with the same? Think of it that use of alcohol or consumption of banned substances also reduces trauma and provides ability to cope up with shocks during troubled times. Should one, therefore, believe that alcohol consumption is good for happiness? On similar lines, even when religions provide support and stability to their practitioners, they can't be linked to human happiness index in any way. Sufferings making any one stronger or better person are, in any case, an absolutely illogical and misguided notion and don't work in real life. Sufferings of all kinds whether faced bravely or meekly, result in leakages from the reservouir of happiness.

One may try looking from all possible angles but religions are unlikely to have visible role that can establish direct link with personal happiness index of their followers. Side by side, it is also seen that people actively participating in religious activities are found having higher level of life satisfactions from their lives. So let us summarize that:

> "Flowers of religion and individual happiness are altogether different kinds. They have their own exclusive seeds, shades and fragrances. But the soil and nutrient they require to germinate on and flourish happen to be largely identical."

Extra efforts have been made to bring clarity about the role of religions for human happiness as many practitioners are seen investing or desiring to invest their time and energy in pursuing their religions rather than exploring other alternatives. It is expected that they should recalibrate their efforts so as to secure better results at the end of the day. It is a matter of individual choice but choices are better made with proper knowledge and preparations and that's about all.

In order to be analytical as well as pragmatic, the role of religions over happiness can also be judged by the annual happiness index of countries. For many years, Scandinavian countries like Denmark, Norway, Sweden and Netherlands are getting top ranking in the global happiness index being conducted annually. It is interesting to note that most of the population living in these countries is placed on the bottom when one looks at the religion practice index of all countries. Actually, all these countries are very close to being symbol of atheism. Residents of these countries are happy because their quality of life is better and that is better because their health, wealth and education standards are better. Opposite to these names we may look at a country like Pakistan (which incidentally came to exist purely in the name of religious identity) where one can see whole lot of religious fervour but pathetic human capital indices on each and every index.

In final conclusion, one may safely say that having the bone of religion in one's body or not having it doesn't seem to cast its impact on the level of his happiness.

Exploring Real Purpose of Life

In our journey thus far, we have talked about happiness as our immediate focus. We tried understanding happiness layer by layer. We looked at factors impacting it. We looked at underlying emotions and their interplay in terms of their influence. We also explored ancient and contemporary ways suggested for ensuring everlasting happiness. This discussion was intended for providing some sort of way forward for pursuing a happy life. These initiatives might certainly have motivated few to make structured changes towards enhancing their respective indices of happiness. But something is not clicking somewhere? The curiosity at the time of starting this book could not get settled? Obvious feeling is that we have already known several of these points and have been attempting many of these suggestions already. What happened to our search for finding that missing spirit that we so dearly wanted to find about?

The murmurs and profound restlessness continues even at this stage without any solution in the offing. The new learning at best could offer only piecemeal solutions. The combined impact of all efforts appears to be far from the real thing that we were wishing to chase. What we get to experience are just moments of fulfillment but it is nothing comparable to bliss that has been talked so much. Neither there seems to be any way for increasing duration of these moments that can be compared to everlasting happiness. For sure, something critical is missing. What is the missing component? Why our yearning for bliss seems to have further intensified rather than getting addressed? Was our goal not proper or the entire goal post moves forward with our onward movement?

We do come across people defining their life aim as climbing atop Mount Everest or bringing ODI World Cup to India. Some may be heard saying creating a masterpiece of art to be the goal of their life. But can such dreams or ambitions be called purpose of life? At best, these may be called important milestones that one may aspire to cross while moving on the path of journey called life. Some of us may have been even lucky to pass by these milestones. But there are many examples where such people felt very disappointed and incomplete after crossing over such milestones. They suddenly got gripped by the emptiness of their void where there is nothing more to do. Some of such people soon get caught by the fear of losing what they got with so much of efforts. Well, for every Sachin Tendulkar, sooner or later, there is always a Virat Kohli in the making. We must therefore explore more deeply as to what is the real purpose of our life and prepare ourselves to focus all our initiatives and efforts to achieve that. May be, the secrets of our success lie there?

People blessed with wisdom could find the right answer to these intriguing questions. They recognized this vacuum and interpreted it as intrinsic restlessness to seek the higher objectives of human life. They identified this longing as a feeling of emptiness that didn't go away even with best possible efforts in place. Finally, they named it as the burning desire for seeking;

Seeking .....wisdom to overcome ignorance,
Seeking .....for real meaning of human life,
Seeking .....for tranquility,
Seeking .....freedom from duality of human life,
Seeking .....evolution from compulsive nature to conscious nature,
Seeking .....the meaning of our very existence on this earth.

This desire is said to be sharply visible and profound when one contemplates about it with pure awareness and consciousness. It is natural and no effort is required to come face to face with this urge. Searching the real purpose of life is natural for human beings simply because we are blessed with reasoning and logical thinking. Most rational and sensible adults, at some or the other time in life, come across this desire from within. The lucky ones get it at the right time and identify the same instantly while the unlucky get it late and fail to spot the same as yet another normal noise.

This is indeed the yearning for undertaking our Spiritual journey.

This is about the journey much beyond filling life with morality and ethics or life dedicated to any particular religious thought or deep desire for committing ourselves to particular doctrine of faith. This one is to explore our real nature in the depths of our own real core. This one is to explore this universe and finding our rightful position out there. If the reader is able to identify with this situation, rest assured, you are listening to the thumping and knocking by your Spirituality and nothing else. Amen!

But this seeking calls for big changes on many levels; it is like diverting ongoing journey to an unknown destination. If and when it happens, one is required to check condition of the vehicle (physical body), rearrange luggage (material possessions), provide for fuel and gas for the long journey (financial resources), be ready for frequent changes in gear and speed (past experiences and knowledge), and recalibrate the highway GPS (conscious intuition) so as to navigate through the unseen terrain and hostile environment. You may have been a very good driver up until now but new surroundings lying beyond the crossroad are absolutely unique. It is like painfully driving through the hills on unpaved roads having twists and turns but also enjoying mesmerizing views of never seen before peaks and valleys. Interesting tales about such new territories may have been heard from those few who have ventured there in the past but not many are known to return and report back in detail. It is said that the beauty of this new destination is so spectacular that those who enter in this land forever refuse to leave.

During our routine normal day-to-day life, we keep getting inkling thoughts for spirituality but there is always a deep mysticism covering it that prevents us from envisioning it with clarity. Most of the time, our thoughts and desires are low on intensity or the frequency of these thoughts doesn't warrant a sense of urgency. Other kind of compulsions of daily life keep shouting at us with far higher decibels and the feeble thoughts for spiritual pursuits remain buried down under. Even after recognizing the true nature of internal reminders, we remain engaged in cramming more activities in our daily routine unconsciously hoping it to be a good measure of success. After all, most of our training until now has been to collect points faster than others and do some more of the same if we get some more spare time. Doing more in same time is a very satisfying feeling for most of us in any case.

There are many books or teachers suggesting that we are more successful when we start and finish more activities on a given day and days after days. But life is beyond the arithmetic. It is neither about collecting brownie points nor keeping their score. Modern management experts are seen taking a divergent objective and advise you to undertake more activities so that you remain busy and unable to tune in to listen to your own conscience. They do it as they know that once you listen to that, you are bound to get disturbed and will get forced to leave behind many activities that you have been doing until now. 'Ignorance is bliss' has been heard many times before but now is the time to understand real meaning of this phrase.

You don't have to agree but the bare and brazen fact of human life is that you are more useful to many others so long as you remain ignorant about your own self. The moment you focus on self, the bridge of attachments with others will develop cracks and they would not get as much from you as you provide them now. It is actually so simple a reality. Unfortunate truth is that the word 'they' used above includes your very own. So, your dilemma is well understood and appreciated.

Modern-day Dilemma and Aim of Human Life

There is no denying to the reality that every other person today is driven weak by the desire of acquiring more; more of money, more of pleasure, more of information, more of news, more of likes from Facebook friends, more of followers at Twitter handle, more of trophies and all such other objects. We have, however, realized that having more is not equal to making our life any better. Having more feeds into more fears of losing of whatever we got. Every time we acquire something, it brings with it additional responsibility of preserving it, protecting it even before using it. Further, haven't we seen the length of the pleasure of acquisition? Don't we start feeling need of getting some more or something different soon after getting one thing? In the process, we completely forget what is more important for our meaning in life and we fail to make a clear choice between self-worth and net-worth.

Many of us are seen justifying ourselves to continue our destination less journey by working harder, forgetting all personal comforts and priorities. We do so in order to meet expectations of parents, children or friends. Many genuinely believe that their life is for family and if they take care of everybody in the family, their own life objective will be achieved. Now, that is the sure shot key to failure. How can one forget that no one has ever been able to please everyone around? Seriously, and who appointed you to be *'Bhagyavidhata'* for your children or for some other person for that matter? Parents have a role to play but that role better be played within well defined boundaries beyond which children have to find their own identity. Helping your children beyond the point is stopping them from growing or standing tall of their own. No human is supposed to be capable of crafting destiny of some other human being and we better know that without any ambiguity.

While it is right that helping others in every possible way is a good Dharma and helps us accumulate good Karma. We all, therefore, must help others as much as we can. But who is going to make things happen in our life for our own liberation? Should we wait for coincidences to let things happen in our life? Or we should take command of our life and commit for everything important? As it is, one has to be strong enough before helping others. How can someone help others when he/she is in desperate need of help for him/herself? Even in airplanes they announce every day that in case of oxygen masks falling down due to reduction in oxygen pressure, you must wear your own mask first before helping others including your children travelling with you. Hope we are able to see the spirit behind that announcement and realize the need to be strong and secure before extending help to others.

As responsible captains of our own souls, we can't run away from the responsibility of not knowing real meaning of this human life. We beings are categorized as most intelligent species in this universe because we are blessed with power of reasoning and logical thinking. Are we not supposed to apply that for attempting to find our meaning? Without the clarity of meaning of our life, we can neither appreciate its significance nor hope for any improvement.

Opting for any kind of philosophy is not going to help at all. There is no point in seeking refuse to philosophies. Philosophers have been speculating about purpose of life for thousands of years but all they could come up are more questions or guesses rather than answers. Surely, purpose of life will be puzzling and people focused on this aren't expected to see easy success but it doesn't mean that we stop trying our best.

How to go about exploring Real Purpose

First of all, a serious seeker who is determined to pursue his or her evolution for higher aim of life is required to hold some hard self-talk. Being similar to a practical workshop, you should move from one step to another well assured of your upward progress. This process does involve some candid enquiry about self even when replies may be quite uncomfortable. One simple advice will be to willingly experiment and keep inhibitions or beliefs away for some time. You might face some questions that may sound very simple but may require deeper unlearning. So being somewhat a sport will lead to good speed and shall be more effective, i.e., your voluntary willingness and motivation to explore your purpose of human life will look that much clearer.

You may like to start by exploring your own self completely as a stranger; check what drives your normal life at present. It may well revolve around some person, some problem, some pressure, some target, some deadline, some position, some guilt, some resentment, some anger, some envy, some atonement, approval or disapproval from a loved one or a combination of one or more such factors. One has to come out of this maze by a series of introspections and explore, dream, set goals, aim high, be disciplined, above all, resolve against giving up. Determining purpose of life certainly has to cross over this entire arduous journey. Soon we will discuss in greater details about steps required to walk-down that path. In the meantime, let us continue understanding other aspects important for the purpose on hand.

It is not that you have been deliberately maintaining distance with your spiritual search. Most of us have infrequent communication with our own conscience. We keep introspecting our situation and actions regularly but while doing so our minds, under the unavoidable impact of visible world, are conditioned by our cultural beliefs, past impressions, influences from external sources and strong hold of our ego. Such a conditioned mind prevents right use of available wisdom and deprives us from benefiting from genuine process of introspection. But our own untrained mind creates numerous obstacles in right introspection because it doesn't like to be questioned and disciplined. It enjoys its lethargy by maintaining status quo. Basic precondition for right introspection is the ability to look at something 'as it is' rather than 'what it should be' – a pure, impartial, unattached, genuine perspective without any influence. Right introspection calls for enhanced and improved Self-awareness and acceptance for real truth perceived by a clear pair of eyes and a willing mind. No, we are not talking about truth contained in complex philosophies or intellectual speculations out here. The desired truth is also not available out of teachings or experiences of others. What is required is the self realized truth realized using our own sensitivity, alertness and consciousness. It is like correct perception of taste realized after eating good food on a hungry stomach being entirely different than the knowledge acquired by someone without appetite from books or opinions of others.

But please be committed. Attempting such major life-changing patterns halfheartedly will not work. If you take a plunge into it without dedication and without complete preparation, you are surely inviting failure with open arms. The casual approach of 'Let us just give it a try' doesn't work. You can't take a chance; it is unlike a game of dice or gamble. Neither is it a relaxing excuse. In reality, it is going to demand more energy and devotion than the toughest exam of your life. It is a serious business and requires utmost readiness. One is also advised to hold practicality in sight where only one out of five people succeed. But once you see the immensity of the benefits, all these initial fears and pains are destined to disappear. Soon you will rejoice the whole thing as a journey towards cherished destination that was worth every effort with so much scenic beauty on the way.

Preparations Required for Chasing Real Purpose of Life

Life shattering, critical and important changes like this don't occur overnight; their origination and germination takes time to fructify. At this stage, our sole purpose is to prepare a willing seeker to glance over this flight path guided by experience of people who navigated their journey successfully in recent times itself. The real exploration is a process where the seeker alone navigates all by himself without any tool or guidance by others. So, baby-steps mentioned below are just indicative hand-holding direction for new aspirants desirous to go down the same path. These steps may be taken as similar to a map of an area providing some description of the contours for the benefit of a solo explorer left somewhere deep down in dense forest; it might not help you quickly come out of the situations but at least indicate signs and hints so as to motivate you move in the right direction.

Be it a tough examination or interview for a dream position, adequate preparations always help us for facing the challenging moments with confidence, courage and conviction. Attempting to explore ultimate purpose of our whole of human life is no less a challenge and hence demand a substantially convincing preparation. The steps listed below are intended to prepare for a well-deserved glimpse into the unknown, unseen, alien environment. Interestingly, this entire unknown exists right in the depth of our own existence away from our vision due to problem in our focus rather than anything external.

Advancement on this path, however, necessitates time and energy in abundance. Freedom from both financial and social responsibilities is, therefore, a strong pre-requisite for pursuing this trail. Financial independence is to ensure that you are not preoccupied for how to pay the bills or making ends meet. Freedom from social responsibilities, on the other hand, allows you the luxury of investing substantial chunk of your free time towards pursuing your newfound passion. Urgency always scores over significance in life. People having incomplete ambitions for achieving in life, can't be expected to shred their urgency of making it in material world over exploring bigger purpose of human life. That is why spirituality knocks on the door of only those who have reached to a certain level of achievement in real life. Family responsibilities, similarly, work as chains blocking one's freedom from eyeing beyond. Incidentally, once you have covered a decent distance in your spiritual journey, your very needs for material resources or family ties become less and less important.

Exploring our real purpose on this earth has to happen in this very life. Life being limited, it must happen as soon as possible. Finding real purpose is very important and should work as a lighthouse. That will aid us navigate our lifeboat in the right direction avoiding risks of grounding or rock crashing. The very perspective of our life influences us deeply and motivates us to invest our most critical blessing of God, our time, accordingly. If we are not even firm about our purpose of life, how we shall evaluate our efforts and what kind of success we can expect? That will be like attending a school class endlessly without any test or exam ever. It is like driving the car at maximum speed using expressways and highways but without knowing precisely about the final destination. The specific steps are:

Seeing through the Immediate

First point is that our life is more important and wider than "here and now". Always remaining focused on these two small words is too contracted a view to invest our life on. Off course, here and now always have instant urgency but what about significance of "Omnipresent and Omniscient." The clarity between immediate and eternal and understanding criticality for the eternal will help us tiding over many issues that presently engage us in vain. The moment we take longer view on life, many things will become much lighter than these feel with short-term view.

Someone dying an untimely death is known to leave devastating impact on immediate family members. But the moment one realizes that death is ultimate reality for every living being and that it has to be God's wish, the same death start sounding more bearable. Similarly, when one looks at similar instances with others and come to realize success stories of those survivors, the same loss is suddenly less intolerable. Our child not getting bagful marks at particular exams is cause of concerns for most of us. But when we realize that final degree is more important or that success in career is not linked with marks at exams, we may not feel as remorseful as otherwise. All those burdens that disturb us so much in short terms tend to become less significant over longer horizons.

Some of us spend a good part of our energy in tracking temporary things like trends, fashions, fusions and popular values; doing all those things that we do to remain relevant among contemporaries. Most of us read Newspaper everyday with so much of eagerness and attention but what is the life of current news? For example, if you were to pick up a one year old newspaper, you will find most of the headlines of that day are most likely irrelevant today. Similarly, what happens to your dresses prepared with in-fashion focus just a year ago? You could recall all the pains you went through to prepare the same but how long that fashion remained in vogue? This realization is true for most temporary things that consume so much of our attention and energy. Let us resolve to live life like a marathon runner. If time and energy saved are time and energy gained, having a long-term horizon has tremendous capacity to suddenly provide us with so much extra time and energy that you will not know what to do with it. More successful people have this thread running common that they always take longer view and use time spared from the worries of present for achieving bigger success in future; to be a creator of history than being a mere commentator of history created by others.

Immediate issues always are known to have urgency but skipping time and energy for long term may prove suicidal. One should always remain invested for longer-term issues; be it people, issues, relationships, interests, values or attitudes. Longer-term view provides you ability to look at things with a wider view and protects you against missteps.

Overcoming Fear of Death

Some of us, who have had the experience of attending funeral of a dear one, will recall the unusual feeling that develops when one is in the presence of a burning pyre or burial as the case may be. That time brings in true realization that the body is just a mixture of physical elements and soul is eternal that continues its journey from one life to another in an endless manner. Let us not think about eternity only while attending funerals. While death is scary but we all know it to be a transition rather than termination. Idea of death can help us remember that we come to this world not for being remembered by others but to continue our journey of settling accumulated karmas in our quest for liberation from the cycle of life and death. Sure thing about death is that it is inevitable. But beauty of death is that it happens only once in life. If you are any good at mathematics, above set of equations will make it easy for you to lose the fear of death for all time to come.

Many of us feel ourselves as more important and significant than reality. We are a miniscule in terms of our existence. There is no point in looking as if we are that significant in making any difference in the running of this world. We should realize that all our prized possessions, trophies and certificates, that we proudly consider our life achievements, eventually be trashed. That is destined to happen sooner than later and by some of our own dear ones. Ask yourself an honest question as to how many achievements of your grandfather were recalled by you in last week or ten days? The answer to this is quite embarrassing. Why expect your grandchild to behave any differently that you yourself. Hence, there is no point in creating a legacy.

Once we know that our life at this earth is just temporary, we should not remain under ignorance and continue remaining too attached with transient objects. After all, for the journey made on this planet, our visa is granted for limited stay and at the end of the tour, there has to be a tour report. There is a very good line from Bible which says '*friends, this world is not your home, so don't make yourself cozy in it. Don't indulge your ego at the expense of your soul.'(1 Peter 2:11 MSG)*. It is really surprising that some people are seen looking at human life as a happy swing or just a game of cards to be lived without any care for the rules of the game.

Going beyond Seeking God with Worship

Some people, at this stage, might suggest, or get suggested strongly, that searching the God is true purpose of human life and one should go for worship with full devotion and selfless desires. There are also similar teachings in ample number coming from Hinduism for propagating and invocating faith and belief through worship and devotion. Well these are the very methods suggested so strongly by scriptures of all religions alike. But worship itself is not so easy to understand. You need to find a God, make a choice of your beliefs and worship methods. The heart of any worship is in surrender before the designated God. But our constant fears, unwise pride and persistent confusions are all great barriers in true surrender.

If our heart continues to remain focused on where our treasures are and we continue counting wealth, where is the possibility of identifying God? Similarly, with all attachments in place, how can one expect to be true about surrender? So, how can we serve God? One has to choose any one between money, desires, attractions or God before complete surrender is aimed. Just for the purpose of shock therapy, visiting temple every day and wishing blessings from God is not worship but perfectly fits into definition of begging. I give you this and expect you to give back me that is the principle of barter trade? On top of it, if one was to factor in the offerings of '*Prasaad*' or '*Chadhava*' (offerings of valuable gifts), the conclusion for the activity will actually get reduced to pure and open bribing. All those people who make conditional offers to their God for doing this and that once their desires/demands are fulfilled actually fall in the discount seeker's category. Few others are doing it to please others. Many people just worship to be seen to be worshipping. Many others are seen worshipping with a long shopping list of items available for free or on offers with deep discounts. Few others are doing it just mechanically. Some are very efficient and wish to keep one eye on God while keeping the other on slipper or purse.

Above words may sound harsh or even offensive. But please, for the very God's sake take a paper and pencil and sit in a quiet corner and search for surrender and devotion out of your entire effort called worship. Whom are we fooling by such rituals carried out with closed eyes, mind and heart alike? In all such endeavours, clearly, the worshipper itself is under focus and not God. No, it doesn't qualify to be real worship. It sounds more like a commercial deal. In our own solitude, let us sincerely contemplate as what we seek from God and what we offer and conclude if what we are doing qualifies as pure surrender? In some cases, yes it may be real surrender but let those be considered as exceptions. Such cases are indeed far and few in between.

Unfortunately, for most beings, worship is a one-way traffic where they are busy desiring from God one thing or the other all the time; be it wisdom, protection from all dangers, courage to face failures, opportunities to succeed, possibilities to make quick bucks, power to rule, ability to stay peaceful, good health without doing exercises, ability to focus, ability to hold on to morals, and the list goes on and on endlessly. It is ignorance to believe that your God is sitting free and His existence is simply to help you with all His powers. Does this approach deserve to be the rightful ladder for providing liberation from this world? As already shared, devotion and surrender are to be at the heart of worship. Surrender is about losing, it is about admission of defeat, about yielding to stronger opponent. Hence true worship requires a complete bowing down with our inner Self before God. We have to remember that God is impossible to be sought with part of our life. He asks for all of our heart, mind and soul along with all of our strength. Shortcuts, similar to many other situations in life, don't work for seeking God. Similarly, seeking God mindlessly is meaningless. Unless the seeker has been able to forget the world around completely, how can he/she establish contact with the God? God also is not impressed with rituals as it rather accepts practical worship. It is not possible to please God with singing praises standing in front of its idols or such other visible forms and continue desire blessings.

Reading through all religious practices let us conclude that forgetting self-centeredness is the most important virtue of every type of worship. Real worship requires His admiration even when you are in pains, remaining in His gratitude even when you are being tested in trials, pillaring your un-wavered trust in Him even when there are hoard of temptations and finally, loving Him in spite of all the distances standing in between. That kind of real worship will be possible only after cementing our 'Real Purpose of Life'.

Differentiate Passions from Purpose

Meaning of passion as used here is strong inclination towards a self-defining activity that provides satisfaction to the doer. Undoubtedly, pursuing passions repeatedly generate positive emotions and that helps in living life harmoniously. It also leads to psychological well-being for the pursuer. But issues like career, family, sports, hobby, wealth creation and preservation, are seen getting sidelined to periphery once we apply the filter of finding Purpose of Life. Engagement in these activities plays an important role in our life. Yes, these issues have their significance in human life but these don't belong to centre of our life. These are just the matters at the outskirts having limited role-play for sustaining our life. It is a mistake to dedicate your life to such small issues. In the context of body and soul, these activities impact the physical body and Ego of the person leaving soul largely untouched.

None of our passions will be strong enough to hold us together as a pillar if and when our life starts breaking apart due to deep crises. Passions are fair weather companions and also have limited shelf life as their relative importance tapers off much before our life journey starts peaking. Any one of us investing good amount of their time and energy on such passions may like to reconsider his priority and should not be ignorant to make these passions itself as purpose of life.

Move beyond Focus on Physical Body

Our body is the only equipment available to the soul to experience this universal drama called life. Similar to any other equipment, it must be kept well in terms of its mechanics and other support systems. Its smaller issues cause interruptions and irritations but final breakdown ends the entire process altogether. But equipment is just equipment. It doesn't have much role besides being used for the final processing of the product it is designed for. In any manufacturing process, once the final product comes out, there is hardly any appreciation for the quality of the equipment used. Think about it, as you have been a consumer of so many things like toiletries, cosmetics, foods, clothes or gadgets. Are we all not just interested in the product without any thoughts for the equipment helping that product to come in existence? How can it be different for soul and body? While sipping a glass of milk, we certainly don't see image of a cow or buffalo. No, equipment does not matter against the products it makes.

We should be ready to look at our physical body exactly as a car to be used for undertaking journey to reach our destination. You may continue shining your car as much you like but it has nothing to do with your reaching at the right destination. While setting our search for the very purpose of our life, we must overcome issues impacting physical body and issues related with it. We are obliged to use the human body and mind systems for identifying and realizing the real purpose of our life. Again, it is no use having shining equipment if our product produced by use of that equipment is NOT as per design, specs and capability of that equipment.

Seeking the Perfume in Place of Flowers

We all like flowers and there is a very wide variety of flowers all around. Each flower has its unique fragrance. But the moment one gets perfume made from the same flowers, the fragrance of flowers is not missed much. Perfume is made basically out of essential oil extracts of the flowers. In addition, there are grasses, spices, fruit extracts, wood, roots, resins, leaves and gums which also get used in smaller proportions to ensure a unique formula for every signature perfume.

Out of about a total 250,000 known flowering plants, merely 2000 or so species contain essential oils having capability for converting into perfumes. Similarly, out of a large number of happiness providing elements, only a very small number have the ability to contribute to our real purpose of life. Each person has his own preference for a particular flower but best of perfume is prepared with blending various perfumes made from a large variety of flowers. Similarly, seeking of real purpose of human life requires blending of different happiness providing elements. Due to the process of blending, happiness provided by each of such elements converge into an unique blend that is certainly much more desirable, fulfilling and long lasting when compared to happiness contributed by each such element individually.

The entire process of perfume making actually consists of various processes such as steam distillations, solvent extraction, maceration and expressions. Similarly, the process of finding purpose of life may include meditation, Yoga, contemplation, scripture reading, Self-awareness etc. In any case, process is just a via media, important point is to obtain final product. The entire process of perfuming depends heavily on use of alcohol, apparently an undesirable but multipurpose substance. Exploring life purpose also depends heavily on the attachment with dedication and sincerity; same attachment when tied with objects creates bondage but tied with dedication it enhances devotion to the cause. Similar to alcohol, attachments also have inebriating capabilities that soon becomes a tough habit that is generally difficult to kick off.

Finally, after maturing over months and years, when the perfume finally gets ready, its odour emulates nature's pleasant smells in all directions and influences every person coming within its vicinity. Having found the purpose of life and having obtained maturity over good periods, the presence of such a soul also radiates its aura in all directions and impacts everyone around. So we all should aspire to achieve our perfumes rather than remain engaged in smelling just the flowers of our choice. Why settle for just one happiness-providing element when you have capability of going to its very condensed form that is well blended, matured and mixed with traces of many such happiness providing elements.

It is a different matter, however, that some people do develop allergy from perfumes. Is it not similar to some ignorant people seen developing aversion towards superior purpose of human life?

True Realization of Real Purpose of Life

Right from the meeting of the fittest male sperm with a female egg, the creation of human life is biologically random and identical to many other animals. With the use of genetically evolved systems, soon human body develops itself to a full-fledged being and starts living life all by itself. This process does explain arrival of life more like an event. But do all these animals and human have a meaning or significance attached to their life? This indeed is an intriguing question with no easy answer. Soon mythologies and religions got evolved to provide external meaning to human existence by bringing supernatural powers by going against all implausible objective evidences pointing to the contrary. No, purpose of human life can't be linked with the fictions of mythologies. We also come across another explanation grouped under the concept of humanism where human life is supposed to be for the service of others by full use of mind, body and speech. But this again sounds more like diversion than anything rock solid. These types of explanations around purpose of human life may allow us to life full of doubts and illusions but fail to provide acceptable explanation with all the objective evidences also pointing in the same direction. Human life is better being something more than random and alive.

The real purpose of life revolves around apparently three short, crisp and basic questions. These questions are undoubtedly simple. But their answers involve complexities of Himalayan proportions. However, once a person is able to figure out their answers, the whole creation gets illuminated with ample clarity. The first of these basic questions relates to our identity crisis where the question is "Who am I?" The second question pertains to our relative importance within this visible world with the question is "How do I matter?" The final question relates to the impact that we leave behind with our existence and the question is "What is my place in this life?"

Each one of us must have read or heard about these questions. Knowing or unknowingly, we may have come across these questions deep inside during our moments of truth. So we know these questions without developing intimacy and identification with the same. A deeper understanding, churning and brainstorming around these three questions alone have the power of leading us to our spiritual orientation and there alone we shall find our 'Real Purpose of Life'. These critical questions have two stark similarities. Firstly, these are all focused internally. There is no reference or significance of what happens in the external visible universe, the world that has absorbed us so deeply up until now. Secondly and most importantly, all these questions relate directly to YOU; there is no family, no reference about children, no place for professions or position or wealth or anything else. It is you and you alone to the exclusion of everything else.

You alone are your real purpose!

Man is the highest fruit on the tree of evolution. It is for man to realize his position in this Universe and understand the true meaning of his life.

The whole elaboration and expansion that enables us to deal with this new found purpose is called Spirituality. Exploration of our Spiritual dimensions alone facilitates our search for the fundamental questions of our life. Let us now concentrate all our efforts in understanding Spirituality in all its forms, meaning and extensions and also penetrate our clarity by putting it side by side all other important issues that have been the centre of our attention up until now.

Part II

Developing Understanding of Spirituality

Spirituality, General Understanding

Strictly speaking, Spirituality can't be defined in very clear words because it is a broad concept that allows multiple perspectives to get developed. But interact with few learned people and few things emerge out immediately; it has something to do with being not materialistic, it seems to be above superficial planes, it is neutral to brackets of religion, cultures, genders or age. Traditionally, spirituality signified having attachment with soul or spirit entirely away from worldly interest. It is also understood to be a state where a human being is fully connected with his deepest core together with other beings, nature, environment and even Divine Being called with whatever name.

Spirituality is something very unique and personal and can be realized or evolved and experienced by someone only by individual efforts. Only academic knowledge about it is not enough. Indeed, it is a personal matter and involves subjective experience that can't be dissected using scientific investigations or tied down to well-defined enclosures. No wonder the question as to what is Spirituality scares many of us. Abstract sounding answers to this question further frighten some more. But hold your breath and there is nothing to feel scared. Here is a step by step effort to make modern day *Karmayogis* understand the whole concept of Spirituality together with steps required to practise the same should the reader get inspired to pursue that path any further.

People familiar with the matter will explain Spirituality as a sense of relationship with something bigger than anything known and a relationship that typically involves a deeper search for real meaning in life. It is said to be universal human experience that touches us all as equals. Also that it is not something that can be explained within boundaries of definitions and explanations but something that can be accepted or visualized by a person based on his own subjective experience. Simply put, Spirituality is an essential process that leads us to an understanding and acceptance of our own true nature. Our body or physical being, by which a person is identified and generally known, is not his real defining identity. Spirituality is also described as a bridge that, when properly constructed, enables one to realize that there is no difference between individual consciousness and universal consciousness.

Spirituality is also about showing respect for every living being, including animals, trees, rocks and even innate objects and leading a healthy, positive and harmonious life with everything else in the surroundings. As an extension of religious beliefs, Spirituality hinges on the concept that some supreme power has put each one of us in this world for a well-defined purpose of living a compassionate, caring and loving life with respect for each other and everything around. But Spirituality rules much above the planes of beliefs and imaginations. Spirituality has more to do with our own conscience, that subtle sense of righteous behaviour that largely, more often than not, get side-stepped or over-stepped under cruel and ruthless compulsions of immediate realities of human life. Our conscience is a part of universal conscience and that is why we hear sages proclaim that ultimate truth resides right inside each of us. Being non-material in nature, Spirituality can be experienced and attempted by understanding, regulating and purifying our mind since all our values, principles, habits, behaviours and controls are all affected by our mind alone.

Just for a quick clarification, Spirituality has nothing to do with religions. Unlike all religions, there are no institutional structures or defined hierarchies governing it. This is purely personal experience and there are no dogmas, beliefs, rituals, scriptures or any other definite form to get identified with it. But Spirituality is an active ingredient of all religions of the world. Ideals propagated by all religions converge seamlessly with ideals of a generally identified spiritualist. In one case, the ideals are like aspirations while in the other those are completely realized.

Spirituality is not about definitions or intellectual deliberations. At the end of the day, it is all about self-exploration and self-realization. Hence rather than looking for words and descriptions, we will try to touch it on personal level. It is like a first time climber standing at foot of the peak and thinking if he has what it takes to climb up to the peak. Any volume of study or sermons from others doesn't prepare him for the unique experience that he is likely to go through on his way up. Unfortunately, on this climb, there is no instructor or trainer to hold hand or extend support when needed. To that extent exploring Spirituality gets that much more self-dependent expedition.

On a personal level I really like the description of spirituality provided by Mr. Larry Culliford, a Psychiatrist based in Sussex, England, who explains it to be similar to an open and vast adventure playground where one can have as much fun as one can experiment and enjoy. Imagine such as playground where rides and riddles are not like the typically modeled parks and games played have no defined characteristics; where presence or absence of other beings don't disturb you as you explore alone, where you play with your own capacity and capability. In this park, a new adventure awaits you every time you are done with the previous. You can imagine the possibilities of endless joy, wonders, fascinations, mysteries, wow moments and delights that await you at such an adventure park!

Spirituality is indeed that expansive, transformative and blissful.

When is Someone Ready for the Spiritual Quest?

Similar to the importance of a strong foundation for a high-rise building, the spiritual structure that one wishes to create shall begin with ensuring that basic foundations are in place. The understanding of these foundations can excite and stimulate the reader to see his very own inclination and readiness to initiate his travel down this road; a road full of hardships and steep climbs and falls but full of extremely rare bounties waiting all over the climb. Complying with the conditions below is just to provide a sort of self-check. Realization about following points is expected to help one in verifying if the seeds of Spirituality are ready to sprout and grow if not sprouted already. An experienced farmer checks before seeding that ground preparation is appropriate, soil is fertile, irrigation source is ready as and when required, provision of nutrients is all in place, removal of weeds will be well catered to and climatic conditions are all favorable for germination. Let us try taking stock of our conditions precedent before knowing our own status on way to our spiritual preparedness. The prerequisites necessary for helping your spirituality growing well are:

1. Firm realization that we are basically spiritual beings (different from materialist and psychological-physical beings) currently going through human experience.
2. During this human experience, it is only body that gets acquired and destroyed. That there is another essence of life which is indestructible and transcends this journey.
3. We are part of this Universe that has no beginning or end, which has been there for ages and will remain there forever.
4. This Universe is the manifestation of the Universal Being (also known as Pure Being) similar to ocean and its waves. Individual life here is just like a small and insignificant ripple in the stream.

If we are sufficiently moved by these realities, we are ready to explore our journey of comprehending Spirituality and seeking the same in suitable proportions. Conversely, if our answer to these questions is not in affirmative, it is a clear indication that we are not there as yet. It certainly doesn't mean end of the road but an alarm that a pause is required for a detour or loop before we hit the highway again. Unless we don't realize above-mentioned statements, we shall not be capable of appreciating Spirituality as a true discovery of our Self.

Continuing the example of the farmer, there are various methods for preparing the ground for the next cycle of intended crop: ploughing and re-ploughing, irrigation, growing cover crop, balancing organic matter, etc. The interested aspirant, accordingly, has to continue his efforts of improving his mental ground preparation so that his spirituality has potential to germinate. The recommended initiatives include scriptures reading, working on moral values and cementing ethical behaviour. The tools available for the same are meditation and contemplation. Also recommended are activities such as participating in social activities, working on compassion and empathy, listening to sermons. Getting access for seeking blessings and directions of a capable teacher also goes a long way for seeking clarity about all possible doubts arising in the process.

Laying the Foundation for Spiritual Seeking

Our spirituality solicits to examine our own nature thoroughly; the nature that normally remains suppressed under burden of various roles that we do play or wish to play in our normal life. Unfortunately, our own true nature is far more complex and intriguing than we may be aware up until now. We keep shuttling in between many roles almost constantly. For example, we keep honing cap of a bread earner, a loving spouse, a caring parent, a dear friend, an intellectual person, a successful sports man, a responsible administrator, etc. Surely, each one of us is quite a unique individual. In addition to all the roles mentioned above, we are a bundle of particular characteristics, feelings, thoughts, personal traits, values, habits, weaknesses and strengths. But all that has nothing to do with our Real Self.

This real 'Self' needs to be differentiated, at this stage itself, with the more recognizable and familiar physical self as well as 'Psychological Self' (more simply understood as 'Ego'). The combined identity of body and ego is also referred at times as 'lower self'. This self, called by whatever name, is more familiar to most of us as it keeps us trapped all the time with all its tricks in action (desires, cravings, attractions, arrogance, attachments, false identity, pride, envy) giving us false projection of self. Our Ego, incidentally, thrives on large accumulations of past memories. Layers of memories and false perceptions soon convert into a thick concrete slab over the true Self. Our Spirituality invites us to examine into our most profound level of being. It helps us explore our real side by making us capable of pushing aside trappings of this world; desires, hopes, demands, memories, history of experiences included.

For sure, most of us may have heard statements like '*Our pure self, the natural state of being has love, peace and tranquility as its original unspoiled state*'. But believing in such a statement needs abundant clarity about all the components involved. But what is true is true. We might take longer time to understand and appreciate the real truth. Undoubtedly, our pure Self is embedded in permanent happiness. In that very state, no one needs to make efforts to seek happiness since it is there already. This state holds many treasures waiting to be accessed. Love, peace and happiness are natural state of human beings but once the Ego brings over its influence, the original happiness gets pushed into distance and it appears as coming and going in bouts. The beauty is that when the being is in its original state, even sufferings can't erase the happiness. Such a state, therefore, is worth making all possible efforts. Intense craving for possibility to reach this state is a great attraction for aspirants to try this path in spite of challenges, hardships and sacrifices.

Seeking our own spirituality requires surrender of the false ego acquired in our normal life existence. It necessitates that we yield to our real Self by sustained efforts of developing ability to go beneath all artificial layers of false self. This process is achieved by sharpening our self-awareness. As the word goes, self-awareness should not be difficult as it is all about self. But real self-awareness is most important hurdle in the entire process of seeking spirituality. We shall shortly be taking up understanding self-awareness in great details and shall realize why it is so difficult. All through our normal life thus far, we have been tacitly feeling and accepting our individual qualities and properties as part of our unique nature. Actually, most of the time, we have been feeling proud about this apparent uniqueness. Most of us have innocently believed being different with pride. Little did we realize that such an unreal understanding has been falsely built over years under reiteration of our past memories or behaviours. We had been busy in repeating it to our self time and again. As a result of these gullible repetitions, we start identifying with these unique traits and soon one becomes what one identifies oneself with.

But once we start working on our spiritual aspect, our vision starts getting wider and sharper which helps in sighting reality in better light. Suddenly we realize that the uniqueness celebrated by us is just false ego that has been working as a deep divide by pitching us against others. By dispensing the glasses and correction of vision, we once again get to see that these attributes were mere shadows of false perceptions and self created illusions. As and when such a transformation happens, one can take it as a new birth after death. This seeing through allows us to appreciate that there is no need of visiting any hell or heaven as this very life and this very world contain both hell and heaven. Yes, once a person is able to walk past its created ideas, behaviours, attitudes and memories, there will be a peculiar and weird emptiness. But such emptiness soon gets filled with trans-personal fullness. It is in such state that false ego gets replaced by perfect harmony, order and integration; where a person starts seeing itself as a universal being with more similarities with the entire external environment and not separateness.

Let us quickly try appreciating why does this ego build up take place in the first instance. One of the realities of life is that it starts with a physical body. That body soon evolves into a person. Such a person is faced with some physical requirements (like hunger and sleep) and some social requirements (family, friends and society). In addition, this person also has optional requirements (thoughts and knowledge) and some fear protection mechanisms (religion and worships). To shoulder all his responsibilities and sustain the physical life, this person has to create and accumulate some wealth. All these activities engage the poor person in compulsions of 'here' and 'now' affairs. This engagement closes his inner eyes and keeps his consciousness suppressed under the burden of never-ending urgency of these issues.

This short-term view on our existence is the sole reason for us to remain blindfolded for our inherent real self. Later, when one is able to move step-by-step on the road for seeking real self, there will surely be realization that life without 'real purpose' is all mechanical, burdensome and uninspiring. This initial knowledge, as and when it happens, will generate flurry of fears but would also feed to yearning for more exploration. Thus, in several steps, we will finally get to see moments of liberation and potential dissolution of our ego laced self. As against this, the newfound Spiritual Self will be found full of endless possibilities for happiness spread over unlimited space with assured peace, tranquility and bliss.

Seeking Spirituality is not meant only for seeking endless joy and bliss. Spiritual aspiration is one of the governing forces of entire Ancient Indian culture. Seeking moksha has been held as the ultimate aim of human life and moksha is nothing but complete realization of one's own spirituality. This is what Sri Aurobindo, the sage of nearer times, precisely explains in 'Arya' published in 1919. He has written that for those of us believing and following Hinduism inspired by Sanatan Dharma, making everyone ready to seek and obtain their spirituality is a core thought of Hinduism. He further explained that all our Rishis and sages have been known to succeed in focusing their whole life on Spirituality.

Dismantling Religion and Philosophy based Barriers

Most human beings have some background of religion, dogmas, worship methods, images, signs, customs, rituals, forms and symbols. These emerge as supporting symbols providing growth opportunity to a person during the making of each person. Hence, these supporting elements acquire integral part of that person's life. These elements get acquired over a long period and can't be wished away just like that. Point under consideration is about potential use of this luggage that the aspirant is endowed with.

Actually, religious-philosophical culture being followed by the seeker plays very crucial role by taking basket full of potential questions out of the way. These supporting structures have good significance for seeking Spirituality as well. In fact, these acquire similar significance as scaffolding required to construct a grand and impressive temple or any other building. These are essential during construction. Individual element of support helps immensely during building, plastering, painting the temple of Spirituality. So much so, the very construction of the temple is unimaginable without such supports. But once the facade gets completed and ready for occupation, the same scaffolding gets removed as an unwanted obstruction. Exactly similar is the role of all religious and social systems of the aspirant; eventually all such supports will have to be left behind when one decides to enter the very temple of Spirituality.

Once the person progresses in finding his Spiritual orientation, he has to necessarily withdraw reliance from all other temporary supports. Spirituality requires him to stand on his two feet without seeking support of crutches. The scaffolding will get dumped in the corner or in some store far away for use, if any, during subsequent repairs or refurbishments. As a result, more often than not, all spiritually awakened persons are known to rise above religious, cultural baggage, sectarian or such other divides and start considering every other human being with honour and respect. Spirituality also necessitate that the aspirant treats each person as equal without any influence of his wealth, position or education or social status what so ever. The temple of spirituality is known to have only one door for entry and exit, which is open, only and only, for ultimate intellectual truth without any rigidity about conclusions or reasoning or logics; because supreme truth requires neither.

Different Notions around Spirituality

Broadly, there are three different lenses that can be used to view the entire spectrum of spirituality. The first kind is based on formal notions and includes viewpoints of various established religions. While there are some common issues running across all religions, their respective doctrines, at times, stand in the way of developing common threads beyond a point. It is similar to all political parties in a multi-party democratic system where each party promises better future of the country without agreeing on what is better future. They have different priorities and approaches and can never get same result. Hence, this lens is best kept in abeyance due to inescapable controversies.

Second lens covers informal notions developed by certain individuals or defined groups. So-called individuals or groups can be seen taking up some parts in bits and pieces and calling that as their own unique feature. In order to bring some uniqueness, they focus on packaging and branding rather than content. At the content level they are hardly different from each other. For this very reason, this lens also needs to be kept out of our discussions. These individuals or so self-proclaimed Swamis, Gurus, Mullas and Preachers, we all must agree, are into it for their own business. Your well-being for them is at best a by-product. They look at spirituality as a product and are busy developing larger number of customers similar to a business corporation working to expand its consumer base. The role for Teachers and Preachers is only limited. To continue the example of scaffolding for constructing a temple, a guru is comparable to an architect who provides a set of drawings of how a temple may look like and what all minimum provisions it should have. Similarly, scriptures can be compared similar to manuals for construction practices.

The third and final category relates to ethical notions, which are based on universal values like truth, mysticism, inner realization and contemplation. Spirituality, *per se* is a universal tradition that has cross-cultural outreach but which remains clear of all types of vested interests. It is here that the seeker expands his/her views on reality, finds subtleties of life and begins to grasp real truth from a unifying ground by continuously growing his knowledge, wisdom and virtues. We will use this particular lens for all our subsequent discussions. Suffice to understand that Spirituality is an independent subject that stands of its own completely broken from the moorings of any specific religious traditions. Spirituality being discussed under this book, for the modern day person, is therefore a truly secular concept in letter and spirit.

Quest for spirituality and growth to be achieved depends purely on self-seeking and self-inspiration. Clarity on this account goes a long way to help prepare a new practitioner. He/she must get committed to be vigilant to fight a lone battle. What makes this battle interesting is that enemy to be fought, battle ground, arms used and strategies made and revised are all well within our own mind. The enemy is none other than our own ignorant, fragmented and divided self. It is the same self that has been able to successfully suffocate the gentle sibling living under its shadow since childhood. We may have experienced losing internal battles in past and may have believed having thin chances of winning against our own self but fight we must!

When to Initiate Spiritual Seeking

Everyone would like to check his own starting point to see as to what is the right time to start. Well, it is not that everyone starts from the same place at same stage of life. There is a theory that differentiates the starting point for each person based on spiritual orientation and accumulated karmic balance. This theory is based on differentiation between worldly knowledge and spiritual awakening. Worldly knowledge, considered temporary, is said to be acquired fresh in every birth cycle and its use or misuse results into karmic debits or credits. Worldly knowledge, however, get subsumed with death and there is no accumulation or carry forward of this knowledge.

Karmic balance, however, is partially settled in each life by undergoing sufferings and pleasures while balance Karmic credits get used for selecting out situation for next birth. But spiritual awakening does not end with life. It remains attached with the soul and takes off, in every new life, from the stage achieved in earlier life. The theory is a theory but it has some appeal in so far as we come across different levels of spiritual status of different people where some take on it in very young age while others remain ignorant all through their life. As such, spiritual seeking can start at any stage in human life and there are no rights or wrongs out here. Since the carry over continues birth after birth, one should try getting initiating into it at the first possible opportunity, however, subject to fulfilling conditions precedent already discussed.

Measuring Spiritual Progress by Any Individual

Like devotion for a God, there is nothing to be used to measure heights or depths of Spirituality desired, attempted or achieved. One has to keep seeking it as much as possible. One has to remember there is no quality or quantity or volume or any other way of quantifying one's Spirituality. Neither can you compare it with that of others. Each one has his own Mt. Everest and he has to climb it of his own taking own route, creating his footprints. Each one has to evolve, search, sharpen, use and discard his tools and support systems for conquering his own peak in spite of trembling or falling on way to this endless journey.

Recently, however, psychology related instruments are finding use for undertaking clinical research of wide variety. Some of these researches are specially focused on use of spirituality in mental health domain. You may also come across a Spiritual Well-being Scale that records data on psychometric properties. Similarly, many other instruments are emerging for measuring spirituality in general, spiritual well-being, spiritual coping and spiritual needs. Let us conclude that as the situation stands today and considering the lens with which we are approaching spirituality out here, defining levels or measuring spirituality in any other quantifiable term is not possible even with the help of any scientific instrument.

Understanding Broad Contours of Spirituality

One of the fundamental reasons for near impossibility of measuring Spirituality is its very definition that is changing all the time. There are no set boundaries that can be applied to include or exclude aspects from the dimensions of Spirituality. As it is, from the spiritual point of view, it does not matter who and what you are. You may be long or short, fat or thin, boss or subordinate, master or servant, famous or unknown, wealthy or poor, loved or hated. When it comes to looking at your spirituality, all the known divisions and categorizations are found unwanted. There is actually no requirement to measure your borders of spirituality in the first place. What matters most here is the internal understanding that your soul is being provided with right experience and expression for its journey in human life using your body as the tool.

All you need to realize is the clarity and continuity with which you are able to listen and communicate with your soul. As we have seen earlier, soul generally remains suppressed under layers and layers of overburden of external and temporary shadows of teachings and learning from books, societies, parents and even elements such as movies and TV. So, one is able to listen and communicate with it only after silencing the noise and vibrations of the overburden. If your frequency is well tuned and as long as you are able to listen to the sounds and signs of your soul, you can be rest assured that your spirituality is in the process of awakening.

Spirituality v/s Common Concepts in Life

At this stage, it is obvious to expect questions where readers are not able to see the borders of Spirituality with other familiar traditional concepts like morality, religion, materialism, sex, career, pleasures, self-improvements, Yoga, peace and tranquility, role-play with different fields of sciences. Bulk of our actions, thoughts, motivations and judgements comes out from these very concepts. Our divided mind has been trained to divide things under multiple forms but now we have to train it to cross over most of these concepts and work on Spirituality. Surely, it is a tough call and complete clarity is required around the borders of all these concepts before we can take Spirituality as an all-compassing subject.

In following few pages, effort is made to take up those familiar concepts and put Spirituality just next to them with the objective of helping the reader develop unambiguous clarity about Spirituality vis-à-vis these concepts. Evaluating something through the process of negation is a very old and time-tested technique. We can use the same process to appreciate as to what is not Spirituality. This proven method will most likely bring better clarity against understanding Spirituality as a abstract subject. This understanding should also loosen the power of the glue that binds us with these concepts.

In our normal life, we do interact with these concepts on daily basis and are quite well-versed with them. Understanding Spirituality vis-à-vis these, shall certainly help us assimilate Spirituality without creating indigestion. This process should sharpen our comprehension about Spirituality in required details as well. If nothing else, the negative, neutral or positive connection of spirituality with these engagements will provide us ways to improve our performance over these concepts to higher levels. That by itself is likely to bring higher fulfillment in our existing life. To that extent, even those of us who are still not listening knock-knock from their own spirituality, will get additional motivations to explore at least the periphery of their spiritual cloud.

Let us take on these concepts one by one:

Spirituality vis-à-vis Religions

> "Religion is the rules, regulations, ceremonies and rituals developed by man to create conformity and uniformity in the approach to God. Spirituality is God's call in your soul".
>
> – *Iyanla Vanzant, an American Inspirational speaker*

Religion itself is a difficult subject matter filled with contradictory views about their efficacies in modern times. As already explained, every religion plays an effective role towards developing ethical and moral discipline among its practitioners to face personal and communal adversities. There is another desirable and important role that deals with enhancing virtues of love, compassion, patience, tolerance, forgiveness, etc. But religions are also infested with a significant undesirable element of constructing walls around their own identities and introducing divisions among people leading to lot of conflicts. History tells us and we continue to see more violence based on religious and sectarian divides than all other issues combined.

Religions are, generally speaking, institutional phenomena and are defined by their boundaries. Particular beliefs, practices and models of social organizations differentiate them from one another. Religions cater to many objectives including cultural, economic, political and social which club them fundamentally as social phenomenon. On the contrary, the entire gamut of Spirituality operates at individual level. As such, a single individual may well be leading a perfect spiritual life together with being religious or vice versa. Group versus individual quality goes on to expand the possibilities for operations of spirituality to endless possibilities.

Religions evolved to provide specific methods to human beings for living a balanced and happy life in harmony with each other. But considering endless fights and destructions faced by the world in the name of religions, it is obvious to raise finger of doubt towards their usefulness for the furtherance of humanity. In modern times, religions are seen erecting barriers than facilitating peaceful co-existence. No wonder, one can listen dissenting voices throughout all societies showing disenchantment and disillusionment towards their respective religions. Unlike any time in the past history of mankind, people are either discarding their religious convictions or pushing them so much away in the corner that they don't impact their daily life in any significant manner. One can clearly see today that most educated and economically competent societies are increasingly turning away from holding hard-line approach on religions and can be seen collectively becoming more and more liberal and secular. Both fundamentalism and apocalypse play significant role only among the impoverished people among all societies. Gallup Poll held in US in 2010 establishes strong positive link between strict adherence to religion and deprivation. Scientists also suggest that religious beliefs help poor people to cope with the difficulties and destitution with the hope that they may have better condition in next life. No wonder, poor among all parts can be seen more religious than their rich counterparts.

On the other hand, spirituality is concerned only with universal, fundamental, original and basic human spirits such as love, compassion, empathy, tolerance, forgiveness, contentment, etc. that are advised to be practised by every single human being for aiming at happiness and fulfillment for self and those in vicinity. Spirituality requires no metaphysical, philosophical or religious belief system to sustain. In a way, it is easy for people to survive without religion but just imagine the plight of any human, howsoever strong or independent he may be, surviving without the universal qualities listed above. The fundamental point to appreciate is that individuals may be branded as religious without any of these qualities while it is not possible to call them spiritual unless above human qualities are practised and absorbed by them in true sense. As another example, a criminal with proven record of offences may qualify to be a religious person but no one will ever accept his spiritual credentials. As soon as any human is able to assimilate this hard reality, his penchant for a religion gets punctured.

However, if any person follows his religion purely on individual level without involving into its social strings, such a follower can be said to be moving towards original meaning of *dharma.* Such a follower comes out of the bounds of religion with respect to our present discussion. Such followers are generally seen being selective in their practices and there is hardly any intolerance, bigotry or orthodoxy involved in their rituals. At that level, religion is nothing beyond personal belief and works just as a spare clutch to be used if and when required. In the process, such followers have no reason to feel offended about the remarks meant for fanatic followers.

Returning back to our discussion, one can easily understand the plight of religions by comparing them to anti-biotic medicines that are liberally used at present. Each anti-biotic works only when administered in specified doses only. Efficacy of medicine is also effective for curing specific disease only. But intensity of ailments keeps changing over the years due to countless effects from surroundings. Prolonged use of any anti-biotic medicines, however, results in the virus developing immunity and it doesn't impact in proportion to doses taken in the past. This situation necessitates different anti-biotic for getting success in treatment. Also, every anti-biotic comes with side effects which vary from case to case. Religions also have their respective applicability, decreasing efficacy, immunity syndrome and side effects. Hence, religions have to evolve continuously to avoid the risk of losing efficacy; those which are unable to evolve and keep pace with newer environment, risk the very relevance as the time goes by.

If you go through the evolution of religions the world over, these can always be traced playing catching up game where time lag has been there almost on all issues. Social issues are changing over the generations and newer issues keep emerging afresh all the time; for example, we have burning issues of 21st century like abortion, drug abuse, global warming, same sex marriages, gay/lesbian rights, pornography, extremism and terrorism where most established religions of the world have a lot of catching up to do in terms of revising their moral codes to effectively provide directions to their practitioners. In the recent past, almost all religions have not kept pace with the fast evolution of humanity and have been falling short of fulfilling expectation of large number of their followers resulting in increasing portion turning docile and passive followers.

There can be another way of understanding importance of religion and all things religious for specific person having unique value system, moral strength, and ethical orientation. Let us assume a person proceeding on a visit to a foreign country for a temporary period. He studies the climatic conditions, availability of food, general living conditions etc. Based on such knowledge alone, he plans to pack his bag. He tries his best to carry every item that may be required to complete his stay with as much comforts as possible. Now, if his destination is changed to some other continent with different climatic conditions, can he carry the same bag? Certainly not. And because you can carry only that much, adding even one extra item, something else will have to be left behind. Every religion is just like a bag packed for a particular foreign visit where its doctrines, philosophies, customs and methods offered are suitable for specific type of requirements. There is no single religion that can take care of human needs for living a balanced and happy life, as there is no single bag, which can be fit for travelling to all locations and destinations.

One is prompted to accept truth of each religion as taught by them. But how can one ignore another truth being taught by another religion. Now, unless you are secular enough to accept more than one truth, you will be faced with multiplicity of truths from all the religions. This calls for ability to develop a genuine sense of religious pluralism but that is a missing component in modern times. This is the turn on which religions are forced to deviate from their journey with spirituality. A particular religion, any religion for that matter, is just adherence to a particular thought process; one which is held to the extreme of not allowing further growth or application of any rationality or providing room for any exploration or any questioning. In most religions, its followers shift responsibility of most things away from self on to their designated Divine Being. (Oh God, only you can do something)

Spirituality, on the other hand, is a guide to human mind and shows people good way to understand their connection with themselves and with consciousness of cosmic world. It does allow truth to come up with churning and mixing of all possible fluids without any restriction or regulation. As there are no walls or boundaries, Spirituality allows explorations for finding answers to even those questions where religions are rather silent or vague or incomplete. Another way of differentiating the two is that religion looks at social aspects impacting people on collective basis while spirituality remains focused on inside of an individual to the exclusion of rest of the universe.

Religion(s) can also be compared to working of a computer based spreadsheet (for example, Microsoft Excel). While we are free to pick up any exercise to operate in the spreadsheet, we will have to work within defined borders (very large but not endless), pick up from predefined formulae and arrive at a predefined answer. A person using excel may feel as if he achieved the result using his own thinking and reasoning but reality is that whenever one desires to compute, he must operate within pre-defined ways and means set by Excel's programmers. Answers are guaranteed but process selected and order followed have to be as already pre-specified. Religions also operate within similar laid out restrictions. In many cases, on the contrary, size of the matrix available also has only limited number of lines and columns to play around with.

In case of religions, with some exceptions to the contrary, the followers are expected to have blind faith in the doctrines set up by their Prophets or teachers. Religions are based on subjective experiences that can't be verified or on perceived doctrines that are not verifiable at all. A follower is not allowed to tinker with the doctrines using his own reasoning or verification process. But Spirituality operates without boundaries or any recommended formulae. The seeker has to be necessarily free from all limitations and is to sail his own boat without any written map or chart or guide; all one gets is general information about contours provided by people who have already sailed through those waters before. No doubt, everybody can tow religion but *spirituality requires the courage of an explorer, mental strength of an inventor, wisdom of a realized man and patience of a sage.* You have to check your own orientation and move ahead or take a U-turn all by your own choice without any one prompting you to do that.

Spirituality vis-à-vis Morality and Ethics

Being a qualitative subject, it is open to different interpretations.

Use of morality and its meaning, at times, is twisted to serve meaning differently depending upon situations. But we wish to deliberate about universal meaning attached with these concepts. Universal approach on morals judges something immoral even when the act was initiated away from the eyes of others. However, society or administration can initiate punitive or corrective action against immorality only when the act, per say, comes in public space and someone complains against it. As a result many acts of immorality remain hidden away from public knowledge. We will see soon how and why this difference is important to understand.

Universal morals and ethics have a very thin line to walkon and are mostly self-administered. Pursuing these involves much more than what the law requires or what is acceptable by the particular social system. Fundamentally, the state of mind and the emotions influencing the overall state of heart and mind at the particular moment when any action is being taken, in my view, determines the true nature of its being moral and ethical. Any action initiated by a self-serving motive or a desire of getting direct or indirect benefit out of it will fail the test of qualifying as a moral action. The point under highlight is that a person's own grounding in the moral codes of his time, region, culture and society are very critical for his readiness to seek Spirituality. Morality helps a person in differentiating intentions, decisions, actions between good or bad, between right or wrong and between good or evil. This differentiation is a desired virtue for Spirituality seeker rather than only legal or social compliance on moral and ethical codes. Once this test is established properly, the entire concept of morality gets subsumed within spirituality without doubt.

Sanatan Dharma and Buddhism go a step further as thoughts under these religions are considered similar to actions. This goes to enhance the responsibility of their followers even further. They have to not only abstain from committing an immoral act but also have to abstain from entertaining any thought about possibilities of committing such acts as well. For example, it is not only hitting someone that qualifies as a violent action but having strong thoughts of harming the other person, in any way, also qualify as violence. Putting it more blatantly, having sex with someone is as immoral as having thoughts of potential sexual encounter with that person.

Seeking of Spirituality calls upon the seeker to develop empathy and compassion. It also requires understanding about the connectedness of a person with humanity at large and universe in general. These requirements help motivating the seeker to take actions aimed at well-being of others. Every action, having well-being of others at its core will pass the test of being ethical and moral. Spirituality helps in transforming our hearts and minds through pursuing ethical means and thereby helps us become better human beings. Being moral in public domain and being really concerned about well-being of others is the difference that needs to be appreciated. Calling some young girl as daughter in public and thinking about her as your daughter is as big or as subtle a difference as the one that exists between not being violent and non-violence.

Spirituality vis-à-vis Materialism

Practically speaking, many of us are seen justifying materialism to a large extent with varying degree of conditions attached. Yes, less or more, all of us require things to survive. But the point to appreciate is the subtle difference between necessities, comforts and luxuries. No one survives on air and water alone and necessities are perfectly acceptable. Similarly, comforts available out of one's own hard earned resources accumulated by operating within moral and social norms, are also acceptable in so far as they help maintain this body, the only instrument at the disposal of our soul to enjoy this ongoing human experience. But luxuries of all kinds and at all times are destined to fail the test of spirituality. Developing this differentiation about luxuries from the other two will come very handy as we try to evaluate materialism in clear light.

Materialism is best understood as unending appetite for wealth and material goods driven by immediate thrill of acquiring something in the first place and ego-inflating thrill of owning it later. The impulse to acquire and own things is said to be natural feeling for most normal human beings. But the desire to acquire under materialism is not driven by hardships or necessities but by inner discontent. It underlies the fact that wealth is the path to permanent fulfillment. Here success of beings is measured in terms of their ability to acquire and own things in comparison to others. Materialism is justified as an evolutionary mechanism that enhances state of alertness and motivates individuals to achieve more. But studies prove that people under its spell lose the sanity of deciding how much is enough? Their restlessness and constant desire to accumulate more keep growing with every acquisition. In north India there is a famous proverb that calls it the "circle of ninety nine" that suggests that every time a person reaches to 99, he/she wishes to achieve one more to reach to next 100 and this keeps going on in never ending circle.

Materialism is known to graduate to become a problem in due course. At some stage of materialism things start controlling the man rather than man controlling things. This is a stage where a person spends more focus on objects (possessions, brands, bootlicker people, trophies included) rather than finer feelings like learning, knowing, peace, relationship and respect for fellow beings. It is a fact that materialism has immense attraction in the first look but problem arises when it starts working as distraction. 'Basic materialism necessary for survival' and 'desire for unending acquisitions' are connected in a blind fluid where normal human being invariably fails to gauge the tipping point. Lust for acquisition is like a dragon fire while access for basic minimum requires a strong insulation of contentment.

Spirituality and Materialism are known to have longest running battle over entire recorded history of human beings. It is because both these share a mutually exclusive relationship with men of all times. Their relationship is similar to day and night, hot and cold or more clearly black and white. In normal situation, desire for materialism survives and flourishes but only until spirituality remains drowned deep. Awakening of spirituality becomes possible only after complete suspension of materialism. It is a perfect either or scenario. There is no meeting ground for these concepts! So any time you come across *Babas* and *Gurus* engulfed in materialistic luxuries, you can safely conclude that they have no connection with spirituality any more.

Biologically, all our five sense organs get tired with the excessive exposure to situations where they have a field day. For example, there is limit to which your ears are ok for best of music or your eyes are ok for the best of scenery. Best of food can be had only up to maximum appetite. But our sixth sense, namely human mind, loves to remain trapped in one or the other greed at all times. Next moment of getting one thing, it fades on that and looks for going to the next. There is nothing new getting revealed here as we see it within us all the times. Theoretically, we know well that greed, egoism and attachments are all insatiable. But there is a genuine problem among most beings for not able to find the tipping point, which differentiates necessity with greed or with acquisitiveness. It happens so slowly like a 'frog in hot water syndrome' that human being is unable to take note of crossing over from necessity to acquiring for accumulation. Because of the presence of colored fluid, even after going deep into the luxuries, we continue thinking that we are still on necessities.

Proper founding in Spirituality alone helps us in seeing through that coloured fluid and help us establish a strong '*Laxman Rekha*', the perimeter line that is not to be crossed under any situation. Basically, man's basic requirements of simple living are not elaborate. Spirituality alone provides us realization that excess over minimum requirement will either remain unused or will get misused. Once a person understands this clearly, he or she will avoid being trapped in the undesirable territory of materialism by clearly seeing the tipping point. As a result, the first step towards human journey for seeking Spirituality requires giving up lust for materialism and all things attached with it. Undoubtedly, indulgence or desire for materialism is a big roadblock on the path for seeking. The real seeker must prepare itself for freeing from all fears of losing life's comforts, possessions, luxuries, social security, human relations and attachment with '*me*' and '*mine*'.

All the points highlighted above are classified as physical materialism. Similarly, and equally important, we have philosophical materialism where the captured being starts developing strong opinions, strong likes and dislikes, strong judgements and strong pretexts under external influences as if nothing else can be truer. Such people develop very stiff attitudes feeding to being in competition with every other person having divergent views. Another weakness of philosophical materialism is identification with strong symbols (in simple words, it refers to Brand consciousness) where everyone else belongs to opposite camps and worth criticism. For example, the feeling that I am from a particular religion and every other person who is not so is inferior, less intelligent, less tolerant or less secular. Youngsters promoting specific brands, supporters cheering for win by their sports team, political followers cheering their leaders, religious followers cheering for their cult leaders are all clear examples of philosophical materialism which is as undesired as physical materialism.

Yet another form of materialism is called spiritual materialism. Examples of this type are temporarily experienced during meditative state, worship routines, undertaking visits to religious places, undertaking philanthropy based activities including conducting camps for donations, arranging free meals for needy and such other getaways intended for uplifting ego by developing a false self image. In reality, all such practices are more of pleasure-seeking trips and provide experiences similar to relief from anxieties post well dosed alcohol intake. These all are temporary in nature and result in confusing our intellectual mind. Anything carried out with the intention of pleasing or praising the self-infested ego, broadly speaking, forms part of materialism and hence strongly advised to be avoided. It may not be easy but one has to see through these adventures as a part of materialism and detest from these as far as possible.

Materialism is known to have immediate younger siblings called fears and frustrations. Materialism is also rumoured to be biological father of jealousy and insecurity. We have to understand that materialism is unable to fill voids in human life. Some people who start believing that they can find a middle path of pursuing spirituality while continuing with materialistic society have to clearly realize that spirituality and materialism are irreconcilable extremes and can exist only in mutually exclusive conditions. The seekers of spirituality have to get ready to leave behind materialistic attitude, of physical, philosophical and spiritual varieties, before starting their very quest for seeking. They should look other side as some people say that spirituality is sought after by those who fail in their pursuits for materialistic world. Let such people embrace their opinion for their own good.

Spirituality vis-à-vis Sex

Some people consider sexual desire as sacred and chaste and they believe that its suppression is false and ugly. They brand it as a problem only where it gets associated with hidden emotions of shame, guilt and anger. These people relate all sexual evils like deviance, lust, violence and abuse with resistance, suppression and repression. They strongly recommend sex in playful manner with focus on expression rather than suppression. Some others applaud sexual energy as a corner stone for feeling of bliss and happiness. One also comes across some odd religious traditions, both in East and West where sex is shown as a door for quick spiritual progress. Some equate male sexual desire with matchstick that flares and exhaust quickly and female sexuality with pot of boiling water that takes time for getting hot and then take time for returning back to normal temperature. They say that clubbing of these opposite poles have large potential energy ready to be discharged and that can be channelized to enhance the feeling of bliss.

But these are all abrasions and stretch of intellectual and imaginative powers of presenting strong arguments in support of something basically wrong. If you fight the case of a criminal knowing well about his crimes, you may be a good lawyer, but never a good human. These ideas need to be rejected and dismissed by seekers of spirituality without much importance. Research after research have proven beyond doubt that even thinking about sexual activity, in any or every way, forces the subjects to become too single minded to be creative. Sexual activity, even between two people loving each other immensely, instigates erotic thoughts inhibiting their capacity to think globally and clearly. Being real people of this very world, we all know it with own experiences. So sex, with all its attractions, forms and situations, clearly is a roadblock on the path of Spirituality and has to be suspended by every potential seeker. Like materialism, there is no middle path out here.

Giving up sexual desire is not considered an exercise of self-denial. Rather it is taken as a preparation of a solid launch pad for obtaining everlasting happiness. Total abstinence from all things sensual comes without much difficulty to every serious seeker as they can see through the momentary nature of these pleasures. We shall, in due course, will be discussing steps suggested to obtain mastery over winning all physical impulses including control over wavering mind, sexual desires, other emotional tendencies such as love, liking, disliking, attachment, envy, etc.

Sex is quite natural as it forms integral part of nature's way to bring new life in this world. It is a different matter than human had acquired expertise in using it in short-circuit mode, using in excess as well as misusing nature's bounty. Nature wrapped strongest possible attraction and laced sexual activity with immense feel of pleasure as facilitation for the process of procreation. But modern day human developed contraception to suspend creation and constantly indulge in enjoying the natural gift just for fulfilling sensory pleasures. Nature implanted this mechanism for use in rare conditions but human indulges in it casually. Nature wanted people in regenerative age only using it but human came out with formulae and concoctions to prolong the use of this mechanism far longer.

Undoubtedly, adults use sex as a toy for repeatedly getting momentary pleasures. It is just like a child getting his kick by playing with toys. But even children get over with toys soon after their physical and psychological development grows. Adults however continue indulging in sex and have to wait for similar development on spiritual level before they get over their lust for sex. Some say that it is a physical need but the moment they understand that physical needs are essential for surviving human body like food and sleep, they are willing to forget about such comparison. Fascination for gratifying frequent sexual urge is not to be taken as natural considering the fact that such a drive has drain on both body and senses. No wonder that all religions of the world teach exercising control over turbulent sexual desires lest these start inflicting injuries on physical and moral health. On this count, human have a lot to learn from even wild animals who use their natural drive only for procreation.

Spirituality vis-à-vis Career or Occupation

For a *Karmayogi*, career remains a corner stone for best part of his adult life. While objectives or expectations out of career undergo changes over the career's life span, broadly speaking, most people focus on following aspirations all through their working life:

1. Work assigned, allocated or forced must remain interesting with possibility of variation so that it remains absorbing and satisfying all the time.

2. Work should help realize full individual intellectual potential and inspire to acquire new and higher knowledge and skills.
3. Organization that one works for should follow good business and ethical practices.
4. Monetary benefits and financial rewards should be equal to or better than competition.
5. The work should be useful to serve society in general and thereby bring in sense of service to humanity at large.
6. Should get opportunity to work with other good human beings in congenial and positivity charged environment of respect and regard.

Most career minded people could be seen focusing on positions, status, power, flexibility of work and time, life work balance and above all, financial rewards. Of late, newer perspectives are getting added to this wish list and these include avoiding loss of meaning in work, loss of self-esteem, avoiding conflict with personal values, craving for self-respect. It is encouraging that perspective of issues that we expect out of work today is expanding. Achieving success in one's career is one of the profound aims of life and must be well pursued with full energy and vigour. But career gets paired with materialism and needs suspension before one turns to be a seeker. As we have already seen, none of us have got energy to do full justice with career, personal life as well as demands of seeking spirituality seriously.

Employers, on the other hand, more so in traditional organizations, focus on factors impacting productivities and involvement and have not been known to worry too much for employee happiness or helping them to seek their personal fulfillments. The volatile economic conditions have forced many organizations to relook at their human development practices rather closely. Not all organizations are blessed enough to respect individual's expectation at a time when their own survival remains at stake. However, there are cases where organizations have been making research on factors influencing choices made by employees while making transitions over to other organizations. The findings, in their early stages, suggest that employees, having good market potentials, have started combining their spiritual objective fulfillment as additional factor high in priority. Also, some sensitive organizations have started taking note of this new requirement. Maybe, soon, synthesis of 'decision making' and 'meaning making' will also start having qualitative parity for those who are in position to make choices.

Spirituality, on the other hand, is the feeling an individual has about the fundamental meaning about who they are, what they are doing and what contributions they are making. To that extent, there is not much possibility of pairing career with spirituality except that one can follow the way shown by Gita. If a person is able to practise Bhagwad *Gita*'s recommended approach of "*Nishkama Karma*", there remains a perfect possibility of finding a meeting ground between career and spirituality. As per this concept, a person must discharge his obligations in a manner where there is no attachment with the result. It propagates that so long as you are doing some action, with all the right intentions and using noble means, within the ambit of your obligation and you are completely detached with the fruits of such action, you don't lose your salvation. Quest for spirituality and continuing in career, therefore, is possible provided the person concerned is mature enough to detach himself with the results of his actions and is blessed having employers who are ok with such a thing. Some combination, yeah!

Spirituality vis-à-vis Family Life

We all are real people from this very world and during our adult life our family consisting of spouse and children remains our second, if not first, important cornerstone after occupation. Adults can be seen toiling hard to ensure that their loved ones can have a good life. Most of us will always be ready to carry extra burden to ensure that our family remains safe and protected. And, in Indian context, most part of wealth that gets created is also passed on to the family through inheritance. No wonder, we wish to be role model for others and desire our family to get best possible of everything in this world.

But, have we ever seriously questioned ourselves to be judged on our performance as a proud head of the family? Before we discuss family's relation with Spirituality, let us sketch out the actual role model that the family head can get compared with. Even if it may be a little bit of diversions from our main focus, the overriding importance of this role in our lives makes it worth a topic for some of our time and attention. Let us first list out important qualities that make someone a successful family head. All these points are being listed at random and their serial number does not indicate relative importance, which can vary from family to family, depending on specific situations:

1. *Be a Genuine Person* – The Head of the family must be a real and genuine person in all interactions with the family – a real person is not trying to look good under all situations, he is willing to appear vulnerable if situation so desires. This is real life and not stage; you can't be wearing role of a character. If you try to be anything more or less than genuine, there will be difficulty in establishing heart to heart connection with family members. No human being is expected to be always perfect nor can you be at your best at all times. Family connects with the real man and not the ideal man; ideals look good but only in external settings.
2. *Very strong communication skills* – Within the family, or even outside the family, the most important aspect of communication skill is ability to listen everything spoken, indicated and subtle. Communication also demands picking up of feelings expressed without words for fear or regard or social customs. Family thrives on feelings; feelings are to be perceived and reciprocated. Ability to express your thoughts and feelings is an art and like all arts, requires lot of practice before getting perfected. There are no born communicators; every person has to work hard to gain perfection. While outside world goes after more on your words, your family goes more what you do rather than say. You get watched inside your house more than you want to believe.
3. *Ability to forgive and forget* – Family members deal with each other without guards on and it better be like that. There are occasions where a member puts her foot in mouth. Let it go. At the end of the day we are all human. Your ability to forget and forgive each other for words spoken, angers off

loaded and outbursts poured makes you family. You may not realize how important is to practise this for developing affection and mutual inter-dependence.

4. *Playing the game with three Aces* – This point is more applicable for parents and grandparents having children in impressionable age groups. Psychologists recommend parents to hold three aces to boost confidence of the young ones. The first ace is 'acceptance', simple unconditional acceptance of how the child is; small, big, good, bad, ugly, intelligent, silent, blatant, outgoing, reclusive, naughty, sporty or whatever. The child is yours and must be accepted with full heart. It does not matter what your child got or not. What really matters is what we do with what we got? One better remember the game of chess where, with proper moves, a pawn also gets upgraded to become queen.

   Second ace is 'appreciation'. Children look forward to their parents for a lot of encouragement. Your appreciation for all their baby steps works like seeds capable of germinating into becoming strong and confident persons in their life. Appreciation leads them to believe in their own actions, views and thoughts. It works wonders as against need for guiding on every step. You have a choice to let them feel respected. Seeking your guidance should be their choice rather than your obligation. It may appear hard to apply this principle when it comes to our own children but this is the key.

   Third and last ace is 'affection'. The real and genuine affection gets across and gets visible very clearly. Parental warmth expressed through genuine hugs, hand-holding and gentle caressing boosts their positivity more than anything else. You may wonder about the ability of the child to sense genuine affection from a distance. This affection is what helps them grow stronger; it is their real support structure. It does wonders towards their psychological and behavioural issues. Lack of it, on the other hand, is often seen in terms of alienation, hostile behaviour, aggressive stances and lower self-esteem.

   Like a game of cards, any one holding one or two aces has his chances to win the hand but the one who holds three at a time is a sure shot winner. Real life is no different.

5. *Let go the blame game* – As head of the family, you must be man enough to own the situation without blaming any one for it. It is not correct to be looking at you versus them. Passing the buck doesn't help in the family. Some of us assume the role of judge simply by our position of the breadwinner. No, your family is not your courtroom where you are self-appointed judge. Don't worry about chaos but it is better to accept the unruly, election based, multi-party, parliamentary system of democracy than the well-mannered, well-educated, well-represented and well-decorated court of a dictator. It requires guts to accept your children as equal but that is the real family and everybody must be motivated to make opinions on subjects of importance. Every family member must also be involved and be persuaded to vote on all important issues of the family.
6. *Never to take things personally* – This ability requires a well-acquired and nurtured skill of having ability to understand standpoint of others from a perfectly neutral position. This skill is simple to apply in work situations but its effectiveness in family settings is more critical. One is expected to be completely detached and that is not simple. As head of the family, you are expected to don hats of a strict coach, a caring therapist and a professional counsellor. It is not hard to assume that these roles work well when you develop the ability to look at your own flesh and blood as totally separate from you. This is one situation where many Indian parents of my generation are not known to score too high.
7. *Aligning Values* –We have to agree that value system of most children take shape influenced by family environment. Especially in Indian context, family is a very dominant institution where nuclear family structure is now the norm for most urban India. An important responsibility of the head of the family is to pass on all those values to the next generations which were, in olden times, passed by grandparents and other elders in a joint family set up. Respect for elders, gender equality, sharing of common pool, mutual support and assistance to each other, independence in thoughts, actions and behaviour are all examples of values

which need to be inculcated among children. These are important issues and leaving it to destiny is like washing your hands off.

You are expected to spend your efforts and energy in helping your spouse and children to build on their abilities. For sure, systematic work on their abilities will get converted to proficiency sooner or later. If they are good at scribbling, you help them to learn writing. If they are good at sketches, motivate them to draw and paint. If they are good at singing, make them learn classical music. If they like exercises, you help them convert their routine to wellness program. Beyond a level, you may like to get service of a trained coach to help them achieve best of what they are good at. Capacity is the ability to do more while capability is the ability to do better; as head of the family, you have an obligation to help your family expand on their capacity as well as capability.

8. *Differentiate between Love and Pampering* – These two are very different traits; one weakens while other helps in growth. Giving tolerance the name of acceptance will leave you with ignoring imperfections of your loved ones. Pampering lets us feel ok what is not ok. Real love must work as a mirror that reflects the image without any addition or deletion. In another example, pampering children is compared to a drinking session that gives a joyful evening followed by a hangover. By being bitter in the beginning but curing later, the real love for your family members, on the other hand, works like a medication. Parents who ignore this simple principle ought to be seen playing role of an enemy of their child rather than a well wisher.
9. *Managing conflicting situations* – No point in ignoring the fact that people within family are likely to have conflicting point of views. To begin with, we must look at it as healthy situation. Only people having opinions can differ from each other and we don't want our family members to be dumb. The role of the head becomes more critical as he/she is in both as a member and as a referee. The respectful discharge of this responsibility hinges on the quality of being honest, being impartial, and ability to take responsibility as a

communicator and impersonal judge. It is easier said than done.

(*Some of the points highlighted above are encouraged by an article of Ms Lorraine Cohen, CEO and Founder of "Powerful Living" published at* www.thebridgemaker.*com dated 23rd November 2009*)

We will realize that all the points listed above require investment of a lot of our time. When inquiring about their time spent with the family, most parents will instantly respond in a big affirmation. But when grilled in detail, all they come up with will be about time spent for eating out, visiting multiplexes, enjoying TV programs together, going on picnic or having vacations together. Wait a second, these activities are all entertainment or relaxation oriented and they have their limited impacts but these will not help extend the required caring, nurturing and strengthening which is so expected from elders. You have to spend time together for attending to household chores, religious services, outdoor sports, learning new craft, learning new language, playing intelligence testing games, discussing current affairs, discussing socio-political problems and solutions, etc. where focus is not on entertainment but on issues, thoughts, ideas, society and learning.

The idea behind listing qualities required in a successful head of the modern nuclear family is to help us identify areas where Spirituality supports or obstructs qualities. In any case, the picture that emerges about a parent is an individual expert in multi-tasking. He/she has to function from being a cook to teacher to driver; from nurse to housekeeper, mediating arguments as well as fights, repeating instructions *ad infinitum.* He/she sounds a very busy person with no vacations and working hours spanning 24/7. As against this, the image of a spiritual soul is about someone sitting quietly, meditating, centered in the midst of chaos, having few words full of wisdom, busy reading scriptures and philosophies. What a contrast? No wonder that parenting and spirituality are never discussed together. But let us go a bit deeper and we will see that spiritual orientation teaches us about focused discharge of all our parental obligations, helps us connect with other human beings on an equal parity and helps us develop detached perspective.

Therefore, a parent or grandparent having attained his/her own spiritual awakening would want children to seek success in place of materialism, will wish them to grow, learn and expand their individual horizon. The parent is expected to impart clear instruction and set consistent rules that will set well-defined boundaries for children so that they feel safe. Such a parent will be honest and open about their emotions that will provide children a clear understanding of the working of this world. He/she would talk and listen and will have children participate in decision-making giving them self-confidence and having their own opinion.

Is there a need of comparing the scoring of a spiritual parent with another who may be authoritarian, indulgent or uninvolved? Undoubtedly, a spirituality oriented householder is expected to discharge his duties better than his other counterparts who remain focused on matters relating to 'I', 'me' and 'mine'. Hence spirituality is a strong thing to pursue with all sincerity for all those doting parents out there as well.

Spirituality vis-à-vis Physical Health

Until few decades back, the answer to the relation between Spirituality and physical health would have been a straight no. These two were two worlds seemingly held poles apart from each other where one referred to material elemental composition called body while the other belonged to unseen, immortal and immaterial part called soul. People strongly felt that physical health was a subject matter under one's own control while spirituality was a pious virtue, which can be bestowed only with the blessings of supreme power, something more like a wishful thinking. But all such views have increasingly seen erosion on both sides of the lines holding them apart.

Direct advice for taking care of physical health starts from early life. Minimizing all types of tortures on body, protecting one's organism to slow ageing process, cutting down on emotional tensions by leading a disciplined life, protecting heart from tearing down, etc., are advices that most adults get from elders and other well-wishers all the time. But what force will help a common person to adhere to such effective advice in the first place? Why is that most people know about these advices but very few opt for practising them? That is where Spirituality steps in by infusing unwavering sense of purpose for responsible living. Spirituality allows a person to relate to making meaning about whatever happens to them. In addition, it works on enhancing positive features of persistence, acceptance, self-motivation and internal empowerment. Similarly, Spirituality also impact how people deal with their joys and sufferings. Spirituality makes people less prone to self-destructing behaviours like drugs or alcohol abuse on one side or extreme tendencies of committing self-inflicting injuries on the other side. No wonder that research after research are now establishing better health index among people involved in spiritual pursuits. It is not to suggest that only spiritual people are healthy people but Spirituality leaves profound impacts on mental state of its seekers and that in turn, enhances coping up skills. This is precisely why post medical intervention recoveries are faster among spiritually inclined people.

Researchers also established that spiritually inclined people are found having thicker cortex which result in providing additional protection against depressions — one of the most dreaded diseases of our times that is working as a silent killer. Even emotionally, spiritually active people are found far off from the roller coaster rides experienced by less spiritual folks. Spirituality also enables you to have courage of letting things go and encourages for opting for responsible lifestyle. Besides all above impacts on physical, mental and emotional levels, Spirituality works on increasing your love for life among all settings, which has unseen but undeniably strong correlation with positive all-round health and general well-being. So if you think that you are very health conscious but not so much spiritually inclined, you have strong reasons to pursue your spiritual pursuits just to significantly improve your health index even further.

Spirituality vis-à-vis Pains and Pleasures

Pains and Pleasures are two sides of the same coin and have an important place in human life. There is no denying the fact that human beings are auto conditioned to crave for pleasures and avoid pains from their life as well surroundings. Hence, going over the deep understanding of pleasures and looking at the link between pleasure and Spirituality will be of real use for establishing clarity about what should we go after and why.

Pleasure may be understood as a unique concoction of several likable human feelings like happiness, satisfaction, enjoyment and gratification. Its feel good factor is worth seeking and hard to resist. But pain is the flip side of pleasure, always there on the other side where human eye is not able to see it in the first look. The moment one withdraws from pleasure, bouts of pain crop up without notice. Going little technically, pleasure's feedback mechanism motivates the organism of human body to recreate the situation again and again and remain in that situation as long as possible. It is precisely because of this system that some weak individuals don't mind even use of recreational drugs to get the same euphoria. However, induced spells of pleasure shall always be visited by bouts of pains in almost equal proportions without fail. Well, it is a nature's law that is far beyond any remedy to the contrary. It is like a swing; if you want it come back fast, it must go to the other extreme with similar force without exceptions.

To understand pleasures in greater details, we can divide them into two. On the one hand, biological (like eating, hygiene, sleep), social (like accomplishment, recognition) or relating to cultural matters (like arts, music, dance, and literature) and on the other hand, pleasure can also be classified under 'sensuous' and 'intellectual'. The sensuous pleasures are those enjoyed by five sensory organs (mouth, eyes, nose, ears, hands) covering feelings of taste, sighting, smell, listening and touch. While the intellectual pleasures of learning and gaining knowledge is solely experienced by our mind. Sex, under this classification, incidentally, falls under intellectual category rather than biological.

Most of us are well aware of only sensuous pleasures, as these are so natural to our priority of survival. Just imagine world of million years in past where finding good food and fulfilling appetite was prime occupation and extremely crucial to human survival; where sexual drive was so essential for procreation; where sighting objects led the primordial human to fend itself from dangerous enemies; and presence of sounds coming from distance indicated presence of other birds and animals indicating existence of a habitable cluster. It is over these millions of years of evolutionary process that those survival instincts got upgraded to pleasures, as human mind has still not forgotten importance of all those cravings and still welcomes them to this day.

But one of the most satisfying pleasure and one that endures its joy to human being is the pleasure of learning, also called 'conscious pleasure'. This pleasure gives rise to imaginative mood that activates the to connect the earlier stored pleasures in our memory, recreate series of memories and impressions and generate currents of sensations to provide newly created pleasures. Knowledge can be called as mother of all conscious pleasures as all the virtues involved in pleasure seeking are conceived and flourished in the courtyard of knowledge. Surely, this pleasure is slow to come by but it is known to stay longer and is capable of getting recreated enumerable number of times. Incidentally, physical pleasures suffer from dependency over external support at all times. So we can say that knowledgeable people have better chances of enjoying pleasures. Not only that, intellectual pleasure is also called the Superior as it is longer lasting and easily repeatable and is not known to have side effects unlike sensuous pleasures.

Finally, Spirituality drives its seekers to access the real source of the conscious pleasure. A man with wisdom will, of its own, develop his/her defence against the temptations of lower stage negative pleasures of the sensory organs. Spirituality divides pleasures into 'agreeable' and 'non-agreeable' and expects them to be treated accordingly. Strong mental state of Spiritual person aims for joy of connecting with his real Self where there are no seeking based on gratifications or temptations; where intellectual thoughts control the mind space; where the mind is connected with genuine Peace and Tranquility and not even looking for instant happiness. The relation of Spirituality is best described in the following saying:

> "Man is created to solely delight in Supreme and enjoy the radiance of His presence and ultimately be one with Him. Everything else in this world exists to bring us to that moment."

Spirituality vis-à-vis Sciences

Science is completely compatible with spirituality in more ways than one. In fact, more and more people are finding these two separate streams complimenting each other. Their coming together is said to result in a whole that is bigger than their combined sum. Science studies physical and natural world through observations and experiments in exactly similar manner of spirituality where internal world of the human is accessed with subjective experiences or consciousness. One aspect of Spirituality is where practitioner makes use of methods that include sitting in solitude in perfect silence and immersing within own psychic following meditation or contemplation. Every scientist also does roughly the same for pursuing most part of his inventions and innovations.

> "Politics and religion are obsolete. The time has come for science and spirituality." — *Vinoba Bhave*

Work on any scientific investigations begins with an idea based on the explorer's intuition about what to look and where, and all his further experimentations are directed towards that idea accordingly. The use of intuition and creativity for furthering spiritual explorations also takes exactly similar route. As a result, the uncertainties and chances of success in both science and spirituality are also similar. Scientific experimentations are carried out in physical laboratories fitted with different kind of equipment. Though the intensity, concentration and efforts required for monitoring results of such experiments are similar for science and spirituality, human mind and consciousness is the sole laboratory and equipment required for carrying out all sorts of spiritual explorations.

In a way science operates below the spiritual dimensions as until now there is no scientific discovery that proves anything substantially in variation of already known aspects of spiritual understanding. Another difference between the two can be that science deals with external visible world and can be documented and communicated through language and documents while spirituality deals with internal world of the human consciousness, which can neither be consigned to words or formulas and must be accessed only and only by seeker's own experiences and initiatives.

Quoting Mr. Max Karl Ernst Ludwig Planck, the German theoretical physicist, the originator of famous quantum theory, which won him the Noble Prize for Physics in 1918, can provide the best example of the relation between spirituality and science and he said:

> "Science can't solve the ultimate mystery of nature. And that is because, in the last analysis, we ourselves are part of nature and therefore part of mystery that we are trying to solve."

Spirituality vis-à-vis Self-improvement

It is mandatory for good human beings to improve and improvise at all times. Many of us, accordingly, do remain engaged in self-improvement or self-development efforts. It may be a good idea to see if such efforts are compatible with our quest for finding Spirituality and if yes, to what extent. Basically, self-development covers efforts for improving status, position, education, skills *etcetera* by one's own efforts. These measures include efforts on economic, intellectual and emotional levels and focus on self-wellness, relationships as well as improved skills.

Spirituality helps us in realigning our sense of self that we had not imagined to have before. It helps us realize that we are greater and more powerful than we ever felt before. By helping us reach to higher level of consciousness, our Spiritual quests push us up in a state where we get connected with God, Nature, with other beings, and deepest part of ourselves. Spiritual energy, therefore, works wonders as a source of inspiration to always look for more and better. There is good saying credited to Ernest Hemingway, on the subject that goes as under:

> "There is nothing noble in being superior to your fellow man;
> True Nobility is being superior to your former self"

Spirituality vis-à-vis Popular Yoga

Before going any further, it is better to understand that what we discuss here in this section is about 'Yogic Asanas', the yogic exercises based system. Now, the Yoga of Asanas is but a small part of *Ashtang Yoga*, an entire philosophy based system credited to Maharishi Patanjali that will be taken up with its entire arch due to its deep connect with Spirituality. However, in its limited context, we shall call Yogic exercises based Yoga as 'Popular Yoga'.

The Popular Yoga as practised across the globe is a system helping the practitioner finding a healthy balance between body and mind. Their regular practice helps well-being and re-energizing of various physical systems and mental systems. The advantages of these Asanas are linked with difficulty involved in postures attempted and frequency followed by the practitioners. It also goes to work on improving general attitude of the practitioner towards positivity and creativity and enhances energy flow for more focused and enriched living. Yoga, at this level, is completely non-religious and helps every practitioner similar to routines at the gym except that it has better contribution on mental health alike physical.

But Yoga of the Asanas has only indirect and passive advantages for working on constructive war on thoughts raged by normal life biases, superstitions, fantasies, memories and frustrations. Similarly, it has only partial and indirect impact on controlling and curbing normal human emotions of anger, jealousy, grief, fear, guilt and anxiety. Against Asanas, Pranayam, the system of breath regulating sequences, do wonders on balancing human mind against its constant oscillations from one worry, pain and conflict to another. Pranayam delivers much better results for a conflicting mind that needs to be brought to focus by letting it concentrate on seeking clarity.

Popular Yoga surely works as a cleansing agent for both body and mind and, to that extent it surely steps into the territory of Spirituality. What needs to be remembered is that Yoga is practised both on and off the Yoga mat. Yoga starts with compliance of specific sets of dos and don'ts. Physical and ethical purity that is a must for continuous guidance to the practitioner all through his normal life, rides only on the strength of strict compliance of these dos and don'ts. In the absence these, the yoga session will get reduced to just another visit to a different type of physical training regime. No wonder, we come across some friends complaining that "no advantage" is seen by them even after going through sessions after sessions of Yoga.

Ethical preparation under Yoga is termed as advance preparation for a long and arduous spiritual journey. In addition, specific Yogic routines help cultivating awareness and consciousness, which once taken to deeper and subtle dimensions of the being, help in practising spirituality. Spirituality deeply influences the entire thought process as it focuses on the inner world of the practitioner. It makes the person aware about his consciousness and its relation with others and the universe at large. That realization works on the super psychological level and thereby has transformational impact by suppressing all thoughts and emotions other than peace, happiness and tranquility. While it may not have direct physical advantages as compared to Yogic exercises but the balancing achieved by Spirituality works on enhancing wisdom, regulating life pattern, tendencies, opting for regulated dietary preferences and encouraging stress-free living. These benefits indirectly culminate into very positive influence on human body as well.

Yogic exercises and Spirituality, both, work in positive direction and complement each other rather perfectly. Due to their positive direction approach and similar looking objectives, both facilitate their practitioner to incline towards each other without any rivalry, confrontation or mutual exclusion.

Conclusions from Comparisons

Having gone over some of the daily life concepts and putting spirituality next to them must have taken away at least one notion out of reader's way that spirituality does not require abandoning everything. On the other hand, it works as a great facilitator for living the normal life in a fulfilling way and can actually be used to raise the quality of our life several notches up. No, spirituality is not only for old and tired who have nothing else to do; it is very much for hale and hearty adults who have miles to go before hanging their boots. They can operate on lower levels during their working period, reap its benefits in living better life as a householder and prepare a solid launch pad for taking the big leap forward when they get ready for escalated stage in life. This will enable them to have the best in both phases of life.

Interpreting Signs of Spiritual Awakening

At this stage of our journey, there are reasons for us to quickly look around for such signs in our own life. This looking around is going to be grounded in personal perceptions picked up after filtering out the chattering of normal life. After all, spiritual possession is not like spirit possession shown by the movies. Neither one is supposed to get some particular kind of tingling, itching, pricking or crawling sensations to identify with spiritual awakening. It is just a matter of subtle realization without any visible signs. In addition, unlike physical maturity that grows with age, spiritual maturity is not guaranteed at all. It is not like graying of hairs that eventually is bound to happen. On the other hand, each one of us living beings on this earth is spiritual to some extent; we may know it or be completely unaware about it. All these factors make it quite interesting to really know about if and how much spiritual we are?

One may also come across books and lectures linking spiritual awakening to opening of *Kundalini Chakras.* People talk about continued practice of prescribed methods leading to activation of one after the other *Chakras.* It is said that each person has got a total of seven *Chakras* where first four are based in lower body and remaining three in the neck portion and above. Explanations about *Chakras* and *Kundalini* involve discussions about unseen and unknown psychological energy fields in different parts of human body. May be some day, Science is able to penetrate into the mystery of the presence of aura fields and prove existence of chakras but until such time, it is safe to take it as imaginative theory worth putting aside. It may certainly be an interesting discussion for many but not for those who believe in this real world, real lives with real issues and still look forward to finding their ultimate purpose. Hence, one needs to have a clear idea about sure signs for their own spiritual awakening.

So returning back to our discussions, we better remain focused only on real and visible indications alone. The points mentioned below pertain to those clear, unambiguous and directly experienced indications which are easy to spot and difficult to ignore. These signs get invoked with the very emergence of spiritual orientation of a normal '*Karma Yogi*' even before he graduates to be a seeker. Please note that sequencing of the points is not important and neither is relativity; just compare your own signs with those mentioned below and arrive at right conclusion about your own status of Spiritual inclination:

- There is recurring yearning for searching meaning and purpose of this life as you no more feel contended to keep running the normal routine involving pains and pleasures, family and friends and material acquisitions in an endless manner.
- You wish to give more than you desire to take from others. Earlier, your obvious response to every proposal was to search 'how do I get benefit out of it?' Now that has changed to 'how can I contribute to the given situation and how can I be a partner to solutions rather than problems'.
- You have stopped feeling like a victim all the time. In your earlier avatar, the feeling was that the worldly forces are combining to join hands to obstruct your destiny and play a spoilsport. But now you feel that your destiny is self designed and you don't see any evil design propagated by others for both negative and positive happenings in your life. You have stopped seeing foreign hand behind everything taking place in your life.
- You no more ride those violent waves of emotional roller coaster that you have been experiencing not so long in the past. The emotions are there but their waves are smooth and curves are softer. No more you lose temper at the drop of the hat. Your level of acceptance of others has seen significant rise.
- Intensities and cravings for both pleasures and pains are much reduced in comparison to earlier times. You no more

oscillate between ecstatic and doom. For happy and not so happy events alike you now operate more on a neutral state such that nothing gives you extreme end of pains and pleasures.

- Making money, managing it or multiplying the same is now more of a headache. Now you sincerely wish to stay away from such options. Surprisingly, the chasing similar situations used to be a passion for you until recently. Now you are happy delegating all financial affairs to others in the vicinity.
- You are no more absorbed in judging others for their words, ideas and actions. Now you are much more ready to accept their deeds without feeling impacted.
- You have developed the ability to perceive things from others' perspective and find their actions and moves much more justifiable and amenable. Others seem to have lost the edge to irritate you unlike before.
- You have stopped searching freedom and happiness tied to external objects and sources. You have full understanding that the real source of joy lies well within each of us and it is ready to be exploited with little efforts. The glitter of objects does not attract you anymore.
- You have increasingly started observing voluntary periods of your silence. Spending time in solitude is found very attractive and peace enhancing. Actually, solitude is your preferred way of enjoying your time. Newspapers, TV or Mobile phones are seen as waste of time worth minimizing to the least.
- Your search of truth now does not lie in seeking strong arguments or undeniable examples but in assimilation of actual TRUTH coming from within. You are open for accepting the new findings without any judging.
- Earlier you strongly believed that truth is only one and you were confident that you knew it better than others. Now you realize that truth can be more than one and you are ok with various versions like my truth, his truth, her truth and truth of others. More importantly you are at peace with all truths being equally right and justified.
- It is not so much difficult now to let go attachments including very close relationships. Things and people do not appear

as important in life as they used to be earlier. Now there is nothing worth ending your life for.

- It does not matter to you even if others in relationship are happy or unhappy about your changed behaviour towards them; the view now is 'if it is so, it is ok, let it be'.
- You feel happier now. Your dreams are no more as scary as these used to be. The fears have stopped bothering. 'What if' scenarios do not occupy mind space as much as in recent past. Investing in insurance policies for life, accident, burglary or even medical does not appear essential any more.
- You have shed away the fear of death almost completely. Now you feel ready for any situation without strong likings, disliking or preferences.
- You have developed more confident views about your needs and necessities. They are no more insatiable. Actually, needs are getting reduced slowly. The urge to own something new and exciting is a thing of past.
- Absence of luxuries in life no more baffles you. Rather you wish to give up all unwanted luxuries and comforts of material world for physical body in a voluntary manner.
- You have stopped measuring or comparing your lifestyle with others; you are perfectly at ease with your own lifestyle. There is no desire to make a show or prove any point, to justify to anyone or to adhere to standards set by traditions or peers or who so ever.
- You have been able to regularly maintain healthy routine involving your walks, gym exercises, meditation sessions, pranayam and yoga sessions with consistency. You no more looking for lame excuses to drop these things for some other pressing requirement like before.
- Your list of books to read and places desired to visit has all undergone big qualitative changes. You are no more looking for thrills and titillations. Fictions are a thing of past. On the whole your expectation from all these sources is to acquire new knowledge rather than erotic or sensual stimulation.
- Your ability to ignore actions of others has gone up. Someone honking or jumping the lane no more disturbs you as much. Similarly, someone in a public place speaking loudly into his mobile phone does not upset you as much.

- You are observing newfound humility. There is no more desire to boast before anyone about anything small or big neither there is a desire to take credit of something done by you.
- There is a new found affinity with all other human beings coming in contact with you. Your responses and reactions to others are no more based on their position or status but more on being human. Your respect for your milkman and your rich neighbour is roughly same.
- You are mesmerized with the very existence of this world and find your own little space as insignificant.

Please take a big moment and try to find out your own identification with some of the statements above. If you are able to relate even with five to seven points out of the long list mentioned above, it is quite likely that your spiritual awakening has touched you already. But these are just murmurs and need to be taken only as early symptoms and act like a feeble knock on your door. Real awakening is a very tedious process and demands lot of dedication and hard work on the way. No one is expected to awaken his spirituality just by chance or simply by wishing. As the process unfolds in due course, you will be called upon to be ready for a big preparation as if you are to proceed on a long journey into an unknown destination.

All these are just a few examples and surely, you may have signs having different intensities. You have to keep your antenna in readiness to check signals that may still be weak and subtle to begin with. Idea is to leave aside philosophical or meta-physical doctrines and abstract sounding dogmas and focus on clear indications of changes that may be occurring in your normal day-to-day life to help you realize that something different is happening to you now as compared to your recent past. We better take note of these changes and solidify our efforts to initiate our spiritual journey so as to take it to its logical destination.

The Need for Seeking being the Real Call of the Day

The required solution for facing the crude reality of this present world is not so much about "*practising spirituality*" but "*seeking*

Spirituality'. Seeking spirituality itself is the most important factor to start the process of unlearning about conditionality and learning right. Without feeling deeply with a sense with intensity and urgency, you don't expect anyone to make real serious efforts of unlearning old teachings, shredding unconscious learning, acquiring right learning and then reinforce it with regular practice. The 'intense need' is the missing component today. So long as one remains ignorant and lives under the illusion that everything is running fine, intensity of this desire remain suppressed under the overburden of what we call modern living.

As seen earlier, one effective way to be a seeker was to respond one's internal call of spiritual pull. But if one is not touched as yet by his own spirituality or if the pull pressure is not very strong, one may even try to develop the spiritual desire through evolution of one's own inner consciousness. Aim should be to elevate our self to the level of being a seeker using pulls or pressures, whatever works for the individual concerned. With due progress achieved on way to honest seeking, personal transformations can't be left behind. Honest spiritual seekers are expected to transcend far beyond institutionalized, conventional and traditional ideals of thé modern world. This transcending inevitably works as a strong mooring to help you remain grounded even during the worst of storms of attractions and attachments. Our yearning to reach to our fulfilling truth shall soon transform into being our pillar of strength. Our truth alone has the ability to be our compass capable of guiding us through to the right direction even under severe storm conditions.

Caution

At this stage, there is a need for a quick stocktaking. Because of any reason, it is possible that you as a person have not yet felt the knocking of your own conscience asking you to explore purpose of human life. It is quite possible as well that the yearning for something important missing from your life has not started hitting you hard. If it is so, I wish to place my suggestion in a candid manner that further reading of this book is not likely to provide you complete benefit. In such a situation you may like to think about using your bookmark at this stage. Whenever you listen to internal thumping or knocking and if that happens at all, you may like to return back later for resuming your journey from this stage onward.

From now on, this book is expected to be more of a practising together. Practice will be feasible only after you have been able to clear all your initial doubts and you are sure about your commitment and dedication to follow the way come what may. Reading only for academic interest may provide you a feel similar to someone making an aerial survey of the trekking route to the peak. Alas, he can't have much clue about insurmountable difficulties as well as wow moments awaiting en route the actual climb to the peak. Please make your choice and move accordingly.

Part III

Spiritual Evolution and Practice

Stages of Pre-Spiritual Evolution

Having identified positive presence of spirituality awakening signs, the next item on agenda is to locate our current position on this beautiful journey. Like for every other normal long journey, we are required to track our position with respect to topography of the path, familiarization with major halts and knowledge about important milestones across our journey. The process for knowing the location of spiritual journey is not much different except that the milestones here are embedded in a new language which needs to be learned in advance. Soon after getting idea about the location, a positively inclined spiritual person would like to know about steps required to pursue the path of further seeking. It is just like preparing for any big journey having decided the desired destination.

Preparations are required about the items to pack and deal with items to be left behind, climatic conditions en route, physical requirements on the entire journey, knowledge about likely stoppages on the way *etcetera.* Detailed preparations are essential to avoid expected problems and hardships. The preparations will ensure that journey get progressed comfortably by avoiding all potential hiccups. Thinking will also be required to travel alone or with spouse, how to spend time while in journey, how to make arrangement for family and other people in life thus far. Actually, this will be more than journey as you are likely to make your destination as your permanent base. It is more like relocating to an unknown new town about which you hardly know much. Such a big life transforming change can never be taken lightly.

Considering all this, it is perfectly desirable to glance over a prospective roadmap. Interested seeker will also get opportunity to better ponder over likely stages to be crossed on way up their search for spirituality. From this point onward, intellectual understanding need supplementation from actual practice in developing complete perception of the concepts and methods. Your actual experience of spiritual practices alone is likely to help you realize the true substance and significance of my personal experience being shared. Individual's own practice will become primary key for appreciating and absorbing the true meaning of words, techniques and doctrines unfolding on the way. Reading will only teach you 'why' part of the landscape. Yes, understanding why part is very important for a perfect beginning but practice alone will help you acquire specific techniques and convert them to become your useful tools for use thereafter to deal with 'how' part of the climb.

See, there are no readymade tools available here. Neither there is set formula that different people approaching the solution of the given equation will get to same answer. You have to try various techniques where some may work and many others may not; some may work more while others may work less. Some of these may work initially and will require changes as you progress along. It is only with practice that you will adopt and improvise what works and discard what doesn't. For example, there are innumerable ways of attaining a meditative stage. Simply learning about meditation by reading alone can't take you anywhere. Each practitioner has to try different ways for reaching to their desired state. What works for A may or may not work for B. Each person has to try out every known technique before settling down what works well. Techniques that work get repeated while those don't work get dispensed with. Some methods prove good in the beginning but stop giving results later. Those who have experienced sitting for meditation will understand what is being discussed. So practice alone takes care of 'how' part of the process. Theory will teach you from the experiences of others but it is practice that allows those experiences to become your own.

Receiving experiences from other is just like receiving raw information. What we are able to preserve out of all information becomes our knowledge. Going over the same chain, what we are able to use later is intelligence and finally, what, where and how much we use it is determined by our wisdom. When we preserve and practise, we are able to gain knowledge and start identifying with it. Practice and wisdom combined enable us to appreciate and absorb true spirit. To be good at something, be it a sport or music or any other performing art, you must practise alongside learning by reading. It is so easy to fall in the trap of learning alone that one becomes paper tiger with no idea of how to bite when the need arises. This reminds me of an interesting line that:

> "In theory there is no difference between practice and theory. But in practice there is big difference."

Our entire journey of exploring purpose of our own life is going to be more like "*Sadhana*" where meanings of several words like learning, practice, exercise, accomplish all get combined into one besides worship of one's chosen God. The God here is our very own "Purpose of Life". So please remember that spirituality demands one's total dedication as a true *"Sadhak"*, worshipper and not as a *"Vidyarthi"*, student alone.

Returning back to stages on way to our destination, attempt here is to identify major stages likely to be crossed. Milestones of the following stages will allow you to undergo a sort of 'Self Assessment Test' also to determine which level you may join in the new institution having a different curriculum than what you have been studying so far. You should also be cautious about likely pitfalls or detours to remain on course. A deep understanding of these stages will also help you measure the pace of your individual progress once your journey is already underway. The details provided under each stage are intended to expose you to big picture so as to provide a feel of things likely to happen. If required, these will also provide you opportunity to apply mid-course corrections.

The identification of these stages is based on personal journey and may please be taken just like an example. It is a sort of recollection of developments experienced in my own journey over last ten years before starting work on the very experience-sharing project, this book in your hands. But we are all different individuals blessed with our own specific cast and mold. Surely, there can't be a 'fit to all' approach. One's own journey is unique due to individual orientation, age, situation, genes, emotional quotient, financial independence, mental make-up, cultural exposure, social background, level of intensity, passion for pursuing and what not. Even when the desired destination of all seekers is climbing the same high peak but the choice and ability to make one's own hiking trail has to be individual choice. Another seeker travelling ahead of us, at best, can share about his trail but such trails on way to seeking spirituality get erased and are not there for others. Here, each seeker has to make new trail.

Each seeker is invited to sharpen his own gauges, find his own location and chart out his own likely route. Efforts are also intended to let you have a broader view of the physical geography of the terrain.

Stage 1
Pre Contemplation

It all starts with intermittent feeling of something important missing in life. You have a well-settled family, sufficient financial resources and creditable achievements in career/occupations but there is a recurring deep sense of void. A vague kind of anxiety about 'what next' or 'is it all' keeps occurring in your thoughts like an irritating thumping. You wish to check about this hissing sound in detail before it grows any further in intensity and frequency. The urge doesn't sound very pressing or urgent but it touches you often nonetheless. Whenever you are alone and wish to have some quality time for your own sake, the depressing feeling of emptiness gets accentuated. It is not that you are losing it completely but your sleep experiences disturbances as if your search for 'what is missing' is getting louder by the day. There is a definite discomfort and mental confusions over main purpose of life and about direction of personal life.

This is something unique and you have not been able to identify it or give it any specific name. You have no clue how to get rid of it or go deep into it. You are not aware of cost and benefits involved in this search. Gush of energy is missing and you don't wish to jump in leaving everything behind. But subconsciously you wish to go after chasing this recurrent thinking and to get acquainted with its very source. You just got a feeble inkling that chasing this search must have sizable potential benefits.

This feeling can set in at any stage of your life. Speaking generally, such knocking is reported to be profound between fifty to fifty five years of mental age. Traditionally it is the same time when you were advised to come out of *Grihastha* stage and move over to *Vanprashtha* stage of life.

Stage 2
Serious Contemplation

You have been touched by your search of finding ultimate purpose of life. You are not yet ready to make a big plunge but you do desire to take some concrete actions towards exploring the issues disturbing you from time to time. You are open for receiving increasingly more information about it so as to look into it deeply. You are also willing to talk to anyone who sounds experienced expecting that some light gets thrown on this scenario. But talks are still more in your mind than in public space. You have just started checking with others and slowly your own courage to commit to the process is on the rise. You are experiencing a new found perception of a greater whole, something that was not bothering you earlier. Exploring more and more about this makes better sense to you and your yearning for giving up of existing materialistic routine is increasing. There is an increasing sense of urgency to explore these issues.

You dare not give up everything but you also are unable to envision yourself in life filled with repetitive boring routine that are called by different names but really means 'money making'. These are like thoughts of early retirement flashing through your mind. There is a sense of excitement and challenge. You are getting impatient to change gears in your life. Your preference for your reading material has changed from fiction to factual and from titillating to scintillating. You no more wish to waste time for entertainment or for sense gratifications. Weekly movies or TV programs interest you no more. Your lust for accumulating bank balance or properties seems satiated. The loss of losing social status or position of dominance makes no difference to you now. You are often visited by perception of a greater whole transcending the immediate world. Issues impacting humanity at large now attract your attention in place of issues impacting you personally. Just for sharing, this whole process in my case took about two full years to bloom and crystallize.

Stage 3
Initiating Preparations

Finally you have decided to go after the ultimate exploration without losing any more time. Hence, you have started thinking about the right time to switch over to new life. Your conscious mind has learned to take control of your impulses leading to new obstacles and weaknesses. But your trouble shooting mechanism has started operating with success. You have started feeling secured and set in spite of ifs and buts that crop up frequently. You have volunteered out of your occupation such that entire time of the day is available to you for committing for reading about and practising various techniques. If you are still engaged in your profession, it is not about money making but solely for preparing next line, sharing experiences, guiding or as social service only while rest of energy and time is invested in seeking spiritual progress.

Moderation is the new operating word for all you eat, for all you speak, for all you think and even for how much sleep you get. Mantra of moderation coupled with serious self–talk enables you to look at yourself from a new angle where you first come out as an individual being before your other hats of being a spouse, parent, colleague, business person, executive or a professional of a particular geography, religion, caste or creed. This change enables you to taste some success towards self-observation, self-analysis and enhanced self-awareness. For the first time, your real nature seems to float near the surface of the muddy pool of multiple bondages with creations of external world. In my opinion, this is most impactful stage as it works as a tipping point; people who are able to cross over it are never known to come back to earlier life. It is like point of no return.

This is also the stage for observing all *Yam* and *Niyam*, the prohibitions and observances prescribed as first two steps of eight steps Raja Yoga. Basically these are dos and don'ts necessary for mastering bodily and psychic disciplines to boost physical, moral and mental preparedness. Good level of proficiency achieved over *Yam* and *Niyam* further empowers you to voluntarily look over materialism without feeling compelled to do so. Aspirant has to constantly pursue superior virtues in his quest for supreme objective.

Constant practice will slowly help in developing discrimination between moral rights and wrongs and between permanent and transient. Holding on *Dharma* helps to stay float on higher plains guarding against violations that can cause pulling down of the entire progress. Idea is to accumulate sufficient conviction, courage and moral controls to pursue the path known to have been travelled by selected few.

This is also a very critical stage in terms of acquiring lots of knowledge about scriptures of different vintage and religious shades. All the heavy concepts like 'this world being an illusion', philosophies, separation of ego and self, mind and matter, death and re-birth and every such other concept must now be taken head on by going deeper into each of these. Until now you have been despising, castigating or detesting these concepts but going forward the essence of all these must be brought to the surface with near complete understanding. It is human to feel fear of everything unknown; so idea is to get over all such fears by successfully delving through these difficult looking concepts.

Towards advance section of this stage, you also become successful in assimilating temporary nature of your ego and its consequences. Your mental focus now is able to frequently endeavour to ride over your ego with some efforts. With awakening of your conscious mind, you are now able to move away from destructive habits of deceit, self-pity, alcohol abuse, refusal to be helped in time of need, and physical and mental neglect. You have developed good understanding of your logical mind and emotional mind could be enslaved with little efforts. There are some spurts of emotional mind seizing the responses but that does not last beyond few seconds. You are now prepared to accelerate the speed of your spiritual journey using higher gears. But challenges and temptations post this process have started emerging bringing new situations to life. This stage will take about two good years to emerge clearly with individual specific points lengthening the time further and further,

Stage 4
Action Initiation

This is the most critical stage for determining both speed and success of all future endeavours. You have started undertaking concrete activities and have started sharpening your skill for the subsequent stages. Issues relating to financial sustenance and income streams are all completely settled. Your process of gathering knowledge has caught on higher momentum and your doubts are decreasing progressively. You have reached to a point of no return and nothing on this earth can now convince you to make a U turn for resuming the former life.

This is the stage where you have started regular sessions for your inner communication by employing all or some of the techniques like prayers, meditations, concentrated thinking and/or contemplation. Quite possible that you were undertaking these practices earlier too but the intensity and regularity is of a different level now. Similar is the case about doing each of these techniques in correct manner. I say so because I have ignorantly believed that few Asanas that I have been doing all my life was practising Yoga. But my Yoga of twenty five years back and that of today are qualitatively two different things with nothing in common. Today I can appreciate it better. Earlier my purpose was to de-stress but now it is finding Self and broader meaning in life. Earlier I was largely concerned to develop right mental capabilities to perform better on job and achieve more but now my approach stands completely shifted to understand better and realize more.

Having arrived at this stage, you are clearly able to see the existence of your own Ego and its interplay in generating likes and dislikes. You are comfortable in seeing those likes and dislikes forming basis about your perceptions of good or bad, judgements about right and wrong. You are also able to decipher the ways your Ego has been operating in self-justification mode by controlling your mind. You now clearly understand your ego's role in creating a false personality and attaching too much importance on that separateness. You realize that so called duality is completely out of sync with the basic and pure human nature of wanting love and peace. You realize that Ego of your past need not be treated like an enemy from the past who wanted to conquer you but as a friendly companion who doesn't know how to say goodbye. It is still hanging with you but in its tamed version. With continued inner communication, you are, at times, able to come out of the grip of Ego and apply logical reasoning more dispassionately. This very new found learning is gradually making you a different person than you have ever been.

Now your drive towards new direction of your life is out there in open as you share your resolve with your family and other people connected with your life. This stage also requires many critical supports from your spouse and children as your decision to pursue new objectives also impacts them. Don't worry about some delays and resistances. Please remember that best of rivers famous for flawless streams don't flow as the crow fly and are known to have turns and twists along the course; final direction is all that matter in the end. You have taken decision and you are on right course. It is generally seen that responses of immediate family members play the biggest spoilsport in this stage as they continue to attach importance to factors that have lost significance for you. But you understand their arguments and worries well and have anticipated most of their views in advance. Your resolve, however, is more firm than before and you are determined to continue on your journey with or without their acceptance for your decision.

Stage 5
Operational Stage

You have settled all issues of earlier stages and have continued remaining engaged in pursuing knowledge from multiple sources of books, scriptures, Internet, discourses and every other possible source of right knowledge. Maximum time of your day is now utilized for your daily routines for conditioning your mind and body for experiencing recommended benefits. Such practices include Yoga, Pranayam, meditation and general physical exercises to keep your body, mind and thoughts healthy and robust. There are immediate benefits that you have started feeling. Your mind is at ease; your body is taken well by positively responding to changed routine. Your higher sensory perceptions are more alert, spiritual links have enhanced, your inner communication is more energetic, and your self-awareness has deepened like never before. Truth appears with sharper clarity with many of its earlier shades disappearing one by one.

The gains in initial period of this stage will be visibly significant.

After few months, however you can expect to hit a plateau. Don't get alarmed, as it is perfectly natural to start facing stress, apathy, boredom and loss of emotional support. There is no need to feel disheartened. Similar to every other new field, the supply of low hanging fruits comes to end making further plucking of fruits comparatively difficult. But the best of fruits on every tree always come from higher branches and Spirituality is no exception. Some backlash is only to be expected.

Spare times must go for studying as much as you are able to willingly absorb. This reading is not similar to fictional material. So, don't be in hurry. Refuse to turn the page unless you have been able to comprehend the contents with full clarity. Now it is not about some exams but for your deeper understanding. Feel free to cross over from ancient to modern sources, from one scripture to another and even from one religion to another. That way you will soon realize that their words may be different but ultimately their essence is almost identical. This realization is to become a firm foundation for your personal enlightenment in due course of time. Lastly, on the time front, it is only towards the end of third year in this stage that you should expect yourself to be completely familiar into your new life.

Stage 6
Initial Success

It is only after six to eight full years (exceptions apart due to individual's situations and the starting point being different for each of us) of your drive into this journey that you expect to climb to the base camp of this last and final stage. You have been able to pursue the spiritual practice with full honesty, integrity and dedication over all these years on a full time basis and that has made you realize perceptible changes on your behavioural side, health status, mental attitudes, feelings and emotions. These changes got integrated in your lifestyle making you a different person altogether. You know that you are a far improved version having significant add-ons and minus of many discarded false images.

Attractions don't allure you anymore, most temptations are under control, emotional outbursts are thing of past, your acceptance for others is at much higher level, your intellectual knowledge about this world and your place in it is much clear, there is no approval required from anyone. Earlier divisions due to caste, creed, region, religion, sect, language, nationality, ethnicity, culture, education, economic status, colour of skin, gender have but all subsided; none of these labels stick on you anymore. You have successfully overgrown out of all such divides and have become a human with childlike, division free nature engrossed in peace and love. Being in harmony with everything is your new buzz word.

Now you have been successful in suspending most of your earlier held beliefs and doctrines. Your past haunts you no more. You are comfortable living in present and you have started enjoying present as the ultimate reality without colours of past or anxieties of future impacting your vision. Future does not scare you any more as your fears stand extinguished. You have been successful in sinking your systems and methods that were borrowed from others; now all you practise are your own systems and techniques evolved with desired improvisations. Any time a situation develops, you are able to form a dispassionate view based on reality check rather than being a self appointed judge. You are absolutely comfortable with your own traits without finding faults or comparing with conditioned false images.

There is no more temptation to go back to earlier world of stress and confusions. At times you get dreams of glimpses of earlier life but your conscious mind is completely happy in present. Now you don't feel part of any cult but more as a part of the universe. Now you are more open in approach. You are able to see through most curtains and you realize them as man-made and nothing but bundle of ignorance. You keep coming across instances of realizations as how little you knew in past and how much more is there to learn and assimilate. You are able to see the immensity of the world and realize your insignificant little existence out there. You have comfortably set into your own timings and styles of regular daily practices. These may be different than learned initially. Your present practices have evolved over the years based on your own practice than theory. Your repertoire of religious, philosophical, historical, socio-political and psychic sources of knowledge is much wider now than you ever imagined and with passing time it only keeps growing.

Congratulations! At this stage you are one out of five people who started their journey from stage number 3 and above. Remaining people either lost their interest or lives or they could not sustain the pressure of this journey. Yes, the success rate can't be more than that; this has been the toughest of all struggles and self-forced expulsions are expected. There are instances of self-evacuations also where people get bored and their restlessness returns.

At this stage your challenge is how to make best use of newfound knowledge with vigour, how to apply your strength gained and wisdom acquired. You also wish to find more potential aspirants and help them progress on their journey by encouraging through sharing. But it is just a good beginning and a lot more still needs to be achieved. Further success will be more individualistic and it is beyond my capability to anticipate or visualize what more can be there in store. Like a seasoned musician, lifelong practice also can't suggest that there is nothing more to learn. The world of our inner psyche is ever expanding and is comparable to this visible universe where more and more galaxies are located every other day; every time you develop a bigger and stronger telescope, you are able to spot few more astronomical objects.

"Similar is the case with your consciousness, the more you go deep, the deeper it goes."

Spirituality vis-à-vis Traditional Concepts

Spirituality was traditionally explained as a process of reformation of the human beings to their original shape. In that respect it has been there for very long time and has been regularly touched by religions and philosophies. Almost all religions are having some or other aspects of spirituality covered under their respective doctrines. Especially in the Ancient India, spirituality has been deeply involved with practices of Yoga and Meditations.

So before we move on to specifics of spirituality, it will be a good idea to disengage it from the other concepts mentioned before. This will essentially allow the spirituality to have its independent contours such that there are no boundary disputes with other concepts. So let us look at each of these concepts in some perspective and decipher its links with spirituality.

Religions and Spirituality

In the waters of religions, Spirituality is the oil that floats atop without mixing or without losing its separate existence. But all said and done, religions do have a large social presence and each one of these does have associated spiritual streams as well. Let us briefly take prevailing position of spirituality in major popular religions of our times one by one.

Buddhist Spirituality

The spirituality of Buddhism relates to the objective of ending one's sufferings, *Dukha,* through enlightened understanding, *Nirvana,* about realities of human life. In due course of time, various branches and streams of Buddhism developed their own spiritual approaches but central theme of all these approaches always remained grounded upon ultimate freedom from sufferings and cultivations of wisdom and compassion.

The unique feature of Buddhist Spirituality is its focus on practices as against beliefs and doctrines. Since Buddhism is not centered solely on presence of beliefs like Christianity and Islam, it enjoys freedom from many questions within the domain of traditional metaphysics. 'Buddha' is known to consider questions relating to creation or eternity of universe, its being finite or infinite or soul being part of body or separate from it etc. as mere unnecessary speculations having no link with human liberation or its fulfillment. He believed that such questions couldn't be settled with certainty and he was indeed so right about this view. Today also, with so much scientific advancements taking place over last 2500 years, those issues remain as grey as they were during Buddha's life. He said he would rather use his energy and time towards quest for wisdom and compassion rather than considering such abstract questions.

In view of the Buddha, compassionate life was to be lived without keeping the self at the center of the universe. Realization that our whole existence does not resolve around 'I', 'me' and 'mine' was to reflect in attainment of right wisdom. In place of self, the spiritual focus of Buddhism was to resolve around the famous "Eight Fold Noble Path" consisting on right understanding, right purpose, right speech, right conduct, right occupation, right effort, right attention and right meditation. All these steps are intended towards helping the human beings recover their essential nature filled with wisdom and compassion.

In spite being one of the oldest traditions, Buddhism comes out having several aspects that attract even the modern world of today. One of the strongest points of Buddhism is its teaching of accepting any thing as truth only after it is based exclusively on one's own experience and not on the basis of order or experience of some other person. This principle is applicable for seeking spirituality verbatim as self-exploration remains the key of all spiritual attainments. Holy life in Buddhism begins as well as ends with practising humanity without holding or being prisoner of beliefs. Further, the teachings of Buddhism are custom made to accommodate the needs of very individual by encompassing several elements that are devotional, mystical or spiritual. These teachings promote peace and happiness by developing the pious virtues of tolerance, non-violence, morality, compassion and empathy.

Buddha strongly recommends focus on quietness and tranquility in every aspect of life as against prevailing noise, hurry, haste and confusion widely prevalent in present day living. One is also compelled to say that Buddhist spirituality is focused on disciplining mind and body by developing ethical and moral behaviour which is best developed by pursuing gentle awareness and contemplation. It tends to aim at immediate issues of this very world right here rather than coming up with doctrinal burden aimed at existence in some other unknown world.

Christian Spirituality

Christian spirituality is defined as a set of beliefs, values and ways of life that reflect the teachings of the holy Bible and revolves around consciousness of fellowship with the Spirit of Christ, uninterrupted by carnality and sin. Spirituality in Christianity is said to develop when a born-again believer makes a consistent and ongoing choice to surrender to the ministry of the Holy Spirits. As per Ephesians (Chapter 1 to 4), when a human being is born again, he or she receives the Holy Spirit who seals them for the day of redemption. Further, as per John (16:13), Jesus promises that the Holy Spirit would lead us into all the truth where part of the truth is taking God's virtuous qualities and applying them to our life. By applying these very qualities to their own life, the believer makes a choice of letting himself/herself be controlled by the Holy Spirit. True Christian Spirituality is based upon the extent to which a born-again believer allows the Holy Spirit to lead and control his/her life.

It is said that when our nature controls us, we are bound to become carnal. The moment a sin is committed, sinful nature is supposed to have taken control of that life. But sheer confession or acknowledgement of our sin to God facilitates taking over by the Holy Spirit again. Apostle Paul tells believers to be filled with Holy Spirit (Ephesians 5:18). This simply means that the Holy Spirit should be allowed to control us rather than we yielding to our own desires and carnal nature. Thus true Christian Spirituality is produced by the Spirit working in and through the believer and his character, not due to his own efforts but by the control of the Holy Spirit. To see the same point in some other words for better clarity, Christian Spirituality involves a choice people make in relationship with Lord Jesus Christ by submitting to the Holy Spirit in their lives. As believers, they make a choice to keep communication with the Spirit clear through confession (1 John 1:9) and by not grieving the Spirit by sin (Ephesians 4:30).

With the advent of medieval period, history of European Christianity started defining spirituality in many more different ways. But Christian Churches emphasized that life includes both materialistic and spiritual aspects as an embodiment of both spiritual ascensions and physical yearnings. Historic conflict arising from such comparisons saw reduction in authority at the disposal of Churches as more and more matters were now to be dealt with under state, the man-made laws and systems. Such a shift is held responsible for famous industrial revolution of Europe where great progress got made on technology-fuelled mass production model. That resulted in unprecedented increase in consumptions at levels that were too much deviated from the past practices. Soon, materialism cropped up as a by-product which only lead to increased focus on sensual pleasures and thus widened bigger spiritual voids among large part of the generally Christian population living all through Europe of that time.

Christian spirituality is also said to be the quest for a fulfilled and authentic life that involves taking Christian beliefs and values and weaving them into the fabric of all aspects of human. God is said to have provided a way to people to spiritually come alive to Him and enter into a deep spiritual relationship with Him through repentance and firm belief in Jesus Christ.

Further, Christian spirituality expresses itself in practical service to mankind in his struggle to achieve human dignity. Christian spirituality is also rooted in prayers and worship as against self-inquiry and contemplation used in Hinduism or Buddhism. Christian worship is aimed at directing human heart, mind and will to God as man's true end. Yet Christian Spirituality is not about running away from responsibilities of life but is to be practised well within complexities of life at homes, offices and factories unlike asceticism and renunciation practised by many *Sadhus* from Hinduism, monks from Buddhism or Sufis from Islam.

In addition to above comments about the Christian Spirituality, there is also a need to look at popular variations, in brief, applicable for major sects within Christianity. Let us start with Catholic side first. There one comes across following important thoughts or streams:

1. *Benedictine Spirituality* – This is signified by striving perfection while grounded in community, liturgical prayers and leaving behind worldly concerns. People from East can very well smell lot of similarity with this brand as it is a form of monasticism within Christian religion. This is credited to St. Benedict (480-550).
2. *Franciscan Spirituality* – This is signified by life devoid of all riches, developing love for nature and helping those in need as much as one can. It was started by St. Francis Assisi (1182-1226) who like Buddha or Mahavira was born in a wealthy family. Followers of St. Francis believed more on experiencing and sharing rather than discussing or contemplating about God.
3. *Dominican Spirituality* – This is characterized by poverty along with love of preaching and devotion to truth. Popularized by St. Dominic (1170-1221), it blamed preachers for many problems of general public. He founded 'Order of Preachers' who were drawn to contemplation of the sacred humanity of Jesus Christ. Dominicans helped people in deepening their relationships with God.
4. *Carmelite Spirituality* – This is characterized by interior detachment, silence, solitude and desire for spiritual progress and insight into mystical experiences. Its roots go back to hermits living on the Mount Carmel in Israel. Some great writings from this stream, mainly credited to St. John, got compiled in 16th century and are considered as spiritual classics until today.
5. *Redemptorist Spirituality* – it belongs to those believers who follow Christ in his incarnation, death and resurrection. They consider Jesus Christ as a divine being, similar to Rama and Krishna from India and believe that He is still around for guiding and supervising the deeds of his followers.

6. *Ignatian Spirituality* – It is the most influential Spirituality movement of modern times and is based on insight of St. Ignatius of Loyola. It focuses on active attentiveness to God who is ever active in lives of people. Also named as spirituality of decision makers, its purpose is to conquer oneself and to regulate one's life in such a way that no decision is made under the influence of any inordinate attachment and by making the practitioner free from their own likes and dislikes but solely by following God's will. Interestingly, this stream is also found increasingly popular among people from Protestants and Evangelicals as well.

Similarly, we can also look in brief at spirituality practised exclusively by Protestants. Besides the religiously and politically conservatives, the protestants are also around in many specific groups including but not limited to Lutherans, Presbyterians, United Church of Christ, Disciplines of Christ, Methodists etc. The voices of all these groups are shaping the emerging paradigm within Christianity making Protestants transforming towards being progressive. They show inclinations and commitment to critical reflection, listening voices of poor and oppressed, concerns for inclusiveness and racial equality. Their practices span over head and heart, love, justice and prayers along with social service as the right methods of realizing God.

Islamic Spirituality

Islamic scholars never considered Spirituality as a separate subject as did the Christians. They maintained their opinion that the matters related to creation of '*RUH*', the soul, were well settled in Allah being the sole creator. Such singular cause does not leave any reason to search any other power. In any case, they argued that *Qur'an* texts also dealt with the matter of *RUH* at length leaving no room for any imaginary explanation. Islam looks at spirituality simply as linking of human actions to the purpose of their life. They believed that doing all actions solely for the pleasure of Allah is spiritual practice by itself as it establishes direct link of material actions with the purpose of life.

Islamic spirituality can be simply captured in following teachings of Prophet Muhammad who emphasized on gaining good character by engaging in constant practice of prayers, meditation, remembrance of God and other such practices that result in changing the heart of a true Muslim and thereby bringing him closer to Allah. In fact, God's consciousness is considered most essential element in Islamic Spiritual practice to the extent that all behaviour and attitude, to the exclusion of Allah, are considered corrupted. But as elsewhere, the very approach of people standing at different levels of spiritual awakening helps them differently in seeking the very learning of Islam. The very word of Quran, the pious words of Prophet Mohammad carry altogether different meaning to an awakened person. Some people, in fact, blame the evils associated with modern day Islam on narrow interpretations by those ignorant practitioners who are sitting on lower rungs of their spiritual evolution.

In a way Islamic Spirituality approach stands just opposite to the popular belief held by many that spiritual growth was not compatible with leading a normal life and that physical self-denial and asceticism, austerities and penances were absolutely essential for development and perfection of *RUH*, the human spirit. Such believers were known to push themselves in killing physical desires by undertaking tough exercises and ascetic practices conducted in remote and isolated places in forests and mountains far way from human habitations. Such views divided the mankind into two separate groups. On one hand were those who were to enjoy and consume all material comforts and pleasures and lived life closer to animals without bringing morality under question. On the other hand were those who viewed that senses should not only be subdued but extra sensory powers should be awakened such that subtle and feeble voice of souls is listened.

Islamic approach, interestingly, differs radically from both of above-mentioned categorizations. As per Islam, human body has been created with the sole objective of allowing the soul to use it in the exercise of its authority. It suggests that human body be looked as a workshop or laboratory rather than as a forced prison. As such, Islam preaches for spiritual development of human beings without turning away from normal life, by turning into any corner or by giving up active participation in the normal working of this world in any way. Islam requires every follower to live and work in normal life and give his best possible account. In any case, God is to conduct the evaluation of all the actions of the being on the Day of Judgement. Thus, Islam rejects ascetic view of life and proposes pursuing spiritual development by living inside this world itself.

Later, discussions about Spirituality in Islam started when Muslims came in direct contact with Hindus from Indian sub-continent. Comparisons got made with the concept of '*ZUHD*,' which meant pious austerities as reported in several references from *Hadith*. Re-emergence of Sufi culture is reported as a consequence of such comparisons. Sufism is identified as best known tradition of mystic spirituality, a tradition that involves strong adherence to the principles of tolerance, peace and opposing all forms of violence. Due to their principles, however, Sufis have faced persecution by Wahhabis and Salafists sects of Islam.

Hinduism and Spirituality

Hindu Spirituality is closely linked to God-realization that is achieved through Self-realization. Further, both God and Self-realizations are rooted in the intuitive awareness that one is in essence divine or an integral part of divinity. Evolution of spirituality in Hinduism is credited to Mysticism right from '*Shramana*' time. It is only in Hinduism that Mysticism has always been a very strong shade of social culture all through the rich history of the sub-continent. Ever since *Upanishad*'s time, the ancient Indian thought has remained concerned with individual's own experience of union with the Supreme Being. For this union, Hinduism is known to offer an array of alternate options which could be followed by persons concerned depending on their own orientation and maturity. Ultimately, all ways recommended lead the practitioner to the Supreme, called by whatever name.

But before we attempt to analyzing Spirituality under Hinduism in greater detail, it will be better to have a brief look at some key issues of Hinduism because it is not as straight jacketed as other religions discussed above. Hinduism is too wide and complex to get commented without understanding proper reference to the context. Hinduism, as being commented here, refers to '*Sanatan Dharma*' that allows one to look at the ultimate Supreme as a God both with and without face, name and form. But even where the God is having a form, there is no advocacy of worshiping any deity in particular. Different people over different periods have worshiped thousands of gods with the belief that each and every God represents different aspects of the same Absolute Brahman. A follower is completely at his own liberty to choose his own preferred method without any demeaning to the others.

As a basic concept of Hinduism, *'Atman'*, soul (which is identical with the transcendent self *Brahman*) continues its journey from one life to other accumulating good and bad karmas on the way. Enduring pains and enjoying pleasures by human body is understood as the way of settling bad and good karmas respectively. Ultimately when all karmic effects are exhausted or settled, irrespective of number of lives used, soul is to achieve salvation and merge with the Absolute. This concept of series of births and deaths is called the principle of 'transmigration', (yet another defining and distinguishing feature of Hinduism when compared to other popular religions of our times).

To understand real essence of *Sanatan Dharma*, let us look at the literal meaning of these two words. *Sanatan* means eternal, universal, abiding, ever present, unceasing, natural and enduring the fundamental principles behind this marvelous universe. Similarly, Dharma means harmony, righteousness, compassion, natural law, divine conformity, cosmic norm, wisdom, purest insight or law of being or moral duty. Putting these together, *Sanatan Dharma* denotes a dharma applicable to all people, at all times, inherent in and inclusive of all, loving to all and excluding none, both immanent and transcendent, the whole and the parts all together. And this is the real Hinduism where finding one's own spirituality is the sole purpose of every human life at all times.

A deep reading of cultures such as Egyptian, Babylonian, Greek, Celts, Persian and Chinese will clearly display that many aspects of the universality and inclusiveness identified with *Sanatan Dharma* have been in existence within those cultures as well. This is to say that before the emergence of prophetic religions on the radar of humanity, all cultures did embrace eternal Dharma in varying proportions. But the same got trampled and gave way to other thoughts in due course of history. Hinduism, however, has survived itself on Indian soil from such trampling simply because it never remained far away from its deep roots embedded in "*Sanatan Dharma.*

One may have a genuine question as to why *Sanatan Dharma* in India allowed diverse forms to get created as vitiated versions of universality. This indeed is very genuine question of followers of Prophetic religions where there is one God, one Prophet, one main scripture, one base philosophy that is too straight, narrow or wide as the case may be. Here is a clear need for understanding and appreciating that *Sanatan Dharma*, by its very nature, is against uniformity because uniformity results in some sort of rigidity and artificiality. *Sanatan Dharma* always recognized that human being are blessed with uniquely different orientations and can't be clubbed under one single band. Therefore, it promoted diverse localization by the people that it served and encouraged all to find their own ways depending on what appeals to them. We can appreciate even in today's context that anything to become universal will have to allow adaptation suitable for local digestion. Sanatan Dharma had recognized this reality all along.

Taking another important aspect under consideration, Hinduism proliferates the idea of an eternal code of human conduct; that which has no beginning and no end; that which is firmly rooted in nature and honours all aspects of natural world including mountains, river, rocks, trees, flowers, birds and considers them all as sacred and holy; which has completely pluralistic approach and accepts and appreciates all methods of worshiping the God in all its forms or human imaginations without the exclusion of any one; which does not believe only in one book but consider every word and every letter as a guide for proper human behaviour.

As yet another unique concept of Hinduism, it does not require any middleman between a human and his God and *encourages every man to contemplate his own inner self and connect with the God of his choice and imagination. It prompts every human to seek his own experience of divinity rather than just blindly follow experience of some other human being from distant past.* Thus, Hinduism accepts multiplicity of beliefs being true and it neither persuades nor dissuades anyone to change his belief under any fear or favour. It considers every being whether living like animals, birds, reptiles etc. or non-living like stones, soil, water etc. as a separate soul by itself with no difference between long or short, thin or fat, black or white, Eastern or Western, male or female.

Hinduism does not emphasize on methods of worship as those are temporary and change every few hundreds of years. Hinduism is not only about how one seeks his/her God but also provides as many ways of seeking to that. Actually, Hinduism also accepts a person as a good Hindu who does not have any God. These discussions may not have a direct link with our subject matter of spirituality but once we are able to delink Hinduism with present day narrow image of Idol worships in temples and rituals and develop understanding about its ancient concepts, its very approach of being largely spiritual than religious will emerge without requiring much effort.

The background discussion is also critical as many may not know and appreciate Hinduism in all its spectacular expanse in terms of its long traditions, its teachings and teachers, its aspects of human religious aspirations, its philosophy of coexisting in harmony with everything alive or dead on this earth, its commitments to non-violence, its spiritual traditions, use of all types of imagery as aspects of God, its beliefs in all sorts of rituals as means of maintaining disciplined life at different stages of life, its techniques and approaches to meditation to connect with the core of humanity well within our own hearts and its practices of Ayurveda and Yoga to ensure a perfect healthy balance between mind, body and soul.

Speaking spiritually, as per Hinduism, the whole human life is supposed to be a unique journey where the individual soul remains in search to reach to the goal of Self-realization that ultimately leads to union with the divinity. Hinduism offers multiple choices of the tools or aids or inspirations that may be relied by the soul aspiring for that union with the divine. Hinduism provides that the karmas one accumulates with each of its thoughts and actions determine the time taken or lives required for such Self-realization. The array of choices on offer for the spiritual journey are observed to be the most attractive proposition influencing new converts from the Western world in modern times.

Sanatan Dharma encompasses a rich treasure of literature created over millenniums, which is larger than written material available for any other scientific stream until today. This speaks volume of contributions made by learned *Rishis, Munis, Yogis,* Philosophers, Scholars, Thinkers, and Teachers. The concepts contained all through its great literary heritage have been refined with utmost collective wisdom of these great souls. Against this, other religions came up with collection of single Saint (or a handful of them at best) and their beliefs where their writings are seen responding to prevailing conditions of that very specific time and place of history.

While Sanatan Dharma constantly talks of inclusivity and acceptance for all, many others focus on rejections, that too, not based on logics or philosophies but simply because their Book says so. Hinduism encourages each person to constantly remain in search of Truth, his own Truth, by knowledge or actions or devotion or Yoga or meditation or a combination of all these options. On the other hand, Prophetic religions simply specify the individual to follow what is told without searching any logic or rationale and that is one of the biggest possible differences impacting religious interface with search of spirituality. So in Hinduism the onus of leading his journey on the road and to pursue his truth is centered in driver's own hand and while there are milestones and directions available for travelling all through the road; the reaching to destination will firmly remain with the endeavours of seeker himself. Contrary to this, other popular religions make the whole process very simple and provide that anyone can follow the truth by simply accepting teachings of the Prophet or seeking pardon for the sins committed.

Quintessential Spirituality being the Essence of Hinduism

In true sense, Hinduism together with other Eastern traditions is largely a spiritual tradition. These traditions are open source, personal and are rooted in objective experiences by each individual. Hinduism does not go for Band-Aid type solutions rather it digs deep inside in very psychology of human to look for possible answers to all the intriguing questions. This very quest led to evolution of Yoga and Meditation, which eventually got heralded as most appropriate and proven technologies for approaching individual's most inner planes and achieve transformation within human being using his own mind and body aggregates as tools as well as laboratory. It is indeed a unique characteristic of Hinduism that it encourages free and open thinking, depending on individual's own capacity to inquire and investigate into the nature of ultimate truth. It encourages seekers to pursue experiencing the divine by focusing inward using either of the many meditative and contemplative practices and improvising the same going forward.

Hinduism also strongly believes that in spite of several ways followed by different people, the ultimate God of all is same. There is a famous mantra from *Rigveda* (1:164:46) that goes as "*Ekam sat viprah bahudha vedanti* – Truth is one, the wise describe it in different words". This very thought has always been the cornerstone of inclusivity of Hinduism that included every approach and every path for believing in a single final destination. It is this very principle that ensures that here is no room for any fanaticism or fundamentalism.

The four stages of life system of Hinduism devotes two full term stages (accounting for second half of total life span of an individual) in every person's life for preparing for and pursuing Moksha as final goal of life to be practised to the entire exclusion of all other objectives. That clearly goes to show relative higher priority accorded to seeking one's spirituality as the very objective of human life. Depending on specific nature and orientation of each person, Hinduism provides them a selection of approaches named Karma Yoga, Raja Yoga, Bhakti Yoga or Jnana Yoga. These concepts shall be discussed in full details in a subsequent chapter.

Talking a bit technically, Hindu spirituality is called non-dual. It holds that ultimately there is a single supreme reality, which may be called with any name like God, Brahman or Atman. It is the same reality which is also called in other traditions as 'Buddha Nature' or 'Tao Spirit', 'Awareness', 'Consciousness' or whatever other similar names. It basically signifies that there is no real separation between God and world, God and Soul and one Soul or other Souls. It also underlines that this ultimate reality is without any form, name, shape, colour, sound, volume or touch but at the same time it is very much present in all forms, names, shapes, colours, sounds, volumes and touches that exist right here and now.

Finally, Hindu Spirituality assumes that any person pursuing self-inquiry sincerely and devotedly is entitled to reach this final understanding where lies the answer to abstract sounding questions of "who am I?" or "what is the purpose of my life?"

More and more analysts now feel that the key concepts of Hinduism like individual seeking and open source structuring, become very important for spiritual experiences as holding of beliefs, even if those are held rightly, strongly and forcefully, kills the very seed of seeking or knowing or experiencing. Opening up of spiritual world to every single individual by providing them with innumerable ways and means, is the greatest contribution of Hinduism.

Devotion and Spirituality

The interplay of spirituality with devotion is yet another intricate but critical phenomenon for many people as both these concepts are linked with very porous boundaries. Let us first try understanding the real concept of devotion. It generally means a selfless affection and dedication towards a person, power or principle. But more often than not, devotion is generally perceived for acts of religious observance. Specially, in Indian context, the very word of *Bhakti* is usually referred to as dedicated and unquestioned complete relationship with one or the other form or name of a chosen God.

The theme of devotion is very wide spread but always aims at having presence of God. The methods may range from one extreme to another or a mix of many but basic aim is to seek direct surrender to God. Sufis from Islam may pursue their devotion by dancing in trance while Buddhists may do the same by chanting and meditating. Catholic may be seen praying with a rosary while Protestants may be seen singing hymns and orthodox Christians may be seen meditating. Jews are seen in prayer wrapping shawls while Muslims may be seen undertaking their pilgrimage to Mecca and Medina. Different faith people may be pursuing formal liturgies or informal gestures but ultimate aim of all these traditions is to establish a link with their respective Divinity. Across all religious practices, devotion is seen helping self-discipline of the devotee improving substantially as a precursor to achieve higher aims of human life.

Hinduism also has seen Bhakti as a major unifying movement among all its sects and branches over last thousand years or so. *Bhakti* movement in Hinduism has brought a perfect level playing field among all its followers as it established a direct contact between the seeker and the sought after. Bhakti allowed the devotee to have a direct physical, visual and passionate transformative relationship with his God. Hindus resort to devotion using various practices like *Jap, Kirtan* or *Dhyana.* Hindus call it Bhakti Yoga where basic idea is that God promises to impart something of divine consciousness to the devotee provided that the devotee is able to completely surrender his self to his God sincerely, and lovingly.

In a way it is part of a discipline that culminates in developing individual souls and spirits. Devotion may be pursued by long or short versions of prayers and meditations, both normal and special. The importance here is not on words or methods but on the state of mind induced by such methods focused on converting once entire life dedicated to the Absolute. It covers all actions and practices followed by individuals and groups with an aim of individualized spiritual path irrespective of the fact that the tricks and tools followed are a mix of little of this and little of that.

Devotion is best understood as a way of connecting with one's own divine within and without. A true devotee is the one who seeks oneness with his God. So, in that sense, devotion is nothing but intense spiritual love for the Absolute, which can come in existence only after sinking attachments with all worldly affairs. Devotion is much deeper than feelings and experiences. Devotion is a deep and intense yearning to reach beyond the phenomenal existence and captivity in this endless cycle of life and death. Devotion moves the soul away from pride, egoism and selfish motives and encourages us to see through this transient existence, which is nothing but source of pains and sufferings. Hence, in its purest form, devotion is just another name for approaching part of complete spectrum of spirituality.

The sum and substance of devotion can be concluded to help the devotee establish clear distinction in personal lower self and higher self. Ultimately, it is only our higher self that inspires us to selfless, broad-minded and principled approach to issues in life while the usual lower self incites us to be selfish, mean-minded and opportunists. It is to the credit of Devotion that it helps its devotees to understand that the higher self is what we originally are; pure, godly, filled with love and peace. To the contrary, lower self is who we think what we are; material bodies and minds which cover and prevent human godly nature. Turning to some other points of comparison between the two concepts under discussion, devotion is something that we do while spirituality is something that happens within us. In that sense both these are unidirectional approaches where one works as the stepping-stone for the other. While undertaking devotion, human beings hope their God will bless them for their needs and desires whereas in Spirituality, we wish to cooperate with Him and His creations. The best way of understanding the relationship between devotion and spirituality is through the example how oxygen flow to muscles improves physical health by undertaking cardiovascular exercises and routines. Pursuing Devotion is similar to cardiovascular exercises aimed at improving spiritual fitness by activating flow of divinity in entire human systems.

Both devotion and spirituality necessitate cultivating virtues such as love, patience, forgiveness and wisdom. Similarly, upgradation of ethical and moral characters is common to both. Thus the road leading to both these is absolutely identical for quite a distance and it is only after climbing up to a decent height that the branching out takes place for separate ways. Surely, that puts matured devotion and spirituality on similar footings. Undoubtedly, Devotion is a direct encounter with Divinity and provides a foretaste of the indescribable which also is the quest of Spirituality. In a way, Devotion prepares a devotee for undertaking hardships expected on way to seek his relatedness with the Universe created by that very absolute.

As it is, seeking a direct contact with the Consciousness that pervades the entire cosmos is never easy. Devotional achievements open that path which leads the devotees to seek their own spirituality and that certainly is a big help in this difficult process. We may, however, come across some learned people in modern times who advocate that accessing the Consciousness is possible by a direct approach, sidestepping devotional practices. They may even be right on that argument. Universal consciousness certainly transcends all forms of distinctions and need not hinge on devotion but the entire process is best facilitated once devotion is able to create that small little crack in search of the road to seek access to that Consciousness.

Spirituality requires a complete revolution in the deepest recesses of the soul in a manner that not only an emotional but also an intellectual reorientation is achieved involving entire life of the devotee/seeker. The seeker is required to go through a complete conversion of his mind and heart before seeking his own spirituality. Devotional achievements facilitate this conversion of hearts by preparing a person for self-surrender. Aiming for self-surrender by routes other than devotion are said to have more and longer detours and risks of loosing ways. In conclusion it may be seen that bulk of people coming from Indian thoughts has climbed their path using devotion in the initial phase of their spiritual journey. For example, one of the most common practices for devotion is self-inquiry through which an individual contemplates in the depths of his own consciousness. This self-inquiry lets the seeker know that faster the bond of worldly attachments are abandoned nearer will be the search of God. Similarly, the practice of meditation helps winning over endless war with distractions of thoughts and centering of mind for uniting with divine. Devotional practices are also able to significantly convert the difficulties in exercising austerities into opportunities for self surrendering to the God and thereby paving the path for progress on spiritual orientation.

Once success is tasted in the initial stage of seeking glimpses of divinity, further continuation of practices keep losing shades of devotion automatically such that shades of pure spirituality replace those very strands. Every serious seeker can find traces of this transition in the life and works of all great spiritual achievers. Hence, it is safe to conclude that the path of devotion leads every serious devotee to be a seeker of spirituality by transcending over the God for merging with Consciousness of the entire Universe.

Samkhya: The Philosophical Connect of Spirituality

Around 800 to 700 BC, in Ancient Indian culture, Upanishad teachings were given a new twist by one of the first and foremost attempt of diving into human consciousness like never before. Being credited as the inception of philosophy, named "*Samkhya*", it was to become a corner stone with most philosophies in India and outside borrowing something or the other from this very source. Credited to Sage Kapila, it can be translated as "Perfection" or "Reflection". Normally, Philosophy and Spirituality are not much related to each other; however the reader will be clearly able to appreciate the process how *Samkhya* prepares the very fertile ground for sprouting of the initial seeds of spirituality. A good understanding of *Samkhya*, therefore, answers the How part of the beginning of spirituality as a separate field, one that is so unique in comparison of other fields of focused knowledge. This section is also intended to make the readers aware how consciousness is at the crux of being at the center of very creation of this visible world away from Gods or some sort of unseen power. To that extent, *Samkhya* is considered a big leap of faith.

While Vedas and Upanishads provide only hints and indirect references, or at best speculations, about important subjects like God, Human spirit, Brahman and such other abstract subjects, other sources up to that time in history also made mere assumptions about universe and its origin. "*Samkhya*" was first ever organized system to study human consciousness and its connect with the Universe in a comprehensive manner like never before. In addition to external visible world Samkhya also immersed into the depths of human mind and intellect opening altogether a new possibility leading to treasures of wisdom. It analyzed the entire cosmos into separate parts and components and went back to the very beginning of entire creation from where this world would have evolved in the first place. Its main objective was to understand various forms of human experience with objective world.

During the time when most thinkers were focused on finding their Gods, *Samkhya* focused on consciousness of human beings. During intense discussions on Brahman and Atman, *Samkhya* had the guts to discard all such discussions as mere estimations and gave a new name, "*Purusha*", to the supreme reality of the world. This *Purusha* was supposed to be an absolute entity, not subject to change, and most importantly multiple in numbers. Every human being in the universe was credited having his own eternal *Purusha* that was not bound by cycle of life and death, nor bound by space or time. Being completely, independent of being's mental or psychological state this essence was entirely different when compared to the more common form named "*Atman*", the soul. *Purusha* of *Samkhya* is without any intelligence as well as desire or attachment. It can be best understood as "Pure Consciousness" or "Transcendental Self". In a way it was the first occasion to project consciousness as the essence of each human life, an essence that was to become a strong base for entire concept of Spirituality much later.

Another important element of *Samkhya* is called "*Prakriti*" which is translated as 'matter' and not 'material nature', an obvious meaning to any Indian mind. Just for repetition, "*Prakriti*" of *Samkhya* has nothing to do with nature. To start with, Sage Kapila begins with the proposition that world is full of three kind of miseries. These were identified as '*Adhyatmic*', '*Adhibhotic*' and '*Adhidaevic*' translated as due to one's self, due to the products of elements and due to super natural causes. Kapila assumed that complete cessation of all three kinds of these pains is the complete end and objective of man. Later still, this very beginning was to influence the thinking of *Gautama Buddha*, who was to call it as *Dukkha,* the ultimate pains of humanity.

It is also interesting to know the impact of cultures and social surroundings reflecting on the thinkers and philosophers all this while. During those times in history, most of the Western thinkers were impacted by peculiar circumstances of their own life and their beliefs can be seen as clear reflection of those individual situations (*Attention is drawn to the Greek mythological figures and their interplay of issues*). But Indian soil in particular was still blessed with calm and quite scenery and bountiful Mother Nature. That calmness inspired its thinkers to patiently inquire into the mysteries of universe as well as human beings. This is one fact which rarely get discussed when one goes through evolution of cultural thoughts of East versus West.

Samkhya identifies three miseries as a result of properties of '*Prakriti*', the matter and providing clean chit to the other counterpart *Purusha*, the consciousness. Matter is held as eternal, subtle, insensitive, spiritless but always remaining in state of constant change. Matter was supposed to have existed before the evolution and was expected to exist forever. It accounts for whatever is physical and visible in this world. But with passage of time, it goes through so much of changes that un-liberated soul is but unable to comprehend its nature. After *Purusha* and *Prakriti,* there is another element called *Jiva* (spirit) that is said to be a state where *Purusha* is bound with *Prakriti* through the glue of desire, and, final culmination of this bondage is the state of *Moksha*, the liberation.

We may try understanding this concept in another simpler way. Our world is filled with objects. Objects are made of compounds. Compounds are made of molecules. Molecules are made of atoms. Atoms are made of particles. Particles are made of a subtler substratum. This chain is quite simple to understand by most of adults of today. While one evolves out of the other, all of these levels of reality coexist and interact with one another in an ongoing manner. '*Prakriti*' is the primordial state of matter, a '*tattava*', even prior to matter, as we know it in the physical sense. *Prakriti* is made out of a proportionate mixing of three *Gunas* (normal meaning is quality or nature but here used as a constituent) called *Sattva, Rajas* and *Tamas.*

Let us try understanding these Gunas in a bit detail for understanding for future:

- *Sattva*: Represents poise, fineness, lightness, illumination, joy and happiness.
- *Rajas*: Represents dynamism, activity, excitation and pain.
- *Tamas*: Represents inertia, obstruction, ignorance and inaction.

The whole idea of evolution of this world revolves around *Prakriti* and *Purusha. Prakriti* remained without manifestation until such time that it did not come in contact with consciousness of

Purusha. That coming together disturbed the set equilibrium of three Gunas and started the manifestation process. Some evolutes of *Prakriti* caused further evolution, as these are evolvents, for example, Intelligence gave rise to Ego. Other elements evolved out of this process are identified as five subtle elements (word, touch, form, taste and smell) and two sets of organs (external organs being sense and action organs and internal organs being mind).

Lastly, from subtle elements arise five gross elements, namely, Space, Air, Light/Fire, Water and Earth. It is imbalance in these *Gunas* and elements that result in creation of identified constituents. It might sound a bit complex to someone exploring *Samkhya* for the first time but this is by far the most authentic and integrated explanation of evolution of everything visible and all scientific discoveries made or proved have not been able to identify any thing contrary to this principle of "*Samkhya*" as to this day.

Ego principle is held responsible for apportioning three Gunas in different proportions to different constituents. This differentiation is said to give rise to visible variations among human, animals, plants and other insensitive items like stone. Ego also provides false image of Purusha to human beings and creates feelings of 'I', 'me', and 'mine'.

As per Sage Kapila, first thing to evolve out of *Prakriti* is *Buddhi* (intellect). *Buddhi* (also translated as "Great One") is said to be supreme aspect of human beings. It is said to be capable of getting identified, isolated and developed whereby it can lead the human being to enlightenment. *Buddhi* gives rise to *Ahamkara* (ego) and *Manas* (mind). Once trapped, most of our energy gets used to serve this false image. In the process, the real *Purusha* develops yearning for liberation to get beyond the pains and frustrations of normal life. And this is the seed that initiates search for Spirituality, as we understand it today. Extending the *Samkhya* argument, so long as our *Purusha* remains attached with ego and mind, the lack of yearning for freedom stops it from seeking spirituality.

Soul, which is neither a producer or produced, is external to manifestation by *Prakriti*. It is not considered as bound to matter nor is it liberated. Soul, therefore, is stated to be a fusion of *Purusha* and *Prakriti* where it is unrestricted by its physical body. '*Samsara*', the bondage (the cycle of death and rebirth) is said to arise when *Purusha* is mistakenly unable to discriminate itself from *Ahamkara*

(Ahamkara is part of Prakriti but Purusha mistake it to be itself). So, the *Samsara* continues until the time this ignorance persists. The moment *Purusha* develops knowledge and ability, by working on intellect and mind, to discriminate the difference between itself and *Prakriti*; the Jiva is called liberated (means *Moksha* attained). *Samkhya* considers *Purusha* and *Prakriti* enough for the purpose of creation and, thus, reduces the whole concept of 'Creator God' as redundant, a phantom of empty philosophy.

Samkhya relies on '*Viveka*', the intuitive discrimination, of a being to guide his intellect to differentiate between *Purusha* and *Prakriti.* Ignorance cast strong spell on the human minds where those minds consider personal thoughts, emotions and desires to be highest and most essential part of human existence and the mind and intellect duo do their best to serve those very thoughts and desires as much as possible. Most part of humanity can be seen engaged in this very complex cycle without any end in offing. Lot of hard work and mental discipline is required to develop the ability to see through this spell. That is where all the self inquiries, meditations and contemplations are directed.

The contribution of *Samkhya* clearly is the diversion it achieved by inspiring people to move their attention away from celestial forces of one or the other kind and focus on internal reality. This again was to prove a foundation laying for spirituality moving over the religious traditions involved in celestial forces under the name of Heaven or hell in one or other such forms. *Samkhya* called upon beings not to seek refuse with Gods and such other powers but work on awakening their already existing pure and real Self.

To that extent, *Samkhya* is undoubtedly the first theory sowing seeds of an altogether new field of knowledge, which got developed and recognized as "Spirituality" in due course of time. It was asking people to get out of daily life confusions and miseries and see the well-covered self by systematically working on self-awareness and not self-indulgence. Tool suggested for this difficult process was undertaking introspective meditational practices.

(**Note:** *For some readers, it may have been first time exposure to Samkhya Philosophy. Metaphysical Philosophies being a wider subject matter known for its finer intricacies, a separate and detailed study of Samkhya is suggested before re-reading the above portion with proper comprehension of connecting Samkhya to evolution of Spirituality.*)

Yoga: The Science of Practising Spirituality

Let us now closely look at the connection between the real and complete Yoga and Spirituality. Before we do that it is essential that we understand the real yoga in sufficient details. The real yoga is practical extension for *Samkhya*, one the foremost philosophical school from India. While *Samkhya* provided a 'theoretical' platform for people to achieve salvation by study, contemplation and meditation, many renouncers of that period were not completely satisfied about 'how' part of working for achieving liberation. The spell cast by ego was too strong to get rid of without any structured and systematic practice with assured chances of success. Thus if *Samkhya* was to be considered as a lab test, Yoga will be taken as the Therapy for treating the identified ailment. That is why it is also called practical aspect of realizing *Samkhya.* Yoga got evolved in ancient time as a way for systematically working towards achieving liberation of *'Purusha'* from the strong entanglement of '*Prakriti*'. That is why the classical Yoga is considered as a twin of *Samkhya* School as they both start and end at the same street. Majority of people today have no clear realization that it was for this purpose that Yoga, one of the fantastic practice being followed the world over for regulating working of mind, body and soul, came into being in the first place.

Evolution of Yoga as a well-defined practice known in current times is credited to Maharishi Patanjali but surely it must predate him, in its original form, by a few centuries or even more. Yoga has been around on Indian soil even before the composition of initial Hymns of *Rig-Veda.* This is concluded based on the sculptures excavated from *Sindhu Sarasvati* (popularly known as Harappa and Mohenjo-Daro Civilization) sites showing *Rishis* sitting in yogic postures, a time much before complete evolution of concepts like spirituality and religion came to exist. The historians point the dating of these excavations to a period around 3000 BC. Even in such an early phase, Indian sages had realized the importance of silencing human mind in an effort to focus on deeper depths of the mind in a serene quietness and away from subjective distortions. Patanjali worked more like an editor or redactor who organized and compiled prevailing Yoga knowledge from all earlier sources. Yoga as an extension of *Samkhya*, was aimed at the idea that if man wants to understand his place in nature and be happy and progressive, he must aim at that physical, psychological and moral development which will enable him to pry into the depth of his own Self. Man must observe, think and act; he must live, love and progress and his development on all three planes must be simultaneous.

Thus original Yoga may sound much different than the relaxation focused, stress buster, position dominated, aerobic routine filled exercise regime as being practised by most followers in modern times. Originally, it was designed as a detailed step-by-step procedure to organize a strong assault on the ego so that it is able to shred away ignorance of considering itself as *Purusha*. It was to happen over a long period of time running into years with very sustained efforts. As discussed earlier, *Samkhya* system proposed achieving the *Purusha* isolation through systematically segregating consciousness from everything such that at the end of the process, only pure consciousness remains.

Yoga practitioners of antiquity realized right in the beginning that human mind needs to be silenced as a prerequisite for accurately reflecting objective reality without its own subjective distortions. Yoga was not to create that reality but it was to prepare the human mind to become capable of apprehending it by assisting it to transform from prevailing noises, clustered thoughts and crowded views to a still position where it is disconnected to not only physical body but to that intellectual state which gives rise to newer thoughts every split of seconds.

Maharishi Patanjali has provided five distinct impulses (*Vritti*) that slave the normal human mind and listed these as Ignorance, Ego, Passion, Disgust and Lure for transient life. These impulses surface and resurface one after the other in inexhaustible sequence and with uncontrolled energy. Since, these are basic part of human nature one cannot win over these simply by study or understanding.

Human beings are deeply conditioned by lust and just having knowledge of it is not enough. Simply said, Yoga is the science of mounting a constant pressure on the subconscious mind to bring it under control and to behave as directed by a controlled mind such that it must follow command like a servant receiving instructions from his master; no questions asked and no excuses offered.

The most effective and most practised method devised to achieve that goal was named "*Raja Yoga*". This is the practice of psychic control or one pointed meditation. Raja Yoga is literally meaning "Royal Yoga" and it allows a person to rule over the vast territory of the mind in manner similar to a king controlling his kingdom. Every individual has as much control over his mind as a king has on his kingdom. Interestingly, those very reasons that converge into success of a king at the kingdom of land, apply to the success of a seeker within his kingdom of mind.

The Raja Yoga

Raja Yoga uses human mind similar to a scientist using his laboratory for scientific pursuits. The only difference being that mind is both laboratory and instrument. The power of attention when properly guided and directed towards the internal world, analyzes the mind. But stopping the mind from going out and focus on inside, concentrate all its power and finally throw those powers on the mind itself, is very difficult proposition but not impossible. Practising Yoga is equally suitable for people coming from every age group or gender or geographical background. Yoga actually works similar to all sciences; any one learning and practising it is assured of the results. It is indeed most secular concept and is already so accepted the world over. Just to prove this point, the Indian proposal for declaring 21st June as the International Yoga day, got positive recommendations from as many as 175 countries of the world. But for its most accepted secular credentials, this feat could not have been possible within a few months of the initial proposal.

Human body and mind are very well connected. If one gets disturbed, the other also gets impacted. With vast majority of humanity, and the readers can vouch it for themselves, the mind is largely under the control of body while it should actually be other way round. But before any attempt to control the mind, one is ought to control the body sufficiently. Here comes the importance of practising Yoga by sitting in stretched postures for longer durations, the practice of '*Asanas*'. But that is only a small fraction of Yoga or just a baby step towards the long journey.

Yoga practice involves gradual step up approach where mastery over first step qualifies for starting the next stage. This journey is to be completed only by practising. Simply getting knowledge of all the steps doesn't help in any way. Jumping over steps or premature climbing will only cause crash landing and every interested practitioner better pay full attention to this caution. The whole process of Raja Yoga is divided into eight steps, namely—*Yama, Niyama, Asana, Pranayam, Pratyahara* (restraint of senses from their objects), *Dharana* (fixing the mind on a single spot, concentration, '*ekagrata*'), *Dhyana,* meditation and finally *Samadhi.*

Undertaking Yama and Niyama brings in essential physical and moral preparedness for undertaking subsequent stages of the process. Let us first look at Yama, prescribed moral ethics which are required to be mastered by undertaking the followings prohibitions:

1. *Adopting complete Non-Violence* – As we may be knowing, *Ahimsa* if much wider than abstaining from violence. Observing *Ahimsa* will include avoiding injury to others in every way, not causing pain to any one, having feeling of compassion towards all living creatures, following practice of forgivingness, having peace and equanimity towards self and others, abstaining from eating animal meats, avoiding actions of all types of cruelty including for animals and other living beings.
2. *Giving up desire for having more than minimum required* – Using minimum possible resources for most minimum requirements is the point being talked here. A person should be satisfied once his basic requirement of food and shelter are met. This acceptance of minimum requirements been met should be with willing attitude, without any grudge or objection. It can be seen that the feeling is as important as the action. The idea here is to give up the desire of hoarding

of objects beyond necessities. Idea also requires giving up without any sulking or suppression. By practising this prohibition, the person is assured of relaxed mind and a feel of peace; a distinct form of happiness.

3. *Not to speak untruth* – Every word spoken must meet twin conditions of being necessary and being kind at the same time. One must speak truth and only truth and nothing but truth, and the truth without any distortion. Speaking truth at all times leads to purity of speech and mind. Every time a lie is spoken, there is a burden on soul and by abstaining from speaking we take a step towards our natural self. It will be a mistake to take this prohibition any easier as holding truth in every situation is known to require metallic strength, conviction and courage.
4. *Total abstinence from sex and intoxication* – For preserving physical and mental powers and enhancing will power, this prohibition goes a long way. Ancient Yogis called highest human energy stored in brain as '*Ojas*'. More *ojas* enables higher physical, intellectual and spiritual capability. As per Ayurveda, *Ojas* is subtle essence responsible for radiance in health, immunity system and contributor for longevity. It is created at the end of the proper digestion and efficient metabolism. The sexual fluid lost is a big drain of *ojas*. Similarly, intoxication weakens the power of judgement. Both these traits shall be required in abundance when we pursue further steps on our way up spiritual growth as well. In addition to sex other activities identified with loss of *ojas* include excessive speaking, excessive seeing, excessive listening and even excessive eating. That is why moderation is the operating word for all these activities.

As a second step, and only upon complete success achieved over the first step of following *Yama*, the aspirant must be able to follow *Niyama*, the personal ethics. Each of the Niyama is intended for mastering over bodily and psychic disciplines. These include:

1. *Complete physical and mental purity for being clean and disciplined* – This requires periodical baths, restricted eating,

regular exercises, sufficient sleep so that the body and mind remain pure and healthy at all times.

2. *Contentment* – It means being satisfied with life in totality. Contentment enables one to enjoy the peace of mind. Mental peace works on stress levels of the heart and mind. Fresh heart and mind are handy for regulating the thought process in later stages. The mind of a contended person gives up desires and attachments for all objects thereby paving the way of seeking spiritual gains.
3. *Austerities/Asceticism* – Common meaning of this ethic is translated as stern and severe self-discipline, determination and mortification. It means putting physical body through intense hardships and sufferings with the purpose to purify it completely. It works similar to a goldsmith working on precious metals to remove last traces of impurities. Fasting, penances, exposing body to climatic extremes are generally adopted methods used by sages to purify their bodies and develop capacity to bear pains and sufferings.
4. *Study Holy Scriptures* – Scriptures are supposed to be full of knowledge about all human aspects. Regular reading of the scriptures has been known to provide encouragement to seekers in order to convert their knowledge into wisdom besides expanding their knowledge on multiple planes. This is also advised to carry forward the wisdom of previous generations for use by future generations.
5. *Developing Devotion* – Complete surrender of individuality to Personal God. This Niyama requires complete abandoning of individual will to Supreme.

The dedication and commitment of aspirant in following these preparatory conditions goes to test and prove his spiritual ambition. Success in these is known to lead the practitioner to be a different kind of human being with a radical moral transformation. Yoga aspirant has to leave his unenlightened self behind, abandon '*Ahamkara*' and behave as if their soul is already liberated. Over a period of time, by sheer dent of practice, these ethical disciplines were to become second nature. No progress can be expected further unless the above-mentioned controls are exercised and psychological transformation is achieved.

At this stage, and only if the teacher was satisfied about the progress made thus far, the aspirant is allowed to initiate the very first *Asana.* Sitting in crossed leg position for hours together, motionless with back, neck and head upward, the Yoga aspirant is supposed to learn to severe the link between his mind and his senses. *Asanas* include a series of exercises, physical and mental to be gone through on daily basis until the higher states are reached. The original purpose of *Asanas* was to achieve severance of link of sense organs with mind. Each person was free to find and evolve his own ways and positions with the aim of achieving the severance of this link. That is how different people perfected different postures and many *Asanas* got evolved. One is actually encouraged to try out newer postures helping the purpose on hand. If some *Asanas* got identified with providing direct benefits for the physical fitness of the body, it was just incidental, a by-product. Keeping body healthy and strong, however, is a precondition for ensuring obstruction free *Asanas.* Point to remember is that Yoga was not so much for the body as for the mind and consciousness. Body is important but only in limited capacity. Body is the vehicle of soul where the mind is navigational steering. Of course, one needs a good vehicle to reach the destination trouble-free; but having reached the destination, the vehicle is left in the parking lot and forgotten. The destination, here, is liberation of soul.

Pranayama, the exercise to regulate breathing comes as the next step. Idea here is to inflict even greater attack on one's subconscious self. Respiration by nature is a fundamental and automatic sequence in every living being. But for pursuing *Pranayam,* one has to inflict a systematic assault to bring controlled changes in that subconscious life giving activity. '*Prana*' is the force that is setting the whole engine of our body into motion. The most obvious manifestation of *Prana* is breath. Entering through the breath will enable us to find out about the subtle forces, the nerve currents that are moving all over the body. It is by controlling these nerves that one hopes to control the body. Finally, the aspirant shall try controlling the mind also.

The person dedicating himself to practise Yoga should try *Pranayam* minimum two times every day and regularity is the key. Doing it only when you have time and skipping on other occasions will result in skipping of success also. Thought is the finest and highest action of *Prana*. Thoughts have different nature, like instinctive thoughts, the conscious thoughts and super conscious thoughts. But all thoughts also are part of *Prana* and regulation of all types of thoughts is the purpose of right *Pranayam*. Human mind is always active like a monkey. Later it gets intoxicated with desires, thus increasing the turbulence even further. Next, jealousy stings it and finally we have the demon of pride. What a deadly combination!

One has to overcome all these hurdles and it is indeed very difficult. Practice to regulate mental activity requires quite sitting for a while and letting the mind run on free. Give it the rein and don't get worried of thoughts entering your mind. Once you practise sitting in Asana over a good period, the number of thoughts, over months, will reduce gradually. In few more months, these will become fewer than before, until at last the mind will be under perfect control. This controlling and not allowing it to join with body organs is "*Pratyahara*".

Having mastered *Pratyahara*, next thing to work on is '*Ekagrata*', one pointed concentration. Important thing is to put away any emotion or association or distractions that try to invariably rush into the mind. Finally, when the mind stuff is confined and limited to exclusively to a certain specific place, '*Dharana*' is achieved. The Yoga aspirant must always practise, should try to live alone as much as possible as the companionship is a distraction of mind. He should neither speak much nor work much. The biggest advantage of Yoga is that it tones down nervous excitement resulting in compressing both peaks and valleys of emotional impacts, brings calmness and enables human to see things more clearly. That is why a Yogi is said to be above emotional influences.

One should also give up all argumentation to avoid loss of mental balance. Talking does not help in realizing things of subtle planes. So, please give up all vain talks. Also give up the desire for nibbling on one idea after another. Having followed all above steps, one comes to '*Dhyana*', the final stage of meditation. When the mind has been fully trained to remain fixed on a certain internal or external idea/action/thought for as long as desired by the Yogi, it is called *Dhyana*. Having reached to this stage, the master Yogi thus sinks deeply into his inner world much beyond ordinary consciousness. This stage is called "*Samadhi*", trance. Here the Yogi is able to completely control his psychic life and he becomes impervious, invulnerable for his own condition.

To recapture the essence of last few stages, we see that *Pranayam* throws out all impurities of the body. By *Dharana*, all impurities of the mind get thrown out and by *Pratyahara* all impurities of attachment meet the same result. Finally, when *Samadhi* is achieved, one reaches to the stage where everything hiding the Soul is taken off. The mind and senses are to be disciplined until the mind process is suspended in complete emptiness and merge with the Self.

Modern versions of Yoga come under the names like *Hatha* Yoga, *Kundalini* Yoga and *Kriya* Yoga and many other names being added continuously. These are like product variants of a market leader by working on branding and packaging as marketing strategies and projecting advantages in catchy phrases without much difference in the base product.

Practising Raja Yoga leads to a deeper understanding of self, including intrinsic positive qualities and innate values. Over long periods, this understanding merges with the practitioner's daily awareness constructively influencing his/her self-image and how they relate to the world at large. Practising Raja Yoga is supposed to lead the person to gain understanding and application for values such as justice, freedom, respect and love by allowing emergence of fresh perspectives based on meditative contemplations.

Basic premise of Raja Yoga is that perception of divine is covered by the disturbances present in our own mind space. Once the mind is worked upon using well-defined eight steps of Raja Yoga, the same mind gets tamed and becomes still and pure. At that stage the real Self comes out shining of its own. Let us understand this with the help of a comparison of two lakes of similar sizes, depth and dimensions. The first lake is having uncontrolled settlements on all banks resulting in discharge of pollution, its sides are open allowing winds to flog it by generating sizable waves, it get muddied by countless tourists flocking in all seasons, different types of speedboats are used which spill variety of oils on the surface of the lake. All these factors result in water remaining murky and dirty. Surely, there is no possibility of seeing the bottom of such a lake.

Well, this lake is directly comparable with the mind of a normal person where the bottom of the lake is 'Atman', the true Self. Surely, the murk and dirt wouldn't let any tourist see the bottom of the lake with any clarity? Now let us look at the second lake. Its banks are well protected by mountains restricting winds from generating waves, the sides are all having green covers and human settlements have their own alternate sewage and storm water drains diverting water discharge to treatment plants. The boats are all flat bottomed and running on solar panels restricting any kind of discharge into the lake. All tourists visiting are made to strictly follow SOPs completely protecting the entire environment. The water of this lake is, therefore, calm, tranquil and still. This helps preserving the lake serenity to its natural form. The clarity and stillness combines to allow clear visibility of the depths throughout the surface of the lake. Even a leaf lying at the bottom of the lake can be seen clearly by any naked eye. Different steps of Yoga are nothing but systems designed to preserve the calm, tranquil and still reflection of all mental processes of a human mind.

Yoga and Spirituality

Having looked at Yoga along with its various forms, it is obvious that the complete Yoga system cultivates spirituality by enhancing awareness about subtle dimensions of the physical body and mental processes. Yogic forms promote its practitioner's perspective towards his/her connect with self as well as the entire universe in a unique manner. Both these disciplines require impermeable moral and ethical attitude, immutable commitment and unfaltering regularity to obtain results. Both Yoga and Spirituality place similar importance on intentions and sincerity. Neither of these is visible by any external signs. Actually, one can go on and on with the sameness of Yoga and Spirituality both in theory and practice. Yoga is one of the best and most proven practices to scale spiritual peak and certainly is the most structured of all the options on hand. The connect between these two is best understood by comparing the same with popular mobile operating systems; if Yoga is to be taken as a proprietary iOS – the OS from Apple Inc. – Spirituality can be looked as Android operating system which is free and open source software where individual developers are free to work on their own Apps without strict conditions applied for Apps conducive with iOS while end purpose of both Operating Systems are almost similar.

Millions of people from all over the world are practising Yoga and are getting benefited towards their spiritual growth besides health benefits for both body and mind. A complete Yogi is a person who is able to consciously unify his body, mind, emotions and soul so that they all work harmoniously in tandem to discover full possibilities of the human existence. As propagated by Bhagwad Gita, Yoga is a way of achieving union with the entire universe, and at that moment, Yoga and Spirituality merge completely in an inseparable way. People practising Yoga even only through *Asanas* report significant progress towards their improved spiritual awareness. One can just imagine the immense impact of Yoga on making spiritual progress if the real and exhaustive Yogic science is directed completely towards that progress. Yoga, in every form and variation, undoubtedly, remains an integral Spiritual practice without any single doubt.

Meditation

The Art of Practising Spirituality

Meditation has been practised since antiquity. It is a common component among most cultures in one or the other form and has been taken as a systematic training to direct own mind to reflect inside. We all may have some exposure towards meditation as a practice, method or technique and expectedly must have attempted it with varying degree of success. But in spite of it being practised by most of us, it has as many meanings as contexts. But with all its variations, the common thread to all types and shades of meditation is voluntary internal effort for self-regulating mental processes in one way or the other. The regulation may include inside reflection for observing the mind's contents and patterns and later guiding the same for inducing desired mode of consciousness. Surely, it encompasses a broad range and varieties of techniques evolved at different times in different parts of the world.

While one can trace Meditation practices to all major religious thoughts, the origin of meditation is associated with Eastern Spiritual Practices right from Rig-Veda times, if not earlier. The most popular and highly revered *Gayatri Mantra* of "*Om bhur bhuva swaha....*" starts with the words "We meditate on....". This goes to prove that meditation practice in India is as old as Rig-Veda in the least. Meditative practices are easily traceable among all ancient civilizations and religious thoughts. In fact, within BC era itself Jews, Confucian, Taoist, Jain and Buddhist have all evolved their own unique meditative techniques besides Vedic practices. Starting at the turn of millennium and in between Philo of Alexandria and Plotinus, even Greek have developed full version of their own meditative practices.

Western Christians also came out with their own meditation practices by 6th Century AD.

Meditation and Its Modern Uses

Having initially originated for the purpose of advancing spiritual growth, the meditation in modern times is increasingly practised for benefits related to stress reduction, relaxation and as a tool for self-improvement. It was the evolution of neo-meditative systems in 1950 that led to a sudden big boost to meditation. It was then that the stage was set for globalized expansion of centres and teachers promising all kinds of meditations assuring benefits ranging from ecstasy to bliss. In a way, meditation expansion also can be traced with popularization of Yoga as both these streams attracted a common pool of seekers falling out of particular aspects of materialism spread in the Western World of second half of Twentieth Century. But everything that glitters is not gold. Different people are seen holding diametrically opposite versions make Meditation a very complex system. On top of that, many of the versions stand far from the real thing.

Its being old and common practice makes it vulnerable for different people to understand it differently. But we also realize that not all practitioners are able to appreciate the real thing and many remain deprived from getting desired advantages from their practices. So, knowing it in proper perspective becomes critical. It becomes all the more important because, as the most effective tool, meditation is deeply linked to the subject under our scanner, the seeking of spirituality.

In its widest possible explanation it might include systems, techniques, methods and routines that govern our internal attitudes and activities. Meditation is supposed to be the most effective tool of regulating our internal awareness and to enhance the same to the highest level where we become the world and the entire world get perceived as our own extension. Comprehending such a deep subject will require practical realization because intellectual comprehension alone, even with use of best possible and precise combination of words, in unlikely to offer much help. Actually, it is much more than practice or comprehension alone. Meditation is more of a discovery.

To begin with, it helps us to be aware about our self at our deepest level beyond our usual divisions and segregations. Meditation involves knowing about our self not only on conscious level but on a much deeper level, the subconscious state as well; it brings clarity and neutrality about our motives, intentions and designs without any colour of what is socially or morally right or wrong. As the whole world is our own extension, any desire of change involves change at our individual level. In the process of such a change, meditation is the tool used for reprogramming our brain and mental working. If our intellect is our CPU, meditation works as software that cleans all the sensors, indicators and activators to ensure correct reading and feedback get exchanged with the CPU and corrective action initiated wherever required. At that level, meditation helps us in making our reasoning more reasonable and our logic more logical. It helps us remove subjectivity and replaces the same with increased objectivity at all levels.

Meditation: What it is Not

Ancient Indian sages have effectively used the process of negation to explain many complex and critical subjects. Under this process of negation, the perceptions get refined by evaluating all the peripheral meanings and negating them one by one such that ultimately pure understanding is the only thing that remains. Considering importance of Meditation as the most effective practice for pursuing Spirituality, let us try and approach it in the same manner by explaining and filtering out on what is not right meditation. Since our purpose is to reach to the very foundation of our understanding, sometimes, very harsh and strong words may have to be used to bring the point home with clarity. Use of such words is a matter of accentuation to coerce removal of all traces of grey areas from reader's understanding of the subject on hand. Let us simply recall the scenarios that are branded as being meditation in normal parlance and look carefully if that is really so.

1. *Meditation is not about controlling mind:* Many teachers, modules, systems and authors might be seen advocating their audience to control their mind or regulate it or redirect it or engage it in particular direction. But this is all farce.

Decades of practice has not helped people to control their mind as all efforts of controlling human mind are destined to result in certain failure. The DNA of human mind does not recognize 'No fly Zone'. One can put as many signs as possible everywhere but mind is meant for wandering free without any rhyme or reasons.

2. *Mechanical repetition is not meditation:* Even when it happens to be the better of best possible systems, repetition at best can be good vocal exercise. It might as well be a good ritual for many but following anything mechanically can never be called meditation. Even if we are talking about proven systems like *Pranayam* and Yoga, the moment a person starts following them mechanically he has already shut down his mind with its own thinking ability. The mind should be active and creative but repetitions don't create creativity; all it can be effective is for robotic actions. That does not help you in reaching to the core of your existence. You may like it or not, repetition of rituals, let it be the best of all, turns you as good or bad as a machine. How can we expect creativity from a mind riddled in set systems?
3. *Following some system suggested by best of expert or best of realized individuals of past or present can't be meditation:* Their system may have worked for them but need not or may not work for others. Both times and systems have changed a lot in the interim period. Following others is reducing you to become substandard beings and such a being can't even understand what meditation is all about. Our own truth has to be learned by us singularly with our own efforts. Experiences of others may just show us the way and nothing beyond.
4. *Meditation is not about sharpening concentration:* Concentration demands strong determination. Experience suggests that strong walls need to be erected in the mind to let it engage in selected thoughts for a longer duration. Every one of us who has tried concentration can vouch how little success is possible in such barricades. Concentration by very definition is coercive in nature and is bound to fail.
5. *Focusing the mind on any object, organ or thought is not*

meditation: Focus, like concentration, involves duality of pairs of forces at conflict with each other all the time; the one watching and the other being watched; the one regulating and the other being regulated; the one seeking freedom and the other that wish to control it. How can a mind involved in ongoing turf war with its own twin sibling, enjoying equal rights by birth, can ever achieve concentration on pure truth? However, proper focus as ability is very well desired for learning meditation.

6. *Meditation is not a worship or prayer*: There is no supreme when you meditate. It is only about you and you alone. It has no connection with any religious strands whatsoever. So whatever works for worship doesn't work for meditation. Worship and prayers generally involve singing or uttering prayers and all such activities take you away from silence. As against this, meditation necessitates a complete silence, a silence of inside where there are no thoughts rising, where emotions are at deep sleep. This is a condition which can't be described in words at all.
7. *Meditation is not about seeking escape from something or someone.* Neither it is running away from real understanding of Self in its true form. It is not to avoid some harsh realities as an escape into emptiness. This emptiness arrives when all questions are answered and all doubts are cleared with pure wisdom and true realization.
8. *Meditation is not about having some profound, godly, spiritual or transcendental experience:* It is neither for pursuing some sort of idealism. Our normal mind is pretty busy in materialistic and sensuous engagements and such a petty mind is not capable for experiencing something great. As it is, experience is defined as an art of accumulating greed for repeating particular feeling over and over again. Experiences are grounded in past. Meditation will involve learning rather than visiting past or dreaming for impossible. The learning can come only when there are no accumulations; when thoughts and motives are being assimilated as a constant process. Meditation involves reaching to deeper levels of sub-consciousness and that is

neither an experience nor any qualitative subject. The state of mind suitable for meditation has to be just pure, complete, natural and spontaneous.

9. *Meditation does not involve any unraveling of mysteries:* Yes, meditation deals with consciousness, something deeper than thoughts but there is no mystery involved. Being natural and spontaneous, it can be logically understood and practised by a dedicated practitioner exactly as most others skills are learnt and acquired. What gets revealed is not something exceptional but the real truth that is always there in the depth of our being and is turned invisible, suppressed or overburdened under ignorance or false understanding.
10. *Meditation is not about relaxation or calming down from any stressful situation***:** It is neither a way of getting a sense of serenity or rejuvenating in any way. Expecting physical advantages alone from meditation, for example, amounts to firing real rockets for celebrating *Diwali.* The practitioner experiences physical benefits purely as incidental and indirect benefits. Benefits for agility, relaxed body and improved working of mind are purely as add-ons or by-products.
11. *Sitting in straight posture and working on regulated breathing with the aim of some sort of unique enlightenment can't be meditation:* These conditions aptly qualify to be called as 'day-dreaming' or 'self-hypnotizing'. People having tried meditation by sitting in such postures can directly relate to their own experiences and appreciate the link.
12. *Meditation can't simply be a self-improvement project***:** Improvements come from change in attitudes and emotional intelligence. Sitting alone and going over 'what is' and 'what should it be' or 'how it can be' may be a self-talk but it has no power to bring changes that are key to slightest variation in human behaviour.
13. *Meditation can't be an obligation or a duty***:** It is not that we sit for so many minutes or hours and we must have some exotic result. No, it is not similar to getting perspiration after going through a particular regime at the gym. There is no direct input to output ratio that works here.
14. *Meditation is not for only saints or scientists, neither it is for*

eccentrics or tricksters: It is very much for *Karma Yogis* of the real world like us. The only condition is that it requires your will of getting transformed into a newer purer soul.

While none of above is meditation, all of these points have to be crossed over to rise to the desired level of achieving transformation of mind. At best, some of above can be considered as initial stages to be climbed. The ultimate purpose of meditation is to learn about patterns and habits of our mind before understanding and trying to redirect or reengage the same. For the required inside focus and access to our consciousness, the mind must be clear, relaxed, awake, alert and ready. But each one of us who have tried observing it knows it well that our mind itself is the biggest obstacle standing between our deeper awareness and ourselves. It is said that the mind has a mind of its own and working around it is easier said than done.

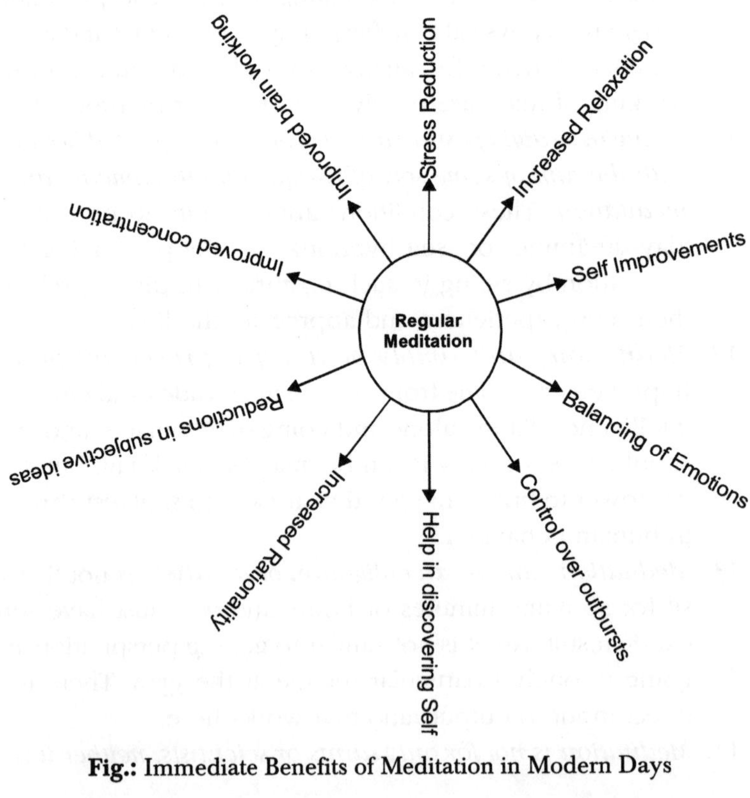

Fig.: Immediate Benefits of Meditation in Modern Days

Understanding Right Meditation

In simple words, meditation is the technique or process meant to help an individual recognize his/her original, pure and universal identity. So, comprehending meditation requires understanding the identity of an individual, an identity that has nothing to do with its name, nationality, religion, physical appearance or any other label or attribute. The fundamental identity of each person relates to that unchanged aspect of one's being which remains intact in every circumstance. Such fundamental identity at the core of a person's very existence is nothing but pure consciousness. This consciousness alone is the essence behind all doing, witnessing, feeling and thinking by that person's physical body and mind aggregate.

This very consciousness, the permanent aspect of every person, is called the Self. As a valid explanation, the whole universe is said to be an extension of the same consciousness. Scientific studies also suggest that at quantum level the whole universe is just a play of energy in some or the other form. The same energy at the helm of entire visible world is spiritually called supreme consciousness where everything moving and dead is taken as manifestation of the same consciousness and that is how the whole world is shown connected to each other in an integrated manner.

> "Meditation is nothing but the art of realizing this very energy, this very Self."

Practically speaking, meditation is the sum total of all techniques and systems used for achieving transformation of our mind aimed at developing a state of consciousness where the mind is free from all scattered thoughts, patterns, conflicts and divisions; where the mind is able to develop focus, clarity of thoughts, emotional balance and ability to see things in their pure natural ways with spontaneity and freedom. In order to do all this, the brain must be perfectly in order. This is the same kind of order that our mind achieves by dreams during our sleep. Each morning when we get up, the mind is much fresh as compared to the time we went to sleep. Similar to mind achieving its order at subconscious level during our sleep, meditation helps to achieve order at conscious level. It can be seen that normal human mind is busy doing one thing, saying another and thinking yet another. Such a mind can't be used for bringing creativity and bliss. It needs to be restored with its order when everything is in one direction, the direction of pure truth and reality. Meditation is the art of achieving that state of our conscious mind.

Buddha was once asked, "What have you gained from meditation." He replied "Nothing!" "However," Buddha said, "Let me tell you what I lost: Anger, Anxiety, Depression, Insecurity, Fear of Old Age and Death."

Preparing the Mind for Proper Meditation

The mind comes out as the most important subject and object for understanding depths of meditation. Surely, the mind must be quiet, should be in order and should be able to stand alone of its own. A quiet mind is free from suppressions, pressures and distortions or influenced from outside elements. In order to reach to such a state, the person is required to sink his unwanted burden of memories, impressions, opinions, explanations, justifications, beliefs and bindings. That is possible only when the duality of 'what is' and 'what should be' comes to an end. So long the duality remains, the ability for pure observations remain suspended. Coming out of these shackles is most desirable preparation for readying the mind for pure contemplation.

Meditation was never something that got achieved by anyone with ease. People do get success but those get it faster who are able to walk away from systems and bookish techniques as that will only promote robotic machines. Simply put, the mind will not get prepared for meditation so long as moral, ethical, compassion and empathy levels of the person have not been upgraded to higher standards. One may try for a year or twenty years, seeds for successful meditation will germinate only on a morally and ethically well prepared ground. The silence of the mind desired must arise voluntarily without any kind of force applied. The mind must be willingly and voluntarily ready to accept, perceive and observe all new and fresh objects. Above all, the mind must be ready to see a thing without need for evaluation or comparison or judgement. One might feel that this is an impossible task but if you don't go for impossible, surely, you are destined to fall for possible.

A practitioner may have a practical curiosity to know if and when his mind is well prepared for meditation. One such technique is simple enough to apply. The practitioner can check his sleep patterns and recollect his dreams. Absence of dreams during sleep of such a person can be taken as a clear signal that mind is well prepared for meditative state. The dreams are a result of working of the subconscious mind in the sleep state based on what the waking mind does during the daytime. If we remain aware with purity and holding truth during the day there will be no need for the subconscious mind to rewind during sleep. Besides a pure mind, a still body is another key requirement for perfect meditation. Body is holding the mind and any activity at body level is bound to generate some or the other impulse in the mind. Accordingly, *meditation practice requires sub sections of the body including its nervous system, sense organs, action organs, sub-conscious system as well as immune system to be grounded in peace.* Regular practice of Yogic exercises and Pranayam comes handy for this very purpose. It is said that gaining physical stillness is comparatively less challenging in comparison of mind.

Ultimately, meditation means finding a way of living where there are no conflicts left to resolve; where a person is able to see reality with his open heart without burdening its mind and without allowing old memories or past conditionings to fume out thoughts about what it should be. Each one of us must have experienced some moments when our heart is able to see and appreciate things as they are without any intervention from our mind. We know these as 'wow' moments. Meditation is just another name for the efforts to experience more and more such moments and for subjects of choice where mere glimpses are replaced by longer durations.

Meditation is all about self and this self can neither be known based on what others say about it. Teachers and guides including books and formulas can only help you showing the mountain ahead, where you alone would have to make your own efforts to climb. You alone will have to select, use and discard your ladders and clutches. You alone will need to find and accept your own truth without explanations or justifications. Be ready for the journey without any timeframe and without having address of the destination. What a journey it is going to be!

Techniques for Practising Meditation

Essential perceptual modes of individuals vary from each other to a large extent. Some of us respond well to sound while others do so to words; some feel comfortable with guided tour while others like to explore all by themselves in isolation; some have strong beliefs while others are open to take on new ideas on merit. Each such group will need a different technique for harnessing and directing energies away from obstructions and distractions to contemplate on any important aspect. The energies mentioned above include emotions, feelings, attitudes and desires. Accordingly, different techniques have evolved over the periods to help people meditate on their own issues. These include use of a *mantra*, focus on some visual symbol, concentrating on flow of energy, reciting lines from a scripture, concentrating on breath, focusing on a body part, focusing on a person or relationship or on any particular ambition. Guided meditation under the instructions of a guru is yet another widely followed technique used by many.

Each and every technique is acceptable and should be taken just like a mutable support system liable to get changed in due course. So, we need not be obsessed with the technique and should move over from one to another freely and make use of what works with us individually. Let us remember that the final destination of any meditation is to reach to the internal empty space far beyond the noise of this visible world. Each of the technique has power of opening some doors or windows of our inner space and we are ultimately required to access entire inner space without leaving any corner dark and dirty. So, we are in any case required to work over all types of techniques without any fixed routine. On a personal note, I even make use of more than one technique in a single session depending on distractions arising on that given day.

More importantly, the technique we adopt should not generate stress for our mind or body in any ways. As such, we should try out every available tool and create our own mantra and revise it as and when need arises. Exploring alternate techniques also becomes very helpful in exploring our own Self-Awareness, an important aspect of our spiritual progress. Irrespective of the technique that we are adopting on a given day, right posture and right preparation mentioned elsewhere in this very section remain of paramount importance.

Sharing of My Personal Technique

In order to help the beginners, I would like to share my own technique of meditation, something which has evolved (and continues to evolve) over last ten years or so. This sharing may also work as exchange of notes with people having similar experience of their own sessions. My preferred time is around ten o'clock in the morning which is clearly after over five hours of waking up. The interim time is normally used for morning walk, Yoga exercises, Pranayam followed by going over news besides bath and breakfast. After breakfast, I attend to mails, messaging, utilities and such other works so that my mind is absolved from all types of urgencies and exigencies of the hour. If I know about prior engagements for the 10 AM slot, I sit for meditation before breakfast but after bath. You may like to select your own time slot that take care of your personal conditions with the desire that when you wish to sit for meditation, let there be no urgency or time pressures or tiredness of body or mind. Urgencies and pressures provide extra strength to our mental processes and that work like a strong wall erected in between mind regulation and its ability to move towards one pointedness on any object or subject of our choice.

It is needless to mention that you should have an assigned corner for your sitting and the place should be clean and free from cluttering of physical objects. I have created my space within my home office where the assigned space is used exclusively for meditations and nothing else. Any sound as well as bright light work as a big distraction and hence this place must be ideal for spending time in solitude. It is funny that bright light distracts even when you are sitting with eyes closed. The carpet and cushion used during meditation is chosen with utmost care for providing comforting support. Initially I used to burn an incense stick but later I dispensed with it after realizing that even the nice smell is an indication of some sort of attachment. In short, please create your special space that is clean, quiet and exclusive. Equally important is to ensure it is neutral to temperature, smell, lighting and space.

My session starts with deep and relaxed breathing. I do not wish to deliberately shorten or lengthen the duration of inhalation, exhalation or the change over in between. Slowly over next 8 to 12 minutes, I slowly move the point of focus from nostrils to the location of heart in the chest along the entire respiratory track consisting of nose and throat mucous membranes, voice box, windpipe and entry into the lungs. The idea is to engage the mental activities exclusively focused on the breathing such that flight of thoughts is diverted from other directions to the inner space bit by bit. It is interesting to feel the temperature, smell and sound of the breaths at different points on the respiratory track. This entire process is aimed at directing the mental activity withdrawn from the external world and redirected towards inner core. Indeed it proves much more difficult than it sounds. But it is also the foundation for the further success of each and every meditation session. So, this process must continue every day and every session until you are able to feel the concentration of all your mental faculties towards your internal space by cutting from the external world in a voluntary manner.

It is essential to keep the whole exercises as relaxing, enjoyable and de-stressing without expecting any sort of exotic experience. Keenly observing our breathing with real feel of each of the palpitation and throb of the heart is a very effective therapy as it works to calm down the entire thought process and help in making us aware about our consciousness. In a way this is the process of entering in our own treasured cave of heart. Many people consider this stage itself as end of meditation. No, this is merely a first glance of things to come and settling just for this is surely a poor bargain. We must ensure that the whole session is voluntary and there are no resolutions made for the session or process. Use of force results in letting the door of this inner cave shut even harder and deprives us from accessing the very inner core.

As I start my session, the thoughts are as usual and as normal but the process of deep breathing with focus on sensations in the entire breathing track helps in moving the thoughts in the background progressively bringing me in peace, silence and in touch with my consciousness. In between there are occasional random thoughts. But redirecting the focus on the rhythm of breathing and feel for its sensations brings back the consciousness to desired space. I have also observed that the number of random thoughts arising in the meditation sessions has progressively reduced. To begin with whole lot of time got wasted waiting for the focus to come back on inner space but with practice, less and fewer efforts are needed to get back to the desired state. The key for this improvement, for sure, is the regularity of practice.

After few minutes when the point of concentration of breathing has reached right up to the lungs, a very narrow opening is assumed on the other side which has an opening into a dormant cave sort of space somewhere around the heart. Taking a crude example to put across my experience, it is like entering into an empty red colour hot water rubber bottle which expands only as much as the volume of water put in. Initially, I assumed various visible symbols being there. One day I will assume *Hanumana* idol, the other day I will assume Lord Rama being installed out there to focus the attention for as long as possible. Some day, I will just assume the space like an imaginary amniotic sac filled with fluid such that all objects/ scenes obstructing concentration are able to swim across gracefully. Over the years, the continued meditation requires no symbols to concentrate on and it is now possible to hold the attention in some sort of void within inner core. By now this imaginative space has turned out to be a virtual space with endless possibilities and dimensions. It can now accommodate visualization of every kind of thought, object or person or even emotions and feelings. However, even today this cave or space is accessed only after the perfect breathing has been experienced for couple of minutes for proper synchronizations.

Now my practice involves quietly peeping into this vast inner space where I enter and position myself in a small corner so that I am able to observe all activities happening in that space as an external observer. At this stage I am just like a bundle of consciousness without any form or shape such that I am there but no one else can see me being there. My imagined inner space is now very flexible and keeps expanding or shrinking at will based on the subject matter of that moment of meditation. Breathing and presence of this independent observer keeps the mind engaged constantly such that it has no time left for chasing/entertaining any other thought(s). The very imagination of reaching to this inner space and synchronized deep breathing itself results into a unique situation where heart and mind feel converged into one identity. At this stage there is no difference in feelings and thinking; mind, heart, intellect, eyes, ears, memory, experiences, knowledge all get converged into this unique identity without any segregation what so ever. I take it as my introduction to my very own consciousness.

Sitting there in that inner space, I am left with no identity tags or personal opinions. In that state all I am left of is consciousness, truth and purity. This space contains its own stage where objects and subjects of meditation keep performing live like a play being enacted at the stage. Interestingly, in this space even thoughts are as visible as a part of body or innate objects like tree, river or mountain. This is the time when there is no connection with the body, ego or intellect. There are no sounds out here, not even from the breathing itself which seems as if it has gone in background. While in this state, I have realized my inability to differentiate if the actual breath is inhalation or exhalation. In this state I could feel the presence of entire world inside me coexisting along with a wonderful silence.

Next step revolves around concentrated thinking on a specific topic. On any given day, it may be an object, thought, idea or process. I don't follow any rigid process for selecting the subject of my daily meditation as I find it easier to let my subconscious throw out the subject for each session. Many times one subject leads to another in a linked or unlinked chain. At times, I just meditate over some encounter of previous day/days where events are gone over for observing real intentions and drives beyond the words and gestures actually spoken and used.

This process allows me to see through things in a different light of clarity. At times, I wish to know the source of my thoughts and this state helps me understand the real me where my real motives are known without any colours of what should be or what is right or wrong. This state also allows me to role play on behalf of others and that brings a lot of peace as acts and words of others get accepted without judgements. This process combines meditation with enhancing pure observation. It also destroys barriers between me and the world outside and allows me to see myself perfectly linked with the rest of the world without boundaries. It certainly allows me to melt my fragmentations and divisions at least during the time my session continues. The entire session spans about 50 minutes to an hour. In the beginning even half an hour used to be big success but continuity has been able to lengthen the duration and most importantly bring reductions into disruptive thoughts creating obstructions. Beyond an hour, my body starts losing its poise. With practice, the mental process has not only accepted the concentrated pointedness on a chosen object or subject but also started enjoying that as a preferred state.

My purpose of sharing my technique is not to propagate the same but bring forth an example well practised to instill confidence with those currently struggling in their initial efforts. Please don't lose hope and please don't worry about your tools or techniques. Everything is ok to try and ultimately you will end up finding your own combination provided you remain dedicated for your practice and you have taken care of the right posture and preparation for improving your ethical behaviour.

In the beginning years, my subjects for meditation were largely related to obvious divisions in the real world. There were more people and situations inviting immediate attention. But over the years, those issues have digressed in background and newer issues pertaining to Self (the whole concept of which will be dealt in greater details in following chapters) and consciousness replaced the earlier issues. I assume that to be a natural progression of spiritual journey. In any ways the subject of meditation having been left to the subconscious system, one can be comfortable that the same keeps pace with our individual spiritual evolution. With years gone by, I assume that success over meditation is linked to our own craving for knowing the hidden inner world; higher the intensity, easier should be the meditation process.

But let us not forget that tools, equipment as well as laboratory used during meditation is our own mind where we wish to observe its patterns and habits and try cultivating newer and more positive ways of being. It will not be out of place to say that, in broader sense, every conscious activity will qualify to be a meditation practice so long as the mind is free from all types of distractions, memories, desires and attachments. That is why many people also call it a way of life more than any technique.

Practical Tips for Effective Meditation

Every single session of meditation accrues some direct and indirect benefits for sure. Each session adds to clarity by removing some doubts and confusions. In immediate terms it makes you calmer, sharper and smarter for sure. Progress into advance stage should result in bringing you directly in touch with your own real self. Once there are no conflicts between reality and temporary identities, there is no inner division in '*what is*' and '*what it should be*'. A person free from such conflicts and divisions will automatically be at peace with self and others. He will no longer need to defend or protect false image or projected forms and hence, he stops perceiving threat from others. Soon, he will graduate to have peace with the world as he starts containing the world rather than the world containing him. Earlier world was able to impose itself on him and influence his feelings and perceptions but not now. No doubt, it is a tough journey but every step in right direction is full of endless possibilities and that is why it attracts best of human minds at all times.

Enhanced self-awareness is the prerequisite for starting advance levels of meditation. Right awareness about self equips the person to appreciate that he himself is world. So, any desire to change the world will be automatically realized as the desire to change self. What we are talking is not about physical change but change in our attitude to look at world with proper pair of eyes, with a neutral vision without any shade of 'what it should be'. Bringing such changes requires reprogramming of our brain several times over. Ability to identify the changes required and opting for right programming to bring those changes is, in right earnest, the beginning of meditation. Later and much later, when one is able to sort out all possible programming requirements and reaches to a level where the core of the being is filled only with voluntary silence, it can be said to be the true realization of meditation.

The main object of focus in advance meditation is the Self that is loving, tender, subtle, and generous. But all these qualities become known only when we are able to end the duality of lower self and higher self. We can expect to access our higher self but only when our own state is able to acquire qualities of love and tenderness mentioned above. The ground rules shared below are some practical tips for beginners. In due course, they can very well grow out of these and chalk out their own way forward. These points are initial aids and may help in early stages only.

1. Your practice requires your commitment; it better be treated as sacred ritual. It also requires regularity. Attempting it on and off or only on select occasions will keep pushing the benefits towards unknown future time.
2. Be ready to invest in a proper place with right environment and ambiance. Worst come worst it can even be a portable little place. Let there be some space or setting that is used for meditation sessions alone. Random selection of place impact results negatively, especially for beginners.
3. Since our body is both instrument and lab to be used for the session, it better be taken care of before starting each session; proper hygiene, well rested muscles, comfortable clothing and near empty stomach are some points that contribute bit by bit to make the lab ready for best use of its finer instruments.
4. If you believe in symbols, create some symbols for the place to be used for your sessions. You may like to make use of a lamp, preparing an altar, lighting a candle, incense burning etc. An untrained human mind accepts external symbols more than we tend to agree. Visual, Mantra, sound or any combination of these may be tried, depending on what works better for you. If nothing else, these symbols help in getting initial preparation in place for the mind to get ready.
5. You just can't be in any hurry. It is a serious business and demands full patience. It is not worship; meditation is not possible with an agitated mind. Complete relaxation of body, mind, thinking process and every other human sub-system is a must for proper meditation. Actually, you are required to perfectly relax to meditate and not meditate to relax.
6. Before attempting each and every meditation session, it is essential to prepare your body and mind with your own

routine of *Pranayam* and Yoga or a combination of some such techniques. The idea is to prepare the mind to be willing to focus inward. These steps are known to positively influence the mind to look inside in a voluntary manner. Interestingly, you will be required to undertake *Pranayam* even after years into practice.

7. Explore your own technique or combination of techniques that allow your mind to rest and stay. Experimenting with alternate techniques will allow you to realize the optimum conditions through your own observation. Don't worry about subjects or thoughts to be meditated during your sessions. This search will keep moving from time to time and that is fine. Please remember that different types of ladders are required at different elevations and slopes.
8. What it requires necessarily is regularity. Any one taking on-off method will fail to make progress. Please remember that sitting every day at roughly same time and at same place for thirty minutes is more important than sitting for four hours on a Sunday or any other day for that matter.
9. While knowing self, be ready to go through tons of shame, disappointment, discouragement, clash of mind and heart. Don't get disheartened your reaction is the proof that you did not know your real self until now. It is not about quality of self but your own clarity about it. Once you graduate to your real Self, qualitative divisions are doomed for sinking anyways.
10. Please remember that you are here to explore depths of your own truth and that has nothing to do what others could or could not do. Have no reliance on others and make no comparisons with others. They never know you as much as you know yourself. How can they help you then?
11. Please remember that there are no set criteria for being eligible to attain success in meditation. It is neither mathematic nor an art form that only few people could excel. Every human being who can think and apply logic is qualified for meditation.
12. It is not a destination but an ongoing process. It is a process that remains in flux all the time. There is nothing static here as everything keeps refining all the time. Be ready to see

changes in your own thoughts and feelings. Practice for longer periods should lead to refinements and that is only sure sign of success.

13. Along the whole journey, be ready to expect many detours, sidetracks, hairpin turns, potholes and unprepared road patches. No, it has never been a smooth journey for any one. Expect days after days when nothing will be working. Our own mind has so many tricks in store and is capable of frustrating your best of intentions on days together. The process of enslaving an intelligent and capable entity was never easy. Brave people don't let courage slip and persistence always pays in the end.
14. Similar to other human relationships, be ready to get impressed by initial looks before ultimate reality catching up. There are going to be a lot of courtship, offence taking, cajoling, complaining, time spending before you and your meditation start living in proper live-in relationship with mutual interdependence. One is advised to remain practical in this period.
15. Do not try any coercive method; it will never give positive result. It is said that by force you can only bring the horse to water but can't make it drink. It is so true for right meditation sessions too. There will be gaps when you don't find yourself ready or motivated enough. Surely, there will be pauses due to one or the other reasons but any desire for exerting force is always going to be counterproductive. Go for concentration but only when your mind feels satisfied to do so. It is a fight among equals. Don't ever try forcing your mind to concentrate. Remember it doesn't need visa to fly across places.
16. Be ready to face frustrations. Knowing your own mind and your sheer inability to bring it under any order is a very challenging and frustrating experience. The good thing is that you are not alone into it. It is so with every other aspirant. Many beginners are seen losing interest in continuing but success comes to those who are dedicated and committed for continuing with determination.
17. If you don't experience sense of peace, joy, comfort and relaxation after the session, review the potential reasons

before you get up. It helps for improving results in the next day session.

Slowly you may like to keenly take notes of your own experiences and make your own chart of things that work and otherwise. It is a very interesting journey and success achieved in initial sessions start feeding to motivations for more and more. Because it is a journey without a destination, the fun never ends.

Effective meditation also requires proper knowledge about breathing and relaxation techniques. It sounds silly but not everyone knows that for superior performance, our mind requires at least three times more flow of oxygen than other body organ. This equation becomes more important in case of aspirants working in offices or such other indoor environments that are generally oxygen starved. The reason behind this starving is the ignorance about necessity of learning to inhale deeply. Unfortunately no system or institution in modern times focuses on this aspect. Most of us don't feel any compulsion of deep inhaling and we don't do anything sans compulsions. Undertaking *Pranayam*, therefore, before every session of meditation is to be considered as very essential.

Next requirement is to make the body absolutely relaxed before starting each meditation session. Use of Yoga posture of a dead body, '*Shava Asana*' works wonders for immediate relaxation of both body and mind provided one undertakes this posture correctly. Relaxed body and mind results in balanced energy of our mind and body aggregate and prepares right environment for getting positive results.

A revisit to this section after completing the subsequent topics dealings with "Self-Awareness", "Finding Real Truth" and "Preparations for Spiritual Journey" should enormously help the seekers to gain greater understanding for their meditation sessions. These topics contain several concepts that will better illuminate the criticality of right meditation. But so far as Spiritual progress is concerned, Meditation, to the very least, is an essential technique for achieving deep Self-Awareness and mastery of meditation helps in somewhat shortening of the process required for Spiritual progress.

Part IV

Understanding Self before Self Realisation

Understanding Self

The Foundation for Spirituality

Be it Meditation or Spirituality, the reference to Self keeps coming again and again. This Self is unmistakably different than the self we always thought we live with and knew so intimately. Indeed this Self comprises of many sub sets where deeper realization is essential for better clarity. Understanding self requires treading in highly complex territory. Actually, knowing the real Self is bound to prove the real test for our learning thus far. Journey involved in exploring real self is tough and so has to be our resolve towards piercing the same with great precision. So let us deal with each of the concepts involved one by one.

Definitions of Self

It is strange that a word that gets used thousand times needs to be looked into as an unknown entity. Going by normal parlance, it should have been so easy to understand and explain. Is it not the same self that we use so casually refer to ourselves? Surely, it might sound strange when suddenly we are called upon to perceive its true meaning and that too with respect to something so important for our life and beyond. 'Self' can get explained as being a personal essential essence that distinguishes it from others and is normally understood as synonymous with Ego, the false perception of mind that mediates between the conscious and subconscious and is responsible for temporary personal identity being taken as permanent real identity. But again, the full meaning and concept of 'Self' is much bigger than what meets the naked eye. Every other dimension associated with Self will fall short in capturing its entire gamut. But hold on, very soon we are going to realize that the small self and Self are two very distinct concepts.

To directly go to its deeper meaning, let us begin to look at Self as a phenomenon without identity. This concept should be easy to grasp by people exposed to Vedic systems which link Self with *Jeevatma*, the soul that is linked to Brahman, the Supreme. The famous *Mahavakyas*, great sayings of Upanishads, "*Aham Brahmasmi*", means '*I am Brahman*', is the right example of understanding '*Aham*', Self as the real ego (Spiritual being) by differentiating it with '*Ahamkara*', the false ego (temporary material body). Some other sources explain Self as something like perception devoid of any kind or reality. But that will be yet another extreme view devoid of justifiable comprehension with reference to our purpose.

Self, however, can't be defined as the subtle essence that gets discovered within clustered and crowded space of mind because that will make it subservient to mind. Self enjoys very special relationship with the mind where, once it is properly recognized, influences the entire thought process environment of entire mind space. An empowered and realized self, the real Self, is capable of regulating thoughts in mind but Self itself can't be thought through by the mind. It is different matter that among normal people with undeveloped Self, the same mind continues to have capability of reducing the powers of Self to self, the ego principle. Going over this entire process where the roles of Self and mind get reversed, in short, covers the entire journey that we call Spiritual evolution. This tectonic shift is so short but offers so many challenges and involves so many transformations that most human beings are unable to cover this distance in entire lifetime.

Understanding Self, and its reference to Spirituality, is due for some interesting revelations and wow moments and we better be ready for the same. But before that, we are required to acquire good command over its entire spectrum from every angle and every dimension. Best way for the same is to try breaking it in parts and then looking at each part in some detail. It would be similar to what an expert explorer studying the mountain to be conquered by studying all its slopes in all directions, all its peaks and valleys, the quality of snow out there, climatic conditions and risks to be guarded against. Knowing every little detail is essential to deal with challenges of climbing the peak as an expert to avoid perishing on the slopes like a novice.

Classifying Self

To begin with, Self can broadly be classified under two distinct forms of Physical Self and Spiritual Self. The same categorization may also be named as Personal Self and Individual Self. Just a word of caution that bifurcating these two to distinct forms and names is just to facilitate better comprehension for the reader. Idea is to divide a very integrated personality into bits and parts so that we are able to appreciate its working at multiple levels. I hope these lines are taken along as a disclaimer of this being any new theory getting proposed to divide the indivisible or separate the inseparable.

Let us take these one by one:

Physical and Mental Self (Ego)

This is the obvious and visible self that consists of body, the mind and the ego. It includes our emotions, likes and dislikes, thoughts, desires, perceptions, memories, and every other thing that can be identified with the word 'my'; basically everything involved with ego. Ego is best defined as lower divine nature of Self consisting of eight fold divisions. Out of the eight divisions, first we have five elements that make up human body (air, water, fire, earth and space), sixth is mind, seventh is intelligence and finally we have false ego, the identity which combines all these elements together. Together, they all make a unique 'me' that becomes beginning as well as end of the physical or material phenomenon. 'Me' is the main motive behind everything in life and quality of this very 'me' determines who we are at the end of the day.

The evolution of this 'me' is very slow and complex process that starts right from our early days as an infant. With every passing day, this 'me' comes in contact with other plural 'me' and external world and starts acquiring their impressions on this 'me' also. To begin with this is just like a fresh canvas where every interaction and experience of real life leaves its colours. Slowly, all through the growing period, the entire canvas gets coloured where further brush strokes continue shading over the existing colours as an additional layer. This all happens in very subtle and slow manner. Over years the entire canvas gets deeply divided in endless fragmentations of different hues and shades in layers after layers. This evolutionary process continues unabated in several directions, gradually growing more and more complex where needs keep moving over from basics to superficial levels without any end in sight. Very limited number of plural 'me', however, are attracted towards their Spiritual dimensions and start seeking awakening towards deeper meaning of questions of human. Understanding ego as this physical identity is simple to miss but difficult to escape from.

This part of self also includes 'Personal Self', which is a person's essential being, his core; specially considered as the object of introspection or reflexive actions. Unique identities associated with the words like I, Identity, Personality, Psyche are all included here. This part of the self is beyond ego syndrome and starts from the place where ego ends. Ego experiences itself only in comparison to others. So it normally deals with only relativity. By very design, Ego provides judgement on others as being higher or lower than itself but never equal. This very uniqueness of identity is the very essence of ego. That is why we have named it as 'me'. But later we will see that real and composite Self sees everything as equal and similar without weighing any type of difference.

> "Ego is just like dust in the eyes. Without clearing the dust you can't see anything clearly. So clear the ego and see the world." *www.wisdomquotesandstories.com*

Over the years of a person's life, all his traits, goals, aspirations, experiences, interests and every such other quality that go to differentiate him from others keep evolving and cementing this 'me' in more and more separate form. Also, this 'me' keep enjoying that separateness and keep fuelling it more and more. This self is so clearly visible in most adults that you talk to them for a few minutes and you get examples after examples of they being very proud of their 'me' to the exclusion of other plural 'me' around. Any other person telling us his or her way of attending any small thing, say, what do they take in breakfast and just observe your own 'me' jumping in the discussions and sharing what you do instead. If you are able to side by side observe the feelings going through in your mind at that point in time, you can't miss that your 'me' is also continuously judging others and passing judgements as how your system is better than those others. This very feeling results in organic growth of ego from small to big; big to bigger and from bigger to even bigger.

But hold on, this 'me' is not something that is to be despised or detested. In fact, this 'me' needs to be revered by us as much as possible because this 'me' alone is our entire existence including our childhood, our adult self, our life companion; it is our real friend and undoubtedly our greatest well wisher. It does not care more for anyone else in the entire universe. It is our sense, our perceptions, our impressions, our memories, our desires, our attachments and every other such thing that normally we try our best to acquire, use and preserve for repeating pleasures in future. All through its existence, all through its initiatives, this 'me' keeps our personal interest higher than any other thing. No wonder we come across many people in love with their 'me' part. In reality, it is hard to avoid falling in love with your own 'me' because of its never ending attention on you and round the clock company that it offers to us. So, it needs to be appreciated and there is no need to hate or envy it.

It is this 'me' part of Self that makes us think and believe that we are doers of all the functions. It is the one that guides us to discriminate rights and wrongs. This 'me' also makes us believe that we are responsible for our own actions. Being our discretion, it brings a lot of understanding as to why our personal and social behaviour should be of particular kind. Imagine there was no power to exercise our discretion by cautioning us against indulging deeper in sense pleasures? Each one of us would have been certainly worse off.

So, where is the problem? The problem begins in ignorance when one starts pampering his 'me' too much. Such a person starts behaving in dictatorial manner with self-centered arrogance and starts actually believing that he/she is superior from others and must be respected, feared and worshipped by one and all. This results in a highly exaggerated self-image. This person gets hurt even with little pricking and starts feeling humiliated and insulted. Thus a punctured ego becomes the source of troubling behaviour and it results into bigger trouble for others in the vicinity.

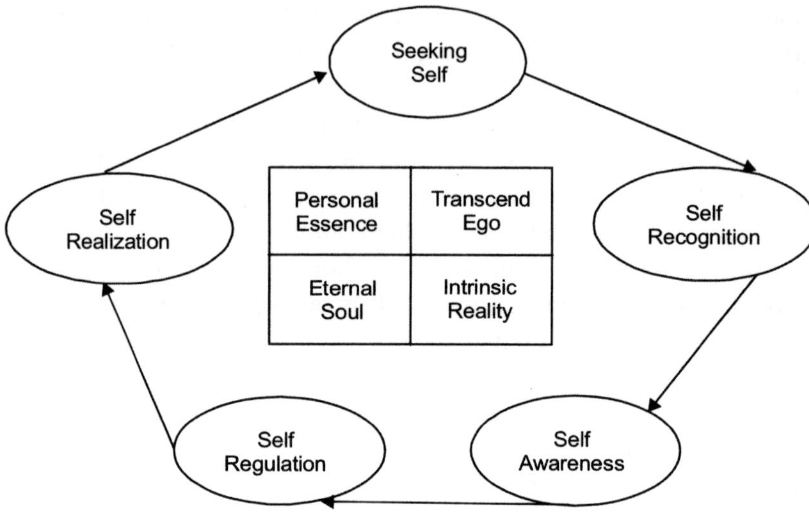

Fig.: Journey of Self-Discovery

Observing or Witnessing Self

When we refer to organs, we will instantly say as 'my hand' or 'my heart' or 'my mind'. It clearly means that my hand is different then myself. A look at this scenario and we are able to clearly conclude that there are two identities involved out here; one which is observer and the other that is being observed; the one that is involved in action and the other one that is working as witness of that very action. For the sake of understanding, we can assume that the one being observed is the "Physical Self" that we discussed above while the other part that is seeing is called "The Observing Self". This is the part of self that survives death of physical body and acquires new body in due course. As per Hinduism, the first is called 'Jeevatma' and the second is called 'Atma'. Incidentally, this is the subtle self that consists of breath, intelligence and eternal bliss. Being without form, volume and expanse, this is what is also referred as "consciousness". This is the self that is sought during meditation sessions. For brevity, we will call it the '*Seer*'.

Understanding these two distinct identities of 'observer' and 'observed' is critical to absorb and appreciate further discussions in this chapter and few others to follow. In simpler words, one may understand the 'Physical Self' as a computer consisting of hardware fitted with CPU, operating system as well as memory. On the other hand, the software to be added for particular function may be considered as 'Observing Self'.

Why call it 'Seer' and not directly spirit or soul? Because this observing self, at best, may be imagined as early form of Soul only i.e., a soul without developed consciousness. Once it get fully realized, we may certainly call it a soul or spirit or Atman or true Self or pure observing Self. All these identities are very well understood as part of universal consciousness, which is nothing but a manifestation of, or reflection of the Ultimate Supreme. But that is the later stage and is to be achieved by each individual with concerted efforts over longer periods of times. 'Seer', the under developed version is there with every person, albeit in varying intensity. But both lower and higher forms of 'seer' are certainly subtle in nature and permanent in character. This is the part that transcends human life and is reported to remain in circulation by those who believe in transmigrations.

Now, on functional level, the 'seer' keeps witnessing everything happening at the level of physical self and continues its constant feedback to 'me' irrespective of 'me' listening to its advice or otherwise. Actually, if the 'seer' was to work only as a witness, it would still be ok. The problem arises when it gets disillusioned by 'me' and start believing that it is by itself is the doer of everything happening at the physical self.

Interplay between Physical and Observing Self

Both the elements of 'me' and 'seer' are pillars of our existence and these are only dynamic forces that are able to help our Self evolve and grow to higher levels of reaching up to the soul and beyond. But their mutual working makes the scenario much complicated.

During the general waking state, the 'seer' starts imagining itself as 'me', the physical self and starts acting accordingly. This mixing up with physical self results into attachment towards things seen resulting in stress, anxiety, fear, insecurity and such other experiences that we as individuals are very well aware of. Of course, this process is complex as these two separate forces are tightly intertwined with each other and are most difficult to grasp without essential degree of clarity.

As and when an individual is able to detach his observing self from body, mind and the ego, the perception for everything around will be clear, deeper, calmer and complete. Such a person will be able to perceive hidden motives and true intentions of self and others without any attachment. No mask or curtain remains invisible for him anymore. This ability to separate the observing self (seer) from the subjective duality (me) is the art to be mastered by learning and practising all the tools available and as long as required. The one who could do that shall be called Enlightened or with such other similar names.

One could bring in tons of material on this topic with heavy sounding words and loaded meanings but our purpose is to understand and appreciate rather than explore intellectual part of Self. So many great Gurus and teachers have already done that for so long without many from general audience being able to really experience the depth of those statements and words. We are here to experience it for our own understanding. The idea is not to impress or get impressed but experience that yes, any normal person walking on the road or working in the office or having his own occupation can also realize the duality of its own Self with ease and clarity before he/she starts working on ways and means to achieve transformations of his/her own Self.

How to Develop these 'me' and 'seer' aspects?

The 'me' part is to be awakened by going beyond the gaze of the observer. This awakening gets facilitated by sinking or dispensing with the accumulated colouring agents such as memories, systems, methods, teachings, experiences, perceptions, traditional learning and everything else that prevent the right access to the genuine truth. It is here that the proverb of unlearning required for new learning gets applied in its purest form. The personal identification with despair, conflicts, competitions, comparisons, aggressions, violence, attachments, failures, faiths, persons, things, views need to be completely ended by seeing through these as temporary. One has to realize that these are momentary in nature and arise due to undesired duality. One also has to appreciate these elements as roadblocks and unwanted overburden for accessing our real self. This could be done only and only by developing real capability to get to realize own truth. Identifying and sinking this entire baggage of colouring agents, listed above, provide unseen freedom to the self. This sinking allows self to regain its innocence, love and peace. Going back to the example of climbing, throwing away this unwanted baggage makes one feel very light to climb further with ease. It facilitates you to move ahead faster. Soon, we are going to overview the entire journey involved in this process.

On the other hand, the 'seer' part is to be awakened by raising it to the level of pure consciousness. The tools available for awakening 'seer' largely relate to moral and ethical conduct and contemplation using proper self-inquiry. The techniques suggested for such results include – but do not remain limited to pure observation – meditation, concentration, yogic exercises, enhancing virtues, disciplining desires and feelings, and regulating emotions. Interestingly, all these techniques help each other in a unique way where all these move up together in a unidirectional manner. The basic idea behind all these techniques is to refute every negative and ignorant knowledge so that, at the end, all one is left with is pure and complete wisdom. At this stage there will be no attachment with the personal self connected with 'me' part of false image. These techniques are also planned to be explained in greater details in following chapters.

Role of Human Mind as Only Instrument

Interestingly, the only instrument available to awaken both kind of self is the mind. In normal state, this very mind is seen as captured by the superficial ego with all its allurements and false trappings. The very mind also works as an important cognitive faculty enabling everything relating to consciousness, perceptions, thinking, judgement and memories. No wonder that most human beings find it so hard to clearly differentiate these overlapping aspects of the same mind.

In a way, we can take a normal householder as Physical Self represented by 'me' on one side and a mountain representing pure consciousness (all other names included) on the other side of the spectrum. In between these two positions, there remains a big void that is too difficult to fill or cross. For the sake of example, we can take it as the deepest and widest wild river. The ultimate objective of the householder representing Personal self is to cross over to reach to the mountain representing pure consciousness on the other side of the river. That being so, observing Self or 'seer' is the only bridge possible to be used by the 'me' to reach to the mountaintop. Systematic growth and evolution is the only method available to 'me' to raise it to access to this bridge. Not sure, though, if this example made matters better or worse than before. Let us try understanding it one more time with yet another example.

Most readers are expected to be well aware about Bhagwad Gita, Upanishad of Upanishads. The entire communication included out there is extension of this very bridge where Arjuna (householder as per our previous example) is represented by 'me' sitting down and faced with dilemma and Lord Krishna is nothing but the developed Soul (the high mountain of our earlier example) that is supposed to be the ultimate aim of human life and all the ways and approaches discussed in Bhagwad Gita are processes for facilitating evolution of 'me', the Arjuna to unite with the very source of all existence, pure Soul, the Krishna. It did require very many steps, it necessitated taking multiple efforts spanning over 18 long chapters but Bhagwad Gita paved way for removing all ignorance from the mind of Arjuna and prepared him to undertake his own right-full obligations without losing his access to superior aim by removing away all the suspicions, hesitations and doubts. All one has to become is Arjuna of today!

Coming back to mind being the only instrument to experiment and experience evolution of the Self, we realize complexities involved in same mind required to bifurcate itself into different parts, to work as observer and observed at the same point of time, work as a doer and witness of all doings, initiate actions and then evaluate the same, get entangled in the lure of attachments and then try getting unattached. It is certainly more difficult than asking the tongue to check its own taste or asking eye to see itself. Enormous difficulties in bringing this clarity invite seekers to try their own methods. Some of their methods may succeed and many may fail. One has heard help from teachers and preachers being available but the 'me' and 'seer' for each individual is different from others. So what works for one may not work for others?

The process of evolution requires simultaneous awakening at both levels. The awakening of personal dimension is to be aimed to cross over all divisions and fragmentations and be at peace with the pure truth without any shades or strands. In addition, awakening of spiritual dimension is required to enhance the status to reach up to pure consciousness, the soul. It is said that soul can awaken only after our very 'me' has been awakened to itself first. There are as many teachings and methods available to work on these aims as suggested by scriptures and teachers.

Understanding Self with Examples

Having understood the form and feel of lower self and having gone over the ways and means of evolving it to a complete Self, we will now move on to its fully evolved form which is its original and unspoiled form to begin with. This evolved form is the one used in Spirituality where it is referred as a source of vastness of consciousness. It is equated to mid point or center of the inner space where we experience our connection with the entire Universe.

Actually, personal identity of an individual has many different aspects at the same time. These identities keep changing over the years. For example, I happen to be father of a child. This father was different when the child was one year old as compared to the father of the same child when the child was, say, twenty years old. So, one can't say that self is name of any fixed or specific phenomena as it keeps changing all the time. One person joins an organization and becomes its CEO but few years down the line, he ceases to be the CEO and retires for good. Clearly, after having ceased to be CEO, this person will only refer himself, as he was CEO between this to this period. Now, Self can't ever be bracketed as a 'has been' phenomena. For sure, being CEO, therefore, cannot be taken as equal to the person's self.

Self is also certainly not identifiable with one or more experiences that one has gone through in the past. Our reference to any real life situation will always relate to an already happened event and hence irrelevant. Similarly, the future is yet to come and not known at all. *Hence, the reference to Self must get limited to an ongoing experience in the very present, this very moment, before it turns over to past.* This emphasis on Self, being referred as a present phenomenon, will prove very important to develop understanding that our past, which at times appears as most precious thing and consumes so much of our time and attention, is as temporary as rainbow after showers. Comprehending about the futility of past and future has immense power of unshackling human beings from chains of unwanted prisons. Each one of us can see the difference in our life if we are able to forget about both past and future and just focus on the present as it unfolds. Such an experience will help us live our life as a fresh flower with all its smell intact and all its love and bliss flowing all around.

Taking the example of this physical world, the Self is both a subject and object. As a subject, it is the 'Observer' or the 'Witness' or 'Consciousness'. In this role, the Self experiences everything by activating the mind which, in turn, makes use of sense organs and generates thoughts to convey all feelings and emotions to the master i.e., Self. On the other hand, Self is also an object by itself, the one that is witnessed or observed as an aspect present from the beginning of our existence. Here it remains the basic form of consciousness, something that becomes obvious and recognizable only when maturity transcends. Thus it is both experiencer and experienced at the same time. This duality requires great efforts to see through. Actually, a major part of our entire journey of Spirituality gets devoted to develop ability to crack this duality. But once this wall develops a crack, we are able to see everything on the other side with absolute clarity.

Imagine for a moment that you are made to enter a dark room with your eyes blind folded. Soon after you enter the room, your folds are removed and the lights of the room are switched on. Obviously, you will be able to spot many things in the room including the furniture, fixtures, colours on the wall, show pieces, shape of the room etc. The light that enables one to see the objects with required clarity, is to be understood as 'Self". Interestingly, all the things were there when the folds were removed but the person was unable to see all those things because there was no light. The light does not see by itself but presence of light enables the person to see all those existing things with clarity. Well-developed and fully evolved Self is that very light in our life. Self alone provides us the actual sense of being and without this recognition we live a life as a blind man in the dark room.

Activating Self-awareness

The importance of Self-awareness is similar to pathological tests for the internist to identify proper diagnostic conditions and prescribe right medications. Enhanced Self-awareness is the key for all subsequent initiatives intended towards bringing required improvements and transformations in one's life in general as well as for spiritual advancements. But its comparison with medical treatment ends at this stage because there are no drugs that can be administered for a fast recovery within weeks/months if not days. Improvements identified for advancing Self-awareness are known to succeed when administered like a therapy, very slowly but steadily. Interestingly, Self-awareness is equally helpful to people who are not pursuing their spiritual growth as it is basically a process of knowledge about self, useful for all endeavours centered on self-improvement. In nothing else, actions of a self-aware person are always better aligned with his personal standards. This alignment itself results in drastic reduction of stress-generating conditions from this person's life.

Visible Symptoms of Low Self-awareness

There are some very peculiar symptoms that clearly indicate lower self-awareness of a target subject. A quick look at these symptoms might help us to identify such a victim from a distance. It might also help to look at ourselves as well and realize if we are also victim of similar symptoms.

1. *Person showing use of power of words or ideas in a bullying manner* – Parent forcing children to do things in certain ways, senior forcing subordinates to work exactly as desired

by boss, one partner influencing other in a coercive manner, anyone using intimidating tactics are all clear indications that the person involved is low on awareness.

2. *Person found using defensive tactics to protect his territory* – Someone refusing to accept reality on face value, someone showing regressive behaviour, someone showing disassociating tendencies, someone showing preference to work in compartmentalized manner or someone showing extreme reactions are all clear examples of defensive mechanism in operation arising out of unsecured feeling due to lack of self-awareness.
3. *Person showing controlling tendencies* – Someone doing micro management of trivial issues, person with habit of picking small things and projecting them bigger than reality and someone making efforts to sound overconfident are also clear symptoms of a person with poor self-awareness.
4. *Person showing signs of vulnerability or embarrassment* – Such people are seen avoiding situations where facts are to be faced. They can make promises casually to avoid confrontation even in a situation where success is not assured. Low in esteem, these people generally cave in too meekly.
5. *Person showing frequent changes in behaviour* – When we come across people with changing behaviours over times or in presence of different people, it is a clear sign that person lacks clarity of judgement and comes under influence of external situations rather easily.
6. *Person seen relying on excuses* – People showing habit of deflecting blame for every small and big thing on others, people identified with pointing finger syndromes and people seen blaming some one or the other for every small or big things in their life, are clearly lacking self-awareness.

But before we move on, it would help to appreciate as to why knowing about self is such a big thing to begin with. We have lived with our self all this while, we have seen our mind taking decisions from close range, and we have seen our emotional response across situations for so long. So, why is that now we are being told that knowing is so difficult?

Barriers to Self-awareness

We got to actualize how serious attempts can lead us to the depths of our own personality and how can we work to bring about the transformation required until the attitude level. Plain reading of this process sounds very exaggerated but when we start practising these steps, the reality confronts as stonewall. At this turn one needs to understand what are the roadblocks that make knowing self so difficult and why removing those roadblocks is uphill task.

One can read from here and there and come up with technical answers to this simple question as to why knowing self is so difficult. But before we jump to solutions let us spend a bit of time in going through real life challenges that work as barriers in the process of developing self-awareness. The understanding of these barriers will guard us to be extra careful on the way to practise Self-awareness techniques:

1. There is just too much to keep track at all times. We all are associated with multiple identities which keep shuffling from one moment to another rather constantly. These identities are undergoing changes all the time. Each of these identities is continuously clashing with other due to divergent interests. So, even if I stop at a moment and try understanding me in best possible measures, sometimes later that understanding will need yet another updating. For example, being father of my 32 years old married and well-settled son today is different than ten years ago when I was father of a 22 years old college going son. Constant changes in underlying identities, with and without the implication of external world, therefore, makes it that much difficult to be fully Self-aware at all times.
2. Another problem relates to conditioning about being socially and politically correct. A good part of perception about self is to do with our wishes than reality. We are trained to know what we 'should be' rather than what we 'actually are'. Most young and not so young adults carry so many wrong notions about themselves because they are conditioned while observing themselves. This process starts in childhood itself where parents keep telling us about what they wish to be

true. Soon other people arrive on the scene and they start colouring our impressions in darker and darker shades. So, at best, even if we know about our self, it was only that carbon image and not the real Self.

3. Each one of us is always in flux rather than a solid or constant identity. We are also under a slow process of evolving where one adolescent turns into an adult in few years and much later evolves into grey hair adult. Besides age, there are objective changes taking place due to learning, knowledge, responsibilities, experiences and relationships. Each such experience adds to our net content in a manner that a person is always subjected to being a 'reference to context' where context changes the reference and *vice versa.* The constant learning keeps changing our shades making it difficult to keep track at all times.
4. In the absence of pure observation power, our knowledge of self depends on our recall value of memories. Now, we know well that both memories and thoughts are glued together with desires and attachments. Our memories are coloured and subjective rather than being true reflection of realities. Our recall of a single event from our past keep changing depending on what are the circumstances under which we are trying to recall that same event. As such, as and when one is sitting to take stock about own self, there are issues regarding wrong and incomplete recollections. Every recall is bound to be a new version impacted by the situation of the time the narration is repeated.

As such, every identity that one tries to recollect in the process of Self-awareness, turns out to be an illusion or just a projection which is temporary, incomplete, conditioned and subject to change over the years. It inhibits a true and complete narrative being available for correct and complete reflection.

Practising Self-Awareness

> "He who knows others is wise. He who knows himself is enlightened." – *Lao Tzu, Ancient Chinese Philosopher*

Each one of us is a unique bundle of our own realities, routines and stresses. Only we know about our own self and know it better than others. Navigating out of our current circumstances will also, therefore, depend on our own efforts. This resolution that we alone can transform our life works like strong foundation for constructing all subsequent super structures required for personal transformation. Yes, there will be inhibitions as knowing self will bring us face to face to this subtle reality. On the other hand, normal human being is possessed with a mind that is too gross to appreciate this reality. Let us focus on practical ways for developing our own ability to be aware about self in first place.

The very first step in that direction is to develop a focused vision to clearly observe every big and small activity going on within our mind. Most of the time we are busy skimming our self but only around the surface. That is not enough. We have to dig deep. You must observe and appreciate complete chain of your thoughts, behaviours, feelings, emotions and motivations. We remain ignorant about these basic processes running through our mind because we are always on the go. Each one of us is always sitting on a long list of 'To Do' that keeps us busy from one moment to another. It is so amusing that normal person of today is unable to let its mind be at ease for some length of time leave alone long hours. And until we exhaust our pending job list, our mind will not be ready to look deep; it is programmed like that.

When we try looking at our self on the surface, all we see is that we are a sum total of number of sub systems. Than inside us, there is a never ending flowing stream of one or the other emotions. These emotions keep rising and falling continuously all the time. These roller coasters possess us with possible combinations of pleasures and pains based on memories and possibilities. Some of these are even shameless and so disgusting that even thinking about it makes me sick.

> "In order to be who you are, you must be willing to let go of who you think you are." – *Michael Singer*

With or without logics, each one of us is also a bundle of strong likes and dislikes for almost everything under the sun. It is unfortunate that holding any label and liking results in narrowing our vision which clearly obstructs us from seeing the full picture. Since all this happens in very subtle manner, the normal person fails to even notice about these divisions in normal course. The self, as previously emphasized, is programmed to thrive on such differentiations. Soon, these divisions result as walls constructed out to protect our likes and dislikes; higher the wall, bigger is the obstruction to the reality. Each of these walls is covered with a different shade based on our egocentric judgemental views. It is quite easy to see shades of so many colours spoiling the real beauty of any beautiful picture. One really needs to develop a very penetrating and focused telescope to see through all these divisions and fragmentations.

A well-developed Self-awareness is that very telescope for us.

But the process required to develop the same is going to be pretty tough as we shall soon realize. Many of us have strongly believed as how good we are about knowing other people. But few steps down the road of self-awareness, we shall realize that how little we knew about our self, leave alone knowing others? More shocking will be the realization that you thought you knew something based on reality but it turns out merely to be your desire to be like that. This ignorance is the main cause of low self-esteem among many. The same ignorance is also the biggest roadblock in our way of developing reliable relationships because if we don't know our self well, how can we interact with others well? This process of knowing oneself will require couple of steps to reach to desired levels. Just a word of caution that this process is similar to our experience in gym for workout sessions; the more we are consistent and regular in practice, more enjoyable is the session. So, patience, practice and continuity will be the key for the success here as well. Let us look at these steps one by one:

Exploring self involves facing some uncomfortable questions posed by self to self. These are totally new questions that have not been posed thus far. Why do I like something? Do I accept command and authority of some other person? Why do I succumb to morally and ethically unacceptable behaviour? Am I really jealous of other person? Do I find the other person being better than me? Do I really mean what I say? Why recognition by XYZ is that important to me? Why am I unable to celebrate the success of that other person? Why do I get so much angry with that particular person? The appreciation by that subordinate is based on my individual traits or just due to my position? Why do I want so and so to use such and such words while talking to me? What is the motive behind my thoughts? The list of such questions can be as long as our patience.

Ability to identify and finding real and accurate answers to these questions is just the first step to be Self-aware. Without finding right answers to all such questions, we can't stand alone, stand strong and stand firm. Right answers will remove the opaqueness from the surroundings and allow right access to the open space for living with clarity and purity. Knowing everything about self and knowing it accurately, is the purpose of entire Self-Awareness drive. The reality of becoming self-aware in true spirit is very different. Pursuing self-awareness as part of practising spirituality is absolutely irrelevant if it is only about talking, reading, thinking or watching.

Some people, and indeed some systems, strongly suggest that self can be met only with the blessings of Almighty but that will be naïve and an effort to pass the buck as no one has ever been able to be sure about Almighty itself. History is full of instances where a number of situations are blamed on the Almighty to encourage the individual to take it as any divine design. No, you alone with your own contemplation have the power of accessing your hidden self without dragging your God into it. You are all real and God is all about imaginations and beliefs. As it is, this universe is very big and poor God must be so busy to have spare time for you? :

What is required is to develop explorative keenness to observe our entire spectrum of existence rather than specific selected fields alone. Some of these may be actions while other may just be thoughts; at some places you may have active role and totally passive role at others; some may be related to your past while other may just be compulsions of present; some may be to your liking and other absolutely undesired; some may relate to livelihood while others may be for leisure. For sure, each one of us is a complex sum of many smaller parts where some parts are good, some parts are very bad; some parts are of a peaceful loving soul and few parts are of a cruel and violent wicked man; part of us may be well educated and sophisticated person while other part may be just a rogue. These fragmentation exist on all levels, be it inward/outward or individual/ social or personal/related levels.

What needs to be watched? Well it roughly includes everything, like the way of talking, way of walking, way of thinking, way of reacting, way of reading, way of listening, way of watching, selection of words used in all types of communications, tapping on intentions going through the mind, motives coming out of mental processes, fears, dreams, aspirations, people and feelings igniting hate and love, indifferences and reasons thereof, what you wish to acquire, what you wish to hold on, what you wish to give away, what would you die for. It includes all aspects of life including but not limited to greed, envy, ambitions, work environment, colleagues, successes, failures. Basically, we are talking of all those things that, in any way, occupy our mental space in normal day-to-day living. We must cover everything flashing through our mind without differentiating anything as big or small, significant or otherwise, important or garbage. Idea is to develop sharper but neutral view to observe and understand the result as it appears, without any colouring or justification or conclusion.

Many people feel that they know themselves very well and they are proud of their neutrality while interacting with the outer world and hence, they don't need to cultivate the habit of watching keenly. They also assume that they can watch things without conditioning. May be it is true, may be it is not. Let us have a quick self-check? Please recall the last entertaining movie that you watched. Please recollect where was your mind, scene after scene? Was your mind busy linking each scene with some previous movie, comparing the character's performance in his/her earlier movie? Did you have a clean slate about story or performance of the actors? How many times you were busy preempting the outcome of scenes? The same applies to songs, direction, story and everything else involved in the movie. Now, a simple question – Did you go to the movie to enjoy or as a critique or you were appointed to pass judgement? What you were doing, in your opinion is closer to keen observation or fiddling with past memories? Were you there for observing or comparing or judging? How many minutes you actually watched the movie with total attention as if you were watching a movie for the first time in your life? Now, if the quality of observation is below par, can the learning out of such observation be ever above par? Pure observation happens with a very quiet and neutral but keen and open mind.

How to develop the penetration of pure observation for enhancing Self-awareness? Traditional studies suggest abandoning of pleasures and avoiding pains as the starting point for exploring self. The roots of this suggestion lie in the belief that pains and pleasures obscure our vision and hide the self like a thick blanket. Many people experience boomerang effect of shunning pleasures and pains as deprivation of these result in uncontrollable craving that occupy the mind space higher than before. In any case, pains and pleasures have reliance on the external world and, therefore, can never be reliable for seeking success. No, this tool can prepare you to attempt it but this cannot get you success.

Reliance on external institutional assistance from Religion, Philosophy or Yoga is another method suggested for exploring self. These may work for a while but a modern mind exposed to global systems is smart enough to realize that these systems have been fossilized over the years in history where original teachings and their impacts have been butchered and liquidated by interest groups and what is left is ghastly picture of lies and divisions serving self interests of selected few. In today's time, one really has to be naïve to ignore insufficiency of any particular religion or system to be taken as all-complete by it. After all, if religions were to be so important part of social life, why more deaths have taken place in human history in the name of religions than any other single reason? Certainly, we have to search out for newer tools.

Modern times require modern solutions. Going forward, we need to develop ability of a part of our observing self to be taken out of our body and focus on self from a distance like an invisible drone fitted with camera and mind reader equipment hovering around us to capture every impulse. Its feedback to us will prove to be the best tool for exploring self as an unattached, independent and unbiased third umpire on a cricket field with access to replay facility from different cameras. This is the system that has been cited as a personal experience under the chapter on Meditation. Traditional tools suggested in previous paragraph are like traditional field umpires in the game of cricket who relied on their own personal judgement and over the years have been seen making wrong decisions. Our own personal drone connected with our very mind is surely the only camera that can investigate most minute activity/thought to help the required exploration.

Our inner space is too personal and vast. It holds much more than we have been able to observe or understand until now. The best tool to analyze this reality is to operate with eyes closed and concentration penetrated deep within. Once you focus your search at the right place, with right intent and unbiased attitude, your own intentions and underlying responses and reactions will get decoded completely as an open book. Then alone, you will have the accurate peep inside you. Once a person acquires that ability, there will be no need of finding the God in temples and churches. While on that journey towards unknown, you will be able to see yourself as a traveller, as the tour guide, as the vehicle and also as your own destination; there will be nothing outside of you.

Developing Key Observation

The step before this was like recording everything happening from a distance so that every activity, reaction, thought or desire gets captured. Obviously, the next step is to absorb the essence of things recorded. Here the appreciation is required to differentiate seeing and observing; while one is mechanical activity the other is qualitative. Keen observation is significantly different than fixing a gaze. Observation goes beyond sensory perception with eyes wide open. More than open eyes, real seeing involves a loving heart and peace filled agile mind. This fact has to surmount our entire process of developing keen observation.

In order to become peaceful and agile, the mind has to be trained to shred its existing inhibitions, its attachments, its existing knowledge and above all, its judgemental nature. What is required is to develop a quality where the mind looks at the activity with the keenness of it being watched the first time without any preconceived notions. Even at the cost of repetition, the mind should sink all its memories and fragmentations/divisions to develop the keenness of watching an activity in its pure perspective. Such observation alone will allow us to see the reality, the real us vesting in the background. In short, the lenses used for observing must be cleaned of every particle of shade, dust or dirt.

In addition to all its complexity, the first challenge in developing such an observation continues our willingness to rise above our divided existence. Trust me, it is going to be very exciting and eye opening. This ability has power to even help us look at our existing life from an entirely new perspective; the life that starts every morning, where you get up and unwillingly have to attend the tiring routine day after day. It is hard to find possibility for much creativity and sense of satisfaction in such a monotonous life. Keen observation will bring you in direct confrontation with many cluttering about hits and misses. But please don't get scared by the sinister results of such observations. As it is, these are already part of your life and you have to face them squarely. Reality does not change or vanish simply because we decide to overlook or look aside. Good or bad, we need to observe every part of actual thing happening in our life on ongoing basis, no less and no more. Train yourself as the camera that captures everything happening irrespective of qualitative aspect of the event. A camera does its work irrespective of even recording relates to birth or death and designed or accidental.

This observation is not like one time stock taking or like visiting a pathological laboratory that we give our blood sample and few hours later we get the report showing all readings and comparing them alongside acceptable limits. The observation for self will have to continue for days and months or may be years. It is only over long periods that we will develop the habit of pure observation without making conscious efforts to do so. It needs to become one's second nature. One has to keep trying until such time that the real intention behind every action and thought comes out as clear as water. This observation without any quality and focus is a continuous ongoing long process rather than test or event or a milestone.

Please remember that this is not the stage for attempting to fix anything but just pure observation.

At this stage we don't have to draw any conclusion at all. Forget about if the observation is good/bad or right/wrong. Similarly, there is no need for comparing with others. It is our life, we are committed to enrich it, we are sure that we alone are responsible and capable of it, these are parts of my life and I alone wish to look at each part of my life keenly and closely. There is no point in running away as it is reality and we do not yet believe that nothing can be done. The only resolution at this stage is that I am here to fix everything required and possible. Behaving like a camel with its head in the bush or running away are solutions and still available as an option. But you started with your own accord, not out of any compulsion?

Embrace Reality without Fear

A keen and close observation on all scattered parts of our own life will indicate that our life is revolving around two important aspects of fears and pleasures. These two things embrace our entire existence in two separate categories. First category is pleasures; and we want more of these in an unending manner. On the other hand, we have fear and we wish to settle for minimum possible fears around. With improved self-exploration and focused observation, we will be able to see these pleasures and fears in every small or not so small activity and thoughts occupying our mind space. It is this desire of fleeing the fears that we start looking for escape from situations. Knowingly and unknowingly, this search for escape from fears directs us to other people in our life. Some of these people are our own close relatives where we genuinely believe them to be part of our own existence. Many others are from external world, some who come to us and many others that we go to. The list of people we start depending for our real life issues soon becomes long enough. But this dependence, like any other dependence, starts inhibiting our freedom and we don't even realize it in normal life situations.

Whenever we come into a problem that we are not willing to face directly, we find people on whom we can rely. These include our teachers, gurus, ideals who are able to provide us ideas for helping us clinging to our situations. But this is absolute loss of freedom as these people develop the control over part of our life. While we have gone to them seeking freedom from fears, they soon turn into direct or indirect controllers. Either they dominate us or we want them to dominate and in either situation, there comes more fear; fear of not being alone any more. Also comes into play related situations laced with inevitable jealousy and anxieties. Also, we rely on close people for burdening our limited life in more ways than one. A quick look around real life and most readers will clearly perceive the point under discussion.

Did we actually realize before that our simple normal life is full of so much of fears and that most people that we thought are there to enrich our life are actually contributing to these fears? Sure, we have heard that ignorance is bliss and not knowing yourself is indeed ignorance, and therefore it is certain bliss. You can live a carefree ignorant life assuming that everything is wonderful and there is nothing to worry. Really blessed are those of us who can isolate/insulate themselves from reality and continue believing that 'all is well'. Without any doubt, we have to develop our self reliance and reduce dependence on others including those we hold in extreme regard. Reality is without fear so long as one is able to comprehend it without judgement.

Comprehending Source of Fear and Pleasure

The real physical or psychological fears are far and few and can be dealt with. But not all pains and fears are real. Many of these are based on just repetitive thoughts that occupy our mind as uninvited guest. In reality, it is harder to deal with fears generating out of our constant thoughts; the 'what will happen if?' syndrome. The logical question, therefore, is to understand their source. I was once involved in a serious road accident some fifteen years back. It still haunts me every time another vehicle suddenly comes in front of my vehicle. Without exaggerations, I have gone through perceived pains of this incident many times more as compared to the actual pain I sustained at the time of accident. Surely, you will be able to identify your life incidents generating streams of thoughts based out of this 'what if' scenarios.

Similar thing also happens to pleasures. Every time we experience some exciting scenery or a work of art, our brain records those events on its hard disc. As a natural tendency, thoughts keep going back to those experiences and we continue desiring for their repeat as many times as possible. That desire for re-occurrence of those pleasing experiences is the seed for pleasure. Thus, similar to fears, our pleasures are also dependent on thoughts. So, our own thinking breeds fear and pleasures and also their repetition over the years. Now, thoughts are also used for almost every other human activity we do including speaking languages, making scientific discoveries, managing all our past impressions. We can't do without strong thinking process in functioning rationally, logically and objectively.

Before dealing about the management part, however, it is advisable to look at thoughts in some detail. In a way, thoughts are like vapours coming out of a big block of frozen ice. The frozen ice here is the bunch of memories, knowledge and experiences stored and compacted in our brain. On physical level, thoughts get generated based on body's sense organs and its characterization by the mind. Now we know that our body is a marvelous sensing device capable of sensing even subtle difference in energy anywhere in the immediate environment. But characterization by mind depends largely on past knowledge and experiences. When the mind is forced to step out of its characterization, it is called creative imagination that is largely based on intuitive guidance. Management of thinking process involves cutting down reliance on stored memories and enhancing reliance on intuitive guidance.

Intuitive guidance incidentally is understood as ability to acquire knowledge without inference or use of reason. Intuition gets strengthened in proportion of our spiritual progress. Intuition is supposed to help us know the reality in a flash. Ideas out of intuition are also rated higher than intellect. In this entire scenario our mind works like a radio that can pickup signals only for the frequency that is tuned in. Signals out of frequency get clubbed as interference or noise beyond comprehension. But the beauty of human mind (when used as a servant) is that it honours any request made to it by intuitive guidance. In this mode, the mind is said to be engaged in learning. That is how all inventions and creations come into existence. That is why spiritual growth requires calming down of all body based sensing so that entire thought generation mechanism is suspended or neutralized. As seen earlier, the entire focus of meditation sessions is aimed at this very requirement.

Management of Thoughts

The next key point, after developing keen observations and understanding thoughts being the source behind all pleasures and fears, is to manage our thoughts. Incidentally, this should not be a big issue after developing intuitive guidance to desired levels. We know very well that once the same mind gets occupied with learning, it is known to replace its earlier impressions or knowledge. So engaging the mind in continuous learning, both voluntary and induced, is the most effective process for managing thoughts. Unfortunately, most human beings allow their minds to operate within its known content where its belief systems are coloured by past experiences. Old and coloured knowledge stop it from acquiring new knowledge. Incidentally each mind is capable of learning until its last day provided the owner is willing to direct it to do so.

> "The mind is by nature restless. Begin liberating it from its restlessness; give it peace; make it free from distractedness; make this a habit. This can be done by ignoring the external world and removing the obstacles to peace of mind."
>
> – *Ramana Maharishi*

After developing keen observation our intelligence is tuned to apply findings in a neutral way. Soon, thoughts motivated by intuitive guidance react with our intelligence and forces the mind to learn something it was not doing before. Beyond this stage, ours 'being human' helps as the logical reasoning prompt human brain to set right anything it comes across as wrong. We are programmed like that and no special efforts are required to activate this impulse. The resistance to change stands only until we are not convinced that something is wrong in the first place. Finally a mind that starts learning is destined to enhance its own intelligence. This is the turning point for all subsequent improvements in entire system and its subsystems.

Once we are well aware of our actions in real life (with the use of self exploration with keen observation fully developed) we will take control of all our initiatives and reactions by making logical choices based on unbiased, unconditioned and un-fragmented new learning in place of our emotions and feelings directing such a choice. After all, it is thoughts that are behind activating all emotions driven mental processes. So when, sharp and clear observation and awareness ignite the generation of creative thoughts, the same mind is directed to learn and take well-informed action. Right actions in turn result in right emotions and feelings as well.

Events and people from external world will still remain active and will impact our life as before but our response to such actions will now be different. Actions by others will no longer trigger our emotions and in turn create the fear under influence of our thoughts. Emotions are chemical molecules that act as command circuits in our body. Emotions also work as bundle of energies that organize and shape our beliefs and behaviours over longer periods. But once our newfound skill of being self-aware is able to put a stop to activating the said circuits, emotions get no role to play in impacting our mind to initiate our actions. Now we will be able to see the development with a fresh pair of eyes without igniting our fears or pleasures.

Imagine so many keen observations being made by our system with an open and active mind disconnected with stored memories and experiences. The new mind is now a learning mind which is engaged in keen observation rather than drawing upon just on the past memories and experiences. The new mind now looks at fear or pleasure as if it is looking at it the very first time. Now there is no set reaction based on stored impressions but fresh processing of keen observation conveyed to mind without any connectivity with the baggage of past.

This indeed is our Eureka Moment!

The same thing could have been said in simple lines that train your mind to process observations without falling on memories and experiences. But could we have understood it how to train that mind? How many times we succeed training our mind? The very first impression the mind sends to new knowledge, in its untrained state, is that "Oh, I know it already." Now this is a response of an unintelligent mind, a mind that is not open to learn. Please remember that every time we wish to learn something new, it necessarily involves unlearning of something old and openness to accept something new. In case of minds conditioned by years of routine live issues with set patterns, the most difficult thing is to unlearn. Ability to keenly observe our own things and conveying the pure observation to the mind without the reflexes of past memories and without the attachment with any particular outcome is the key and indeed much more difficult than it sounds.

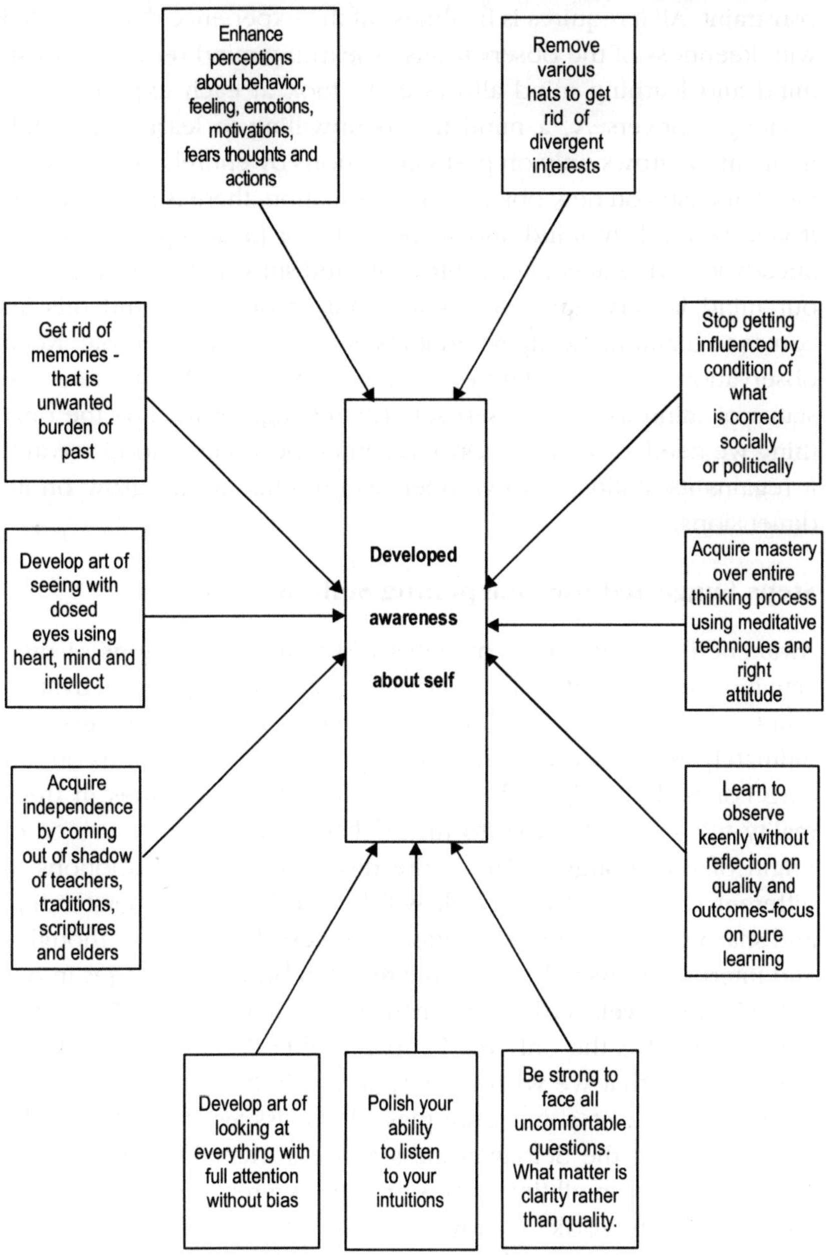

Fig.: Managing Self-Awareness

Learning itself depends on the intensity of the passion with which the learning is pursued. Learning is not limited by age or any other constraint. All it requires is freshness of the experience that is related with keenness of the observations. A learning mind remains a fresh mind and learning mind allows us to look at each experience as exciting. Conversely, a mind that is unwilling to learn is a dumb mind and it grows only on past impressions by entirely blocking the vision focused on new objects. In this situation, there is no freshness. It is at best a lazy mind and works only for justifying that what is already known is accurate, appropriate and sufficient. Unfortunately, our mind is very good at making fool of ourselves and this art comes to it automatically when it takes over the master's role. Keen observation based constant openness for new learning reduces the status of mind as a good servant. This change of roles is the only thing we need to work on. Once the mind becomes a good servant, it regains its ability to do wonders to help his master grow on all dimensions.

Steps Suggested for Sharpening Self-awareness

Awakened self-awareness operates when the observations of own activities and thoughts are used for contemplating and activating mind to make desired changes in activities, thinking process and ultimately in behaviour. Through series of such observations on our core issues, both big and small, and founding the issues in fresh reality we should be able to make changes in the very source of origin of our thoughts. The entire discussions about Emotions in different chapters of this book will be the key for understanding and sharpening that transformational process. Regular new thoughts and interpretations will eventually result in bringing changes in our behaviour as well as help in managing our emotions. Long and painstaking, it is the only road capable of taking us towards long-term changes that we wish to bring in our individuality.

Let us look at some examples of the issues that need to be focused during the Self-awareness process. Actually, the purpose here is to focus on all tiny details on our own real life activities. But we can surely look at few examples for developing better understanding. Some of the examples (which are by no means any exhaustive) are listed here under:

1. What is my most important objective in life at present?

2. What is that I am trying to achieve?
3. What are my weaknesses spreading over my personal and professional life?
4. Which are the areas where my behaviour needs immediate change?
5. Which issues I can bet my life for? What is there to die for?
6. Do I have activities giving positive results in my transformative drive?
7. Am I well aware of my activities not yielding positive benefits?
8. Am I fair in extending respect to all people interacting with me?
9. Is my intensity for pain of different people is same and if not why?
10. Which critical issues or people ignite my defensive mechanism?
11. Why did I make excuses in the recent past?
12. Why did I get aggressive on those recent occasions?
13. Are my preaching and practising in tandem? Where do I see double standards?

It is advisable that we make this exercise as a journalized testimony. If nothing else, the process of writing down your thoughts periodically requires a churning of views and removes the grey areas from the periphery of real intentions and drives. Review of the same list over periods will help you access our own progress or otherwise. We are also better advised to identify people close to us who are used for recording the behavioural issues in particular because behaviour is better evident to others. I could count many instances where my wife's analysis about my behaviour was different than my own and, like always, she was right more often than not. Needless to mention, however, that extreme care is required to choose people to be involved in this intimate exercise. People chosen have to be impartial, objective and intelligent enough to observe subtle changes in your behaviour and share with neutral attitude.

Periodical balance sheet of assets and liabilities of personal traits is yet another tool some people use to evaluate progressive growth. The self-swareness exercises including mind training must continue with the purpose of developing subconscious reflexes for correct responses (by applying logic and reasoning using intelligence) becoming reality. Improving your own attitude is exactly as playing golf. You can read everything about golf in few days but being there on the ground and working on clubs and ball takes years before you are comfortable with your performance on the actual course. Basically you play with yourself, you have the entire course open to you and you have your own clubs to choose from. Finally, you have a stationary ball that needs to be hit to reach to different holes. You continuously keep looking at temperature, humidity, altitude of the ground, wind velocity, wind direction, quality of the ground and grass and so many other factors every time you hit the ball. How many strokes you take to reach the final hole depends entirely on your training, practice and concentration. Players who are unable to forget mistakes made on earlier holes or by co-players are never able to graduate to elite club because the very thoughts of earlier mistakes cost them more strokes in remaining holes. Self-awareness, similarly, has the final goal of getting desired actions and thoughts; various techniques available are the clubs to be used; entire psychological space is the golf course one uses; number of shots taken to reach the destination is the period required to reach to final goal. Finally, the role of a teacher or guide is no different than that of an experienced caddy.

The art of Self-awareness may also be compared with learning of solo dance. As we know, dance sequences involve movement and synchronization of every part of own two feet, hands and the entire body. On top of it there is music, beats, rhythm and floor space. One also has to remain conscious of all other people involved in the performance at the same point in time. There can't be any set steps as each dancer explores his own moves depending on his body shape, physical condition, age and inherent flexibility. But every good dancer has to find limits of his impulses for movement and experiment with them in sync with the music. And each dancer achieves his progress purely on self-paced developments.

Surely, an accomplished dancer is able to bring out a good performance by managing all these attributes simultaneously. A good dancer, in spite of all such difficult sounding techniques in operation, stands out even in a large crowd. But that crowd will better know how much time that dancer must have spent to perfect those moves.

The same principle applies to a person who is able to enrich his Self-awareness.

Using Self-awareness for Self-improvements

Right awareness is the stepping-stone for entire process of reinventing our own self. It leads to learning how to make wise decisions based on one's strength and weaknesses rather than feelings and emotions. It helps us discover our own true self simply by tuning inside on our own source for thoughts and decision-making process. It is precisely because of this advantage that modern management gurus are using this technique increasingly to bring about major behavioural changes among management practitioners by helping them improve their decision-making. After all, self-awareness makes one stand strong with full realization about how his thoughts and feelings impact his actions and behaviours. More importantly, it makes you aware about your strengths as well as limitations. Once you are in know with your core as a clean mirror, your own reflections are more likely to be in right proportions. Somebody rightly said that:

> "When you know better, you think better and finally you do better."

Self-awareness is a unique new invisible muscle that needs to be developed in our body. Sure, it requires persistent practice and lots of patience to grow. But once you are able to grow it well, with time, it will provide wonderful and never seen before variety of strength to your entire working system of mind and body. Since this muscle grows in mind rather than body, it effectively works towards regulating our emotions and feelings unlike other normal muscles that work only for increasing power of the particular body part.

Interestingly, the barriers in the process of enhancing Self-awareness have stronger grip only in the beginning of our contemplative process. In due course, the process of enhancing our self-awareness eventually becomes smooth. We require stronger resolve to keep our courage and conviction in place and continue contemplative sessions. Lack of gaining tangible benefits in initial sessions should not deter us to suspend our contemplative sessions.

It is by far the most fulfilling trait that a human can acquire. So, it is ok if it proves more difficult than other traits acquired by us in our earlier life? The success achieved with greater difficulties and against all odds always tastes sweeter. Undoubtedly, desired success in searching self requires tons and tons of contemplation time. But the results waiting at the end of the tunnel are worth all the efforts required and that is a promise.

Practical Tips for Enhancing Self-awareness

Self-Awareness is all about present; here and now. You are what you are at this moment. Present as it exists, without any qualitative aspect or evaluation or judgement, is the ultimate reality. Keen observation focuses on here and now and increases purity of observations. That results in decreasing reliance on past, knowledge and experiences included. We are not what our past was. Past is not going to be helpful in letting us know what we can be. Past is a 'has been' status and does not matter. Hence, each one of us must make a fresh beginning here and now.

> "Live quietly in the moment and see the beauty of all before you. The future will take care of itself...."
>
> – *Paramhansa Yogananda*

Contemplation enables you to get over your past and it unburdens you to see what you really are at the moment. Let us take the first step of staying away from evaluating self as good/bad or right/wrong. There are no qualifying marks or cut off list. Awareness is a live and dynamic process where pure observation leading to decisions based on logic and wisdom is all that is required. It will not be premature to mention that once you reach to the base of your humanity you realize that quality and evaluation has no role out there. In the pool of purity only the neutral colour can enter.

So, please throw away your measuring scales and score sheet and get ready to practise your observation. There will be difficulties to begin with but that is normal. Soon positive results will tend to be visible to motivate you continue further exploration. Just for the beginners, please focus on studying your inner depth even if it is difficult to do it, you are unable to do it completely, it is coloured or conditioned; one has to start from somewhere. Also, try listening to your real inner voice by calming down external noise and making efforts to make your mental processes quite. A finely tuned radio station always improves the audio quality. It is normal to come across lot of rattling from your mind but don't give up. Sessions and sessions of contemplation will help in getting success in feeling the silence of your own mind. Following any known meditative practice will help you sit calmly and direct your attention inward. Explore freely and stay with any practice that works initially. Later, you can always be selective and innovative.

Also important is to stop all tendencies involving imaginations and speculations. You will have to remind yourself that you are here to observe the reality rooted in self-experience by completely shunning all the borrowed knowledge or tutoring from others. Forget completely what has been read or preached or believed until now. That was past and past doesn't help in developing awareness. Awareness requires the functioning of our own conscious focus on present to the exclusion of all other faculties. It is like you are first time watching live stream of some new sports without any recording or commentary. Ability to blank out both past and future and still maintaining high degree of interest has tremendous advantage for developing awareness in present. Even otherwise, creativity or learning always happens only in present. Forget pursuing spirituality for a while, anyone who lives in present is always happier than those grounded in past or furrowing the future.

And remember that practice is the key. How much practice will start showing positive results will depend on your current location on your long journey. Gaining Self-awareness is the key to further progress on this audacious path. Please remind yourself that consummation of spiritual journey transpires only upon attainment of normal self, hidden deep within you beneath the thick layers of ignorance and incomplete knowledge. Later you have to try reaching to your true Self, the ultimate Self, but before that you have to start from smaller self, the one bundled with ego or intellect.

Interestingly, recognition of the difference between your smaller self and bigger self clearly indicate the success or failure of your training at this moment of your long journey.

Emotions and Rational Minds – Part of Awareness

Ending up doing certain things as a reflex and finding it difficult to control their outbursts ignited by particular situations is one of the constant complaints by many practitioners during their journey for seeking Self-awareness. Their inability to control their instant reactions, keep inhibiting their ability to act based on well-thought out and logically reasoned actions. This leads to a situation where they want to make changes in the way they observe things but their quick reflexes don't permit them to apply logic as their mind reacts in split second of the trigger or, at times, even before there is a real trigger.

This is a very interesting subject for all seekers and deserves proper attention. Well, our mind is responsible for many things like receiving perceptions, thinking, arrive at judgements, management memory and imaginations. But, our mind is divided in two specific compartments, called emotional and rational. Emotional mind is more intuitive, thoughtful and subjective while Rational Mind is categorized as logical, analytical and objective. The emotional mind jumps into reaction to any signal far more quickly while the other mind likes to take a moment or two to check what should be done. Long time back, when survival carried much more urgency for human, emotional mind indeed helped human survive many scary circumstances. After all, it had the unique ability of spotting any actual and perceived danger that much faster. But off late, survival is not that much critical and overriding as most of us live in secured and safe environment, exceptions apart.

Interestingly, there are two very important studies that have contributed a lot towards new insights in the working of emotional and rational parts of the human mind. Their results are very convincing to help us know the working of both these brains and provide useful tips in looking at how these findings help us focus self-awareness in more effective manner. The studies are credited to Mr. Paul Ekman, who heads the Human Interaction Laboratory at University of California, US and Mr. Seymour Epstein who came out with the study called 'Cognitive-Experiential Self-Theory' focusing on how people use two separate systems dominated by 'analytical and rationality' on one side and 'intuition and experimental' on the other extreme. Bulk of the arguments listed below are having roots to these well acclaimed and highly quoted theories that are accepted as ground-breaking in understanding the link between emotions impacting human response under different situations.

Our emotional mind is faster in responding to emerging circumstances both inside and outside. People using this part of brain, come up with quick reactions. But their reactions are also based on strong sense of uncertainty. It is because an emotional mind reacts to overall situation in a jiffy. It doesn't waste time to wait for complete and detailed view of the situation. It looks at the situation in a rather simplified way. So the time of trigger of the particular emotion and eruption of response is in split second. Its speed is so fast that the subject does not even enter the conscious awareness. Its quick and dirty variety of emotions laced reaction does not even wish to ponder as what has actually happened. What matters here is speed and not accuracy or reasoning. First impressions here is taken as representative of entire overall condition without wasting time. There is no time to go for thoughtful analysis and checking different aspects of the situation in a holistic manner, as no time should be wasted in reaction.

Many a times these responses are ill advised, ill founded and ill timed. We can spot people around us who, under influence of their emotional mind syndrome, should not have said the words that they spoke or reacted in the manner they did or should not have perceived others' view even before listening. These are all clear examples of people dominated by responses coming out of their emotional mind. Some of these, later, may be seen even repenting and regretting their quick responses. It is their emotional mind that takes snap shot of emerging situation and, drawing upon past memories, shoots out the first option at its disposal. Response here is out of defence mechanism rather than thinking through. Speed is important always but speed at the cost of accuracy is held dangerous behaviour under any setting involving others.

Extending the examples, we may also come across many violent incidents committed by such people where they lose their ability to reason or logic. The 'shooting from the hip' syndrome is aptly coined for such situations. People have fired shots at their loving family members while mistakenly sensing presence of intruders in their homes. We come across many examples in daily life where people use emotions as an excuse for their behaviour. Interestingly, responses to most of the basic emotions, including falling in love, are known to be without linkage with logic/reason. How many times we see people falling in love knowing weaknesses of each other? Their simple answer is that they got possessed by emotions and had no control to decide their actions. So, emotional mind is at the base of quick actions or quick words of quick thoughts getting fired without analyzing consequences.

On the other hand, the rational mind takes a few moments to register and analyze the emerging situation and come up with a measured response. Actually, in first category, the response is from spontaneous instinct while in the second category it is guided by logically carried out rational thinking. In a rational dominance scenario, it is not the feelings but articulated thoughts that activate the response. It is reported in the studies that people having logical mind dominance in their personality are found low in their beliefs and in following customs or rituals, and it is easy to understand why. These people will always ask 'does it make sense from rational point of view?' These people have only tentative beliefs and every time there is a new argument or new evidence, they are ready to evaluate the same rationally and are open to change their belief without much problem. On the other hand, an emotional mind has beliefs cast in concrete blocks. Such persons take their own beliefs to be so true that they are not even open to evaluate new evidence or argument. Arguing with such people is a sheer waste of time. Whenever we find a person holding on to his/her views and unwilling to even look at contrarian views, it is a clear signal that the person is possessed by an emotional mind.

So how does this division of mind under emotional and rational categories help us in our drive to master Self-awareness? This is where we have a twist; and the twist is the ability of emotional mind to exercise control over rational mind. To understand this, we have to go back to thousands of years ago when it was still period of early stage of human evolution. The emotional mind got evolved fully much before rational part was to arrive on stage. It is like birth of two brothers in the same family with a long age gap in between. Due to the age difference, surely, the emotional mind is the big brother. As a big brother, it has unique capability to befool the younger one, rational mind, by engaging it in search of justifications and arguments so that quick reactions by emotional mind can be justified as well reasoned, if the situation so desire. As a much younger brother, poor rational mind has to toe the line taken by big brother in front of every outsider. In such a situation the rational mind is seen behaving like a capable and learned spokesperson of a political party towing its party line even in matters that are totally wrong as per public perceptions.

We can also understand its working example of a legal environment where emotional mind works as the Law Enforcement Agency. In this example, the Intellectual ability work as the Judge while rational mind is working as a Public Prosecutor. Let us say that the Inspector (emotional mind) has taken a quick action for any situation. In addition, he considers it as its right to influence poor public prosecutor (rational mind). Surely, the inspector wins the judgement in his favour from intellectual judiciary by influencing the public prosecutor. This is how many of us actually utilize our rationality to justify whatever wrongs we keep committing in our daily lives. Remember that these conclusion are completely backed up by authentic studies carried out in recent decades, hence, deserve our total acceptance rather than being brushed aside as a flight of fantasy.

Art of Making Rational Mind Strong

Agreed that a well thought out action coming out of rational mind has, in most situations, merit in replacing instant response from the emotional mind. So, if we wish the judge (intellect) give a well considered judgement, the public prosecutor (rational mind) must acquire his independence by arguing the case with proper facts by working free from the influence and control of the offender (emotional mind). Every justice seeker will agree with this scenario for sure. Even a layman understands that independence of lawyer from the police is a must for expecting fair trial and impartial judgement.

Self-awareness advocates keen and pure observation about every action and thoughts without letting the conditioned images influence the process. Needless to mention that such an observation involves careful view that requires few extra moments. This step is likely to function exactly as a time delay device. This simple process of delaying the instant reaction by just a fraction of second itself brings out a wonderful change. *The moment there is a slight delay, by virtue of genetic coding, the matter is seized by rational mind in place of emotional mind.* We may relate it with live instances where a few moments of delay stop us from uttering some unwanted words or opinions specially under highly charged situations. The aggravation turning to normal situation varies from individual to individual but the process sets in for all beings.

So the fractional delay results in the matter been taken over by rational mind. Rest is all handled by rational mind that is known to be comparatively free from the impromptu approach of the emotional mind. Now, logical mind considers our deeper and real motives and helps us in synchronizing our moves similar to an accomplished dancer. By appreciating the working of logical and intuitive minds and working on it consciously for as long as required we get critical access to a very important weapon in our hands. So, one has to promote the rational mind and suppress the emotional by ensuring that every action we take, every word we speak and every thought that we allow to generate in our minds are processed by our logical mind.

The basic idea behind developing Self-awareness to a higher level is to spot the moment when emotional turmoil is about to begin within you. By consciously opting for use of rational mind and focus on present to the exclusion of past and future, you will be able to prevent animal instinct capturing your decision-making processes at all levels. *This change alone has the power of silencing the cluttering of mind and allow you to listen to critical voices from within so as to avoid trigger of emotions giving rise to angers and fears.* No wonder all spiritual souls are always seen having peace filled aura and speaking softly as if they are weighing each word for its meaning and intensity. Indeed, they have been able to put to sleep their emotional mind and have handed over all mental processes exclusively to the rational mind operating with deeper and clear understanding of a well-evolved Self-awareness. Each one of us is equally entitled for that state but only if we are able to practise the techniques suggested.

Finding Real Truth Using Self-awareness

Finding Truth is a simple question with most complex and difficult answers. It is expected to be something factual and real at the same time. By definition, it is easy to find and firm to stand of its own, something beyond doubts. But in practice we really don't comprehend it with so much clarity and conviction. Truth also keeps changing with people as it is not same for everyone and every time. One can see constant struggles going on to establish one's truth being different and superior as compared to truth of other(s). How can truth be right or wrong? But we do see truth being judged by people devoted to lies all the time. No, we are not deviating from our central theme as these are very important questions having far reaching implications in our quest of our Spirituality. Understanding and identifying truth along with developing ability to use that truth as a foundation for building a strong temple housing spirituality is a fascinating but intriguing challenge to deal.

One of the basic definitions of truth state that "Truth is what conforms to reality, fact and actuality". But even this basic definition itself is open to a wide variety of interpretations about reality, facts as well as actuality. We all can visualize that perceptions colour reality as well as facts all the time. One also comes across many references to truth in religious and philosophical material and most of all in scientific studies. But not all these specialized branches of knowledge paint a common picture of simple truth. Philosophies complicate it further by branching it into subjective or objective. It also categorizes it into relative or absolute states. One also comes across references of it being logical or factual and moral or ethical truth being somewhat different from each other. We better grasp real truth simply because finding the real, the true, the final Truth is very important for our Spiritual advancement. After all, we ought to guard ourselves against spending energy on anything other than the real Truth?

Let us, therefore, take the ancient system of understanding it by applying the theory of negation. Travelling down on this lane one can say for sure that:

- Truth is not convenient; it can very well be something that does not work at many a times.
- Truth is not easily understandable; at times it is difficult to grasp.
- Truth is not always 'feel good'; there are times when it is very unpleasant.
- Truth is not what the majority says; numbers don't matter here.
- Truth is not always comprehensive; more often it is narrow and straight.
- Truth is not how we know about it; it is rather what we know about.
- Truth is not simply what has been believed for ages; history is full of many lies served in disguise of truth.
- Truth need not always be logical; there are times when it defies and contravenes logic by miles.
- Truth is not dependent on visuals; it is same for a blind and a person having eyes.
- Truth is not dependent on knowledge; there are times when it stays with ignorant.
- Truth is not always firm and definite; at times it appears quite elusive, evasive and deceptive.
- Truth is not always clear and perfect; there are numerous distorted angles covering it.

Some of the fundamental pillars that support truth at all times are its being permanent, narrow, straight, fresh as well as first hand. It should also be absolute in nature such that it is not relative to the person observing it. Most importantly, the beholder must have directly experienced it. Somebody telling what it is or we reading about it or what we learn from Gurus and Preachers is not what is experienced by us. Hence, if direct comprehension about the reality is a precondition for the truth being so, anything not comprehended by self better not be taken as truth. We need not be siding with anything neither we need accepting, denying or advocating any variety of truth. All we are concluding is that a truth told by others may be their truth which for another person shall be, at best, a second hand truth. *Nyaya Darshan* (Indian Philosophy based on Reasoning), which may be taken as the very first effort towards laying out the entire road map for finding truth, emphasized '*Pratyaksha Parmana*', direct perception, to be the only ultimate source of right truth. Every other type of truth was made to pass through fourteen layers of filters that, among others, included doubt, purpose, example, doctrine, hypothetical argument and wrangling before reaching to final truth. Readers are requested to undertake basic understanding of *Nyaya Darshan* from their independent sources in order to appreciate clarity about truth established on direct perception versus all other sources.

Clear Truth Necessitating Clear Eye and Willing Mind

So, we need to have very clear understanding and knowledge for reaching at the Truth. That clear vision to understand the truth will be possible only for an eye free from the dust of prejudice. Such an eye must be free from all types of resistance, pressures, discrimination, partiality to visualize the truth from right angle. The mind connected to such an eye must not be moulded in any particular cast. On the contrary, it better be willing, capable and ready for pure perception. Truth requires a pure and clean gaze at the reality present without any theory, image or memory colouring the view in any manner whatsoever. Also important is to have the ability of eye to convey what it sees to the mind without referring to any speculative imaginations or preconceived forms and substances. Such a pure vision alone is rightfully capable of being called 'direct perception'.

The mind required for having direct perception is the same mind that young children are blessed; one that is filled with purity and is devoid of all types of fragmentations. Over the growing years children, forced by their surroundings, end up losing that innocence and their minds get cluttered, divided, prejudiced and conditioned. If we are able to, somehow, go back to state of mind of a child enjoys, we will get equipped again to experience that clear vision. Alas, there is no magic wand that could achieve this miracle for us. But it is not impossible; we come across many people who seem to have done that. Why can't we?

> "The pursuit of truth and beauty is a sphere of activity in which we are permitted to remain children all our lives."
> *–Albert Einstein, German Theoretical Physicist.*

How to Move Away from Ready-made Truth

Modern world inspires most people to crave for all kinds of ready-made stuff and desire for instant gratification. This also applies to seeking spiritual growth. Most of people today are interested for finding right thing through words of others. It is human nature to look for help on offer whenever one is in some sort of trouble. Being social animals, seeking help from others comes to us naturally. Most of us want the wheel but have no interest in inventing it. Going after someone else's advice sounds rather safe option to try. Actually, it is more out of sheer convenience that we are happy being lazy. In most situations we prefer not putting any pressure on our own brains. But please let everyone be aware that only an incapable little person will hold a finger on offer. Strong and capable always wish to lead rather than be led. So there is nothing great in seeking help from others.

If you are interested to change your dependence on others and become self reliant, one small beginning has to be made now. All you require is a simple resolution that from now on you will stop relying on words by others blindly, be it elders, cultures, customs, traditions or even Gurus. Decide that you will hold opinions or agree/disagree only on issues that are self-experienced of your own. You might like to take a pledge that you will attempt to self-explore your own truth rather than follow the given. Let this principle apply to most of the thoughts you wish to hold your opinion for. Let your own self-analysis be the base of arriving on every view. Please hold only a neutral view on anything not filtered with logically conducted self-analysis. So what if the list of issues having neutral views is longer than before? This simple step will help you to make a humble beginning of becoming first hand individual free from shackles of borrowed or emotional opinions. Exploring your logical reasoning on each issue comes out a good technique to quicker concentration of mind away from other abstract issues. This will help you practise baby steps towards your aim for in-depth focus on entire working involving your thoughts generation and opinion holding system.

Every day when you sit for your contemplative session, you can spot a real life issue where you wish to bring clarity. Being a real issue, you will generally know bulk of required details. Now you start concentrating your mind on the issue under observation. Efforts will be required to let go the existing learning about it because blanking your existing knowledge is indeed difficult. Soon, your cluttering shall reduce and you will be able to arrive at your own view with your self-contemplated logic and reasoning. The real life issue may be as simple as a headline from the daily newspaper or should you go for a particular movie or not. With little practice, the quality of issues is expected to begin improving to higher impact matters. And in due course you will see your issues climbing to rather serious level on way to your spiritual journey. Soon you realize that you actually enjoy the process of seeking your Truth as it involves keen observation, better focus, increasing self-awareness and finally arriving at real Truth with your own efforts. Properly activated practice of searching for self-experienced truth works wonders by diverting your mental faculties to focus on reasoning and deflecting recurrent generation of repetitive thoughts from the maze of memories or fears.

Relative Truth or Absolute Truth

We also come across intellectuals raising another boggy about truth being relative and subjective. It is like statement of secularism that your truth may be different than my truth. By agreeing to accommodate your truth along with their own truth, they may only be trying to project their image of being tolerant or progressive. Relativity, at any level, may apply to only perceptions but not to truth. Perceptions are indeed subjective and differ from person to person or for the same person over different time periods. But perceptions are at best half-truth. Truth is fundamental, universal and steadfast at all times. It does not change due to time or circumstances or even over evolutionary process. Truth is like law of gravity. It impacts similarly to everything living and dead at all times. One may or may not have the intelligence of realizing it but its own character remains firm. For example, Science discovered the gravity very recently, but it was there as long as this Universe itself. Similarly, two plus two equals to four is a truth. One may make mistake in computing or interpreting but two plus two will always remain four. Speaking conversely, anything that is not able to stand firm on its own feet under all circumstances may be understood as anything but truth.

This very absolute truth resides within each human in form of our conscience. Each one of us can vouch for its being there and being correctly aware about love, peace, compassion, sympathy, generosity, tolerance being positive. One person may remain ignorant about his conscience or suppress it but no sooner the same is properly touched, its judgement of separating rights from wrongs becomes obvious to one and all. That is the power of absolute truth. So, one need not remain confused with relativity of truth at all. It is absolute and has been universally accepted being so in all cultures, religions at all times. So, your truth and my truth must mean the same thing if we are indeed talking about Truth.

Difference between Guided and Self-explored Truth

Let us understand the love for ready-to-serve stuff and importance of following the self-searched Truth. Let us take a practical scenario where each one of us can identify directly. Please make an assumption as if we are standing in the foot of a beautiful hill lying spread in front of us with its impressive peak visible in far distance. Standing where we are, one can only see the interim slopes covered with forest with many large and small slopes having all kinds of shapes and sizes. Also visible are some odd signs of housings of living beings. It is a very common sight for any hill in our vicinity. Let us say that we are mandated to reach to the peak where our Truth is told to lie buried. The question is how to reach to the top and come in contact with our Truth?

We are also told that many people in the past have faced the same scenario. Over a period, a road got laid by the side that can take you to the peak rather quickly and without chances of getting lost on the way. Over the years, the road got added with proper bridges, culverts and gradients to take care of smooth ride. There being many people visiting the top, there are various kinds of vehicles available for hire. Some are public transport standards while other others are private standards sturdy automobile that can take you to the peak within hours. Also available are automobiles with varying degree of luxuries thrown in together with trained drivers or even guides speaking your language. In extreme cases, even the helicopter service is possible for a direct ascend taking you in minutes.

The road here is synonym with religious traditions brought into present form with lots of digging and leveling over long history involving labour of generations and after exploring many cuts and short cuts. Similarly, automobiles are synonym with Gurus and Teacher/Preachers of various shapes and sizes, just functional or luxurious, offerings sermons in open areas or air conditioned auditoriums. Surely, depending on your own budget and propensity to spend, you can decide your option and soon can reach to the peak within hours without much tiredness or discomforts.

As against this, we have another explorer who decides to climb on foot, of his own, guided by only footprints left by infrequent visitors. Such explorer comes across a wide variety of vegetation that changes with the altitude of the area, he comes across animals and birds, soils and stones, peaks and valleys, water streams and rivers, grass and shrubs, flowers and fruits and all such other things that are expected on such tracking. The explorer keeps looking back and forth all the time so as not to lose sense of direction. He is forced to make some detours and, at times, has to walk a long way to manage approaching valleys. Due to dangers of unknown territory, he is forced to be cautious about safety and security all the time. He is able to constantly experience difference in prevailing feel and smell as he climbs more and more. On the way he comes across many wow moments. Indeed, he ends up learning many new things that he had never imagined at the start of his exploration. Yes, he ends up taking much longer time to reach to the same hilltop as compared to people taking vehicle plying on the road.

Who do you think is better prepared to assimilate the truth about the surroundings from base to peak of that very hill?

When you use a road made by others, certainly you move faster but you are unable to know the real beauty of the place before the road was there. Similarly, Teachers/Preachers can offer you comfortable ride with guide by the side but that same comfort snatches away chance of experiencing the reality of the journey. Now climbing to the peak can't mean the same to people taking divergently different options for the same purpose? In our search of the Truth also, the beauty lies in the process rather than final wisdom. A climb on the shoulders of others can lead one to the knowledge of the destination but not to the wisdom of the mountain as that will come only to the explorer who experienced it firsthand.

Role of Scriptures in Seeking Truth

You need not rely on scriptures. This statement applies to all scriptures irrespective of how great those have been and how long those have been established (exceptions apply). May be those very scriptures benefited lot many people in the past but past is past and may not hold same amount of relevance now. Today's world is different than past and rate of change in surroundings is faster than any time in history. Our issues are different and so are the challenges. Solutions that worked well, say, one thousand years back, fail to offer solutions now. Surely, the basic principles were, are and will be relevant for all ages but access to those principles is not dependent on any external source, those exist in your DNA waiting to be activated.

With all humility, each scripture is a collection of imaginative dreaming of a single author or a battery of contributors. In that sense, each scripture is a book varying in size and contents. Since idealism has always been the theme of scriptures, most likely there are no real life situations explained in most scriptures of all shades. Now ideals have, at all times, been far away from realities as is the case today. It is to the credit of accomplished redactors or authors that real events are also projected as larger than life and with a great deal of idealism. Now idealism looks good on paper or in words but it doesn't do much good to help the common man to live his life.

So, we have to stop looking for Truth in books or in words of others or in lives of others.

For the true wisdom and genuine truth, there is no need to search or rely on any external source or object. Your true doctrines shall be read and understood by you as your real scripture but only with your eyes closed. There is a true Self in our own being and it is waiting to be explored but only if bigger small self makes way for the smaller big Self within. The approach and the key to this secret door also lie well within and no one else in the entire world can lead you there except you alone. One has to understand without any doubt that every individual is a microcosm of the macrocosm. Hence, there is nothing external to what is already there within. Once properly explored, working within our own laboratory consisting of the mind body aggregate can access our own core. All types of divine experiments can be conducted guided by our own inner core to the entire exclusion of physical world.

> "Your visions will become clear only when you can look into your own heart. Who looks outside, dreams; who looks inside, awakes." – *C. G. Jung*

Having decided to go alone and go within, you will have to develop new vision and new perceptions. Going within with improved self-awareness and dedication will certainly bring about change in how you look at the world and what kind of role you find there for yourself. You will, however, have to shred your entire moulded images of each and every type. You will have to somehow go back to your original and pure Self, which is well grounded in reality away from all types of vitiation of images and roles.

Finding Truth – Fighting Your Fire, Alone

Truth has to be searched alone. Best of educational degrees, experience or position in the material world has no importance in one's search for enlightenment. Just imagine that you are all alone and there is a fire in the house. It is all up to you how you wish to quench the fire. Does your being of any religion, age, educational background or profession, in any way, impacts your ability to fight that fire? Will your deposits and financial securities sitting in the lockers have any role in fighting your fire? Surely, the answer is a big No. Our desire to seek our own Truth is in no way less critical than fighting the fire at home.

Yes, transcendent truth is very subtle and human mind is very gross. The mind is joined with ego as the beneficiary of the selfish self. Our own dear mind is successful in hiding the truth within our own depths by manipulating us to focus on other critical issues of normal life. But we do come across cases of particular individuals who come to know this trick. This clarity bundled with their own efforts and sincerity prevails over their mind and brings it under their control. In those few cases, the same mind becomes a happy servant ever eager to serve the master with all powers at its command. You can certainly be one of those few. Just be strong and bring control over your own mind.

Making progress on that route will require you to get ready to become your original self. You will have to learn and practice for focusing on Self and not on your conditioned images. Divisions referred here means your own identification with a particular image of your existing physical self that gives rise to only conflicts and works as roadblocks on the path of your Truth seeking journey. Your Truth alone has the promise to end all such conflicts. End of conflicts has the power of opening doors for your heaven (on earth itself). Ending the conflict does not mean living a robotic life or leaving this world for the forests or mountains. That may have been an old concept. But heaven has its charm only if one gets it here and now, while living this very life amidst all that is visible for sure. It is to be realized right here living a normal human life else it is just an illusion and of no use.

Concerted efforts for searching the pure Truth paves the road for access to pure love, care, peace, compassion and acceptance for everything around, both inside and outside. With this supreme realization with you, there is no more expectation of finding the heaven as a separate plane or seeking bliss or rebirth in the next or better world. You will feel free from subjective world and law of Karma right here and now. You will feel identified with supreme consciousness and at that stage of your personal growth, you will be able to experience what Vedas identify as *Swarga.* It is here that the biggest of sorrows shall be faced lightly; life will become more natural and confident. At that stage losing or gaining shall become irrelevant. Actions or words of others will not be able to leave negative impact anymore. Fears and anxieties will be destined for disappearance. Changes in external conditions will neither matter nor disturb any more. The life will just flow by itself and . . . . what else is true living in *Swarga*??

Practical Tools for Seeking Truth

Search for truth also involves discussions on critical issues of '*what it is*' and '*what it should be*' but with a twist. The first aspect of '*what it is*' requires sharpening one's observation. Observing anything requires two entities, the observer and the one to be observed, the subject and object respectively. Assigning these two roles to the same mind and intelligence and still expecting them to do full justice to each of the assigned responsibility without mixing is the art required. This art needs to be both acquired and perfected similar to any other form of art. Normal observer, the one existing before new learning, is the one grounded in past memories and conditioned experiences gathered with fragmented personality. So its quality of performance leaves much to be desired. As we know already, past memory is a reconstruction over original structure influenced by current beliefs and attitudes. Not the actual individual events from our past but our general perceptions of present links our current recall of the past. Interestingly, with passage of more and more time, one tends to become antiquated and fossilized. As a result, older the memory higher is chance of its vitiation. Why do we have to give so much importance to memories? Memories inhibit our Mr. Observer in doing its job by serving it with readymade stuff as and when the need arises.

Let us see this logic through an example of watching, say, a beautiful flower. As soon as you look at the flower, your memory prompts that it is, say, rose and you accept that immediately. But if you had never seen the rose, may be you would have focused on its leaves, shape and pattern of its petals, its colours and its smell with far deeper attention. But the moment your past image of rose is played back, the real observation gets killed. In the process, you ignore the beauty that otherwise would have prompted positive feel linked with watching a beautiful arrangement involving rose, the special flower. Surely, it is our loss as we keep missing so much beauty and grace all our life by not looking at things with the attention that they deserve. It is same with dealing with people in our life. Unfortunately, we are doing this injustice to so many other things all around us. The real problem here is person's inability to see the blessings and they are always busy regretting that they got too little too late. This is the other way of saying that we remain thankless to so many good things given by Supreme simply because our Mr. Observer (who operates under our own direction and control) fails to do its job properly. For such a poor performance, it deserved to be sacked or given an appreciation?

Yet another classical example of the same fault is the way most husbands and wives interact with each other. The longer they spend life together; tougher is the image they built for each other. After few years, the husband stops looking at the wife as a real alive charming person and the vice versa. Both of them end up making each other's solid image by preempting every move, every step, even words. Soon, not their real individuality but their created images take over bulk of their mutual interaction and communication. At this stage, they interact more like two robots than real human beings. If and when this stage arrives, it is indeed difficult to save such robotic relationship from the staleness? Relationship, by very definition, requires ongoing genuine and fresh interactive exchange. There should be no place for nagging habits coming on the scene.

Why does it happen? Actually, our subconscious system get repetitive exposure of these interactions just like someone watching the recording over recordings of similar behaviours. Ultimately repetitive watching turns into habits. Soon such recordings convert to hard images. Earlier our Mr. Observer was just lazy but now it is rendered without any job as there is no need for him even to try. All these hardcore habits are due to poor work done by our own gaga Mr. Observer sitting right within our hearts. Your first impression may be to ignore this process as inconsequential. But please wait a minute; this is exactly how ice and dust, two soft sounding substances, become stone over longer periods.

Second aspect relates to '*what should it be*'. Once the right assessment of our observer is in place, the subsequent part is rather simpler. As soon as we re-energize our Mr. Observer and force him to work better, results can't be far behind. By keeping him engaged in keen observations of the current scenarios, we deprive him of his old habit of referring back to past memories or image or prejudices. The moment that link gets disturbed, the same old-fashioned mind will start appreciating the vision in true colours. This change brings a lot of freedom; freedom from conditioned view, freedom from frozen images, freedom from fossilized habits and freedom from formula based options. This freedom immediately brings in clarity in the vision, increase in focus, purity in applying right logic and prompt response without distraction and without prejudices . . . . What you realize now is pure Truth.

> **This is the truth we have been longing to find all this while.**

Use of freewill and freedom of thoughts activated by pure Self-awareness is the key for reaching here. It is quite likely that new truthful revelations will bring to surface new side of Truth. The new truth may be quite contrary to your earlier held assumptions and beliefs. But don't try to find any defence or continuity for face saving because none is important. That will only make matter worse and bring in complications. Overlook everything other than pure Truth. Trust me when I say that other than you, nobody on this planet is really interested in you. So you alone are responsible for swimming across your troubled waters. You are most important to you and you alone. Your own truth protects you like no one else. Please push out all others from your drive of seeking Truth as they have little role to play. They are beneficiary of what you got but they have no time or desire to really help you out of your inhibitions. You alone are the captain of your ship, so sail it to the right direction.

Primary concern of every human should always be about himself. It is only after our own needs are fulfilled that others should be invited on the scene. The very search of happiness, peace, harmony or even spiritual realization is also to consolidate our own position within our inside. To accept this fact is not to say that we have to convert ourselves to being super selfish. No, focus on self does not ask you to give up your support for others. Others are inseparably connected with us and more often we help others to help our self. In any case, it is our illusion that we are responsible for dependents on us. Yes, up to certain age of dependents this obligation may be true but not for ever. There is no dependence, it is all about attachments and it is not good for both – you and others involved. Please gather courage to accept the reality of this physical world where each and every soul is responsible for its own destination. To accept the soul's individuality is a practical and correct understanding for starting your spiritual quest.

Humanity is bestowed with mind, an active organ blessed with ability to apply logic and reasoning. Being a unique blessing, humanity is under obligation to make use of this faculty and contemplate on its own spirit of inquiry. But regrettably, this very spirit is grossly underutilized by large proportions of humanity. This original ability needs to be reactivated by people up their journey of 'Self-aware' to 'Self-understanding of Own Truth' to 'Self-improvement' to finally, 'Self-realization'. Make no mistake that our knowledge shall get filtered to become wisdom only after pure assimilation of real truth. This newfound wisdom shall help us to look at things in clear perspective without any wrapper or brand stamping. Once we are able to grow our vision pure and clear, we can see this world as well as our role in this world with harmony and balance. When there is Truth, the love, happiness and peace are never far away. Truth is hard coded and strongly etched within hearts of each human being. Anyone willing, prepared and dedicated to go to the depths of his heart, can access its source. It is really that straightforward.

Tools for Spiritual Practice

"Watch your thoughts; they become words.
Watch your words; they become actions.
Watch your actions; they become habits.
Watch your habits; they become character.
Watch your character; it becomes your destiny."
–Lao Tzu, an Ancient Chinese Philosopher

Our journey for seeking Spirituality is a discovery mission about finding who we are and what is this life and world all about. We also learnt why this discovery has to be undertaken after sinking all accumulated beliefs and divisions and without any external help. It is identical to going on for discovering some new unknown continent using your own small boat. Surely, a journey of such dimensions and importance will deserve best possible preparations to succeed. Expecting this journey to be carried out sitting still with eyes closed in some small corner of the house is but a big mistake.

At times we come across people getting motivated to pursue spirituality under a crisis misadventure of some variety. No, that is not the right time to start your journey. Seeking recluse not being equal to seeking spirituality, we intend to discuss right preparations required for making good progress. Going over these preparations before knowing about challenges of searching Self-awareness and finding right Truth would have given only theoretical exposure. Since it is all about making inroads in our eternal paradox existing in between ego and soul, the preparations required are also directed towards reducing the scope of our ego and strengthening attributes of our soul. (Just as a small clarification, the reference to the word soul here is in terms of that unseen power or light or energy or called by any other name that survives death and that transcends every known attachment.)

The preparations suggested for practising Spirituality are the principles focused completely on ethical advancements. There are only five simple looking steps that are considered sufficient for initiating proper seeking. These are *Dama, Dana, Daya, Aacharan and Sahanubhuti.* Let us look at each of these in some details:

"Dama" – Self Restraint

The closest English word to represent Sanskrit word *'Dama'* will be Self-Restraint. Self-Restraint may be defined as restraint on one's emotions, desires and inclinations. It is also explained as exercising self-control and self-discipline in all personal and social activities. As a tool for pursuing spiritual progress, Dama include all steps required for physically preparing the mind body aggregate to get ready for realizing subtleties of our own core. Practising Dama brings us to detach from unwanted and unhelpful noise from all types of engagements with others in the vicinity. This Self-restraint works fully only when it is voluntary in nature. Coerced restraint on the other hand brings down your growth as it increases the cravings for suppressed attractions and attachments. Importantly, the restraint needs to be applied on what to think, what to wish, what to speak, what to do and what to see. Exercising Dama is further classified into following four distinct steps.

a) *Austerities* – These include severe self-discipline on desires of body and distractions of outer world. Effective methods for austerities include Asanas, prayers, self-analysis, fasting, sexual abstinence, living aloof away from attachments and social connections and giving up luxurious life. Continuous practice of multiple austerities as per one's own capability adds to increased ability to resist.
   Resistance enhances power of controlling temptations. Once the human craving for its fleshly desires is brought under control, the mind gets motivated to seek and enjoy ultimate tranquility. Renunciation is considered even higher than austerities. It will be interesting to go over few lines from an

old Indian Scriptures in so far as it provides us the recommended sequence to follow:

"*The wise man overcomes anger through mind-control. Lust is to be controlled through the renunciation of desire. He can attain mastery over sleep by developing quality of Sattva. He should protect the organ of generation and the stomach through staunchness. He should control hands and feet with eyes. Eyes and ears should be controlled using power of mind. Mind and speech should be controlled by conduct. He should shed fear through constant vigil. Finally, pride is to be overcome by service of the wise.*" (Brahma Purana 235. 40-42)

b) Chastity – Chastity must be understood as sexual purity and being morally clean in thoughts, words and actions. Thus, it is not about sex and sexual desires alone. Celibacy is absolute essential for making progress on spiritual journey. This is practised with a willing freedom from erotic imaginations and not by suppression. It is most potent weapon against evil forces of lust, anger and greed. Chastity is also highly recommended for opening of '*Shushmna*', the astral tube running through the spinal cord, the housing of all the *Chakras,* i.e., if one holds belief in that system.

The entire process of celibacy consists of four different stages. First stage consists of control over sexual desires and *Vasanas.* Second stage involves conservation of sexual energy. Third stage involves channeling the entire preserved energy towards spiritual growth. Finally, this accumulated energy is to be converted into '*Ojas*' by resorting to continuous practices. *Ojas,* also called as spiritual energy, in turn, contribute to spiritual progress in more ways than one.

c) Keeping the mind quite – Keeping the mind quite is a lost art. Peace of mind arising from a quite mind provides best possible opportunity to reflect and discover Spiritual enlightenment. Quite mind is known for revitalizing both brain and body and significantly enhances concentration powers. It also fosters deeper contemplations on core issues that remain out of reach under cluttering of living in community.

"*A quite mind does not mean that there will be no thoughts or mental movements at all, but that these will be only on the surface, and you will feel your true being within, separate from them, observing but not carried away.*" – Sri Aurobindo

People who are able to get opportunity to make friendship with their peace of mind can vouch for great solace awaiting them. In short, a quite mind allows you luxury of focusing on self. That focus alone helps you in self-discovery away from shadows of others. Intensive introspection requires a quite mind. Our ability to withstand our temptations is best tested away from the gaze of others.

Regular periods of a quite mind must be practised even when we are outwardly engaged in our occupations or conversations. The sheer presence of others in the immediate vicinity with their movements, words and actions leaves you vulnerable for unwanted excitation of mental activities. Keeping the mind silent works as a buffer from pressures of worldly obligations and allow you to explore your creative self at its best. Best of writings, researches, music, visioning have all been created by people having quite minds.

d) Silence–Silence is essential to open ears for tapping the tunes of spiritual journey. Speaking involves hearsay, backbiting, flattery and loss of energy in making others understand your actual meaning and intentions. All these activities work as drains storming away your spiritual orientation. Silence is necessitated for leading the soul forward to connect with the Ultimate. The 'still feeble voice' of the Supreme can be heard but only in silence.

"*All other knowledge are only petty and trivial knowledge. The (silent) experience alone is the real and perfect knowledge.*" –Ramana Maharshi

All types of daily routines leave wear and tear on our spiritual practice and observing silence enables our heart and mind to regain that loss of balance. Both Ancient cultures of Hinduism and Buddhism have been promoting observing silence as a pre-requisite to spiritual purification and growth. Progress in silence is equated to progress in realizing of spirit. A soul well balanced in silence joins itself to the silent creative power of God.

Silence also is getting scarce in modern times. People can be seen moving from one activity to another without a silent moment in between. The onslaught of electronic and social media facilitated by handheld devices with 24/7 connectivity has turned out a disastrous recipe for engaging human senses from the moment of waking up until going back to sleep. Many of the individual disorders rising in the societies in modern times are directly attributed to extinction of moments of silence.

But silence, as being discussed here, does not apply for sounds alone. Beyond the decibels, we need to practise silence of our eyes, tongue, ears and most importantly that of the mind. Silence is the language of divine power. For attaining real wisdom and clarity of thoughts, the power of silence is much more productive than thinking. Willful silencing of all sense organs and mental faculties allows harmony and balance between our exterior and interior. Silence provides the best environment for flourishing the saplings of joy and happiness. The melodies of nature require silence at all levels to reach to our very core. Constant chattering of thoughts work as inner speech and inner speech is as disturbing as external speech.

Many beginners report transformative advantages out of their very initial meditations. In reality all those advantages come out of their spells of practising solitude and silence of senses and thoughts. Meditation is a very difficult art and one can hardly rise to meditative stage in initial sessions itself but silencing can be achieved instantly. Silence is a great stress reliever and prepares our mind body aggregate to be receptive. Once you start experiencing even brief spells of total silence, you realize how much energy gets drained out in activities involved in active verbal and mental processes.

"Dana" – Self Sacrifice

Dana is giving away part of material possessions that one has been bestowed with for the welfare of others in need. Ability to give away is a powerful negative freedom from greed. On positive side, this amounts to assisting others. Dana is a celebration of natural law of mutual dependence. It is towards realizing bonding of entire humanity. It is towards understanding that what one owns is also to be shared for the benefit of others. Material possessions in excess of basic necessities are condemned under all religious thoughts the world over. Sitting on pile of worldly possessions which are far beyond meeting essential needs takes you away from seeking spirituality.

Further, mere giving is not enough. Right giving has to meet some minimum qualifications for qualifying as effective giving. Giving must be to an appropriate recipient, one who is genuinely in need. You should give liberally. Giving must be with modesty. Giving must accompany with genuine sympathy. Giving away with these qualities alone shred selfishness. Giving without these qualities is reduced to more than non-giving.

Buddhism also differentiates in pure and impure motivations for giving. Clause 4:231 of the '*Anguttara Nikaya*', a collection of texts in the '*Sutta Pitaka*', provides instances where donations made qualify as impure motivations. Giving for avoiding shame, giving due to intimidation, giving as *quid pro quo* or giving just for feeling good about self are all giving with impure motivations. Right giving has to be with pure intentions of sharing your fortunes with those in need. Giving should be without any reward and attachments to either the giver or the recipient. Perfect motivation for giving should be for release of greed and self-clinging. Giving requires a big heart and giving with right qualities is really transformative.

The concept of giving away should also involve some sort of sacrifice on the part of donor. So long as you are giving but that giving is not asking you to make some sacrifice, it will not qualify as rightful giving. Sacrifice here means that you get impacted personally in some measures that it results in you being forced to bear some sort of compromise for your own use. Ability to make sacrifices in giving is important for all moral qualities but it specially enhances qualities such as, tolerance, strength, determination and firmness of purpose.

Giving entails parting with our possessions which requires great courage and sacrifices. Most common of all reasons is identifying a deserving person or cause. Fortunately, today there are many NGOs engaged in specific causes and one may like to be part of their activities. One may also look at opportunities through their social circles. For example, a dear friend has been supporting school education for girl children from poor families. Initially he contacted a few schools in his neighbourhood and expressed his desire to help the deserving children. Soon the word spread around and cases started coming directly to him. When contacted he meets the child and her family and talks to teachers and pays for fees. He also keeps full eye on the academic progress by the child concerned and interacts with the family and school regularly. Continuation of his support for the child in higher classes is linked to academic progress. Over the years that he has been doing it, a good workable systems has taken shape that nearly meet all the prerequisites of *"Dana"* as detailed before.

One can identify similar other social causes they wish to associate with. It may be from the obvious fields like health, sanitation, self-help, social awareness, eradication of social evils, gender equality, etc., meeting their own choice. Alternatively, one can get associated with organized institutions and be part of their fund-raising. If you have no money to donate, donating your time may equally qualify this virtue. Right giving, in any form of choice, meeting above qualities accrues karma credits that in turn bring future happiness. Based on personal experience, I can proudly share that the satisfaction derived from right giving is many time more than keeping that sum in your bank. You have to do it to really enjoy that unique joy you experience when you see the happy faces of the real needy beneficiaries, Amen.

"Daya" – Compassion for All

The other Indian words that also get subsumed into the meaning of *Daya* include '*Karuna*', '*Anukampa*', '*Kripa*'. Each one of these words ultimately connects to a desire to extend your shoulder to mitigate the sorrows and miseries of others in as much as such sorrows were your own. Compassion in English comes nearest to Daya of Hindi. Compassion is both a value and human attribute and goes a long way in creating an all inclusive, all connected, all interrelated, interdependent humanity where each person feels for each other at par.

Compassion can also be defined as a state of mind where there is no trace of any kind of violence, not even a thought of harming anyone. It involves giving up aggression entirely. Desire to help others in becoming free from their sufferings, oppressions and pains become the underlying principle here. It is also like being in peace with everything around. Compassion originates with the understanding that, as human beings, we all are connected with each other and all of us have equal right for being happy and free from sufferings. The affinity desired under compassion is not out of benevolence but genuine sense of belonging and togetherness. There is no one up scenario where one individual passes on his charities to others to obtain a thrill or a false sense of personal well-being. Making charities does not involve feeling of closeness and oneness in operation but compassion activates that very much. Compassion, once fully developed, brings down all walls erected between friends and/or enemies as it makes all beings standing side by side as equal in all respects. Forgiving is also important part of compassion as it frees a person from grudges against others. Forgiving cleans accumulated toxic waste from our hearts.

Compassion should also not have any string of attachment. Attachment with a person or thing brings in the desire to control or to seek love in return for love. This intention gives rise to biases and partiality. But real compassion has to be practised away from all types of associations. The real compassion has to emerge out of the understanding that every one shares the world and each human being has natural desire to be happy and is indeed engaged in overcoming their sufferings just like us. In any case, this is just pure statement of fact. Unfortunately, most ignorant people fail to realize this fact with required intensity and depth. Sense of equality and commonality is the basis for letting the affinity and closeness evolve in compassion. Acceptance of equality is the basic theme out here. This feeling of togetherness fills all types of voids that separate people in terms of friends and enemies, relatives or strangers, known or unknown, good or bad, rich or poor and weak or strong.

By growing thoughts for compassion in our minds, our attitudes towards other people changes automatically and we start feeling good about them. This very feeling for others, of its own, starts chain reactions where there is reduction in fear and increase in openness. This way, compassion helps growing seeds of connectedness with other beings. Besides fear reduction, compassion works for enhancing kindness, generosity and tolerance, which contribute significantly for our moral and ethical dimensions.

Developing compassion opens us to sufferings of others and that mental state is entirely different than going through your own sufferings. Own sufferings make us go through the feeling of burden and helplessness. But compassions allows us to develop the feeling of determination and dedication to do our best while still remaining comfortable; this is yet another understanding of '*Nishkam Seva*' the principle of service without expecting anything in return as popularized by 'Bhagwad Gita'. Under this feeling you get encouraged to connect with others with a feeling of freshness in spite of sufferings involved there in. Developing compassion goes a long way in improving one's own psychological and emotional health as it leads to a calmer mind, gives rise to feeling of joy and eliminate factors contributing stress and depressions.

Further, compassion is much stronger an emotion than intimacy. Intimacy is generally sharing a beautiful relationship between two people where there is also trust and confidence. Intimacy is known to bring in improvements in both physical and psychological well-being of people involved whereas compassion connects a person to large number of people resulting in similar benefits if not more. Gautama Buddha is credited for likening compassion with a mother who protects her child, her only child with her own life. Buddha called upon everyone to cultivate a heart of unlimited love and compassion towards all beings. Compassion is supposed to melt the human fear better than sincere worship.

Jainism also attaches foremost importance to compassion when it provides that all life are essentially interrelated and interconnected and that all living beings should be considered sacred and respected alike. This very belief forms the basis of their doctrine of "*Ahimsa*" which means much more than mere non-violence. Real meaning of Sanskrit word '*Ahimsa*' includes every action and thoughts besides physical injury, which directly or indirectly, results in harm to others. In addition, speaking unkindly to any one or even getting a strong adverse feeling in the mind gets covered in its definition. *Ahimsa* needs no explanation as most Indians of post independence era are aware of its true power. But with reference to our discussions, the same '*Ahimsa*' is nothing but 'dynamic compassion'.

But the best of all description of compassion is by His Highness, the Dalai Lama, who, as quoted in 'Voice from the Heart' by Eddie Shapira, explains compassion as under:

> "A mind committed to compassion is like an overflowing reservoir – a constant source of energy, determination and kindness. Or this mind can be likened to a seed; when cultivated, it gives rise to many other qualities, such as, tolerance, inner strength, and confidence to overcome fear and insecurity."

"Aacharan" – Cementing Ethical and Moral Behaviour

Focus on external aspects of life by ignoring inner dimensions inevitably leads to doubts, anxieties and fears and pushes away awareness for self. Now, practising various austerities mentioned under "*Dama*" can attain control over external aspects of physical body but regulation of inner dimensions can be attained neither by exerting force nor by specific techniques. Inner conditioning gets impacted by our personal conduct through our actions and has to be approached in subtle manner. It must be attempted through voluntary self-inspirations alone. This is where ethical and moral aptitude plays all crucial roles.

To appreciate the importance of being ethical as used in our discussions here, let us first understand in simple manner what is not ethical. In our day-to-day life, we keep undertaking many actions. Most such actions do impact other people around us in varying proportions. Lack of appreciation of impact of our actions on others is unethical behaviour. Focus on self to the exclusion of others involved work as the shield preventing us from seeing the impact of our actions on others. Ethical behaviour involves holding respect for key moral principles of honesty, fairness, equality and dignity towards others at all times. Dilution of ethical behaviour creates voids between the world and us. Ultimately, this void hits back on us by making us lonely and frustrated beings.

While working on our way up the spiritual path, we necessarily keep cementing our principles of ethics and morality. Like other measures discussed so far, lot of time is required to let our actions meet the spirit of ethics. Each unethical behaviour results like a hole in our pitcher holding nectar of spiritual earnings. All our actions must hold true to the test of being ethical without exception. These are perfect either or situations where either one is ethical or otherwise.

Thankfully, human ethical hardwiring is pretty strong to the extent that feelings of repentance engulf even hardened criminals at some time in their later life. Since, unethical actions are known to ride over negative emotions; winning over negativity from our emotional spheres helps to improve our being ethical. We must remember that unethical actions corrupt our morality much more severely than loss of physical health. Physical health can be gained back more easily with medical intervention but once a person ignores his ethical behaviour, he wrecks his pursuits for higher life altogether and there is no simple cure for the same.

Developing ethical and moral attitude is a tough task. Steps required are simple to understand but difficult to practise. The steps include avoiding every situation or activity that encourages negative feelings. It is here that our in-depth knowledge of emotions and feelings comes handy. To divert something, we must know how to spot the same in the first place. Secondly one must work to promote feelings on the positive spectrum. Negativity at attitude level comes only after longer exposures to unwanted situations. Surely, it will take even longer to move over to positive side. The right knowledge and conviction to pursue positivity and blanking out on negativity is the art that needs to be perfected for winning over ethical and moral turpitudes.

> "Spirituality automatically leads to humility. When a flower develops into a fruit, the petals drop off on its own. When one becomes spiritual, the ego vanishes gradually of its own. A tree laden with fruits always bends low. Humility is a sign of greatness." –*Shri Ramkrishna of Ramkrishna Order*

"*Samvedna*" – Empathy

The last step required for practising our spirituality is to develop empathy, the ability to experience situations exactly with the similar intensity as some other person is condemned to experience. It involves understanding and sharing needs, concerns and emotional states of others while they are forced to experience pains in life. In nutshell, it is like standing exactly in their shoes at the same moment and feeling their pains and tragedies with same depth and intensity. Developing empathy again is a difficult process and needs transformational efforts. But a man who has made satisfactory progress in exploring his own self and is ready to find his connection in the world will find it natural to grow his empathy to desired levels.

By nature, empathy is selfless and requires us to focus on others more that we normally do. Empathy is much more than sympathy. Sympathy involves expression of pity or sorrow for the situation of others. It operates in the environment where one side is a victim and the other side is there to extend physical and emotional help. Sympathy involves separateness and disconnection. Empathy, on the other hand, fuels a sense of connection. If sympathy is '*feeling for*', compassion is '*feeling with*' then empathy is '*feeling like*'. Growing empathy levels necessitates all of the following four elements:

1. It requires looking at the prism from exactly same angle. Difference in angle provides a different view of the same object. Developing perspective of the given circumstance similar to the one held by the affected beings.
2. Staying out of judgement – It necessitates complete absence of judgement for the situation of the other person. If you have a victim whose poor quality house got destroyed in earthquake, empathy involves feeling their pain of devastation without having any room for feeling that they suffered as they didn't took care of constructing quakeproof house.
3. Recognizing emotions of others – Empathy requires to develop detailed and complete understanding of emotions of others. Being a matter of feelings, pains of others cannot be appreciated and felt exactly like them unless we are able

to comprehend the nature, intensity and overlap of their prevailing emotions.

4. Communicating with similar emotions – Lastly, real empathy will get activated only when we are able to communicate with others with emotions that are similar to their own emotions.

Thus, one can learn about empathy only after understanding emotions of others. Interestingly, a person practising empathy is to use more of his emotional mind rather than logical mind, probably the only exception to the general rule propagated until now.
Appreciation of empathy is to promote our understanding that all human beings share common basis and all of us are born similar and we are destined for similar end. Actually, these are indeed fundamental similarities but walls erected by stronger nippers around false ego stop us from developing our appreciation for the same. Initial spiritual progress itself results into loosening of the grip of

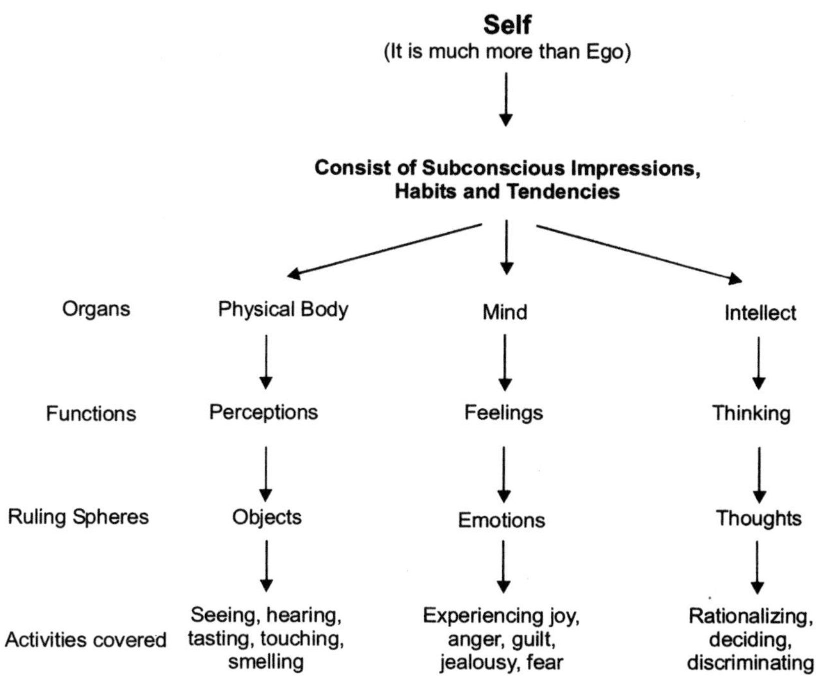

Fig.: Developing understanding around Self

ego and soon we regain our ability to realize increasing similarities among humanity at large. At that stage, empathy gets developed with little efforts.

Finding common grounds on similarities, in spite of harping on differences helps us find space for establishing trust and faith every time we deal with others. This approach yields result in worst of political, social or historical stalemates. This connectedness with others leads a seeker further up in his spiritual quest by letting him know that differences in education, money, power or positions are neither important for own happiness nor these are factors of any significance, hence, we should not let these come in between our dealing with other human beings.

Practising Practical Spirituality

Once a wise man was crossing a big river sailed by a simple middle aged boatman. The wise man got in discussion with the boatman and, upon learning that the boatman has not learned his religious scriptures, pronounced judgement that half of his life has just been a waste. When they reached around the middle of the river, a hole developed in the bottom of the boat and water started filling the boat with great speed. The boatman quickly asked the wise man if he knew about swimming. The wise man said that he has read many books about swimming but could not practise it in the waters. The boatman spoke back, "Sir, looks like your whole life will soon be a waste because the boat is likely to sink and swimming could have been the only way to save your life right now." The teachings of this small story apply exactly to Spirituality; having theoretical knowledge about it doesn't help us in our hour of crisis.

Practising spirituality is similar to aiming for a perfect health target which demands regulated diet, exercise regime, adopting healthy lifestyle, controlling dairy products and other oils, control sugar intake, sweating out at the gym for balancing cardio, calories burning, strength building and muscle forming routines. Above all, you should be watchful of not succumbing to temptations at all times. Both health targets and spiritual aspirations need disciplined life, dedication, self-motivation and practice and some more regular practice. Again, only reading about it can't help you achieve your health target and so is the case with Spiritual progress.

Practising Spirituality is not limited to prayers, meditations, chanting, breathing, ceremonies or rituals. It requires living life within spiritual knowledge and disciplines. Practising Spirituality is not an activity that needs to be done only on selected hours of the day. It calls for change of entire life style. It calls for all round vigil. You have to practise for your body, for your mind and above all for your spirit. Mental health necessitates being watchful of your thoughts, words, actions, emotions, logics, habits and attitudes. More importantly, it is like cooking and eating; bit-by-bit, item-by-item, several times a day and every day of the year. The practitioner has to indeed remain occupied similar to a traditional Indian Lady of the house who goes to extreme details to prepare breakfast for entire family every day. No sooner that breakfast is over, she starts preparing for lunch. Lunch hours follow the preparation and arrangements for dinner. Whatever time is available in between, that is used for sourcing ingredients, growing some vegetables at the kitchen garden, preparing special combinations for use in particular dishes and for preparing snacks for small bites in between. Yes, practising Spirituality is a round the clock penance, a real '*Tapasyaa*'.

Interestingly, all the suggestions involved in practising spirituality squarely fall within our own controls. All these are fully focused on us alone with no one else is involved. This self dependence is, however, a double edged sword; practising involves arduous pains and not practising involves obligation and accountability. One can't hold other people or situations responsible for failures and neither can accelerate the process with the help of others. So, the success in practising spirituality depends purely and squarely on our own initiatives and commitment.

Steps listed below cover a whole range of dos and don'ts. The steps cover our entire life spectrum simply because Spirituality is not practised as an add-on exercise. Recommendations of these practical steps are based on personal experience and may provide encouraging results to other practitioners as well. You may like to make required tweaks factoring your own ways and means, your own situation, orientation, targets and such other real life issues.

Spending Time in Solitude

In normal life we are mostly advised to tightly pack our daily schedules so as not to have time for thinking about pains and sufferings. People take pride in working long hours and running from professional engagements to socializing and to vacations, living life like a sprint.

We grew up learning that an empty mind is devil's advocate. So, mind should remain preoccupied with one or other assignments at all times. Our monkey mind loves such scenario as it enjoys jumping from one thing to another without any control from the owner. But spiritual seeking works just the other way. It requires you to keep as much free time as possible by deliberately shunning away such activities. Here you need to practise by withdrawing your mind from activities to emptiness; basically to get bored. This pause plays a critical role towards our spiritual practice. It is only when we have nothing urgent to do that our mind gets motivated to look inside voluntarily. Having a pressing schedule is a big diversion pulling you away from concentrating on something as significant as Spiritual practice.

> "To make the right choices in life, you have to get in touch with your soul. To do this, you need to experience solitude, which most people are afraid of, because in the silence you hear the truth and know the solutions." –*Deepak Chopra*

Time available without any immediate pending 'to do' list allows us to observe our tendencies in new light. Pure observing leads to enhanced understanding about the very source of our thoughts and intentions including origin, motivations, intensity and underlying reasons of all that it craves. This process brings us face to face with our realities, something that we never knew before. Free time on hand prepares our mind to be ready for undertaking contemplation. Spending regular time alone is, therefore, new habit to develop towards practising practical spirituality. Every human interaction is a drag on your mental concentration. Quality of interaction doesn't play any role here. So, you need to create your exclusive corner where you spend your time away from all types of noises, interactions, pressures and diversions. How much time of the day is good for solitude? Well not the entire time of the day. Out of personal experience, practising solitude just for three to four hours should be enough for setting the mental systems in right direction. So, one is still left with all the time in the world for interaction with others as well as attending to other matters of importance. So, it is more a matter of rescheduling than shunning human interactions.

In today's chaotic situation, it is equally important to be deliberately away from your mails, messages and mobile phones including other social media mediums. All these things can wait while you find time for deep contemplation. Finding regular spells of quality time spent alone is bound to prove very nourishing for refining your own knowledge about self as well as this Universe. Time spent in solitude allow you to connect with yourself and develop genuine self-perception. Solitude is bound to enhance your creativity by several notches and that will certainly help you even in other areas of your life. It is a lost treasure that doesn't command many seekers today but it has great advantages. You try it just for few days and see the instant positive effect yourself.

> "My yearning is my cup, my burning thirst is my drink, and my solitude is my intoxication; I do not and shall not quench my thirst. But in this burning that is never extinguished is a joy that never wanes" –*Khalil Gibran*

Focus on Breath

Sitting in a comfortable pose with eyes closed, one should practise focusing on breath daily for 30-40 minutes. Later you might like to increase the time as also the frequency. Time recommended is in early morning and evening, the meeting point of night and day and vice versa. Let the mind focus observation not on the nostrils but somewhere near the end of nose, around the nasal area. The flow of the breath, both at inhaling and exhaling, is to be regulated in conscious manner by bringing the mind to concentrate on the nose end point. The mind will keep going to other thoughts but the practice requires bringing it back to focus on the breath. You can also practise to locate some other point of attention with the sole purpose of engaging the mind on breathing sequence all the time so that it doesn't get opportunity to fly away. In addition to being highly relaxing, this practice helps us master pure observation. Once perfected, you can also make it your pre-meditation routine.

Don't worry about getting stagnation as this simple practice offers large variations that help the mind remaining engaged over long periods. While breathing is a simple looking activity that every living being is undertaking subconsciously all his life but it will be very interesting to note how many variations are possible within this simple activity. The sensations while inhaling and their changes at the exhaling, the change in temperature of the air breathed in and out, the pressure of breath felt at inhaling and exhaling, the rhythm and flow of breaths, the smell of the air going in, the feel of breath at the throat glands, soreness in throat with change in climatic conditions, the feel at thyroid gland, the variations in some or all of these factors are enough to keep the mind engaged for years. Later these variations can be linked to kind of food or drinks you had the previous day, the impact of quality of sleep at night, impact of physical exercises etc. All these points need to be observed by the mind while breathing under keen observation every day.

This practice soon leads you to the habit of observing without judgement. As already seen, the art of pure observation goes a long way in furthering our spiritual progress. It sharpens our awareness and search of pure truth together with silently working to take the ego out of our conscious system. The multiple impacts of pure observation are the sole reason that this point gets highlighted at repeated places. Capability to observe things without colour and judgements is the single most important milestone on this interesting journey called spiritual evolution. This stage arrives only after certain degree of success in advancing moral, ethical and emotional levels is achieved. Without any doubt, well-developed pure observation is the real tipping point from where the rest of the spiritual journey moves over in auto mode.

In due course, your awareness about things in your own life will start improving. You will realize clearly if you have been living a fresh or stale life. The clarity and purity of observation also brings realization of issues relating to peace and happiness. Please take caution to constantly work on increasing length of the breaths for each inhaling and exhaling and accordingly increasing the total time utilized for each daily sitting.

Daily Sadhana

The key to practise spirituality is *Sadhana*, self-enrichment by undertaking regular exercises of self-inquiry. It is not something done to please some other person (which is the case for worship). It is a process of churning, brainstorming or shaking your understanding exactly similar to the process of bringing out butter out of creamy curd. It must be carried out daily under your own way for searching that ultimate purpose of human life bit-by-bit. Self-inquiry is required for cleaning our heart and mind similar to cleaning the best of mirror. Mirror requires daily dusting and cleaning to maintain its ability to reflect the image accurately. The idea is to clean your consciousness so that you are able to connect with your conscience, the infinite self, without any pride or prejudice.

Various effective methods helping people to conduct proper self-inquiry include one or the other ways of Meditation. As discussed earlier, there are many different ways that one can meditate. Those are all effective systems and you have to find your own combination that works well for you. In any case, you should keep making variations as and when required. Feel free to alternate from one method to another. Remember that we are after end results and not committed to means; means are dispensable while ends are sacrosanct. The key, however, is regularity. As you would like to do it daily, you should better keep it enjoyable but meaningful.

The basic principle for effective self-inquiry requires silencing of our speech, mind and will. This silencing enables to listen to the pure voice from our core without serious efforts. In terms of time, again, you may like to know that *Sadhana* is said to be most effective during the early morning time; the time when birds have started chirping, night is in the process of bundling down, body is well rested after a good night sleep, mind is reconditioned, daily pressures of normal life are still in deep sleep. But one should explore it out by practising on other times of the day and should be guided by results rather than recommendations. In any case, rested body, happy stomach, silent mind, eager intellect, comfortable environment and plenty of free time is an essential list whenever you plan to go for your *Sadhana.* Once we are able to meet these essentials, any number on the clock or AM/PM does not matter at all.

So feel free to go for it as it suits you best. You may like to do it alone or in group, it may be carried out on empty stomach or after meals, it may also be carried out before or after bath; let it be your own way, your own time, your own preference in every way except that it must be regular and pure inquiry to help you contemplate on purpose of human life alone. Suspension of mental activity and withdrawal into depths of interior is the ultimate purpose. Once there, our spirit is able to get absorbed in fruitful silence of Divine Supreme.

Practising Yoga, Pranayam and other Absorbing Activities

As seen earlier, Yoga exercises need preparations in terms of strict practices of *Yama* and *Niyama* on regular basis. Continuous focus on them uplifts our moral and ethical behaviour in baby steps. Awakened morality brings in peace at heart and connects us to our universe without conditioning. Hence, Yoga's role for spirituality is much more than on physical and mental levels alone.

Regular practice of *Pranayam* is another important must for practising spirituality. Pranayam routines bring in balance among the three *doshas* of *Vata, Pitta* and *Kapha*. It provides unmatched exercise to internal organs contributing significantly for physical health as well. It is excellent in making mind cheerful for long periods and adds to enthusiasm level of the practitioner. Pranayam adds significantly to positive thinking and thereby takes out a lot of negativity of emotions out our system.

> "The degree of freedom from unwanted thoughts and the degree of concentration on single thought are the measures to gauge spiritual progress." –*Ramana Maharishi*

Every session of Pranayam helps in concentrating our mind on desired topics. Above all, it prepares our mind body aggregate for undertaking fruitful meditation for hours together. Your study about Pranayam will expose you to a number of practices but the eight selected pranayam popularized by Swami Ramdev of Patanjali Yogapeeth are a good starting point. These include *Bhastrika, Kapalbhati, Bahaya, Ujjai, Anulom Vilom, Bhramari, Udgita* and *Pranav*. The sequencing, intensity, time practised for all these will later on offer great opportunity to find your own best possible capsule by accepting what works and keeping aside what doesn't work with you and for you. Each one of these pranayam offers tremendous scope for evolving your own style based on the stages of your practice.

Caution must be, however, taken that basics relating to sitting with backbone straight, neck and shoulder remaining stable, taking pauses in between changing over to next pranayam, all through the practice must always be followed strictly. Doing it mechanically will only get you physical advantages; for spiritual advantages, you have to carry out your Yoga exercises and Pranayam like worship for seeking your God. The loop of '*study to practice to perfection to study to practice and further perfection*' has to be always on irrespective of how many years of practice one has gone through. The more you will practise, the more you will know the faults in your previous practice sessions. In a way, practising of Yoga exercises and Pranayam cycles are similar to a master musician who keeps improving his art all his life and still keep realizing as to how much more could be learned for improving his art further.

In addition to Yoga and Pranayam routines, the seeker is also advised to identify and work on selected activities that are able to absorb his/her faculties and keep the intellect challenged at deeper levels. Depending on the comfort levels, your creativity and past expertise, it may be dance, singing, playing musical instrument, writing, reading or some other art form. Idea is to have a channel that is able to suck all your free time by absorbing you completely.

Reading... but with Patience, Attention and Gratitude

Reading is by far the fastest way of gaining knowledge riding over the wisdom of others. But reading can be abrupt, casual, callous or contingent. In our normal life, we sometimes do take words as nothing more than group of letters but reading for practising spirituality is a different ball game. Here one has to go deep into words for searching and absorbing their true subtle nuances rather than mechanical meanings alone. More important question than what to read is why to read and how to read. Once we are able to sort out why and how part, the rest of the process is always smooth.

Be it a book or an article or a web page, we should always start with the attitude of gratitude. Every word written by its author, either today or thousand years back, have evolved out of enthusiasm of sharing wisdom. And if it is old, it must be worth reading to have survived and being available to you today, else it may not have been in your hands. In any case, you are likely to read a book that you have not read before and relating to a subject of your choice. So, we better be hospitable for its content and intent to ensure that we are able to learn all that is new for us. Let us always remember that it was our choice to pick up the book and we are here to learn rather than comment or judge the author. If we are unable to adhere to these primary requirements, our efforts of reading it will fail to fire our imaginations and fail to expand our circle of compassion. If it so happens, loss will be entirely ours.

The reading for practising spirituality is entirely different than, say, the way we were reading fictional novels where even the names of the lead characters barely stay in our memory only so long we reach the last page. Fiction or subjective reading required us to reach to finish line at the earliest. But in absolute contrast reading as a spiritual practice requires very open and slow approach. The focus is on searching notions rather than mechanical meaning; we better chew the words and sentences until we are able to extract its delicious juices. Let the subtle nuances conveyed by words sink in our system with clarity and conviction. Such reading alone will let words nourish our inner spectrum quickly and heal the wounds lest they exist. After all, we wish those words to travel through our mind and reach to our heart, and that is quite a distance.

The focus here is not on number of pages read in a session or in a day. Volume or number of words is meaningless for spiritual reading. We are after essence and that requires intensive churning. So, patience is of utmost importance. So often, we don't get our own thoughts come to surface easily, how can we expect the entire thought process of some other person get registered with us in an instant? Let us allow ourselves to be surprised by the author. Surprise can happen only when we are truly open to let the author be understood. It is our duty to make this reading a sacred activity and that is possible when we value each moment with the book as if we are sitting in private contemplation.

Since you have already made some progress on your spiritual journey and you have prepared well, anything not having ability to help you learn is not going to catch your attention as it is. Your hands will refuse to pick up a book unless it has potential contribution towards your spiritual progress. Hence, the question of what to read is no more an obstacle for you. Your changed orientation will help you ride over distractions. But don't limit your horizon to particular language, time period, religion, faith, nationality, zone or any such other limitation. With any such condition operating, you get deprived off the treasures available out there in open. To apply limits to your choices is depriving yourself for sure. So open up your choices, be discreet but be liberal in your pickings. Words of wisdom coming from any part of the world, history, language are all valuable experiences of others and their authors allow us to come face to face to their lifelong learning. As it is, by now you are universal in your outlook far beyond tight boundaries applicable to normal beings.

Aligning with Interest Groups

Joining like-minded people for a cause is very helpful for scaling up your interest even further. All of us without exception end up delivering more in a collective environment where there are people involved to motivate or encourage each other to do higher and better. Interest groups also make the efforts stress free. It is here that common interest groups like Meditation Circles and Yoga Groups come handy for helping you better your spiritual practice routines. Since each one of us will be going for spiritual growth after our professional circles getting somewhat deactivated, such groups also provide you opportunity to connect with new set of individuals and help you meet your social requirements.

> "Align yourself with people that you can learn from, people who want more out of life, people who are stretching, searching and seeking some higher ground in life."
>
> – *Leslie Calvin "Les" Brown,*
> *A multi faceted motivational speaker from America*

Having access to such groups provides an excellent opportunity for clearing your doubts and evolving solutions desired for mid course corrections. Others also help you identify faults in your practising techniques in their capacity as an independent external observer. But for others, you may not realize those obvious faults for long times. On the other hand, acknowledgement of your achievements and appreciation for your progress by your fellow travellers has great motivational impact on providing further boost for your efforts. Working in groups also forces you to shed lethargy on few days when, of your own, you would have skipped the routine.

But to be practical, you must be ready for unexpected difficulties in finding the right kind of group. Since Spirituality is not so common, you may not get interest groups in immediate neighbourhood. Please don't lose your sleep as connecting to some other sources through other options may serve the purpose in some proportions. For example, there are so many blogs available online and you can get sufficient insights even while sitting at home at the time of your choice and convenience. What we need to remember is that spiritual growth requires a unique combination of intellectual capacity utilization, continuous development of character and values and enhanced awareness about spiritual self. None of these depend so much on group working than individual endeavours. Access to like-minded groups, at best, helps to reduce the pains of the process.

Stepping out of the Comfort Zones

People involved with inspirational sciences can be heard encouraging us to get out of our regular routine and do something strange every now and then; something that we normally would not do otherwise. Besides other advantages, such adventures are sure shot ways of pushing our boundaries beyond the known comfort zones. Practising our spirituality also gets helped by pushing aside our normal routines once a while. We all get comfortable with our set routines and known surroundings operating well within familiar territory resulting in no risk, no stress and enough mental security. Comfortable routine ensures peace, happiness and low anxiety. Stepping out of comfort is pivotal for our evolution and growth. Our bigger and better version hinges on our willingness to go beyond what we already are. Comfort zone is said to be a happy space but it is known to restrain further growth. Hence, periodical trips away from happy space are highly recommended.

Operating within our comfort zone also kills productivity and subdues our creativity in general. Whereas pushing our boundaries invariably results in faster results riding on new outlets and forced brainstorming sessions. The important point is to identify the area where you may try expanding your horizon? Well it can be in any practical field that sounds challenging to begin with. If you happen to be typical Indian male with cooking not being your forte, cooking for the entire family for one full week including shopping for groceries can be a good example. Organizing a close group where you deliver one-hour chat on some topic of their interest may be another example if you have not been good at public speaking. Getting up in the middle of the night and having mid-night meditation sessions can be another thrilling experience even without anyone even knowing about it. Joining some forest camping group involving trekking and surviving with least possible essentials can be yet another example. A long visit to the land which inspired you in some subject of your interest is also a well pursued path taken by many people with good results.

Personally for me, writing down my own memoirs about my early life in a village was one such effort. Having become a city dweller from college time onwards, I imagined that my grand children might not have remotest chance to know about real life in a typical North Indian village of early nineteen sixties. So, writing down all my recollections of first sixteen years in my village came out as a unique experience. I had never attempted to write something serious other than usual business/office communications or few letters to would be wife during courtship days. I can never forget the difficulties I went through in penning down about sixty odd pages. It was so difficult to find right word and composing correct sentence besides making use of tools on offer from Microsoft Office Word. Writing was actually concluded by me to be very frustrating to begin with. Who could have imagined that learning from that initial effort will slowly lead me to write full volume books on topics of my interest, just about ten years down the line?

So, you need to identify your fears and commit yourself to work against odds. In a way, seeking your spirituality is a never-ending improvement course with rolling targets. So, all techniques known to work in real world are equally applicable out here. The best part is that you are no more undertaking these things as a dictate from your boss or to cover adverse points mentioned in your annual appraisal report. You are breaking out your comfort boundary for your own sake, under your own inspiration and for the pure love of expanding horizon of your own creativity.

Practising Renunciation, the Art of Willful Sacrifice

Normal meanings attached with Sanskrit word '*Tyag*' include giving up, disowning, surrender but the most appropriate meaning for our purpose is 'willful abandonment', leaving a thing without intention of ever reclaiming it back. It is much more than sacrifice *per se* as simple sacrifice involves some sort of coercion and an activity carried out under some compulsion. But *Tyag* is entirely voluntary in character and there is never an eye on any '*quid pro quo*'. It is more like offering than giving; you part with something that is dear to you and parting of which will certainly create some strains for you. Practising *Tyag* is a very effective tool for getting rid of attachments and fears. It makes you emotionally and morally stronger than before.

> "A sacrifice to be real must cost, must hurt, must empty ourselves…." *–Mother Teresa*

It may please be noted that *Tyag* is much superior to even '*Dana*', donation. Donation or charity involves parting with some of your extra possession caused with an aim of earning some merits. Now best of merits, based on even Indian mythological stories, can get you a place in heaven. But spiritual seeker is looking for liberation and not heaven. Sacrifice on the other hand, involves voluntary giving up of something important to you, something that makes some effect on your own life, something that involves going through sufferings.

Spiritual seekers are advised to prastice giving away from all pride possessions with a view of practising detachment including but not limiting to financial fortune, some material objects, some talent, some time, some thoughts, some professional capability, some knowledge and some wisdom. To practise detachment, we should be ready to part a thing that is being used by us; parting of which does matter to us. So writing a cheque of some amount that does not affect our life style in any manner is, at best, sharing the excess money that was most likely to remain unspent after your final departure from this world. That is called philanthropy. Such giving can't be expected to bring us desired credits. It is a different matter, however, that you decide to part with a good part of your estate for some charitable cause.

Our time is the most important and exhaustible resource at our command. Hence, it qualifies as best possible sacrifice. Sharing of our quality time with someone and his benefiting out of that is a real sacrifice. Other examples of sacrifices made with merits intact may include sharing our professional expertise for the benefit of others, rendering our expert services to those in need, active participation in thankless social works, regular blood donation, arranging for donation of our organs for others, etc. Each such voluntary act contributes bit by bit towards our successful spiritual practice. To become generous in all our actions and behaviours involving others is also equally important component of practising *Tyag*. So, be as generous as possible in your dealing with others. This will sure help out compassion and empathy quotients to grow in the right proportions as well.

Invigorating 'Sankalpa', Determined Willpower

The larger is our muscle of *Sankalpa*; stronger are our strides on the path of spirituality. *Sankalpa* signifies the visualization of the positive outcome of a likely experience or event much before reaching anywhere near to that point. It requires a very interactive combination of *Ichcha, Kriya and Jnana* (desire, action and wisdom) where this combination is used to draw on the energy of subconscious nature to motivate us to do everything that furthers our pre-determined purpose. Practising for this art involves setting targets with stretched levels of both capacities and capabilities. Then one has to work hard to achieve the same. This involves both doing a few things and NOT doing many others.

Most important point is to arrive at our main purpose using all our intellect and increased awareness. That is to be followed with the determination to direct all our conscious and subconscious energy towards achieving that purpose. One may start with short term and comparatively smaller targets to begin with. Success achieved over initial targets will lead you to raise the bar progressively until you are able to say that all your actions and behaviours are on desired lines. This entire process is based on positive motivation and not on suppression or deprivation.

Against *Sankalpa*, we have English words like Self-control or self-regulation. We must understand and appreciate the significant difference in their meanings. Control or regulation is entirely based on denial, camouflaging, getting over short-term temptations and petty desires for gratification. That is too narrow an area for a spiritual seeker to work on seriously as he would have crossed those hurdles in his initial stage itself. Instances like eating that extra serving, drinking that extra peg, skipping the gym session, over sleeping on Sunday morning and avoiding morning Yoga on a wet or cold morning are common examples showing lack of will of saying no to our self. The seeker is not willing to entangle in these petty matters only. These examples may be taken at the level of flowers or fruits where the Seeker is better advised to work on the level of seeds and roots of tendencies giving rise to such desires.

Strength of will power to carry out our well thought out targets is the main point under focus out here. But please be cautioned that willpower is a limited resource. Each one of us is blessed with less than infinite quota of willpower. The success or failures of use of willpower depends on selection of right situations for applying the same. Normal people spend their willpower on trivial issues revolving around satiating the insatiable desires and temptations. People with wisdom, on the other hand, preserve this scarce resource for use it only to deal with testing situations. So please use your discretion of using your willpower very discreetly; it is similar to limited stockpile of your missiles which better be fired only in extreme situations. In normal situation, a machine gun or firing mortars may be a better option.

Let us look at a practical tip. Exercising will power is comparatively difficult when one is physically and/or mentally exhausted. The idiom 'nip in the bud' is most appropriate for exercising willpower at the most appropriate time. The winners are those who are able to avoid the very situation where temptations start arising in the first place. For example, maintaining glucose level by eating in right proportions at right times is far easier than controlling the desire of picking up unhealthy food stuff while visiting a food court on a hungry stomach. It is ideal to avoid going to darker corners than being there and controlling your fear. The issues discussed earlier about emotional and rational minds again have a key role to play out here as well.

"It is easy to avoid temptations than resist the same."

Seekers of spirituality must keep an eye on the big picture always and focus on positive long-term benefits. Self talk and repeated self-reassurance about pitfalls of giving in to desires and gratifications is more doable than fighting the real temptation. Fortunately, issues of self-control will trouble you much more in the beginning of your journey. Once you have been able to shed links with attachments and desires, the very situations of testing your self-controls will progressively reduce.

Purifying Ethical and Moral Self

Purifying individual's moral and ethical self, similarly, requires series of tedious efforts. We have discussed all the options for moral upliftment already where major focus was on practising renunciation and penance. But towards being practical, one should be free to explore every other option and opt for what works. Idea is to ensure that every word spoken, every thought and every action is moral and ethical. These processes, no doubt, involve lot of hardships and sufferings but those are inevitable as one has to get rid of natural human weaknesses of anger, envy, lust, greed, pride and possessing. Pursuing redundancy for these weaknesses is difficult only to begin with. Once you start seeing initial success in your efforts, you start getting real inner encouragement for giving up these weaknesses progressively with increasing speed. Subsequent progress neither proves as hard nor are the sufferings as insurmountable. In advance stage, in fact, there are no more sufferings, as it becomes a norm. The key is to show determination in initial stage.

This is age-old theory and still as effective as ever. Individual personality can be as shiny and glittering as pure gold. But Gold does not come to its shining self just like that. To begin with, at the ore level, gold forms complete series of solid solutions with silver, copper, nickel, platinum and palladium. To process all the unwanted metals, its processing involves a long series of tedious processes of pyro-metallurgical or hydro-metallurgical processing, selenium separation, smelting, reduction, refining together with leaching, precipitation and filtration. Not only that, gold processing necessarily involves dealing with very hazardous items including arsenic and selenium. Those familiar with Gold processing can vouch that over twenty ton of best quality ore is processed for obtaining one gram of pure gold. But all those going after gold are not discouraged in a bit with all its friends and foes. Efforts involved in improving our morality and ethics, similarly, have to go through arduous journey of refining over and over again. But ultimately, that very morality shall make us one among equals as gold becomes precious among so many other metals.

Getting Habitual of Sinking all Known Systems/Methods

One has to develop this habit of dying to relations, attachments, possessions, objects, pleasures, fears and dangers. No sooner our mind dies to its past learning, it acquires its original freshness of being receptive for unconditional grasping. Reaching to this stage enables one to experience each day as a new incarnated day. In this state, the mind is completely protected from all kind of harms and hurts and that is precisely the innocent mind we were blessed at the time of our birth.

Our mind becomes receptive for acquiring fresh knowledge only after we are able to forget what we already knew. A fresh mind is open for pure learning without any conflict. Meditation practitioners with certain degree of expertise achieve this state for brief periods during their mediation sessions. But advanced practitioners should not find it very difficult to continue in this very state for longer periods. Following already established systems and methods, irrespective how good and effective these have been to others, end up making our mind and thoughts stereotype and robotic. Robotic thoughts can never promote genuine and fresh imagination that is a hallmark of human brain. Being lethargic is another important characteristic attached with human mind. The moment we agree to follow what has been told to us, it is natural to expect the brilliant mind to assume lethargy and stop imagining about it.

Known systems work as invisible cage that imprisons our skill for imagination and makes our mind completely docile. Just for example, if one is to ask any practitioner of popular Hinduism of the day if 'Rama of Ramayana' was real life hero or simply a mythological character, thumping majority will favour against Rama being just a fictional character. It is not that most of them are having no intellect to see through the mythology but it is just that strong belief in Rama automatically shuts off their reasoning valve. Let us never have any valve anywhere in our basic thinking. In order to retain its freshness and basic nature, water needs to flow through like in an open river rather than within concealed pipes. Pipes are bound to have elbows, reducers or enlargers on the way. How can water flowing through such pipes have freshness comparable to the river water?

When logic gets applied and imaginations are put into work, pure inquiry for genuine truth becomes feasible. But for that to happen, it is essential to have a routine free, system free, method free and belief free mind. Such a free mind alone is capable of finding answers to questions surrounding exploration of our blissful nature and our comparative place within this Universe. Let us see around us for a while. Among all the knowledge streams, basic sciences promote working exactly on the lines mentioned above. No wonder, then, basic sciences see more discoveries when compared to all other streams of knowledge. Just imagine the results that can be expected by scientists working with strong beliefs, going over only existing routines under already laid out systems. No, such an approach can only promote status quo.

Belief systems are strong shackles preventing us from applying the gift of nature by way of opening the logical mind for acceptance. This applies to all types of beliefs that our religious or cultural background forces on us consciously or unconsciously. Let us take the example of a well accepted and rock solid belief like 'law of karma' that suggests that every action will create a karma effect that will have to be settled in this or some subsequent life. Now every Hindu child is made aware of this since its early childhood. But if you think minutely, holding this belief allows you to leave the karmic effect settlement for subsequent lives. Does this postponement bring in some sense of lethargy? If nothing else, the belief in rebirth takes away the sense of urgency that anything done wrong will create consequences to be faced here and soon. Surely, the strongest and most logical sounding belief creates dilemmas.

Putting an end to every known belief system will make you free and will encourage you to settle everything here and now, and that too not by abstaining from but by undertaking right actions. All stories about next lives are just fictions being told as no one has ever been there. Beliefs drag you away from becoming a living human being. Think through your own self-aware mind using your brain and intellect and do what is right thing to do. Let us not leave things for later as this is the only visible life and this can end any day. Sure, there is a need for great urgency.

Ending Duality of 'Observer' and 'Observed'

Let us recall some cherished moment like being on the banks of a still lake on a summer afternoon or walks through a serene park or visit to the hills etcetera that absorbed your total attention. You may have experienced a unique feeling like never before. Rare occasions like these let us forget everything else that existed nearby. Now let us try repeating similar experience one more time. This time let the lake be even bigger and more beautiful. For sure, you will fail to get the repetition of original experience. Actually, you can't get that unique feeling repeated even with a better surrounding as your mind will lose pure observation and get engaged with comparisons and evaluations. The moment we engage in comparing, we stop enjoying. The mind gets engaged is recollecting earlier impression and the beauty of pure observation gets lost.

As also discussed in a previous chapter, allowing our mind to operate both as observer as well as being observed at the same point of time, takes away its ability to see things with neutral clarity. This leads to generation of deep divides and inevitable conflicts. One has to master the art of being a pure observer by shunning away all comparisons, expectations and judgements. By cultivating the art of ending the duality of observer and observed and focusing attention on pure observation, everything observed will get experienced as a blissful experience. Please attempt it with full knowledge and credence that it is entirely possible to develop such an attitude with practice. This single capability, once acquired is capable of transforming this very world as a beautiful place to live with thrills and wows all around. Such a man realizes how many bounties on offer have been missed by losing our ability of pure observations. Such practitioners are right when they boast that this world is a great place to live for one and all.

Stopping Passing Judgement on Every Issue

Coming to any conclusion, and more so where others are involved, requires understanding of a bag full of information that we normally don't have. Think of a judge who verifies all evidences of every case coming before him meticulously, go through points raised by both complainant and defendant, and allows cross-examining of witnesses by lawyers of both sides and look around for every other important detail about the case under his consideration. Later alone he arrives at any judgement with folded eyes but only after going over all facts, evidences, arguments and precedents. Judging is a serious business and taking it casually is gross injustice. But inadvertently, normal people can be seen passing judgements all the time even after having next to nil information about matters being judged. We forget that we are all different people and what is right for one may not be right for other and more importantly that both types of truths may have good reason to stand scrutiny.

Why did she say what she said? How dare he misunderstand my words like that? No, that is not the right way of doing this job. Why can't my son call me at least couple of times in a week? Should I not have been informed about it earlier? This is the least, they could have done? Should they not have taken my concurrence before committing on this? . . . . One can go on listing all such situations where unknowingly we are constantly working as a self appointed judge and passing opinion about the thing to be right or wrong. Invariably we want others to do things the way we consider right. We may have our reasons to see these observations as logical and absolutely obvious ways of recommended behaviour but in reality these are inadvertently passed judgements on our part.

In any case, when was everybody perfect? Are we perfect on all counts? Do we always do to others what we expect them to do to us? In any case, only person we need to worry about and have right to pronounce judgements about is our self. Accept words and deeds of others as their best and learn to devise your own actions and thoughts based on your best ability and morality. This single point, if perfected to desired levels, is possible to drastically reduce our tensions of normal life and improve quality of life a few notches higher. Expecting the world to dance on our tune is just impossible and needs to be so understood. The only option we have is to respond to situation presented by external world. Get trained hard for keeping our self at the centre of all the improvements required in this universe. Completely forget what others could or should contribute. The moment we stop passing judgements on others and focus only on self, a whole lot of ugliness, pettiness, shallowness and selfishness will disappear from our life.

What to practise and how? Well, handing over actions to the command of our logical mind and concentrating focus on self under all situations are good points with assured success. We need to improve our craft of finding 'action for self' under each and every daily life situation. Let us stop worrying for things relating to others, external forces of all types included. Our untrained mind is expert in fixing responsibility on others for everything wrong in our life as well as in the whole world. Simply put, we have to train our mind to do just the reverse under each and every situation.

Going Beyond What Others Tell, Write or Speak

Surely, you can access to best possible scriptures, knowledge books, sermons to learn from or even have the luxury of a Guru available to hand-hold and guide you at every step. But all that wisdom will be based on experience of others not yours. Anyone who says that he learned something from others is only talking about secondhand learning and can get only second hand meaning. That is not going to help you to seek your own truth. At best other's learning can only satisfy your desire of knowing. But we have to be after wisdom and not knowledge. Real wisdom shall only be gained through self-realization; by grasping the truth about it by using one's own faculties of imagination and finally by absorption of the same.

No, the suggestion is not to throw away books and scriptures. Study of scriptures helps to understand the horizon available to be explored and that itself is a big advantage to begin with. These are good tools to help you design your canvas but not what to paint. Words of others will help you only when their contents match with your own understanding, perception and discrimination. Simply reading them and believing in their content doesn't convert that knowledge into your wisdom. To make it your own truth, you have to complete your own process of pure inquiry involving for prolonged shaking, churning and storming. It is indeed possible that your own conclusions also coincide with what was said by the scriptures or other people in the first place but let this conclusion be drawn after your own inner churning of contemplative processes. Let us not forget that every word contained in scriptures is word by some person of a different age. Attributing any word to a divine power is ignorance. Words are written in languages which were always man made, period. Today, world is different by miles from the past. So, keeping ancient words aside is no disrespect to those noble souls in any way.

Words spoken or written by others spoke about their wisdom but may not have any significance for us unless we also develop the underlying views and opinions as a strong springboard from where those views get thrown out. You have to understand that a visit to real heaven necessarily involves death. If you are not willing to die yourself, forget about knowing heaven authoritatively. The fundamental principles of wisdom are never available for embracement. No one gets wisdom without working hard for acquiring it. Wisdom is not an entitlement or inheritance. It needs to be pursued and assimilated the hard way. By very design, it can't be ours unless we get it of our own. Please see through the falsehood of promises made by so many commercial preachers promising readymade realization. Promises of readymade or fast track realizations are just sham and need to be ignored and dumped. You alone and none other have the power of letting you obtain your own wisdom.

Accepting Realities of Life

Accept that world is what it is and each one of us is just a tiny small dot with virtually no significant relevance for the running of our nuclear families, let alone our societies or this universe. Accept that most of the trophies that we collect by spending our life will turn garbage sooner than we expect. Please forget about desiring how things should be and start accepting things as these are. Acceptance is a virtue and is fundamental in nature. Embracing reality releases tons of energy that can be used for creating wonders in so many areas of our existence. Let things happen without your approval. Allow all others to take lead and move on with what they deem fit, kids and spouse included. As soon as the desire of approval moves over to genuine acceptance, a whole lot of mental agony vanishes in thin air. Besides plugging the holes on the reservoir of our happiness, acceptance allows us time to pursue other passions. Spare time in hand is like a bag full of uncut diamonds. You are at liberty to discard them without their value being ever known. Alternatively, you can improve on them by cutting and polishing and convert them into gems. Acceptance enhances our kitty of raw diamonds. Later, how do you make them shine and use it for ornaments depend solely on choices made by you?

However, acceptance carries the risk of getting confused with passivity. No, it is not to be used as an excuse for not acting where one is obliged to act responsibly. Acceptance allows us to look at a situation in 'this is what it is' scenario. It is not that you don't see the need for improvement. Of course, we shall have to take a good look at it and take steps to make it right if need be. Acceptance is totally different than tolerance. No, we are open for improvements but that is by identifying what can be done by us, not others.

Suspending Mourning the Past or Restlessness for Future

Most memories are a collection of inconsequential possessions with years passed over the expiry dates. Memories are dead moments and deserve to rest in peace inside the coffin buried deep down in the ground. Past is delinked with present as well as future. Past is dead wood and hanging it around the neck is inviting trouble when you are in deep waters, your hours of crisis. We may not realize it but memories occupy space of our mental hard disc and in some cases, it does occupy sizable portion of the total space. If nothing else, unnecessary stored data in our computers reduces the response time and thereby adversely impact potential use of the computer. We all can recall on personal experience that dumping of old non-usable furniture allows a lot of precious space in our homes. Sinking memories does the same to our mental space. Living in the present moment wisely and earnestly brings about real results in our lives. Learning to divert our mind and thoughts from both good and not so good parts of past is an art worth learning. Recollecting past and worrying for future fears equally work as drain on our limited time and energy. Appreciating this fundamental point is a great life-simplifying step. There is a very famous quote credited to Alice Morse Earle. This saying is aptly applicable for spiritual practice as well:

> "Yesterday is history. Tomorrow is mystery. Today is gift. That is why it is called present."

Seekers have to remind themselves that feeling like a victim of past events and blaming others for our failures makes us feel good but only in the short run. Blaming others, situations and people included, makes us powerless. Worrying for things to come may be helpful when it spurs you to take actions and fix problems. But thinking about future by allowing the brain to go over 'what ifs' and engaging it in 'worst-case scenarios', results into big problem. As already seen, worry is known to give birth only to negativity; the more we worry about some eventuality, worse will be the possible outcomes.

Living in present is reality and brings joy. Present is the only important moment in our life and rest is indeed an illusion. Let us not behave like a tourist who reaches to scenic place and instead of observing beauty of the surrounding, gets busy clicking pictures. You think somebody may enjoy that beauty later by just imagining when he has not enjoyed it while he was physically out there in flesh and blood? If you fail to live the present, its memories in future will never be worth remembering. Let the feeling of joy and a long smile on the face be our only possession to survive. Work hard to your full potential but remain ready to let today be the last day of your eventful life.

Discontinuing Comparisons with All Others

Quite unknowingly and at every stage in life, we keep comparing ourselves with others. It is considered harmless and some of us rely on it as a source of motivation of doing better in life. But measuring yourself, both with your own self and with others, can easily spin into tail chasing mania that invariably results in self-doubts. There is famous line credited to Mark Twain, the American Author and humourist who said, "Comparison is death of joy". Let us not glance over this saying just like any other one liner good for sharing on the social media with their impact being felt for a few moments. Crushing capabilities of comparisons have been the basis for several scientific studies that convincingly link comparison with feeling of envy, low self-confidence, depression and most importantly inability to trust others.

Sometimes we get advised to compare ourselves with less unfortunate people hoping that we will be better off after finding them lesser privileged. But that approach is as deadly as comparing self with those considered better privileged. These comparisons end up promoting negativity of feeling good about the unfortunate plight of others, a direct cousin of competition and sense of jealousy. Comparing in all situations and forms is not focusing on what is reality but wishing and worrying for what it should be - the 'observer' and 'observed' delusions. Studies have successfully decoded the double whammy principle that works in comparisons where the tendency is always to overestimate the positivity of others and failing to detect their negativity.

So, please be assured that you have no right information to compare in the first place and your weights of measuring the possessions of others are not at all correctly calibrated to help you reach the right spot. Making comparisons with any one at any time and with respect to anything is possibly the worst way of reducing your importance as well as your true worth. Taking things as these are, without any measurement or evaluation has potential of reducing your burdens, stresses, strains and fears. Be what you are, it is your life and please don't waste it on others. Others are not important for your life as much as you normally were thinking. Others have their own life and you have yours. The only comparison permitted is to compare your previous self with your present self. Also permitted is you comparing your actual condition with your potential. These comparisons are centered on you alone where you have all the facts first hand. For comparing your findings, just remember that being human deserves that you are better today than before and all your potentials are fully utilized. Amen!

Listening More and Speaking Less

The very activities of listening and speaking are much more significant and critical as one generally understands. Listening is not about letting others pour their verbal sound into your ears. That will be too mechanical a meaning for it. Listening is also not about passing such sounds to your mind. Unfortunately, in our day-to-day life that is what we do most of the time as we end up listening everybody through our mind. This mind, we all know, is so smart and it makes us believe that it already knows about the matter even before the other person is through with his words. It doesn't listen but gets busy to draw comparisons with some pre-recorded information and gets engaged in reassuring you about it. That doesn't qualify even as mechanical listening.

Effective listening is listening in silence of mind, silence of attachments, silence of desired outcomes, silence from desire of others agreeing to our point of views and most importantly, silence from any desire of comparisons or judgements. Listening with internal chattering going on at high pitch prevents you from grasping the spirit. In that state it is just robotic. Similarly, letting our mind step in between words of others is a crime we all commit without even realizing.

Right listening is listening with open heart; listening as if the words are being received for the first time, with full attention and without any prejudices. Listening with heart allows us to feel the essence of communication and thereby making it more interactive. Listening should be done for learning, for understanding, for finding out, for developing realization, for feeling the pains and pleasures of others. You can go for a quick self check about it. Pick up any normal talk with any member of your own family. Just try to attentively listen every word spoken by the other person with open heart and acceptance. You can't fail to realize that differences of opinions earlier felt by you during previous verbal exchanges with the same person get reduced substantially, if not vanish completely. Effective listening indeed is known to substantially reduce the need for convincing others.

Speaking, on the other hand, is a very overrated virtue. Barring transactional exchange of messages, speaking is known to create more trouble. Most of the arguments used in history can be traced as seeds of conflicts rather than anything else. Resolution of conflicts hinges on compassion, empathy or accommodation than on arguments and logics. No wonder, Mother Nature blessed us with two ears and one mouth. So the divine design was always programmed for at least two times listening to speaking. In fact, our mouth doubles for so many more activities in addition to speaking. How come, Nature didn't feel the need to create a special organ exclusively for speaking?

Your efforts to explore and realize yourself require you to develop the habit of listening everything from everyone as if you don't know how to talk. Words of others should have impact on you as if those are genuine, forceful and spoken with well-meaning intentions only. Forget what you thought about others as others are not important. We are here to explore what can be done to improve our own conditions. Seekers, having practised to reduce speaking as part of exercising control over mind and emotions, will vouch that it takes multiple efforts to speak as against listening which can be done in rather effortless manner. No wonder, speaking can tire you quickly while listening can go on and on. While total silence may not sound practical, we can cultivate habit of:

a. Speaking only after other person has completed his speaking in full. This will certainly reduce the need for unwanted speaking.
b. Not speaking unless spoken to; you will be surprised how much can be talked simply by gestures.
c. Use only those words that convey your meaning without ambiguity. Time taken for evaluating right words may slow your speech but will fasten listener's understanding.
d. Speaking only when we have full attention of the listener. Speaking to someone who doesn't have his heart to you is wasting your energy. Walls and furniture don't respond how much you cry out there.

Such simple steps shall result in preserving lot of latent energy within our physical system that we generally keep wasting in unwanted talking. Speaking is a pure strain and avoidable most of the time.

Relying Only on Self-Experienced Truth

Seekers shall continue their practices with full devotion towards seeking their self-experienced truth. Applying unconditioned reasoning, logic and analysis allow emergence of one's own truth. The truth we are talking may look abstract to an untrained mind but a seeker on way to his progress understands it as the process of extracting butter out of milk. As we know, the butter is used for making Ghee which has a far long shelf life than milk and many fold applications. Well-contemplated and reasoned truth, clarified based on pure observation and right awareness, also gets converted as an altogether different form of its earlier form in terms of precision, purity, application and shelf life. But it is not a one-time exercise. It requires constant reiterations. This truth is too based on pure observations as against pre-fixed or formed images. Chains of dependence on cultures or traditions or second hand knowledge do not burden such a truth. Books and teachers can't influence such truth as it is based on direct perceptions by your pure, open and free mind.

Developing such an approach is completely feasible. Any intelligent human being is perfectly capable of approaching the source of their own pure intelligence by keeping away all divisions and conflicting distortions of identifying self with any one or more divisions and fragmentations of all types of hues and colours. Every division obscures your vision from discerning genuine truth and subconsciously directs you to take a position in a biased manner. This position taking pushes away real genuine Truth from your reach.

It is only real, pure, self-experienced, directly perceived Truth that effectively allow you to deal with your entire surrounding and allows us to access our love, peace and joy; the pure human nature at the very core of our existence. This Truth will create a heaven like environment 'here and now' where the enlightened soul is perfectly at ease with everything living and not living alike. At this stage, the human being, living life within this world, will be capable of observing beauty of every aspect of this vast Universe. It is here that we will see no separation with other objects in the entire surrounding.

Concluding Remarks

Practising spirituality necessitates all above activities undertaken on a very regular basis. Commitment, dedication, determination and patience are the key words. Spirituality can be cultivated only bit-by-bit manner. The pace is bound to be slow. It is greatest transformation ever undertaken by you. Expecting overnight success in doomed for failure. We can now clearly appreciate why practising spirituality is always referred as 'walking the path'; because it is indeed a walk that has to be taken on our own feet in a step-by-step manner, without any equipment or tool; something that can't be just achieved by sprinting out in a quick time. It is always destined to be a journey, a slow journey, a self-paced journey, a lonely journey, an arduous journey, a long journey where the seeker continues making his progress for '*walking the talk*'.

Yes, it is always going to be for the daring and brave hearts. There are bound to be scars and blisters and so will be pains and sacrifices. But not significant and transformative virtue was available for free to any one in any case. Continuity of practices mentioned here and before will, in due course, start showing positive benefits. Those initial fruits will help you realize blessings of progressive internal healing. There will be other low hanging fruits available in terms of indirect impact on peace of mind, happiness and emotional balance. The satisfaction of knowing yourself intimately will itself cover up many difficulties and sacrifices.

In due course of time, and based on positive progress attained, the need for other practices may progressively reduce. Space so vacated should get filled up by *Sadhana*, the daily contemplation practice such that towards the final stages of your endeavour, it is *Sadhana* and *Sadhana* all the way.

Spiritual Realization

Stages of Spiritual Realization

Spiritual growth of a human being can be seen evolving in discernible stages similar to growth experienced for physical, mental and psychological dimensions. However, spiritual growth differs with all others as growth on all other dimensions, by and large, grow automatically as the time progresses. But Spiritual growth can't be measured by calendar. Spiritual growth defies rules of accrual with time. It needs to be earned the very hard way. It was always so and will remain same for all time to come. Yet another appreciable difference is that spiritual evolution can't be identified with defined milestones. Actually, its very destination is moving all the time. There is nothing to announce its arrival and nothing to measure the distance travelled or remaining to be covered. Spiritual growth is also not a module-based system where one can clear one module after the other and project the time required for completion of all modules. Spiritual growth is all about being substantive than quantitative.

The spiritual journey, to a large extent, is similar to finding one's way home from a stranded unknown location in a dense virgin forest on a hilly terrain without much support or guidance available. All you got there are few natural landmarks such as sun, winds, stars and sounds. Obviously, a person stranded in such a situation has to make his way back by clearing bushes and shrubs and for sure it is too much to expect a clear roadmap or time table for his reaching back home. Forget about certainty of time, he can't even be sure of his reaching back at all. At best, this lonely person may use his tentative knowledge of slopes, contours, water streams and vegetation to help him find his way back but most important of all shall remain his willpower and determination to cross over every hurdle. The plight of any spiritual seeker is no way different than this stranded individual.

Spiritual practitioners have to deal with yet another problem. To begin with, there are not many examples of people who have completed their seeking as the ultimate spiritual realization is not very common. To make the matter worse, most people reaching to higher levels are generally not interested to leave behind their trails with sufficient clarity to help beginners. They rarely come back to normal life and share their experiences with others. As per some estimates, over ninety per cent of successful seekers aren't interested anymore to share their success stories. It is not difficult to imagine why as most of the realized souls are so mesmerized with the unimaginable bliss that leaving that peace and tranquility is almost an impossible option to go for. In any case they realize the importance of individual's own penance being at the core of desired progress. This makes penetrating spiritual citadel becoming even more impermeable.

Thankfully, growing spiritually is truly an evolving process where practitioners start getting unique experience from the very beginning of their efforts commensurate to their sincerity and dedication towards the practice. Surely, defining different stages involved over the entire journey, or grading those stages in terms of significance is quite impossible. Every single stage of spiritual awakening is no less or more significant from others. Still, it will help the beginners if some sort of estimated road map is made available for their benefit. Even tentative understanding of evolution at different stages will provide a new practitioner necessary idea about vastness of the territory to be covered, possible indirect milestones for estimating progress achieved, knowledge about the topography of different stages, choice of tools and equipment to be kept handy and a general idea of what more is expected to follow. The description below is just an attempt in that very direction. Let us spread the entire spectrum of identifiable stages with best possible understanding and imaginations at work.

Majority of Populace Happily Ignorant

To begin with, we have big chunk of population which is blissfully ignorant about spirituality. These people sitting at the base of a wide bottom and low height pyramid are happy leading a mechanical life engrossed in material world. This chunk is happy meeting physical and social demands of their human life and inflating their egos as big as possible. Their mantra for life is to seek some pleasures even if it comes with inevitable pains. They have no desire or capability to look outside their self-centered, self-consciousness, self-indulgent and self-serving routine they call life. Regretfully, these people occupy biggest share of the pyramid accounting for ruthless majority of humanity of today.

This chunk is happy enjoying their selfish pleasures even if it means pains to others. Material comforts and sense objects are good enough toys and they don't feel tired playing with them all the time. They keep pampering their respective egos and blissfully believe that they are far superior to many others. They don't want to be distracted with uncomfortable questions about morality, ethics, divinity and issues relating to afterlife. Actually, their core is tightly covered all around with a thick layer of darkness of ignorance. As a result their voice of conscience has been put to deep sleep and their internal system is unable to even spot its feeble voice. Their ego is well fed and well kept with constant and undivided attention on 'I, me and mine' issues. Now, we have known that ego and spirituality are two swords that can't fit in any single sheath. These are mutually exclusive prepositions. So long as one is predominant, the other can never stay with that person.

Some of them follow one or the other organized religion for the sake of tradition but that may be to create a hollow identity to the entire exclusion of all others. In reality, they fear from God as much as from every other unknown and unseen power. Good thing is that they rejoice fearing multiple concepts all the time be it religion, culture, customs, rituals, traditions, social norms, gurus, etc.

The combination of Body and Mind occupy most of their attention and resources. Emotions rule supreme in their decision-making. They are happy in getting floored caring their own exclusive sense of fashion, looks, styles, habits, tastes and such other irrelevant momentary issues as their focus is only on gross issues. It is not that they don't enter in relationships but that is always for self-serving objectives. Relationships for them are manipulative tool for seeking some selfish benefit. Many of their stands, if they have some, are unprincipled and guided by instant emotions. Their own preferences or wishes are seen switching between moments. Own ambitions rule supreme. These blessed ignorant individuals are not yet touched by spirituality and hence, there is no point in creating any category for them. In so far as our discussion on spirituality is concerned, these people are as good as inanimate objects and, hence, need not be counted for proposed staging.

After happily ignorant, we have category of people currently engaged in one or the other stage elaborated under our chapter "Pre-spiritual Evolution". At best such people can be counted under different stage of germination or seedlings getting ready to those requiring cross-plantation. But for the purpose of categorization, all those people may also be considered clubbed under the lower part of the pyramid just discussed until such time that their spiritual signs gain visible forms and strength. As soon as their resolve to pursue spirituality takes solid form, they will get qualified for claiming their place in the planned stages of spiritual progress. But that has to wait for the moment.

Stages of Spiritual Realisation

On the other extreme, we have absolutely enlightened individuals who have fully realized their Self and have been able to sink separation with the Universal Self. They have achieved the pinnacle of spirituality and have achieved merging of *Atman* and *Brahman*. Now, one has only heard about such beings. There are hardly direct accounts from such realized individuals. Discussions about such people or such possibilities, therefore, involve speculations and may not help our practical desire to know real situation for sure. Speculations can't be the basis of actionable agenda. Hence, we are better advised to keep this extreme topside of the pyramid also out of our present discussions centered on staging.

Leaving both extremes away, one can broadly have four distinct stages to map out entire journey of spiritual evolution in a manner that can be actually followed by potential practitioner. Let us look at each one of these stages with sufficient clarity. This should help us to find out our present location on the journey, to measure progress made over specific period of time and sensitize us with respect to remaining part of our journey. But please be reminded that the following stage description is based on personal experience only and should be taken just as an illustration. It is to be taken like an effort to explain the unknown, to picture the emptiness or to bifurcate the indivisible. The only purpose is to attempt a rough sketch to meet obvious basic curiosity of new practitioners and nothing beyond.

Inclined Enthusiast

This is the stage where seedlings of spirituality are planted in newly prepared bed. The person is grappled with questions about real purpose of life even when there are no clear answers on the horizon as yet. Daily routine is fully occupied by spiritual seeking efforts. There is a far deeper and focused longing to study subjects relating to diverse cultures, religions and divinity as well. There is an increasing desire to know about own place in the universe at large. One is regularly getting quality time for self and on most of such occasions the mind and body are joined by intelligence and discrimination to explore basic issues that were outside the horizon earlier. Rational mind shows readiness to plunge for taking control more often pushing the emotional mind into background. There are many issues and people that cause immediate irritation but in many other such cases, the level of irritation has come down. One can patiently lend his ears to even those he was totally allergic to in the past. Tendencies of bullying, bulldozing, making fuss, leg pulling, false pretentions etcetera no more provide the kick, as was the case in the past. One is more aware and sensitive towards heart burns of others. There is a new found neutrality which suggests that jumping to immediate conclusions about anything and everything is neither desired nor a good idea. One fully realizes that old habit of coming out with instant 'off the hip' response is not the right lane to travel.

The desire now has changed to live for others rather than total centering life on self. The ability to withstand discomforts and sufferings in general is on the rise. Comforts are still desired but lack of luxury creates no panic like before. Gadgets of all types continue to be important functionally but not as fashion statements. One still participates in social gatherings but the topics of interest stand gravitated towards substantial matters. You develop ability to see through prevailing social norms generally accepted and valued. Criteria like position, status, ability of people to gather crowd, length of their car or width of their house are no more as important. Individual's humanity, equality, empathy, knowledge and wisdom are the factors influencing your approach towards people coming in your contact on day-to-day basis. In short, you start valuing a person with his qualities in place of external influence.

Lure for money is still strong but not its insatiability. Questions like how much is sufficient to sustain have replaced earlier thoughts of 'let me have more and some more and some more'. The ruling emotion has shifted from fear (which includes anxiety, apprehension, misgivings, concerns and panic) to enjoyment (including joy, relief, contentment and amusement). Hold of sensual pleasures still exists and so is the attachment with ego. But there is perceptible reduction in anger, outrage, exasperation, animosity, violence, hatred and annoyance. All these changes result in drastic transformation of the personality where poise and confidence have taken over replacing arrogance and impiousness.

The adamancy of 'my way or the highway' has now mellowed down and there is increased capacity for not only withstanding to criticism but also for taking it more objectively. Both praise and prejudice have stopped going to head instantly. Sycophancy stands identified immediately as false. The ability to see through people has increased together with increasing self-awareness. There is a newfound respect for better views even when it comes from others including adversaries. One has started seeing through the narrowness of religious divides. The approach to look at people from other religions or states or cultures is much softer than before. Actually, most of the man-made barriers stand shortened with increasing universality taking over the space so vacated.

There are short glimpses of own spiritual experiences here and there but not in very coherent or consistent manner. There are occasions when meditative churning throws up not seen before variety of truth leading to fresh outcomes to complex real life issues. There is an increasing desire to share your experience with others from previous life so as to motivate them also to change course. Good thing is that all above changes are getting accepted and appreciated internally with due humility.

Restless Seeker

Up until now we have made references to the word "seeker" at times in casual ways. In right understanding, the seeker is that spiritual practitioner who has successfully crossed over the stage of 'Inclined Enthusiast' explained above. A seeker by very definition is someone who has become enlightened in the ways of the universe by accepting they know little about it, someone who is continuously and eagerly searching, asking, trying for something less known. Seeker's position is very critical as well as fulfilling in the spiritual growth. This stage revolves around self-discovery. There is a desire to live and experience life differently. One has already come out of 'nine to five' routine aimed at money making and is pursuing a life where searching real meaning takes over the lust of multiplying bank balances. Material abundance in excess of genuine requirements to meet a decent life is now felt like an unwanted burden. When it comes to possessions, there is a new desire to limit life within less and less. The principle of having less and less now also applies to people, things, relationships, thoughts and notions as well.

There is a perceptible shift in matters relating to opinions, habits and view-points. These factors have started appearing, to a large extent, as irrelevant. There is a paradigm shift towards very definition of truth. You now start realizing that there is more than one truth. Own truth and truth of others are seen overlapped and coexisting with each other without any confrontation and animosity. Unpleasant urge to shout for dislikes is now well harnessed. Earlier, there was a desire to explain things under right perspective with proper clarity and strong arguments. But now maintaining a mysterious silence has arrived as a new option that was never valued earlier. Now there is no inhibition to directly address any question, how so ever disgraceful or disappointing its answer may be. There is a new art form developed, named swallowing. Earlier situations resulting into instant implode of bout of anger are now handled with ease and calm responses. There is perceptible difference in terms of facing opposition both on personal or philosophical dimensions. All these developments are increasingly contributing to mental peace and harmony. The span of responses for both ends of emotions is constantly reducing making you lesser happy and sad as compared to past.

Success is achieved in matters relating to controls over body and mind. The diet control was easy to come by and so was maintaining healthy routines like walks, yoga and exercises. The ongoing practices of Pranayam and Meditations now involve lesser efforts and breathing is more synchronized than ever before. Similarly, meditation sessions are more regular, longer and number of thoughts entering mind in each sessions is substantially reduced as compared to previous stage. The mind is more relaxed and takes to concentration quite willingly. It keeps going back to its previous avatar but shows readiness to retrieve to the neutral zone with relative ease.

Mindless speaking stands curtailed as the mind is tuned for peace and wishes to avoid all types of unnecessary discussions and arguments. Fun laced social interactions, mindless get-togethers and eating outs have become rare rather than weekly affair. Bulk of the available time is used for intense reading to quench the thirst of spiritual knowledge. As an avid seeker, one has so many more topics of interests to learn about. The expectations from close friends are now entirely different. Friends are no more about entertainment or having good time together. Actually, the very definition of good times stand changed at this stage. Now you enjoy talking most about your practice related experiences with friends not so much to impress but to learn from each other with the aim of achieving faster progress on spiritual path.

The mind is seriously occupied in judging on self. With the help of self-awareness practices, there is a new dimension of evaluating own thoughts and actions and constant process of identifying fault lines within self. The standards for thinking, forming opinions, offering suggestions, social conduct and expectations from children and other close family members have all moved to higher levels. There is a constant feeling that you are being watched by someone from far above all the times. Ongoing practices have yielded positive results making strong moral and ethical foundations which get reflected in entire behaviour. There are no more strong temptations of sense gratifications or actions induced by greed or selfishness.

At this stage of one's spiritual growth, there is an increased focus on big picture in every sphere of life rather than fragmentations. This person has crossed over all segregations. By now he has become part of the big family called humanity. The important point is content. There is no preference for the source of the same. Good content from any and every background or source is found equally appealing. It is no more 'we versus they'. You no more wish to spend time in any religious disputations or arguments. One has reached to a point where all religions are seen as personal ways of realizing respective Gods and nothing beyond. Actually, all religions have been found insufficient to address the new questions being grappled at this stage of spirituality. At seeker's stage, the openness and receptivity is all about the Universal connect with every being and thing.

The key emotions working in this phase of spiritual evolution are curiosity and excitement; first for learning more and then for the deep sense of pleasure of knowing and experiencing the hidden treasures of tranquility and peace. The negative emotion operating at this stage is impatience; the feeling of failure for not having learnt it in the past and inability to learn it fast enough in the present. Impatience is also about loss of valuable time for practising more quickly. In a way, there is a deeper eagerness to cover up for lost time. The glimpses of spiritual experience are quite often. The intuitive mind is able to foresee many things coming well in advance. The sessions of meditations are more and more productive with good sessions of contemplation on many issues. But the desire to share experience with others has almost vanished. The seeker is quite mesmerized with his new found knowledge about self and others that convincing others is realized to be a waste of time and energy. Both praise and criticism are treated as unwanted at par with each other. The veil of ego falls quite often and there is a good familiarity with the real Self without any feeling of awe or wow.

Protagonist Believer

This stage of spiritual development is being called as believer because the practitioner has made sufficient progress in his drive and has perfected his own awareness and made good progress in seeking truth. On the other hand, he has also started realizing his place in this universe together with his connection with other beings and non-beings. Even the most ardent believer in God is known to turn into being non-believer at this stage as God is not identified as a separate power with or without name or face or form. The seeker of this stage can be called a skeptic as he is highly submitted to principles rather than powers. For him, there is no pending search for the divine power. The whole of universe seems filled with divinity.

The practitioner of this stage acquires complete individuality as his social links fall apart from earlier chains of specific relations. Interaction with humanity is no more seen in terms of relations and affiliations; every living being is equally close or related without any preference or priority. It does not, however, mean that the person has become anti-social. Contrary to that, the person in this stage becomes deeply involved and committed to social causes. But these causes are humanity based and not specific identity based. One interacts with human beings at a single platform of equality irrespective of different age, position, social background, financial status, levels of wisdom or whatever. In present day example, the practitioner of this stage is fine tuned to provide similar respect to a taxi driver or a waiter or a political leader or a successful businessman owning big empire; he is able to look at all of them simply as fellow human beings without any segregations.

At this stage, the mind is completely captured by strong intuitions where most questions arising on the surface are dealt with logic filled analysis and scientifically established findings. At this stage Emotions are sent to deep sleep. There are no grudges, no conflicts, nothing to settle with anyone anymore. There is no need of making speculations even for the most serious issues. Past does not bother and future does not generate any concern. Thus, life gets centered completely in present in 'here and now' principle. Stability achieved on all fronts like emotional, mental, psychological, time, space and universal connectedness leads to profound peace and tranquility in inner space.

The person has already practised all paths available for seeking spirituality. Such a person is perfectly at peace for undertaking his daily spiritual practice, enhancing his knowledge further to the exclusion of any other activity. Now the seeker has turned to be believer and has started enjoying spiritual *anubhav* with fair regularity. The inner conscience is constantly in communication.

Mystic Master

It is said that dualistic ignorance of a person in this stage gets completely passed over for the divine knowledge. The Truth is said to have been realized. Now, everything is well revealed from beginning until end where there is no beginning to begin with and no end in the end. The place of human is seen just as a temporary character of a small scene being enacted on a big stage called this visible world. Raising and falling of curtain is well realized just another moment in the ongoing enactment.

Inner space is filled up with bliss, love and peace. Awakening is almost fully completed as most doubts and questions have been properly sorted out from well within. All attachments have been severed. Now there is no family, no son and no daughter as all are equal. Soul is now completely cleared of all wrappings of ignorance or smoke screens. Now there is no divide between Self and Universe.

All types of beliefs and opinions are pruned and purged out of one's system. The life is being lived with full integrity and right truth. Now, the practitioner's intuition is fully developed and it is found capable of coming up with right answers to all questions in an effortless manner grounded in pure wisdom. Teaching, mentoring, sharing and guiding are the only reasons for this person to enter in any interaction with humanity and that too happens only and only when there is a deserving audience. There is nothing left to be known or proven to anyone.

Guided by developed intuitive knowledge, at times, such realized souls come out with predictions in form of pure glimpses of things to come. Others see it as miracle because all such predictions are seen proving accurate. All available time is spent in contemplation, meditation, reflection and prayers while remaining connected with entire humanity. Truth and wisdom are the only states that have their approach to such a master.

It is not that reaching to this stage of spiritual growth is unachievable. Ramana Maharshi, Shirdi Sai Baba, Ramakrishna, Narayana Guru, Meher Baba, Nityananda, Nisargadatta, Dadaji (Amiya Roy Chowdhury), Neeb Karori (Neem Karoli) Baba, Padre Pio, Gemma Galgani, Maria Esperanza, Mother Teresa, Thich Nhat Hanh, Taungpulu Sayadaw, Dipa Ma, Ajahn Chah, Hsu-yun, Hsuan-hua, Cheng Yen, Kyongho, Mangong, Daehaeng, Kusan, Harada Roshi, the 14th Dalai Lama, Dilgo Khyentse, 16th Karmapa, Sheikh al-Alawi, Hazrat Babajan, Anasuya Devi, Anandamayi Ma are some such names from several thousand other sages, saints, adepts, prophets and incarnations who have achieved this stage in very recent times. Yes, they come from all cultures, regions or traditional streams.

General

When a practitioner is struggling on the lower rungs of the spiritual ladder, there are many instances of vertical and horizontal oscillations. After all, such a significant development of human life cannot be expected to have a smooth process. It is not like switching on the car and approach the nearest express way and off you got to the top gear. All through this beautiful journey of spiritual advancement, there will always be regular patches where the journey keeps getting bumpy due to pot holes or rough driving. It is similar to an untrained climber frequently falling in his initial efforts of climbing.

Yes, many people do get fed up with their failings during initial stage and they quietly return back to their earlier life. But if your calling was strong and your preparations were in place, you should remain determined to face these oscillations as expected events on this path. Every sailor knows that the waves are stronger around the shores and once you reach the mid sea, the sailing is rather smooth, except off course when storms arrive on the scene. That is why the sailors get sufficient training to face strong winds, torrential rains, vociferous thunders, violent lightening and even strong snow fall or all of these testing situations in combination. The way forward to pursue spiritual journey, similarly, requires best possible knowledge, commitment, practice, resolution and purity of purpose to face all emerging situations on the way. After all, it is the most important project of the entire life and deserves the best of our ability and determination.

So, practitioners are advised not to get disheartened with such oscillations. The swings from normal to spiritual experiences shall have their pangs but these are like vibrations used for perfect settling of concrete during pouring into the cast. In due course, these swings will become lesser and lesser and finally will seize to exist. But that stability is to be expected only when the practitioner has climbed to the higher rungs of second stage.

The Theoritical Aspects of Self-Realization

The field of Spirituality is no different than competing subjects of sciences, philosophies and psychologies. It is so because use of superior human intellect and wisdom with dedication and determination is the basis for making progress in each of these fields. Thinking holistically, one concludes that each of these knowledge streams is engaged in discovering the unknown part in their own influence areas. Each of these involves experimentations and observations of phenomenon from the natural world and there is no room for unsubstantiated opinions or beliefs. Spirituality is about discovering real eternal nature of the being. To progress on this line, the seeker uses his mind, wisdom and intellect as tools and laboratory. But unlike Sciences, Spirituality does not base itself on undeniable facts, hypotheses, laws and theories. Spirituality depends more on realization than on theories. Being so personalized in nature, Self-Realization, the ultimate stage of being spiritual, will mean different to different people. It might depend on their own individual level of evolution, progress achieved or tradition and school one belongs to or several such other factors.

Like other streams mentioned above, study of Spirituality also involves investigations about two basic interlinked aspects of 'object' and 'subject'. But the 'Self" as understood in reference to Spirituality is interestingly a unique combination of both object and subject. Self is both observer and one being observed at the same point in time; it is the doer and witness combined into one. It is this intricate composition that renders comprehension and realization of this very 'Self' so much more difficult. So long as one is not having complete clarity about his own identity, so long as one continues to be subconscious and so long as one is not having developed level of reflective consciousness, a person will not be able to comprehend true nature of Self. The comprehension of true nature of Self is, in simple terms, the real Self-Realization.

Now we are here to explore practical realization as applicable to modern day perspective that has nothing to do with established connotations about Self-Realization. However, continuing our approach of expanding on practical aspect after in-depth comprehension of traditional approaches, in due course of time we will also briefly look at well known concepts of Nirvana and Moksha as associated with Self-Realization. But before we do that, let us understand the significance of Self with reference to the entire Realization. Self is advocated to be an experience to be acquired by realization rather than developing theoretical understanding alone. The learned teachers and successful seekers warn us strongly that 'Self' can't be understood completely until the same very 'Self' is fully realized. So the unique equation is a classical case of 'Catch 22' situation as it reads as:

> "To understand the Self, you have to Realize the same and to Realize the same, you have to grasp it completely."

This being so, the seekers are compelled to experience great deal of doubts and confusions on their climbing up to full realization. In many cases, people get more confused once they are able to climb to certain altitude than they ever were during their stay at the base camp. But most seekers, with perseverance on their side, come to realize the subtle dimensions of Self and intermittent doubts and confusions inspire them even more to explore deeper levels of insights into their own realm of essence. Basic objective at this stage shifts to prepare the reader-cum-practitioner for facing the hard realities of Spiritual realization. But any effort towards simplifying the process required will not do justice to the realities involved in gaining success towards objective in hand. So, we better get prepared to take head-on all the complexities involved in this final ascent. Because Yogi Paramahansa Yogananda says:

> "Truths are not truths to you unless you realize them within yourself.
> Without realization, they are just ideas. For spiritual perceptions, spiritual consciousness lies not is vague theoretical ideas but in acquisition of self-realization."

Having understood the concept of personal and individual self under a previous chapter, Self-Realization will involve the third and final self, called the universal self. Universal self is related to the Supreme as part of the creative force known by whatever name. We are referring it to be the ultimate of all energy or power reasoned to be behind all creative mechanism responsible for existence and continuation of this Universe. Realization of Self in its final state is nothing but awakening of that very source by entering in its own realm. This state is to be reached only by penetrating to the depth of the very Soul, as much as it takes to go there.

Reaching to its realm actually refers to the situation where mind is just empty, peaceful and totally quiet, where one is devoid of all attachments and desires. It is the perfect vacuum position where one becomes merged with the source of creation. By merging with the inner realm, as the most final leap, soul transcends the dimension of presence. If physical self (body and mind) is pile foundation, Personal self and Individual self may be understood as vertical and horizontal columns for the entire building structure. Universal self-realization, in continuation of the example of superstructure, is like the roof sitting atop this entire structure and working as final layer protecting the structure it sits on. Now, we know already that any pillar is as strong as its foundation allows it to be and any roof is as stable as the structure supporting it. In absolutely similar manner, the realization of Universal Self is expected to be as firm and stable as the other components of its structures are.

Soul's Surrender, the Key for Traditional Self-realization

The degree of a soul's readiness to merge with its ultimate source depends on the level of its own surrender. It is said that more a soul surrender itself more is the degree of actualization. Thus, Soul's own evolution into itself (by crossing over the bridge of Personal Self via Individual Self) and later its own surrender into the beyond is the two-step process recommended for complete Self-realization. Like in every other case, it is the first step that is more difficult to achieve.

An individual can be said to be fully surrendered when it is able to clearly realize its place in the universe similar to a finger attached in a human body where it has perfect understanding that it is part of the large body without having its own existence and that it is its duty to serve the whole body or anything else that the body may desire of it. Having realized our own place in this universe exactly as the finger in this example will make us ready to be fully surrendered.

Traditions of Self-realization

Human history is full of several traditions, branches and sub-branches or lines of thoughts exploring the notion of human beings as self or as subjects. Generally speaking, all the traditions conclude that understanding the relationship of human and its existence in the world and its relation with the divine reality is the basic spirit of self-realization. To put it in other words, spiritually inclined thinkers are of the view that the state when the human self comes back to its original primordial form is the real state of the self and therefore is called the real Self-realization. The entire spiritual struggle, in their view, therefore, stands concluded when efforts for bringing back the self to the same original form from where it started its journey of vitiation in the first place see success. Different traditions are simply the bracketing of thoughts from different thinkers around the simple conclusion mentioned above. In any case the three most common segregations of traditional human thoughts are as under:

1. Western Philosophy revolving around Platonic and Neo-Platonic traditions imbedded in the views of Greek Philosophers like Plato and Plotinus.
2. Modern Psychological research and practice particularly from the perspective developed by Psychologists beginning with Sigmund Freud, the Austrian neurologist considered as father of psychoanalysis, and developed with the subjects of Ego psychology or Self-psychology.
3. The Eastern Traditions such as Buddhism and Vedanta, which have developed enormous bodies of understanding of the nature of Self and mind based on powerful techniques of inquiry.

Since our basic purpose is to limit the discussion with respect to spirituality, we better ignore the first two categories that are more scientific than spiritual. One does, however, recognize well that the Self that we are after is much more than self-improvement projects or psychotherapies or psychoanalysis. But understanding the thoughts forming part of Buddhism and Vedanta shall add to our understanding of this complex matter in greater depth, especially with respect to its application for Spiritual growth. Hence, we should look at these two in some details.

"Nirvana", the Buddhist Self-realization

Nirvana is difficult to define in words because it was never intended for intellectual discussions. It is best understood only by self-experience. Gautama Buddha himself shared that understanding Nirvana by an unenlightened individual is difficult. In fact, Buddha advocated that only an enlightened individual could aspire to appreciate the Nirvana state of being. Nirvana was not to provide personal trance but direct access to one's own inner heaven that enables a person to live with his pains; to experience profound peace even in the midst of sufferings.

Thus, Nirvana is to be taken as a natural state of one's own being, deep within one's own heart that is neither bestowed by some supernatural power nor to be achieved by a supernatural saviour. Nirvana is cultivable by everyone who walks down the street of enlightenment as assiduously as Buddha did for himself. Thus, there are no concepts or words that can be understood but only and only personal experience gained by self-practice and living the life taught by Buddha based on his own personal example.

It may be briefly recalled that Buddha has provided for physical, mental and psychological preparation for a noble life rooted in five prohibitions of violence, lying, stealing, intoxication and sexual conduct. These prohibitions, incidentally, were very close to the "Yam" provided under Yoga except that Buddha found prohibitions alone not fully effective and worked on to enlarge their scope by developing positive sides of each one of those five prohibitions. The change of focus from prohibitions to developing positivity was the single largest add-on by Buddha on his original Vedic knowledge. Non-violence was to be followed by gentleness and kindness towards one and all, not speaking lie was to be completely replaced by reasoned, accurate and beneficial use of speech. Stealing was to be replaced with rejoicing in whatever alms were available without any preference. Buddha's prohibitions were focused on prevention of negative connotations by articulation of positive behaviour. Simple suppression of desires, in Buddha's view was insufficient to be effective. Therefore, he advocated developing voluntary acceptance of the prohibitions by cultivating positive values of non-violence, compassion and empathy. Those familiar with both Yoga and Buddhism can directly see the undeniable common foundation of both these traditions.

In yet another departure from the concepts of its time, Buddha's enlightenment was all about the middle way as it strongly avoided extreme on either side of the spectrum that shunned physical and emotional self-indulgence or extreme asceticism. Before getting enlightened, Gautama had resorted to extreme asceticism himself and completely realized the futility of such practices. Buddha's enlightenment revolves around three-fold of plan of actions consisting of morality, meditation and wisdom. Morality involved right speech, right action and right livelihood and all these stages got called "*Kushal*" states. Enlightened person is not expected to grab or hold on something forever. Everything is temporary and this understanding was to be deeply rooted. The emphasis here was on developing compassion and empathy towards one and all and thereby preparing oneself well for subsequent stages.

With morality taken care, one was supposed to work on sinking deep within by learning and practising meditation that is so indispensable to proper enlightenment. Buddha's *Dhamma* was to be understood by an aspirant by suspending selfishness in totality and by bringing their body and mind under revised Yogic microscope of observation. It is here that Buddhist meditation is different than vedic meditation as vedic meditation is focused on reaching beyond oneself to the Ultimate Reality, Brahman that transcends rational understanding of human being. Buddhist meditation, on the other hand, revolves around being fully aware of everything one does including mundane activities like eating, drinking, talking, tasting, seeing, listening, thinking, sitting, sleeping or abstaining from each of this kind of activities.

In addition, observation focuses on flows in the streams of desires, frustrations and irritations, etc. such that one becomes mindful to the smallest detail of change that disturbs the peace of mind. It is through this mindfulness that one becomes fully aware of the sufferings and the desires that give rise to such sufferings. The definition and scope of sufferings must be well understood to appreciate Buddha's doctrine. Besides being physical, sufferings include proximity to things one doesn't like and separation from what one loves and likes. Thus, sufferings are happening every moment and desires remain unfulfilled, as no sooner one gets what he wanted (and suspends the suffering of seeking it), the fear of losing the newly acquired object becomes another source of sufferings.

This stage accounts for important steps of the famous 'Noble Eight Fold Path' of Buddhism namely, 'right effort', 'right attention', and 'right meditation'. These efforts ensure placing the mind where it should be. The wise are able to train their mind to give total attention to one thing at one time, here and now. This training leads the aspirant to right wisdom that is nothing but virtue of right understanding and right resolve.

Thus, Self-Realization through Nirvana of Buddhism translates to extinction of three fires of '*Raga*', '*Dwesha*' and '*Moha*', the three prisons of passions, aversions and ignorant attachments leading to human sufferings. Freedom from these sufferings is achievable by each and every person following the Noble Eight Fold Path where focus is more on practice than conceptual understanding. As against this, the Upanishads teach that chief cause of sufferings was ignorance and once a seeker acquires deep knowledge of his true Self, the seeker is able to insulate itself from pains and miseries of such sufferings. So, one approach is doctrinal while the other is based on practice.

"Moksha", the Vedic Self-realization

It goes to the credit of Upanishad era of approximately 800 BC to 500 BC that three goals of human life (Consisting of *Dharma, Artha* and *Kama*) promulgated by Vedas were given the fourth dimension of "*Moksha*". More importantly, it was hailed as the highest of all goals. Moksha was meant liberation from the bondage of remaining engulfed in the ignorance of 'I' and 'mine' having a separate and independent existence that results in the cycle of Birth followed by Death. We have earlier seen how this sense of false separateness leads to all human miseries, lack of peace and feeling of frustrations. Essence of all Vedic schools implied that acquiring right *Vidya* helps in removing the delusion caused by the ignorance under influence of *Maya*, this illusionary world of visible objects.

The concept of Moksha varies from one extreme to another among different philosophical schools of Hinduism. Some of these consider it available only after death while few others consider it to be available in this very life. Against this, the heterodox schools deny the very existence of soul or afterlife Moksha. In general, the underlying assumption of Vedic streams run on the premise that worldly man seeks joy and happiness in the wrong sources. Human being is seen trying to seek bliss in achievements, family, wealth, position, property, name, fame and power. This chasing of the shadow is taken as turning away from truth and waste of human existence. This shadow chasing is compared to the dear musk realizing little that the scent being chased is having its origin deep within.

For taking our journey of Spiritual growth to its full potential using Vedantic lenses, we have to bring in critical aspect of Individual Soul and Super Soul. The first is called *Atma* or *Jiva* and is said to engross in using the body to taste the fruits of various activities that result in pains and pleasures. The second called as *Parmatma* is explained as the localized expansion of Supreme Power, the Brahman. Both these are said to live in human body like two birds sharing cage on a tree. Super Soul is said to witness the activities of *Jiva* and when *Jiva* begins to tire of ups and downs of material life, it looks up to Super soul to seek help for liberation. Here the Moksha is described as the state of freedom where *Jiva* achieves spiritual oneness with *Parmatma* by practising Yoga and through guidance of a spiritual master.

The study of this aspect thrives on one of the most important concept of Hinduism being the belief in an ultimate reality called '*Brahman*' that is supposed to be the source of all living and non-living things in this Universe. Vedantic scriptures are the sole source of the concept of 'Brahman', the 'Universal Self'. These scriptures explain 'Brahman' as the ground for all realities and existence. Brahman is explained as uncreated, eternal, infinite, all-embracing, immanent and ultimate cause of every object that exists. Vedic scriptures suggest that everything emanate from it and returns back to this very source.

In another explanation, some Vedic Scriptures provide that a person's realization of the identity and unity of *Atman* (the Soul) and *Brahman* (the Universal Soul) is believed to bring about the liberation called '*Moksha*'. Once this happens, a person is said to be free from all restraints of the mind and body and thereby transcends all distinctions and experiences ultimate togetherness with everything present in the Universe. The understanding of *Moksha* kept evolving all through the Upanishadic, Yogic and Bhakti periods and similar to all other concepts associated with Hinduism, *Moksha* also kept taking different meanings and methods but the essence of all these developments have been common. *Moksha* is taken as a stage where there is nothing left to get or to know; it happens bit by bit where each effort takes the seeker from personal or individual consciousness to universal consciousness, where there is no separateness of existence. It is the state where there is no difference between self and 'Self', where personal identity expands or dissolves into impersonal Universal Being. Thus, it is the liberation from the bondage of what the being is not and where there is realization of the true nature. This meaning is very well summarized in the famous words "*Tat Tvam Asi*" (That is What You Are) from 'Chandogya Upanishad'.

But the real push for Moksha, many centuries later, came along with Advaita Vedanta, the non-dual philosophy credited to Adi Shankaracharya which suggested the path of moral alignment and intense meditation as the key to approach Moksha as ultimate life objective. The focus here is laid out on use of intellect for leaving behind what is unreal and developing true understanding of what is indeed real. This multi stage process is suggested to be completed like peeling off onion, layer by layer, wherein seeker sheds his ignorance and duality leading to merging of 'Atman', the true self of an individual or his soul with 'Brahman', the unchanging, highest, ultimate reality. This *Atma-Jnana* emerging post shedding of the ignorance is considered the real Vedantic self–realization. Simply put, *Atma-Jnana* is the knowledge of self beyond both delusions and identification with material phenomenon. It is a stage where ego identification has completely melted and the person achieves his self-identification as part of the Divine whole. The concept was developed by Advaita Vedanta thinkers, which defined God as *Sat-Chit-Anand.* It is a stage where thirst of soul for material existence is perfectly satiated.

Different Vedic schools suggested different ways of achieving the ultimate objective of Moksha and finally consensus emerged on four distinct but intertwined paths of *Karma Yoga, Bhakti Yoga, Gyan Yoga* and *Raja Yoga* which laid emphasis on the path of action without attachments with results, unconditional devotion towards *Ishta Deva,* gaining knowledge from scriptures and practitioners and intense meditation on Supreme respectively. Each seeker was left free to choose his path depending on his orientation with the freedom of switching from one to other at any time and at any stage of his spiritual journey.

In yet another streams of Vedic knowledge, Self-realization is linked with intricate interplay among mind, *Chit,* ego and visible world. Here big focus lies on extinguishing the ego involving 'I' and 'my' with complete clarity. A Self-realized *Jnani* is said to know that the real I, the Self, is completely separate from everything that is 'mine'. He knows well that mind, intellect, *Chit* and ego are physical phenomenon and are part of body. As such all these faculties have forms and patterns and that pure soul has nothing to do with any or all of these faculties. Under this concept, mind always remains inside the human body. The one that goes out wandering from one thing to another is identified as *Chit. Chit* is also understood as the 'Observer', the one that sees scenes. Intellect provides advice and makes decisions while ego goes over all three and endorses either one of them or a combination of some of those faculties. This stream was largely influenced by *Sankhya* school of Indian *Darshan.*

In yet another explanation of interplay between Atman and Brahman, some learned teachers explain about separate stages involved in the final dispensation of the soul. In the first stage, it is expected to be fully awakened itself through its centres of consciousness and by unifying all centres under a composite and complete state. In the second and final stage, the soul is fully realized by its merging with the realm of '*Shunyta*', the state of complete emptiness and becoming one with the very source of creation. Transcending this dimension of presence is the real meaning of Self-realization, the supreme stage of attaining one's spirituality. At this stage, Personal Self-realization, Individual Self-realization or Universal Self-realization merge with each other and become perfectly interconnected and identical.

Having gone over some of the main schools within Vedic thoughts about Moksha, the final Self-Realization it becomes clear as to why the journey of realizing self was told to be so difficult. It is understandable as to why most people attempting the same did get only partial success and majority of them ended up with frustrations. The whole Vedic concept is founded on the strong assumption that there is an Ultimate power named God or Brahman or Ishwar or called with any other similar name, that continues to be at the helm of existence and smooth working of this Universe. But thinking loudly, this very belief in God and reincarnation is but a big If?

Most people from country like India have believed in it because they grew in the cultural landscape where all this has been believed even before they open their eyes. But there are so many others, like those living in atheistic environments of Russia or China, who get amused by the very belief about God. All of them may not be held as much wrong about existence of God as we can be held right about it. What will happen to their spiritual endeavours? Going by Indian systems, bulk of humanity is not even eligible to qualify for searching Moksha. Hence, there remains a wide-open possibility for searching some other approach that ensures self-realization without pre-condition or pre-supposition of any kind. Let us focus for such a search more sharply.

Understanding Real and Practical Self-realization

Following regular practices for spirituality advancements, over as long as it takes, we could raise ourselves to a higher level of spiritual seeking. But at the end of the day, we continue to be real people with real issues. Even with all added knowledge and wisdom, most human beings are seen desiring solutions that are practical in supporting a real life; where we can take concrete steps to achieve what is well realized as an intellectually exciting and spiritually realized destination. This is where traditional views on realizations fall short for modern day seekers. Traditional views of Self-Realization may have been great intellectually stimulating and provocative but what we get out of those excitations are more questions than answers. At the end, we still face critical question "is there nothing that opens gate for seeking self-realization for normal people like us living our humble life here in this very world of whatever qualitative description it may be painted with?" We are not here to appreciate or get impressed with intellectual superiority of people from past but to explore and add value to our own existence here and now.

Fallacy in Traditional Approach to Self-realization

As someone engaged in navigating daily life in present day turbulent environment, all references to heaven, after life, death, rebirth, liberation, Soul and God appear mere fantasies, theoretical volts, conceptual celebrations and imaginary assumptions with no real substance. After all, we have no one to provide a believable first person's account about all these concepts? Who is there to share with us anything with definite knowledge and live examples? An approach to seek first hand evidence for evaluating these concepts will force us to accept that, in addition to being contradictory to each other at times, these concepts are unreal, deceptive or even fictitious. We have started our search for real thing but traditional views provide us only intellectual projections and assumptions. Therefore, it would definitely be construed as a mistake to rely on such concepts for searching meaning for most important question of our existence. We are certainly not ready to leave essence of our deepest aim of life to projections imbedded in second hand knowledge. No, we would better keep away all such concepts in favour of individual's own and real perceptions and experiences. That has been our line of focus all through and we can't deviate from the same for the final realization.

For this most important endeavour of our life, we better focus on perceptible and realizable ways and means that are far from intricate presumptions and difficult sounding doctrines. It is just a simple practical approach when we ask a simple question as to what is the use of an improved afterlife if the present and real life remains full of confusions and doubts. I see no absurdity when a simple human being like us prefers an approach that improves his real life being lived in the present world, preferably amidst all his hard earned possessions and among people connected with him through blood and flesh. Living existing real life in turmoil and contemplating bliss in afterlife is impractical and uncalled for.

Under the previous chapter "Practising Spirituality" we have already gone over a number of very practical steps for achieving the real and practical realization right here and now. Those steps can be taken as a loop where the seeker may continue going back to the beginning and evaluate progress achieved. Surely, this is a long journey with no finality. Once some solid progress is made, one is unburdened of all doubts as clarity prevails in all directions for all issues, for all people and all purposes. At that stage the very desire for practising graduates into auto mode without requiring deliberate efforts.

At this stage, Self-realization is inevitably compared to the process of climbing atop rugged and treacherous snow-clad peak. Nearer one goes to the peak, the trekking becomes more and more difficult.

Final stages of climbing such a peak involves sharp turns, slippery slopes, avalanches (of passion and desires), de-tours and what not. Word to word, the same terminology applies to every spiritual seeker at his final stage. But just like a true explorer never loses sight of the peak, the true seeker also remain focused on the ultimate objective irrespective of challenges involved and hardships to be endured. No wonder, only handfuls of people are able to climb very difficult summits just like exceptional seekers alone reaching to their Self-realization. So as not to scare a serious seeker, we may keep trying our best to avoid comparing it with climbing Mount Everest but the realities involved in reaching Self-realization are expected to prove as challenging, if not more.

True Realization being Similar to Death

One of the greatest fears known for every human is the fear of death. Almost everyone is scared of this eventual reality of human life. Generally, this fear keeps growing with advancing age as older the person becomes, closer is the knocking by death. Even young, adults and intellectually active people often come across this reality due to death of relative or other persons within immediate vicinity. We know that death brings end to all the learning of life time, relations with the family, owning of the hard earned possessions together with end to all the disgusts, failures and achievements alike. These are the things that define any man of form and understandably every person is ought to feel afraid for losing all these identities and attachments. Actually, the fear is not so much of real death but of losing defining attachments of existential life.

Let us closely look at these known attachments that create the fear of death. To begin with, all of us have a bag full of memories and experiences. Similarly, we have bundle of desires, worries and more importantly relations that were used as toys during our life bringing pleasures and pains. This bundle also creates a basket of insults, empathies and embarrassments. Now, during our meditations, we have already realized difficulties involved in getting rid of few thoughts. As such, one should take death as a fantastic opportunity as it takes away our entire burden of acquired knowledge, impressions, pains and pleasures, in a single stroke. That way death also helps us achieve Spiritual growth as the entire process of finding our own Spirituality is aimed at getting over all these accumulations? Certainly, if death has the potential of injecting such understanding, love, peace, joy and beauty, there is nothing to get afraid of such death. One would rather embrace it with pleasure every day or even more than once every day.

> "Practical and real Self-realization is exactly similar to having death every day."

Once we had experienced death just this morning, our Self is not burdened with memories of the past or impressions or fears or failures accumulated over years. A pure and fresh Self will be freely able to operate within its original, peaceful, loving and compassionate state of being. So in most simple words, practical Self-realization is nothing but a fresh new beginning each day, for each object, for each thought sans all impurities and divisions of yester years, months and days included. Hence, Self-realized person should be defined as a person who is able to die each day and who is able to rise each morning having a absolutely new, fresh, innocent and positively energized mind that has the ability of looking at everything afresh.

Developing such an attitude and understanding empowers the Self-Realized to move over the cycle of life and death. This state to me is the real *Moksha* or *Nirvana*. This is the state where theory of reincarnation loses its relevance. Such a realized person has no need to contemplate merits or demerits of death as a real or potential end to life cycle as each day is a new day for him.

> This is indeed ultimate liberation and living in bliss ever after.

Annexure

Questions and Answers

The questions dealt here are based on feedback from people out of the target audience of the subject matter. The concept of the book was discussed with selected few, starting from simple desire of leading a normal happy life to the meaning of real happiness, ways available for seeking such happiness and right up to seeking spirituality being the appropriate human aim for a fulfilling and blissful life. Discussions were held to let them come up with issues faced by them in their journey as real life scenarios. A select few were also invited to offer their comments based on their reading of the initial draft of the script. Doubts and difficulties so accumulated were redrafted as questions requiring further explanations. Since the questions are picked up from among the normal life people in a random basis, the order of the questions is also purely random. The idea of expanding on some of these questions is to help a reader go over the issues felt by other fellows. May be that you, as a reader, may identify yourself with one or more such question and benefit with answers provided. Since these questions emerged out of real discussions with the people, it was beyond me to ignore or set aside their views without properly explaining my views about the same.

Question: Does meditation help only those who are already spiritually inclined or others also stand benefited?

Answer: Simply put, meditation is a name for all activities centered on communication with your internal core where you talk and listen to yourself to the entire exclusion of the external world. Meditation indeed is used for multiple purposes. It is known to improve physical health, reduce stress, improve sleep patterns, enhance vitality, increase energy levels and enhance memory besides helping practitioners on way up their religious, philosophical and spiritual quests. Meditation is gaining popularity all over the world among people coming from extremely different cultures, geographies and religious backgrounds. Surely, there is more than one benefit on offer that suits one or other expectation of practitioners.

Meditation can be seen helping individuals on three levels. Firstly, meditation awakens the mind. This awakening results in creation of several mental conditions that ignite the faculty of imagination. In short, meditative practice makes a person more imaginative. Secondly, meditation enhances individual's intuition by using and preempting information and knowledge even from outside of individual's own mental space. Meditation helps us in developing our empathies and let us know our own feelings. Properly worked, meditation enables the practitioner to pickup thoughts from the minds of other persons. Pooling of information and knowledge of multiple minds leads to enhance intuitive power resulting in ability to know about things to come. There are stories of people picking up not only emotions and feelings of other human being but communication even with animals or inanimate objects using the powers of intuition.

Lastly, meditation works on enhancing inspiration to reach to the highest mental state possible for human. At this level, meditation can lead the practitioner to rejoice self-induced state of '*Paramanand*', the bliss. At this level, all differences of even time and space lose relevance and the person experiences real truth and uniformity with divine. This is the ultimate stage filled with spiritual consciousness that is the final subject of this very book.

The first two benefits relating to imagination and intuition are to benefit every person even those without any religious or spiritual orientations. These will work well for the student attending college, a sports person opting for competing sports as much as an executive aiming for excelling in his career. Meditation is also being used increasingly for its therapeutic benefits for controlling modern day ailments or for post medical recoveries. Undoubtedly, considering the multiple benefits at multiple levels, meditation in all its forms and practices is likely to find more and more takers with multiple expectations.

Question: Is wealth such a bad word? Why every religion and every scripture always keeps advising to maintain distance from wealth?

Answer: As a matter of fact acquiring wealth has been one of the basic tendencies of human all through the history. Common man of today is no exception to this continued practice. Wealth is generally taken as precious material possessions that, at the elementary level, work as a provision for sustaining life and at the upper level allows enjoying luxuries and abundant consumption at present as well as in times to come. It is indeed true that wealth is generally taken as a bad word and considered an obstacle in the path of salvation and liberation more or less by all leading religious traditions of all times. But what is criticized or deadly feared is not the wealth but attachment with it and tendency of getting identifying with it. Also important are the ways and means of acquiring it. For example, so long as someone is engaged in an activity that he or she likes to pursue and find satisfying, any generation of financial rewards will be considered as a by-product, incidental to the process. Wealth rightfully generated using fair means is never considered a roadblock to the path of liberation. The just reward so bestowed must be utilized for meeting personal requirements and/or sharing with others in need or for all types of social objectives. Similar to just acquisition, just spending also does not get classified unwanted or undesired.

But acquiring the same with dubious means as well as accumulating it to enhance one's power over others is exposed to questioning. So, it is not the wealth that creates problems, it is the issues relating to its acquisition and developing attachment with the same that go in determining its qualitative aspect. Just imagine someone who goes after accumulation for creating a personal empire by overlooking genuine care of nature or other beings? Such a person would inevitably get branded as excessively preoccupied with wrong accumulation. Wealth also qualifies as a negative attitude because of its increasing insatiability; more one gets higher is the desire to get more with no upper limit in sight. Obsession with wealth knows no boundaries. Human history is full of examples of powerful people pursuing wealth accumulation by undertaking increasingly unacceptable means. Most of these accumulations have been traced with resulting falling social and personal standards and that may be a different point to prove its uselessness in long term. What happened to the all the rich people from history? Did their legacy survived more than couple of generations? Resultantly, all scriptures from all cultures, traditions, time periods and religions consider it mandatory to guard against this obvious human weakness.

All attachments and identifications work as shackles and prevent the person from rising above the material world. That is why all texts from time immemorial are seen recommending path of renunciation as the right path to pursue. The important point to appreciate is that renunciation required is from desires and attachments and not from wealth *per se*. A human being is truly free only when he has no desires and having or not having any thing, including wealth, becomes immaterial to him. Unfortunately, most beings are unable to differentiate desire from wealth and ignore this approach as an impractical approach to follow. I say with my own example that one can cross over the desire of accumulations without the need to love or hate the wealth. It is just a matter of developing well contemplated right understanding.

Taking our understanding of wealth to right levels we see that knowledge, power, relations, ideas and experiences are all elements that individually and collectively signify true wealth. Factors such as purity of means, balancing, superiority, social benefits that apply to material possessions equally apply to all these belongings. To an individual these provide as much happiness and sense of richness as the monetary wealth. But there is a stark difference as well. All the other forms of wealth, to the exclusion of material wealth, grow with sharing. Money is the sole exception of wealth that reduces with sharing. So, one is advised and encouraged to acquire other forms of wealth as much as possible. Those can't be stolen that easily and don't need as strict guarding as money. Besides risks of losing, it is comparatively easy to grow non-attachment from these forms as against monetary wealth. There is a famous Chinese proverb that says *"If you love something and wish to own it, throw it to the wind. If it really belongs to you, it will get blown against the wind and will return to you forever"*. This proverb equally applies to real wealth in this world. What comes back to you after getting thrown into the wind is really yours and worth possessing? Rest was never yours in the first place.

There is yet another danger of wealth. Generally it comes with various types of debts. These debts may be in form of emotional upheaval, grudges, favours, envy, jealousy, malice, curses, etc. besides financial. All these debts shall have to be settled sooner or later. We all know that debts always carry interest in one form or the other. Continuation of accompanying debts, therefore, will continue dragging the wealth towards depletion and ultimately will leave the person debt ridden. However, if someone can accumulate the wealth without attachment and without incurring any debt in any form, he will qualify for progressing his journey of spirituality without much problem. The only problem is that these simple conditions are not so simple to apply to real life situations.

Question: Can we encourage or convince some other people in our life like spouse, friend or child to pursue Spiritual pursuits along with us?

Answer: Can you force your esteemed guest to eat most delicious food available at your dining table when he has no appetite for the same? Even if the guest shows some courtesy to you and overeats, will he really enjoy that eating? Spiritual hunger must be there before any one is expected to go forward on this journey. One must understand that spirituality, like so many other things, can't be forced down the neck of any other person. His or her own orientation and stage of evolution will determine if any one of your close relation or friend can be inspired to explore spiritual practice. If we have someone who is too much involved with ego principle and is unable to see beyond his/her individual happiness, any amount of convincing to move towards spirituality will result as vain attempt.

One must remember that each one of us is an independent and individual soul. The fact is that we come together in relationships for a very limited purpose. Coming together does not bind our souls together. Each one of us has our own baggage of karmas and each one of us alone is responsible to settle these in due course. Even when we live together, each one of us generates fresh karmas of entirely different proportions. Let us recall that it depends not on the work but the attitude maintained while discharging the work that determines karma to be positive, negative or just neutral. Relations, and all relations for that matter, are social in nature and facilitate living together for mutual benefits. Spiritually speaking, the importance of such close relations is much lesser as Spiritual journey needs to be travelled alone.

It is natural to expect that our close relations also gain right knowledge and they also are able to expedite their spiritual exploration with as much earnest as we feel for our own sake. But it is a desire and too much attachment with it is not good even for our self. Desires lead to expectations and expectations lead to attachments and attachments lead to bondage. Bondage pulls you down from your own spiritual growth. To work as a facilitator and share your experience with your relations is normal and must be done with all sincerity but only as much as you would like to do for any other eligible seeker. You are embarking on the journey to establish oneness with the universe, so how can you afford to give special preferences to those joined with you socially?

As such, you must work on yourself and observe your desire to favour your spouse, children or friends as a drag on your own efforts. One comes across many cases where a parent is wrongly possessive about the child and hold him/her self responsible for their failures even in later lives. It is a clear mistake. Is it so difficult to accept that, as a parent, you had a very limited role of a provider under an environment of affection, trust and encouragement? To take over responsibility far beyond your assigned role is ill-advised and futile. It is useless to feel responsible for our children's success or failures in their adult life. One can't influence his own destiny; forget about destiny of spouse or children for that matter. They are separate souls and you should have the ability to treat them as other adults around you; anything more than that is attachment and ego perceptions.

To return back to the question of convincing any one of them, the answer is clear no. Spirituality requires yearning from within and not intellectual arguments from outside. You can continue arguing until you turn blue in the face, or as they say, until all cows return home, but you can never convince anyone who does not wish to be convinced. And who wishes to be convinced, doesn't require any convincing with strength of arguments or persuasions. Best is to continue your own practice where your gradual growth should generate its own visibility and positivity, which should be good enough to invite them to try it in their own lives, provided they are ready to walk in that direction.

Question: Is being women in any way indicative of difficulty in pursuing Spirituality? In short, is there a gender bias? Also, how do husband and wife approach Spirituality with their obvious differences?

Answer: First thing first. Let us be clear that what we intend discussing here is with reference to typical gender based generalities. Exceptions of all types are possible and have been kept out from following discussions. Let us approach this question with above disclaimer.

There is no denying to the fact that biological differences exist between genders. Also, these differences ultimately impact psychological working of individuals belonging to respective genders. Then genders in general have difference in their wiring of emotional quotients as discussed in detail in our chapter on 'Emotions'. Lastly, there are significant impacts of cultural and social conditioning over centuries, especially for women. As a combined effect of all these differences, women do have higher levels of self and social focus. Women value social skills and relationships of all types over intellect, logical deductions and reasoning. Men are known to be less emotionally advanced and are expected to have difficulty in accessing emotional spheres.

These differences are there to see in real life situations. Generally, women are overly emotional, overly attached to children, husband and family and the very pursuit of spirituality is placed low on their priorities. Whereas, men will be seen more reserved but thinking through more clearly guided by rationality rather than emotions and feelings. Other natural and very visible instincts relate to passivity prevailing in women while men wish to forge forward, conquer and acquire new territories. Women take care of children and others at home while men are wired to extend protection to their clan. However, none can be said superior or inferior. This is just the way nature has wired them and made them complimentary to each other and programmed them to function in tandem.

A good husband is expected to have concern for welfare of his spouse and family while she is expected to have yielding approach. But all the roles are to be played out of consideration and affection and without any presence of fear or authority. Yielding here applies to wife being able to accommodate her husband's desire as far as possible and without suppression and giving up her right of expressing conflicting opinion. With this scenario in operation, it is still far away from being branded patriarchy since there is no dominance or force involved rather it is just recognizing ideal role play well within the biological, social and emotional variations for respective genders.

Coming back to women and their inclination towards Spirituality, it is amply clear that they are programmed to be preoccupied with micro management of the welfare of their children and wards. This pulls them deep in the worldly life, makes them more social, requires them to invest more time in relationships, develops deeper attachment for worldly possessions. They are genetically programmed to want more and more of what they already got; more possessions, more relationships, more of family, more of materials etc.

This very tendency was responsible for sages in ancient past declaring that women are not suitable for liberation or seeking Moksha. Certainly, that approach will get classified as parochial. Flaunting of feminism, on the other hand, will equally divide the void and create confrontations between two types that are typically designed by Mother Nature to work as complimentary to each other. Both approaches of extremes, therefore, are open for criticism and need to be discarded altogether. There is no superior or inferior here, both genders have well appropriated set of strengths and traits and are complete only when they operate together with love and respect.

But women are certainly blessed with higher degree of devotion and lower ability to withdraw the mind from attachments and the cardinal principle for focus on inner Self requires complete detachments with all worldly possessions and relations. For this very logic, even Yogis of ancient past recommended worship to be more suitable for women than seeking Spirituality.

Question: How does one realign living in this very world with harsh realities and still pursue divine objectives like Moksha and Liberation?

Answer: Each one of us must continue growing till the very end of this journey called life. Any one believing in this dictum will realize that material and spiritual objectives have to be met living this very life here in this very world. Wisdom lies in finding the right balance rather than either or scenario. As and when one starts appreciating this equation, rest of the journey becomes easy to pursue. Intelligent people from ancient times itself have been facing this dilemma and have well provided desired steps required to deal with it. While remaining within *Grihastha Ashram*, one is advised to work as hard as possible, enjoy the pleasures that this world has to offer and accumulate as much of energy including knowledge, power, relationships, money, experience as feasible within the ambit of Dharma. The next stage advised is of *Vanprashtha* where one has to start working leaving attachments and preparing for higher objectives in a slow but steady way.

There is no necessity to give up the world all of a sudden as if one is making a big sacrifice. No, that is not the advice of Yogis. Giving up this world like that will not work and they realized it well. Accordingly, they provided a full quarter of life to prepare for the ultimate stage of *Sannyasa*. To anyone who is able to understand the need for spiritual pursuits, this transition will be easy and natural. Anyone realizing this as a big shift is still not clear about the criticality of pursuing higher objectives. After all, pursuing those objectives is just a logical culmination of a fulfilled life befitting to a species blessed with reasoning and intellect. To continue living without enhancing awareness of higher objectives is certainly sub human living.

Anyone who has lived life of a *Grihastha* must have seen the transience of pleasures and the eventuality of pains following pleasures. One also will realize that continuing in the *Grihastha* would leave lesser time for preparing for *Sannyasa*. Such appreciation will eventually lead to urgency for graduating to final stage of life for fulfilling most critical objectives of human life. This very urge and realization will automatically start ringing the bell for preparing for a quick shift. If the bell is not starting to ring for you, it simply means that you are not yet ready for pursuing higher objectives of human life.

Lastly, every serious occupation demands entire energy and dedication with full vigour. Nobody is known to become a world champion in any sports without working extremely hard with maximum energy and drive. Seeking Spirituality for pursuing transcendent objectives of human life is also a serious business and can't be taken as a hobby. So, anyone interested for pursuing serious pursuits of liberation or Moksha will have to give up the attachments of the material world that grip the person like chains and hold them back. Beyond very initial stages, pursuing material world and spirituality is an either or scenario and there is no way to continue growing with both at the same time. Anyone trying to cross the ocean with feet on two different boats is surely due for sinking. Pursuing higher aims of human life and continuing with the allurements offered by this material world are distinctly separate boats. Choice is yours.

Question: It appears that, at this moment in my life, I am not cut out for following Spirituality. So, what should I follow in life – pleasantness or pleasures?

Answer: Any human being wishing to remain limited to physical and bodily pleasures can be blamed for bringing down humanity to the level of animals. Exclusion of intellectual and emotional aspects out of our desired objective of human life is a bad bargain for any sensible human. So, if one is intelligent enough to conclude that evolving spiritually is no more an option with them, they should still focus for fulfillment of mental, emotional and psychological aspects of their humanity. Else, it will be a waste of human life.

Seeking pleasure can never be a source of seeking happiness as one is externally motivated and the other is internally generated. Pleasure is fleeting and requires increasing stimulus for getting same level of experience. Contrary to that, happiness requires decreasing efforts and has no side effects. Pleasure revolves around gratification; sensual indulgence and such other sources of worldly enjoyments fired by ever-inexhaustible desires and are too situational. Desire for happiness, as the least expected aim of human life, is never dependent on external circumstances. Such circumstances, at best, can influence it for a short period and to a small extent. Therefore, no one can be happy chasing fulfilling pleasures as an objective of responsible life and those who have tried that in past have met with dangerous ends. Certainly, you don't want to have another name added on that list?

Question: Does specific health condition matters for pursuing spirituality or such other higher pursuits of human life?

Answer: A balanced regime of physical fitness and controlled diet is actually fundamental to get best of start for progressing on the road of higher objectives in human life. Spirituality is not for a person having weak will or weak physical strength. The regimes for progress involve too much capability for concentration, control over breathing, exercises involving sharpening observations and contemplative sitting in Yogic postures for longer durations. These practices necessitate a functional and healthy body with active, agile and responsive mind. Another most important requirement is to have a positive attitude, which also requires healthy body to a large extent.

Human mind is said to cooperate better with positive impulses. Negative impulses create complicated mental conditions that ultimately lead to pessimism. A pessimist can't pursue an intangible, incorporeal and discrete activity such as Spiritual evolution. So, one ought to have highly positive attitude to begin with. Positivity here is not merely a wishful desire or just having hope. It is neither a matter of having strong faith and beliefs. That will aptly be called laziness or indolence. Mere wishing and not working hard is more like daydreaming and share borders with escapism. Positivity means having abundant energy and drive for undergoing a major transformation with full vigour in search of Self. Simple advice for those waiting to grow old before starting exploring Spirituality is that such an approach is most likely doomed for failure. During old age you will be found gasping for breath with all the pressures that pursuing spirituality demands. Get ready now that you are perfectly healthy and your reservoir of energy is brim full; lest it will be too late.

There is no point in hoping that old age will make us wiser and hence our journey will be easy. Let us be clear that age and wisdom have no direct correlation. Pursuing Spirituality is not just another intellectual pursuit that will not need physical health. That is a wrong assumption. Besides, what is the use of acquiring a living capability like this at the far end of the life? Start early and put in your best and you will continue enjoying the fruits of peace and bliss over your most advanced years adding to fulfillment over longer years.

Why wait to see the heaven on the last day of life when you have chance to make that your home even at young age?

Question: Does any particular age bracket work as a facilitating or inhibiting factor for pursuing spirituality? I am of 55 years of age and sincerely wish to know when should I pursue higher goals of life?

Answer: As they say, age is just a number and what matters more is the attitude. The journey for seeking spirituality depends more on evolution of a particular individual. It is a serious business and needs full time and energy and that too after leaving behind all the attachments and allurements of the material world. Practically speaking, one will find it hard to give up the worldly attachments without providing for the remaining years of expected life. This contrast of having enough material accumulation as well as sufficient balance time results in a perfect 'catch 22' situation for many of us. If you wish to stop earning early, you will need to support yourself that much longer. If you continue earning too late, you are left with lesser time to pursue spirituality and then enjoy the fruits of the same for longer period.

Surely, there can't be a straight answer to such a subjective question. But it is expected that by the time you are 55, your children must have settled well and you will not have any major social obligation towards others. So all you need to check before you call quits is to have sufficient financial kitty to serve you well for your physical and medical needs for expected remaining life. Accumulating too much more is a curse. You will appreciate this point no sooner you start seeing your inner Self with close proximity as every accumulation needs protection, every land needs fencing, every FD needs extension, every asset needs care, every fear needs insurance cover and not all these things can have any foolproof hedge. You will see all these activities as unwanted burden once you are able to see through the futility of material possessions on way to seek your superior goal.

So don't worry too much. As it is, your very material needs are inversely proportionate to your spiritual progress. As you progress, your needs are sure to get less and less as you will have no interest left in foreign travels, five star dining, annual holidays, branded apparels, trendy jewelry, shiny cars or such other luxuries of life that need big money. Thankfully, most basic needs of life do not cost fortunes even now. So if you have saved enough and you have invested your savings in inflation proof options, you can plan to hang your boots sooner than later. Being fifty five is slightly late as you should have been on step two by now.

Question: I am waiting my stress levels to normalize before I am able to concentrate on spiritual journey? Does it help for controlling stress also?

Answer: Let us first be clear that practically all pleasures, excitements, worries, fears or every other kind of emotion at play create stress in our daily life. Many people don't realize the basic fact that seemingly contrasting aspects of enjoyments and unpleasant experiences have identical role for generating pressures and stress. Logically speaking, the stress levels of any person will go down once he/she stops going after pleasures and excitements. So the question gets changed to – Does Spiritual progress reduce the pleasures and excitements and the answer is a big Yes.

Spiritual journey involves understanding your emotions along with its source. It enhances your ability to deal with such issues in a matured manner. It also involves systematic work on improving your empathy, sympathy and compassion besides improving your very approach to deal with all other beings and things. As proven even scientifically, all these developments are pressure relievers or stress busters. A simple look at the face of any spiritually advanced person and you come to realize instantaneously that stress doesn't reside at this address. All you can spot there is serene peace and bliss.

The problem with some of us is that we get so occupied with our stresses that we can't live without intense pressures around us at all times. Pressures have unfortunate tendency of becoming addictive force in our life. It leads to a situation where some of us genuinely start believing that we are at our productive and creative best while under stress. They get so dare devil and dumb with this false notion that even decline of their own psychological and physical health goes unnoticed. Anyone so ignorant has no hope for his survival and is too weak willed to even attempt Spirituality. As must have been seen already, the entire subject matter of Spirituality revolves around self-awareness to self-realization via the route of self-acceptance, self-improvements, self-control, self-analysis and self-restraints. A stress loving person like mentioned above will surely get crumbled in initial stages itself. Hence, such people should just be happy to accept that everything is not for everyone. But anyone who has read this book until this stage can't be a weak willed person, so why should you worry?

Question: Why should one aim for attaining full-scale concentration in Yoga when mere Asanas and Pranayam are seen providing visible and direct health benefits in an instant?

Answer: Discipline of Yoga is not to improve only physical health as believed by many. Suppressions of anxiety and stress management are also just low hanging fruits of the concentration techniques of Yoga. These can at best be classified as by-products. Yoga is primarily aimed at mastering the art of bringing unconscious mind under self-regulation. As you may know, unconscious mind is entirely different from the rational mind used for thinking. Actually, thinking involves only a small part of human mind. Use of Yoga for a purpose other than remaining fully conscious is but a partial benefit. Asanas and normal Pranayam exercises certainly provide fractional visible benefits but letting go of the big potential advantage is a sure under-utilization and should not be settled even commercially. Why settle for steel when even gold can be had?

Question: Attachment involves a sense of longing and desire to provide best of attention and effort to hold it, why than it is always criticized as a bad thing? Is detachment the right answer for losing attachment?

Answer: Attachment to something leads to desire for dominance. One is also tempted to have full possession of the thing sought. This feeling for dominance and possession leads to fear of loss. Fear also breeds to violence as much as desire breeds immorality. Inevitably, this feeling of loss is what ignites jealousy. So every time you see attachment, jealousy can be traced there like a shadow. But detachment is never the right solution to overcome attachment. Detachment leads to withdrawal and resistance, which is even worse. The recommended solution lies somewhere in between these two extremes.

Question: I have listened to many great sages at different times and have felt a great feeling of learning great things from them. But soon the influence of those words loses importance and life returns to earlier state. Why their words and their learning is not able to transform my life for longer time?

Answer: Listening to some other person will be effective only when we listen with neutral attitude and are ready to transform our life style to implement what we understand as being desirable. Imagine a blackboard in a classroom that is filled with so many things already written on it from all sides and shades with no empty space available at all. Imagine you overwriting something new and important over some existing writing. What are the chances of you making out right meaning from the over written message? Similar to the blackboard in the classroom, our normal mind is already cluttered and overcrowded with so many old written messages in form of our opinions, conclusions, point of views, beliefs, assertions, memories, and experiences that we are already saddled with. How can any new message, let it be of great value and importance, remain stuck for long time?

Unless we clean our mind from all the crowded messages and bring it back to its original clean surface, it is foolhardy to believe that we can absorb anything new on sustainable basis. Developing genuine Self-Awareness by rising above all existing baggage is the requirement for proper listening. Listening is key to learning but listening and comparing with what we already know is no listening. Proper listening requires an open mind, a mind having ability to observe and absorb, a mind that is sensitive to feel, that is attentive and which is in no hurry to come to any conclusion.

Bibliography

Abbe, J.A. Dubois, *Hindu Manners, Customs and Ceremonies,* Rupa and Co., 2006.

Acharya Vedant Tirth, *Rigveda* (in Hindi), Manoj Publications, 2008.

Acharya Vedant Tirth, *Yajurveda* (in Hindi), Manoj Publications, 2008.

Armstrong, Karen, *The Great Transformation, The Beginning of Our Religious Traditions,* Anchor Books, A Division of Random House Inc, New York, 2006.

Brahm, Ajahn, *Mindfulness, Bliss and Beyound: A Meditator's Handbook,* Wisdom Publications, Boston, 2005.

Burton, S. R. (1883). www.sacred-texts.com.

Chamine, Shirzad, *Positive Intelligence*, Greenleaf Book Group Press, 2012.

Chopra, Deepak, *Buddha: A Story of Enlightenment,* Harper Collins, 2007.

Cohen, Lorraine, CEO and Founder of Powerful Living, Article published at www.thebridgemaker.com 23.11.2009.

Compilation of The Complete Works of Swami Vivekananda Volumes 1 to 9, 11th Edition, 1989.

Covey, Stephen R., *The 8th Habit: From Effectiveness to Greatness,* Free Press NY, 2004.

Coway, Timothy, PhD, *Our Real Nature,* article published in 1990 available on www.enlightened-spiritual.org

Easwaran, Eknath (introduced and translated by), *The Bhagawad Gita*, Nilgiri Press, 2007.

Easwaran, Eknath (introduced and translated by), *The Dhammapada*, Nilgiri Press, 2007.

Easwaran, Eknath (introduced and translated by), *The Upanishads,* Nilgiri Press, 2007.

Gandhi, V.R. *The Systems of Indian Philosophy,* In D.K. Dixit (ed.). Sri Mahavira Jaina Vidyalaya, Bombay.

Gardner, Howard Earl, *Frames of Mind: Theory of Multiple Intelligence,* Third edition, Basic Books, 2011.

Goleman, Daniel, *Emotional Intelligence: Why it can matter more than IQ*, Bantam Books, NY, 1996.

Goleman, Daniel, *Social Intelligence: The New Science of Human Relationships*, Bantam Books, NY, 2006.

Golgbery, Phillip, *American Veda*, Crown/Archetype, 2010.

Gray, John, *Men Are From Mars, Women Are From Venus*, Harper Collins Publishers, 1993.

Hanh, Thich Nhat, *The Art of Mindful Living* (Audio Edition), Sounds True, 1999.

Henry and Richard Blackaby, *Spiritual Leadership: Moving People to God's Agenda*, Broadman and Holman Publishers, Tennessee, 2001.

His Holiness The Dalai Lama and Howard C. Cutler, *The Art of Happiness: A Handbook for Living*, Hodder and Stoughton Ltd. London, 2009.

His Holiness The Dalai Lama, *The Path To Freedom*, Abacus London, 2002.

Jung, C.G. (Forward by). *The Spiritual Teaching of Ramana Maharshi*, Shambhala Boston and London, 2004.

Karen, Armstrong, *Buddha,* Phoenix, 2000.

Keller, Warner, *The Bible As History*, William Morrow and Company, Inc, 1981.

Kempton, Sally, *Meditation for the Love of It: Enjoying your own deepest experience*, Sounds True, Colorado, 2011.

Krishnamurti, J., *Inward Revolution*, Shabhala Boston and London, 2006.

Krishnamurti, J., *The Awakening of Intelligence*, Harper One, 1987.

Lawrence, Richard, *The Meditation Plan: 21 Keys to your inner potential*, Judy Piatkus, London, 1999.

LeDoux, Joseph, *The Emotional Brain: The Mysterious Underpinnings of Emotional Life*, Simon and Schsuster, 1998.

Luce, Edward, *In Spite of The Gods: The Strange Rise of Modern India*, Little Brown, 2006.

Lyubomirsky, Sonja, *The How of Happiness: New Approach to Getting the Life You Want*, The Penguin Press, 2008.

MacDonell, A.A. (1900). *A History of Sanskrit Literature*, D. Appleton and Company, New York.

Miller, Susan B., *Disgust the Gatekeeper Emotion*, The Analytic Press Inc. USA, 2004.

Mininni, Darlene, *The Emotional Toolkit: Seven Power-Skills to Nail Your Bad Feelings*, St. Martini's Griffin, 2006.

Myers, David G., *The American Paradox: Spiritual Hunger in an Age of Plenty*, New Haven: Yale Nota Bene, 2001.

Olsen, Gary, *Current living master of Master Path*, article on www.masterpath.org/articles-dilemma

Radhakrishnan, S., *The Hindu View of Life*, Harper Collins, 2009.

Radhakrishnan, S., *The Principal Upanishads*, Harper Collins, 2011.

Roberts, Bernadette, *What is Self?: A Study of the Spiritual Journey in Terms of Consciousness*, Sentient Publications, 2005.

Rodwell, J. M. (Translator from the Arabic), *The Koran,* Phoenix, 1994.

Rosenthal, Norman, MD, *The Emotional Revolution: Harnessing the Power of Your Emotions for a More Positive Life*, Kensington Publishing Corp., 2003.

Sasson, Remez, *Founder of Success Consciousness*, Article at www.successconsciousness.com

Sen, Amartya, *The Argumentative Indian*, Penguin Books, 2006.

Society, A. (n.d.). *Jati : Caste System in India.* From www.asiasociety.org.

Tejomayananda, Swami, *Living Vedanta (Vedanta Cintnam)*, Chinmaya Prakashan, Mumbai, 2014.

Trungpa, Chogyam, *Cutting Through Spiritual Materialism*, Shambhala Publications USA, 1973.

Tyagi, Ashok, *All about Hinduism: From Vedas to Devas and Past to Present*, Shipra Publications, Delhi, 2015.

Warren, Rick, *The Purpose of Driven Life: What On Earth Am I Here For*, Campus Crusade Asia Ltd, Singapore, 2005.

Wendy, Doniger, *The Hindus: An Alternate History*, The Penguin Press, New York, 2009.

Yogananda, Paramhansa, *Autobiography of a Yogi*, Yogoda Satsanga Society of India, 2010.

Zohar, Danah, *Rewiring the Corporate Brain: Using the New Science to Rethink How We Structure and Lead Peganizations*, Berrett-Koehler Publishers, 1997.

Index